ROMANS 9-16

A Commentary in the Wesleyan Tradition

*New Beacon Bible Commentary

ROMANS 9-16

A Commentary in the Wesleyan Tradition

William M. Greathouse
with George Lyons

BEACON HILL PRESS
OF KANSAS CITY

ISBN 978-0-8341-2363-2

Printed in the United States of America

Library of Congress Cataloging-in-Publication Data

Greathouse, William M.
Romans 9—16 / William M. Greathouse with George Lyons.
p. cm. — (New Beacon Bible commentary ; vol. 2)
Includes bibliographical references.
ISBN 978-0-8341-2363-2 (pbk.)
1. Bible. N.T. Romans IX-XVI—Commentaries. I. Lyons, George. II. Title. III. Title: Romans nine-sixteen.

BS2665.53.G75 2008
227'.1077—dc22

2008000972

10 9 8 7 6 5 4 3 2 1

DEDICATION

For Kara and Nathanael,
my children, who have always been my joy and God's gracious gift

With love,
Your dad
George Lyons

COMMENTARY EDITORS

General Editors

Alex Varughese
Ph.D., Drew University
Professor of Biblical Literature
Mount Vernon Nazarene University
Mount Vernon, Ohio

Roger Hahn
Ph.D., Duke University
Dean of the Faculty
Professor of New Testament
Nazarene Theological Seminary
Kansas City, Missouri

George Lyons
Ph.D., Emory University
Professor of New Testament
Northwest Nazarene University
Nampa, Idaho

Section Editors

Joseph Coleson
Ph.D., Brandeis University
Professor of Old Testament
Nazarene Theological Seminary
Kansas City, Missouri

Robert Branson
Ph.D., Boston University
Professor of Biblical Literature
Olivet Nazarene University
Bourbonnais, Illinois

Alex Varughese
Ph.D., Drew University
Professor of Biblical Literature
Mount Vernon Nazarene University
Mount Vernon, Ohio

Jim Edlin
Ph.D., Southern Baptist Theological Seminary
Professor of Biblical Literature and Languages
Chair of the Division of Religion and Philosophy
MidAmerica Nazarene University
Olathe, Kansas

Kent Brower
Ph.D., The University of Manchester
Vice Principal
Senior Lecturer in Biblical Studies
Nazarene Theological College
Manchester, England

George Lyons
Ph.D., Emory University
Professor of New Testament
Northwest Nazarene University
Nampa, Idaho

Jeanne Serrão
Ph.D., Claremont Graduate University
Dean of the School of Theology and Philosophy
Professor of Biblical Literature
Mount Vernon Nazarene University
Mount Vernon, Ohio

CONTENTS

GENERAL EDITORS' PREFACE

The purpose of the New Beacon Bible Commentary is to make available to pastors and students in the twenty-first century a biblical commentary that reflects the best scholarship in the Wesleyan theological tradition. The commentary project aims to make this scholarship accessible to a wider audience to assist them in their understanding and proclamation of Scripture as God's Word.

Writers of the volumes in this series not only are scholars within the Wesleyan theological tradition and experts in their field but also have special interest in the books assigned to them. Their task is to communicate clearly the critical consensus and the full range of other credible voices who have commented on the Scriptures. Though scholarship and scholarly contribution to the understanding of the Scriptures are key concerns of this series, it is not intended as an academic dialogue within the scholarly community. Commentators of this series constantly aim to demonstrate in their work the significance of the Bible as the church's book and the contemporary relevance and application of the biblical message. The project's overall goal is to make available to the church and for her service the fruits of the labors of scholars who are committed to their Christian faith.

The *New International Version* (NIV) is the reference version of the Bible used in this series; however, the focus of exegetical study and comments is the biblical text in its original language. When the commentary uses the NIV, it is printed in bold. The text printed in bold italics is the translation of the author. Commentators also refer to other translations where the text may be difficult or ambiguous.

The structure and organization of the commentaries in this series seeks to facilitate the study of the biblical text in a systematic and methodical way. Study of each biblical book begins with an ***Introduction*** section that gives an overview of authorship, date, provenance, audience, occasion, purpose, sociological/cultural issues, textual history, literary features, hermeneutical issues, and theological themes necessary to understand the book. This section also includes a brief outline of the book and a list of general works and standard commentaries.

The commentary section for each biblical book follows the outline of the book presented in the introduction. In some volumes, readers will find section ***overviews*** of large portions of scripture with general comments on their overall literary structure and other literary features. A consistent feature of the commentary is the paragraph by paragraph study of biblical texts. This section has three parts: ***Behind the Text***, ***In the Text***, and ***From the Text***.

The goal of the ***Behind the Text*** section is to provide the reader with all the relevant information necessary to understand the text. This includes specific historical situations reflected in the text, the literary context of the text, sociological and cultural issues, and literary features of the text.

In the Text explores what the text says, following its verse-by-verse structure. This section includes a discussion of grammatical details, word studies, and the connectedness of the text to other biblical books/passages or other parts of the book being studied (the canonical relationship). This section provides transliterations of key words in Hebrew and Greek and their literal meanings. The goal here is to explain what the author would have meant and/or what the audience would have understood as the meaning of the text. This is the largest section of the commentary.

The ***From the Text*** section examines the text in relation to the following areas: theological significance, intertextuality, the history of interpretation, use of the Old Testament scriptures in the New Testament, interpretation in later church history, actualization, and application.

The commentary provides ***sidebars*** on topics of interest that are important but not necessarily part of an explanation of the biblical text. These topics are informational items and may cover archaeological, historical, literary, cultural, and theological matters that have relevance to the biblical text. Occasionally, longer detailed discussions of special topics are included as ***excurses.***

We offer this series with our hope and prayer that readers will find it a valuable resource for their understanding of God's Word and an indispensable tool for their critical engagement with the biblical texts.

Roger Hahn, Centennial Initiative General Editor
Alex Varughese, General Editor (Old Testament)
George Lyons, General Editor (New Testament)

AUTHOR'S PREFACE

Romans has become a familiar friend. In 1968 my first commentary, "Romans," was published as 275 pages of volume eight of the ten-volume *Beacon Bible Commentary.* In 1975 my devotional commentary in *Beacon Bible Expositions* was published. This third effort is not a revision of either. It is a fresh commentary, coming after monumental developments in Romans scholarship in the intervening years. Two publications sparked what has become known as the "new perspective" on Romans: *The Romans Debate,* edited by Karl P. Donfried (rev. ed., 1991) and Ernst Käsemann's *Commentary on Romans* (1980). Fine summaries of the new perspective appeared in the July 2004 edition of the journal *Interpretation.*

One notable effect of the new perspective is a significant loss of confidence in the objectivity and certainty of Reformed Protestant readings of Romans, emphasizing personal redemption and the Lutheran understanding of justification. This pessimistic understanding of Christian living had prevailed in Western Christianity from the time of the Reformation. In brief, it viewed God's righteousness as simply the gift of justifying faith, understood mainly as a change of relationship and status for believers. In this view, justified believers remain *simul justus et peccator* ("at once righteous and sinful") until death. Christians, therefore, remain the sin-victimized "wretched man" of Rom 7:24. The gracious gift of justification, however, does relieve the *angst* of guilt and the fear of death, producing in the believer a peaceful conscience. Any talk of true ethical righteousness or sanctification in this present life, however, is ruled out by definition. Any "righteousness" or "holiness" ascribed to Christians is only "imputed." This pessimism served to widen the gap between Protestantism and Roman Catholicism.

Ironically, it was Lutheran Ernst Käsemann's 1980 *Commentary on Romans* that first seriously challenged the Lutheran consensus that God's righteousness was simply the gift of justifying faith. He argues that God's righteousness is

> primarily a power rather than a gift. . . . The phrase "the righteousness of God" in Paul . . . speaks of the God who brings back the fallen world into the sphere of his legitimate claim . . . [in] the Son of God . . . as our Kyrios, the one eschatological gift of God to us. (28-29)

God's righteousness is both God's *gift* and his *demand;* the Giver always unfailingly accompanies the Gift. Käsemann thereby opens the way for a real doctrine of Christian ethical righteousness and sanctification—precisely Paul's doctrine in Rom 6—8 and 12—15.

It was this understanding of Romans that the Oxford don turned itinerate Anglican evangelist, John Wesley, vigorously defended during the eighteenth century. More recently, it is the view supported by Anglican bishop N. T. Wright's treatments of Paul's theology (see, e.g., his 1993 *Climax of the Covenant*). All these developments are good news for Wesleyan scholars, whose approach to Romans was regarded with jaded eyes as special pleading motivated by dogmatic considerations. Today, NT scholars of every stripe, many of them highly regarded Romans scholars, espouse an "optimism of grace" much like Wesley proclaimed. Such grace promises Christians a righteousness and holiness that are genuinely ethical and realizable in the life of the Spirit now (see July 2004 *Interpretation*).

The Romans debate of the 1970s further illuminates the nature of the Roman letter, restoring as it does confidence in the unity and integrity of Romans. Jewish in its origin (and in its continuing struggle with the Torah), the Roman community, by A.D. 57-58 had become predominantly Gentile in the interim following Claudius's A.D. 48 edict, which evicted all Jews from Rome (see Acts 18:2). Upon returning, Jewish Christians found a totally new situation developing, a mixed Gentile-Jewish community. These facts illuminate chs 14—15 and support ch 16 as integral of Paul's letter.

The forty-year span between the BBC and the NBBC, I spent preaching, lecturing, serving my denomination as a general superintendent, and most recently in retirement. It was also my privilege during those years to teach classes on Romans at both Nazarene Theological Seminary and Trevecca Nazarene University. These assignments necessitated the joyful task of keeping abreast on Romans scholarship in new commentaries and professional journals.

Admittedly, writing a verse-by-verse commentary from the Greek is another matter. It is here that the assistance of my editor, George Lyons, has been invaluable. His Emory University Ph.D. in NT studies and his proficiency in Greek, sharpened by daily classes at Northwest Nazarene University, have enabled him to give this commentary a scholarly quality and authority it would not otherwise possess. Both the author and the readers, therefore, stand in special debt to George Lyons.

I would be unforgivably delinquent not to express appreciation also for my wife Judy's unfailing encouragement for me to give the best hours each day for the past three years to the grueling work of writing, rewriting, and then e-mailing daily offerings to Dr. Lyons. Most of all, I am indebted to the illumination of the Spirit, flickering as it sometimes was, as I sought divine guidance and strength for the task of writing. *Soli Deo Gloria*.

William M. Greathouse

ABBREVIATIONS

With a few exceptions, these abbreviations follow those in *The SBL Handbook of Style* (Alexander 1999).

General

A.D.	anno Domini (precedes date) (equivalent to C.E.)
B.C.	before Christ (follows date) (equivalent to B.C.E.)
B.C.E.	before the Common Era
C.E.	Common Era
cf.	compare
ch	chapter
chs	chapters
e.g.	*exempli gratia*, for example
esp.	especially
etc.	*et cetera*, and the rest
f(f).	and the following one(s)
i.e.	*id est*, that is
lit.	literally
LXX	Septuagint
MS	manuscript
MSS	manuscripts
MT	Masoretic Text (of the OT)
n.	note
n.d.	no date
n.p.	no place; no publisher; no page
nn.	notes
NT	New Testament
OT	Old Testament
s.v.	*sub verbo*, under the word
v	verse
vv	verses

Modern English Versions

ASV	American Standard Version
ESV	English Standard Version
HCSB	Holman Christian Standard Bible
JB	Jerusalem Bible
KJV	King James Version
MOFFATT	*The Bible: A New Translation*, James A. R. Moffatt
NAB	New American Bible
NASB	New American Standard Bible
NCV	New Century Version
NEB	New English Bible
NIV	New International Version
NJB	New Jerusalem Bible
NLT	New Living Translation
NRSV	New Revised Standard Version
PHILLIPS	*The New Testament in Modern English*, J. B. Phillips
REB	Revised English Bible
RSV	Revised Standard Version
TEV	Good News Bible: Today's English Version

Print Conventions for Translations

Bold font	NIV (bold without quotation marks in the text under study; elsewhere in the regular font, with quotation marks and no further identification)
Bold italic font	Author's translation (without quotation marks)

Behind the Text: Literary or historical background information average readers might not know from reading the biblical text alone

In the Text: Comments on the biblical text, words, phrases, grammar, and so forth

From the Text:	The use of the text by later interpreters, contemporary relevance, theological and ethical implications of the text, with particular emphasis on Wesleyan concerns

Apocrypha

APOT	*The Apocrypha and Pseudepigrapha of the Old Testament.* Edited by R. H. Charles. 2 vols. Oxford, 1913
Bar	Baruch
Add Dan	Additions to Daniel
Pr Azar	Prayer of Azariah
Bel	Bel and the Dragon
Sg Three	Song of the Three Young Men
Sus	Susanna
1—2 Esd	1—2 Esdras
Add Esth	Additions to Esther
Ep Jer	Epistle of Jeremiah
Jdt	Judith
1—2 Macc	1—2 Maccabees
3—4 Macc	3—4 Maccabees
Pr Man	Prayer of Manasseh
Ps 151	Psalm 151
Sir	Sirach/Ecclesiasticus
Tob	Tobit
Wis	Wisdom of Solomon

OT Pseudepigrapha

Ahiqar	*Ahiqar*
Apoc. Ab.	*Apocalypse of Abraham*
Apoc. Adam	*Apocalypse of Adam*
Apoc. Dan.	*Apocalypse of Daniel*
Apoc. El. (H)	Hebrew *Apocalypse of Elijah*
Apoc. El. (C)	Coptic *Apocalypse of Elijah*
Apoc. Mos.	*Apocalypse of Moses*
Apoc. Sedr.	*Apocalypse of Sedrach*
Apoc. Zeph.	*Apocalypse of Zephaniah*
Apocr. Ezek.	*Apocrypon of Ezekiel*
Aris. Ex.	Aristeas the Exegete
Aristob.	Aristobulus
Artap.	Artapanus
As. Mos.	*Assumption of Moses*
2 Bar.	*2 Baruch (Syriac Apocalypse)*
3 Bar.	*3 Baruch (Greek Apocalypse)*
4 Bar.	*4 Baruch (Paraleipomena Jeremiou)*
Bk. Noah	*Book of Noah*
Cav. Tr.	*Cave of Treasures*
Cl. Mal.	Cleodemus Malchus
Dem.	Demetrius (the Chronographer)
El. Mod.	*Eldad and Modad*
1 En.	*1 Enoch (Ethiopic Apocalypse)*
2 En.	*2 Enoch (Slavonic Apocalypse)*
3 En.	*3 Enoch (Hebrew Apocalypse)*
Eup.	Eupolemus
Ezek. Trag.	Ezekiel the Tragedian
4 Ezra	*4 Ezra*
5 Apoc. Syr. Pss.	*Five Apocryphal Syriac Psalms*

Dead Sea Scrolls and Related Texts

Q	Qumran
Gk. Apoc. Ezra	*Greek Apocalypse of Ezra*
Hec. Ab.	Hecataeus of Abdera
Hel. Syn. Pr.	*Hellenistic Synagogal Prayers*
Hist. Jos.	*History of Joseph*
Hist. Rech.	*History of the Rechabites*
Jan. Jam.	*Jannes and Jambres*

Jos. Asen.	*Joseph and Aseneth*
Jub.	*Jubilees*
L.A.B.	*Liber antiquitatum biblicarum* (Pseudo-Philo)
L.A.E.	*Life of Adam and Eve*
Lad. Jac.	*Ladder of Jacob*
Let. Aris.	*Letter of Aristeas*
Liv. Pro.	*Lives of the Prophets*
Lost Tr.	*The Lost Tribes*
3 Macc.	*3 Maccabees*
4 Macc.	*4 Maccabees*
5 Macc.	*5 Maccabees* (Arabic)
Mart. Ascen. Isa.	*Martyrdom and Ascension of Isaiah*
Odes Sol.	*Odes of Solomon*
Ph. E. Poet	Philo the Epic Poet
Pr. Jac.	*Prayer of Jacob*
Pr. Jos.	*Prayer of Joseph*
Pr. Man.	*Prayer of Manasseh*
Pr. Mos.	*Prayer of Moses*
Ps.-Eup.	Pseudo-Eupolemus
Ps.-Hec.	Pseudo-Hecataeus
Ps.-Orph.	Pseudo-Orpheus
Ps.-Phoc.	Pseudo-Phocylides
Pss. Sol.	*Psalms of Solomon*
Ques. Ezra	*Questions of Ezra*
Rev. Ezra	*Revelation of Ezra*
Sib. Or.	*Sibylline Oracles*
Syr. Men.	*Sentences of the Syriac Menander*
T. 12 Patr.	*Testaments of the Twelve Patriarchs*
T. Ash.	*Testament of Asher*
T. Benj.	*Testament of Benjamin*
T. Dan	*Testament of Dan*
T. Gad	*Testament of Gad*
T. Iss.	*Testament of Issachar*
T. Jos.	*Testament of Joseph*
T. Jud.	*Testament of Judah*
T. Levi	*Testament of Levi*
T. Naph.	*Testament of Naphtali*
T. Reu.	*Testament of Reuben*
T. Sim.	*Testament of Simeon*
T. Zeb.	*Testament of Zebulun*
T. 3 Patr.	*Testaments of the Three Patriarchs*
T. Ab.	*Testament of Abraham*
T. Isaac	*Testament of Isaac*
T. Jac.	*Testament of Jacob*
T. Adam	*Testament of Adam*
T. Hez.	*Testament of Hezekiah*
T. Job	*Testament of Job*
T. Mos.	*Testament of Moses*
T. Sol.	*Testament of Solomon*
Theod.	Theodotus, *On the Jews*
Treat. Shem	*Treatise of Shem*
Vis. Ezra	*Vision of Ezra*

Josephus

Vita	*Vita*
Life	*The Life*
C. Ap.	*Contra Apionem*
Ag. Ap.	*Against Apion*
A.J.	*Antiquitates judaicae*
Ant.	*Jewish Antiquities*
B.J.	*Bellum judaicum*
J.W.	*Jewish War*

Apostolic Fathers

Barn.	*Barnabas*
1—2 Clem.	*1—2 Clement*
Did.	*Didache*
Diogn.	*Diognetus*
Herm. *Mand.*	Shepherd of Hermas, *Mandate*
Herm. *Sim.*	Shepherd of Hermas, *Similitude*
Herm. *Vis.*	Shepherd of Hermas, *Vision*
Ign. *Eph.*	Ignatius, *To the Ephesians*
Ign. *Magn.*	Ignatius, *To the Magnesians*
Ign. *Smyrn.*	Ignatius, *To the Smyrnaeans*
Ign. *Phld.*	Ignatius, *To the Philadelphians*
Ign. *Rom.*	Ignatius, *To the Romans*
Ign. *Pol.*	Ignatius, *To Polycarp*
Ign. *Trall.*	Ignatius, *To the Trallians*
Mart. Pol.	*Martyrdom of Polycarp*
Pol. *Phil.*	Polycarp, *To the Philippians*

Greek Transliteration

Greek	***Letter***	***English***
α	*alpha*	*a*
β	*bēta*	*b*
γ	*gamma*	*g*
γ	*gamma nasal*	*n* (before γ, κ, ξ, χ)
δ	*delta*	*d*
ϵ	*epsilon*	*e*
ζ	*zēta*	*z*
η	*ēta*	*ē*
θ	*thēta*	*th*
ι	*iōta*	*i*
κ	*kappa*	*k*
λ	*lambda*	*l*
μ	*my*	*m*
ν	*ny*	*n*
ξ	*xi*	*x*
ο	*omicron*	*o*
π	*pi*	*p*
ρ	*rhō*	*r*
ρ	initial *rhō*	*rh*
σ/ς	*sigma*	*s*
τ	*tau*	*t*
υ	*upsilon*	*y*
υ	*upsilon*	*u* (in diphthongs: *au, eu, ēu, ou, ui*)
φ	*phi*	*ph*
χ	*chi*	*ch*
ψ	*psi*	*ps*
ω	*ōmega*	*ō*
῾	rough breathing	*h* (before initial vowels or diphthongs)

Hebrew Consonant Transliteration

Hebrew/ Aramaic	***Letter***	***English***
א	*alef*	ʼ
ב	*bet*	*b*
ג	*gimel*	*g*
ד	*dalet*	*d*
ה	*he*	*h*
ו	*vav*	*v* or *w*
ז	*zayin*	*z*
ח	*khet*	*ḥ*
ט	*tet*	*ṭ*
י	*yod*	*y*
כ/ך	*kaf*	*k*
ל	*lamed*	*l*
מ/ם	*mem*	*m*
נ/ן	*nun*	*n*
ס	*samek*	*s*
ע	*ayin*	ʻ
פ/ף	*pe*	*p*
צ/ץ	*tsade*	*ṣ*
ק	*qof*	*q*
ר	*resh*	*r*
שׂ	*sin*	*ś*
שׁ	*shin*	*š*
ת	*tav*	*t*

BIBLIOGRAPHY

1944. *The Book of Common Prayer.* New York: Oxford University Press.

Achtemeir, Paul J. 1985. *Romans.* Interpretation. A Bible Commentary for Teaching and Preaching. Atlanta: John Knox.

Alexander, Patrick H., and others, eds. 1999. *The SBL Handbook of Style for Ancient Near Eastern, Biblical, and Early Christian Studies.* Peabody, Mass.: Hendrickson.

Allchin, A. M. 1991. "The Epworth-Canterbury-Constantinople-Axis." *Wesleyan Theological Journal* 26, 1:23-37.

Augsburger, Myron. 1961. *Quench Not the Spirit.* Scottdale, Pa.: Herald.

Augustine. 1955. *Confessions and Enchiridion.* Trans. and ed. Albert C. Outler. Vol. 7 of Library of Christian Classics. Philadelphia: Westminster.

Bangs, Carl. 1971. *Arminius: A Study of the Dutch Reformation.* Nashville: Abingdon.

Barclay, William. 1957. *The Letter to the Romans.* The Daily Study Bible. Philadelphia: Westminster.

Barrett, C. K. 1957. *The Epistle to the Romans* in Harper's New Testament Commentaries. New York: Harper and Brothers.

———. 1963. *Reading Through Romans.* London: Epworth.

Barth, Karl. 1933. *The Epistle to the Romans.* Trans. from the 6th ed., Edwin C. Hoskyns. London: Oxford University Press.

———. 1959. *A Shorter Commentary on Romans.* Trans. Edwin C. Hoskyns. Richmond, Va.: John Knox.

———. 1993. *The Holy Spirit and the Christian Life: The Theological Basis of Ethics.* Trans. R. Birch Hoyle. Library of Theological Ethics. Louisville, Ky.: Westminster/John Knox.

———. 2004. *Church Dogmatics.* 14 vols. Ed. and trans. Geoffrey W. Bromiley and others. Edinburgh: T&T Clark.

Bassett, Paul M., and William M. Greathouse. 1985. *The Historical Development.* Vol. 2 of *Exploring Christian Holiness.* Kansas City: Beacon Hill Press of Kansas City.

Bauer, Walter. 1979. *A Greek-English Lexicon of the New Testament and Other Early Christian Literature.* Trans. and adapted William Arndt, F. Wilbur Gingrich, and Frederick W. Danker. Chicago: University of Chicago Press.

Beet, Joseph Agar. 1885. *St. Paul's Epistle to the Romans.* London: Hodder and Stoughton.

Benoit, Pierre. 1973. *Jesus and the Gospel.* Trans. Benet Weatherhead. Bristol: Herder and Herder.

Benson, Bob, Jr., and Michael W. Benson. 1989. *Disciplines for the Inner Life.* Hendersonville, Tenn.: Deeper Life.

Beyer, Hermann Wolfgang. 1964. *"eulogeō, ktl."* Pages 754-63 in vol. 2 of *The Theological Dictionary of the New Testament.* Ed. Gerhard Kittel and Gerhard Friedrich. Trans. Geoffrey W. Bromiley. Grand Rapids: Eerdmans. 1964-76.

Bietenhard, Hans. 1976. "Please." Pages 814-20 in vol. 2 of *The New International Dictionary of New Testament Theology.* 3 vols. Trans. with additions and revisions from *Theologisches Begriffslexikon zum Neuen Testament,* ed. by Lothar Coenen and others by a team of translators. Grand Rapids: Zondervan, 1971-78.

Black, Matthew. 1973. *Romans* in *New Century Bible Commentary.* London: Oliphants.

Blass, Friedrich, Albert Debrunner, and Robert W. Funk (BDF). 1961. *A Greek Grammar of the New Testament and Other Early Christian Literature.* Trans. Robert W. Funk. Chicago: University of Chicago Press.

Blue, B. B. 1997. "Food, Food Laws, Table Fellowship." Pages 376-79 in *Dictionary of the Later New Testament and Its Developments.* Ed. Ralph P. Martin and Peter H. Davids. Downers Grove, Ill.: InterVarsity.

Bonhoeffer, Dietrich. 1995. *The Cost of Discipleship.* Trans. R. H. Fuller. New York: Simon and Schuster.

Bray, Gerald, ed. 1998. *Romans.* Vol. 6 of *Ancient Christian Commentary on Scripture: New Testament.* Ed. Thomas C. Oden. Downers Grove, Ill.: InterVarsity.

Briscoe, D. Stuart. 1982. *Romans.* Vol. 6 of The Communicator's Commentary. Ed. Lloyd J. Ogilvie. Waco, Tex.: Word Books.

Brooke, George J. 1992. "Testimonia." Pages 391-92 in vol. 6 of the *Anchor Bible Dictionary.* New York: Doubleday.

Bruce, F. F. 1963. *The Epistle of Paul to the Romans: An Introduction and Commentary.* Vol. 6 in The Tyndale Bible Commentaries. Grand Rapids: Eerdmans.

Brunner, Emil. 1959. *The Letter to the Romans.* Trans. H. A. Kennedy. Philadelphia: Westminster.

Bullinger, E. W. 1898. *Figures of Speech Used in the Bible.* London: Eyre and Spottiswoode.

Bultmann, Rudolf. 1970. *Theology of the New Testament: Complete in One Volume.* Trans. Kendrick Grobel. New York: Harper.

Byrne, Brendan. 1996. *Romans.* Vol. 6 of Sacra Pagina. Ed. Daniel J. Harrington. Collegeville, Minn.: Liturgical Press.

———. 2004. "Interpreting Romans: The New Perspective and Beyond." *Interpretation* 58, 3:241-52.

Calvin, John. 1960. *The Epistles of Paul to the Romans and Thessalonians.* Trans. Ross Mackenzie. Repr. Grand Rapids: Eerdmans.

———. 1970. *Institutes of the Christian Religion.* 2 vols. in one. Trans. Henry Beveridge. Repr. Grand Rapids: Eerdmans.

Cell, George Croft. 1935. *The Rediscovery of John Wesley.* New York: Henry Holt.

Cerfaux, Lucien. 1959. *The Church in the Theology of St. Paul.* Trans. Geoffrey Webb and Adrian Walker. Freiburg: Herder and Herder.

Chilton, Bruce D., and Jacob Neusner. 1995. *Judaism in the New Testament.* London: Routledge.

———. 2004. *Classical Christianity and Rabbinic Judaism: Comparing Theologies.* Grand Rapids: Baker Academic.

Clarke, Adam. n.d. *The New Testament of Our Lord and Saviour Jesus Christ.* Vol. 2. New York: Abingdon-Cokesbury.

Collins, Kenneth J. 1997. *The Scripture Way of Salvation.* Nashville: Abingdon.

———. 2005. *The Evangelical Moment: The Promise of an American Religion.* Grand Rapids: Baker Academic.

———. 2007. *The Theology of John Wesley: Holy Love and the Shape of Grace.* Nashville: Abingdon.

Cragg, Gerald. 1951. "The Epistle to the Romans" (Exposition). Pages 353-668 in vol. 9 in *The Interpreter's Bible.* Ed. George A. Buttrick and others. New York: Abingdon-Cokesbury.

Cranfield, C. E. B. 1975. *The Epistle to the Romans.* Vol. 1 of The International Critical Commentary. Edinburgh: T&T Clark.

———. 1979. *The Epistle to the Romans.* Vol. 2 of The International Critical Commentary. Edinburgh: T&T Clark.

———. 1985. *Romans: A Shorter Commentary.* Grand Rapids: Eerdmans.

Cullmann, Oscar. 1953. *Peter: Disciple, Apostle, Martyr: A Historical and Theological Study.* Trans. Floyd V. Filson. London: SCM.

Denney, James. 1970. "St. Paul's Epistle to the Romans." Pages 555-725 in vol. 2 of *The Expositor's Greek New Testament.* Ed. W. Robertson Nicoll. Repr. Grand Rapids: Eerdmans. 1897—1910.

Dodd, C. H. 1932. *The Epistle to the Romans* in The Moffatt New Testament Commentary. New York: Harper and Brothers.

Donfried, Karl P. 1976. "Justification and Last Judgment in Paul," in *Zeitschrift für die neutestamentliche Wissenschaft und die Kunde der Alteren Kirche* 67:90-110.

———. 1987. "The Kingdom of God in Paul." Pages 175-90 in *The Kingdom of God in Twentieth Century Interpretation.* Ed. W. Willis. Peabody, Mass.: Hendrickson.

———. 1991. *The Romans Debate.* Rev. ed. Peabody, Mass.: Hendrickson.

Dunn, James D. G. 2002a. *Romans 1-8.* Vol. 38A. Word Biblical Commentary. Dallas: Word.

———. 2002b. *Romans 9-16.* Vol. 38B. Word Biblical Commentary. Dallas: Word.

Erdman, Charles R. 1925. *The Epistle of Paul to the Romans.* Philadelphia: Westminster.

Fitzmyer, Joseph. 1993. *Romans. A New Translation with Introduction and Commentary.* Vol. 33 of the Anchor Bible. Ed. William Foxwell Albright and David Noel Freedman. New York: Doubleday.

Gamble, Harry, Jr. 1979. *The Textual History of the Letter to the Romans: A Study in Textual and Literary Criticism.* Grand Rapids: Eerdmans.

Garlington, Don B. 1990. *"The Obedience of Faith": A Pauline Phrase in Historical Context.* Wissenschaftliche Untersuchungen zum Neuen Testament 38. Tübingen: Mohr Siebeck.

Gaventa, Beverly Roberts. 2004. "The Cosmic Power of Sin in Paul's Letter to the Romans: Toward a Widescreen Edition." *Interpretation* 58, 3:229-40.

Godet, F. 1883. *St. Paul's Epistle to the Romans.* Trans. A. Cusin. New York: Funk and Wagnalls.

Goppelt, Leonard. 1964. *Jesus, Paul and Judaism.* Trans. Edward Schroeder. New York: Nelson.

Greathouse, William M. 1968. "Romans." Pages 18-292 in vol. 8 of *Beacon Bible Commentary.* Kansas City: Beacon Hill Press of Kansas City.

———. 1975. *Romans.* Vol. 6 of Beacon Bible Expositions. Kansas City: Beacon Hill Press of Kansas City.

———. 1998. *Wholeness in Christ: Toward a Biblical Theology of Holiness.* Kansas City: Beacon Hill Press of Kansas City.

———. n.d. *Romans.* Vol. 6 of Search the Scriptures. Kansas City: Nazarene Publishing House.

Greathouse, William, and H. Ray Dunning. 1989. *An Introduction to Wesleyan Theology.* Rev. ed. Kansas City: Beacon Hill Press of Kansas City.

Grieb, A. Katherine. 2002. *The Story of Romans: A Narrative Defense of God's Righteousness.* Louisville, Ky.: Westminster/John Knox.

Hardy, Edward Rochie. 1954. *Christology of the Later Fathers.* Vol. 3 of *The Library of Christian Classics.* Ed. Cyril C. Richardson. Philadelphia: Westminster.

Hays, Richard B. 1983. *The Faith of Jesus Christ.* Society of Biblical Literature Dissertation Series, 56. Chico, Calif.: Scholars Press.

———. 1993. *Echoes of Scripture in the Letters of Paul.* New Haven, Conn.: Yale University Press.

———. 1996. *The Moral Vision of the New Testament: Community, Cross, New Creation, A Contemporary Introduction to New Testament Ethics*. San Francisco: HarperSanFrancisco.

Heitzenrater, Richard. 1995. *Wesley and the People Called Methodists.* Nashville: Abingdon.

Hill, Craig. 2003. *In God's Time: The Bible and the Future.* Grand Rapids: Eerdmans.

Hodge, Charles. 1950. *Commentary on the Epistle to the Romans.* Grand Rapids: Eerdmans.

Jewett, Robert. 1971. *Paul's Anthropological Terms: A Study of Their Use in Conflict Settings.* Vol. 10 of Arbeiten zur Geschichte des antiken Judentums und des Urchristentums. Leiden: Brill.

———. 2007. *Romans: A Commentary.* Hermeneia. Minneapolis: Fortress.

Jones, E. Stanley. 1942. *Abundant Living.* New York: Abingdon-Cokesbury.

Kallas, James. 1964. "Romans XIII.1-7: An Interpolation." *New Testament Studies* 11/4:365-74.

Kallistos, Bishop. 1976. *The Deification of Man.* Minneapolis: Light and Life.

Karkkainen, Veli-Matti. 2004. *One with God: Salvation as Deification and Justification.* Unitas. Collegeville, Minn.: Liturgical Press.

Käsemann, Ernst. 1969a. "On the Subject of Primitive Christian Apocalyptic." Pages 108-37 in *New Testament Questions of Today.* Trans. W. J. Montague. Philadelphia: Fortress.

———. 1969b. "'The Righteousness of God' in Paul." Pages 168-82 in *New Testament Questions of Today.* Trans. W. J. Montague. Philadelphia: Fortress.

———. 1980. *Commentary on Romans.* Trans. and ed. Geoffrey W. Bromiley. Grand Rapids: Eerdmans.

Keck, Leander E. 1995. "What Makes Romans Tick?" Pages 3-29 in *Pauline Theology.* Vol. 3: Romans. Ed. David M. Hay and E. Elizabeth Johnson. Society of Biblical Literature Symposium Series, 23. Minneapolis: Fortress.

———. 2005. *Romans.* Abingdon New Testament Commentaries. Ed. Victor Paul Furnish. Nashville: Abingdon.

Kirk, K. E. 1937. *The Epistle to the Romans in the Revised Version with Introduction and Commentary.* Clarendon Bible. Oxford: Clarendon.

Knox, John. 1951. "The Epistle to the Romans" (Exegesis). Pages 353-668 in vol. 9 of *The Interpreter's Bible.* Ed. George A. Buttrick and others. New York: Abingdon-Cokesbury.

Koperski, Veronica. 2001. *What Are They Saying About Paul and the Law?* Mahwah, N.J.: Paulist Press.

Kuhn, Karl Georg. 1964. "*Israēl, Ioudaios, Hebraios* in Jewish Literature after the OT." Pages 359-68 in vol. 3 of *The Theological Dictionary of New Testament Theology.* Ed. Gerhard Kittel and Gerhard Friedrich. Trans. Geoffrey W. Bromiley. Grand Rapids: Eerdmans. 1964-76.

Leenhardt, Franz J. 1957. *The Epistle to the Romans.* Cleveland and New York: World Publishing.

Leith, John H. 1973. *Creeds of the Churches: A Reader in Christian Doctrine from the Bible to the Present.* Rev. ed. Richmond, Va.: John Knox.

Liddell, Henry George, Robert Scott, Henry Stuart Jones, and Roderick McKenzie. 1996. *A Greek-English Lexicon.* Rev. and aug. throughout. New York: Oxford University Press.

Lightfoot, J. B. 1913. *St. Paul's Epistle to the Philippians.* London: Macmillan.

Lincoln, Andrew T. 2002. *Ephesians.* Vol. 42 in Word Biblical Commentary. Dallas: Word.

Long, Thomas T. 2004. "Preaching Romans Today." *Interpretation* 58, 3:265-75.

Lossky, V. 1973. *The Vision of God.* Crestwood, N.Y.: St. Vladimir's Seminary Press.

Luther, Martin. 1961. *Lectures on Romans.* Trans. and ed. Wilhelm Pauck. Vol. 14 of The Library of Christian Classics. Philadelphia: Westminster.

Luthi, Walter. 1961. *The Letter to the Romans.* Richmond, Va.: John Knox.

Lyons, George. 1985. *Pauline Autobiography: Toward a New Understanding.* Society of Biblical Literature Dissertation Series, 73. Atlanta: Scholars Press.

Malina, Bruce J., and John J. Pilch. 2006. *Social Science Commentary on the Letters of Paul.* Minneapolis: Fortress.

Mare, W. Harold. 1992. "Zion (Place)." Pages 1096-97 in vol. 6 of *The Anchor Bible Dictionary.* Edited by David Noel Freedman. New York: Doubleday.

Martyn, J. Louis. 1997. *Galatians: A New Translation with Introduction and Commentary.* Vol. 33A of the Anchor Bible Commentary. Ed. William Foxwell Albright and David Noel Freedman. New York: Doubleday.

McCant, Jerry. 1981. "The Wesleyan Interpretation of Romans 5—8." *Wesleyan Theological Journal* 16, 1:68-84.

McComiskey, Thomas E. 1980. "(*qadash*) be hallowed, holy, sanctified; to consecrate, sanctify, prepare, dedicate" in vol. 2 of *Theological Wordbook of the Old Testament.* Ed. R. Laird Harris, Gleason L. Archer Jr., and Bruce K. Waltke. Chicago: Moody.

McCormick, K. Steve. 1991. "Theosis in Chrysostom and Wesley: An Eastern Paradigm on Faith and Love." *Wesleyan Theological Journal* 14, 1:38-103.

McGonigle, Herbert Boyd. 2001. *Sufficient Saving Grace: John Wesley's Evangelical Arminianism.* Carlisle, U.K.: Paternoster.

McGrath, Alister E. 2003. *A Brief History of Heaven.* Blackwell Brief Histories of Religion. London: Blackwell.

Metzger, Bruce Manning, and United Bible Societies. 1994. *A Textual Commentary on the Greek New Testament, Second Edition: A Companion Volume to the United Bible Societies' Greek New Testament.* 4th rev. ed. New York: United Bible Societies.

Meyer, Heinrich August Wilhelm. 1889. *Critical and Exegetical Hand-Book to the Epistle to the Romans.* Trans. John C. Moore and others. New York: Funk and Wagnalls.

Mitton, C. Leslie. 1953-54. "Romans—vii. Reconsidered," *The Expository Times.* 65:78-81, 99-103, 132-35.

Moo, Douglas J. 1996. *The Epistle to the Romans.* Grand Rapids: Eerdmans.

Morris, Leon. 1988. *The Epistle to the Romans.* Pillar New Testament Commentary. Grand Rapids: Eerdmans.

Moule, H. C. G. n.d. *Ephesian Studies.* London: Pickering and Inglis.

Moulton, James Hope. 1978. *Prolegomena.* Vol. 1 of *A Grammar of New Testament Greek.* 3rd ed. Edinburgh: T&T Clark.

Munck, Johannes. 1967. *Christ and Israel. An Interpretation of Romans 9—11.* Trans. Ingeborg Nixon. Philadelphia: Fortress Press.

Murray, John. 1959. *The Epistle to the Romans.* Vol. 1. Grand Rapids: Eerdmans.

Nanos, Mark D. 1996. *The Mystery of Romans: The Jewish Context of Paul's Letter.* Minneapolis: Fortress.

Noble, T. A. 1999. *The Foundation of Christian Holiness.*Unpublished. Private circulation.

Nygren, Anders. 1949. *Commentary on Romans.* Trans. Carl C. Rasmussen. Philadelphia: Fortress.

O'Keefe, John J., and R. R. Reno. 2005. *Sanctified Vision: An Introduction to Early Christian Interpretation of the Bible.* Baltimore: Johns Hopkins University Press.

O'Neill, J. C. 1975. *Paul's Letter to the Romans.* London: Pelican.

Oord, Thomas J., and Michael Lodahl. 2005. *Relational Holiness: Responding to God's Call.* Kansas City: Beacon Hill Press of Kansas City.

Pelikan, Jaroslav. 1971. *The Emergence of the Catholic Tradition.* The Christian Tradition, vol. 1. Chicago: University of Chicago Press.

———. 1974. *The Spirit of Eastern Orthodoxy.* The Christian Tradition, vol. 2. Chicago: University of Chicago Press.

Peters, John L. 1956. *Christian Perfection in American Methodism.* Nashville: Abingdon-Cokesbury.

Polkinghorne, John, and Michael Welker, eds. 2000. *The End of the World and the Ends of God: Science and Theology on Eschatology.* Harrisburg, Pa.: Trinity Press International.

Purkiser, W. T. 1983. *The Biblical Foundations.* Vol. 1 of *Exploring Christian Holiness.* Kansas City: Beacon Hill Press of Kansas City.

Purkiser, W. T., Richard S. Taylor, and Willard H. Taylor. 1977. *God, Man, and Salvation: A Biblical Theology.* Kansas City: Beacon Hill Press of Kansas City.

Quimby, Chester Warren. 1950. *The Great Redemption.* New York: Macmillan.

Rack, Henry D. 2006. "Some Recent Trends in Wesley Scholarship." *Wesleyan Theological Journal* 41, 2:182-99.

Räisänen, Heikki. 1986. *Paul and the Law.* Philadelphia: Fortress.

Reed, Millard C. 2005. *From a Pastor's Heart.* Nashville: Trevecca Nazarene University Press.

Reumann, John. 1966. "The Gospel of the Righteousness of God." *Interpretation* 20, 4:432-52.

Ridderbos, Herman. 1975. *Paul: An Outline of His Theology.* Trans. John Richard DeWitt. Grand Rapids: Eerdmans.

Robinson, J. A. T. 1952. *The Body.* London: SCM Press.

Royo, Antonio, and Jordan Aumann. 1962. *The Theology of Christian Perfection.* Dubuque, Iowa: Priory Press.

Russell, Jeffrey Burton. 1998. *A History of Heaven.* New ed. Princeton, N.J.: Princeton University Press.

Sanday, W., and A. C. Headlam. 1929. *A Critical and Exegetical Commentary on the Epistle to the Romans.* The International Critical Commentary. New York: Charles Scribner's Sons.

Sanders, E. P. 1977. *Paul and Palestinian Judaism: A Comparison of Patterns of Religion.* Minneapolis: Augsburg/Fortress.

———. 1985. *Jesus and Judaism.* Philadelphia: Fortress.

Sangster, W. E. 1954. *The Pure in Heart.* New York: Abingdon.

Schleiermacher, Friedrich D. 1956. *The Christian Faith.* Trans. and ed. H. R. Mackintosh and J. S. Stewart. Edinburgh: T&T Clark.

Schnackenburg, Rudolf. 1965. *The Church in the New Testament.* Trans. W. J. O'Hara. New York: Herder and Herder.

Schreiner, Thomas R. 1998. *The Law and Its Fulfillment: A Pauline Theology of Law.* Grand Rapids: Baker Academic.

Schrenk, Gottlob. 1964. *"patēr, ktl."* Pages 945-1022. TDNT. Pages 359-68 in vol. 5 in *The Theological Dictionary of New Testament Theology.* Ed. Gerhard Kittel and Gerhard Friedrich. Trans. Geoffrey W. Bromiley. Grand Rapids: Eerdmans. 1964-76.

Scobie, Charles H. H. 2003. *The Ways of Our God: An Approach to Biblical Theology.* Grand Rapids: Eerdmans.

Scott, E. F. 1947. *Paul's Epistle to the Romans.* London: SCM Press.

Seesemann, Heinrich. 1964. *"pateō, ktl."* Pages 940-45 in vol. 5 in *The Theological Dictionary of New Testament Theology.* Ed. Gerhard Kittel and Gerhard Friedrich. Trans. Geoffrey W. Bromiley. Grand Rapids: Eerdmans. 1964-76.

Spross, Daniel B. 1985. "The Doctrine of Sanctification in Karl Barth." *Wesleyan Theological Journal* 20, 2:54-76.

Stählin, Gustav. 1968. *"prokopē, prokoptō."* Pages 703-19 in vol. 6 in *The Theological Dictionary of New Testament Theology.* Ed. Gerhard Kittel and Gerhard Friedrich. Trans. Geoffrey W. Bromiley. Grand Rapids: Eerdmans. 1964-76.

Stein, Robert H. 1989. "The Argument of Romans 13:1-7." NTOA 31/4:325-43.

Stendahl, Krister. 1963. "The Apostle Paul and the Introspective Conscience of the West." *Harvard Theological Review* 56, 3 (July 1963): 199-215. Republished in 1976 in *Paul Among Jews and Gentiles.* Philadelphia: Fortress.

Stirewalt, M. Luther. 1991. "The Form and Function of the Greek Letter-Essay." Pages 147-74 in *The Romans Debate.* Rev. and expanded ed. Ed. Karl P. Donfried. Peabody, Mass.: Hendrickson.

Stowers, Stanley K. 1981. *The Diatribe and Paul's Letter to the Romans.* Society of Biblical Literature Dissertation Series, 57. Chico, Calif.: Scholars Press.

Stuhlmacher, Peter. 1994. *Paul's Letter to the Romans: A Commentary.* Trans. Scott J. Haffeman. Louisville, Ky.: Westminster/John Knox.

Stuhlmacher, Peter, and Donald A. Hagner. 2002. *Revisiting Paul's Doctrine of Justification: A Challenge to the New Perspective.* Downers Grove, Ill.: InterVarsity.

Tannehill, Robert C. 1967. *Dying and Rising with Christ: A Study in Pauline Theology.* Beihefte zur Zeitschrift für die neutestamentliche Wissenschaft 32. Berlin: Töpelmann.

Thielman, Frank. 1994. *Paul and the Law: A Contextual Approach.* Downers Grove, Ill.: InterVarsity.

Thomas, W. Griffith. 1947. *St. Paul's Epistle to the Romans.* Grand Rapids: Eerdmans.

Tyerman, L. 1882. *Wesley's Designated Successor.* London: Hodder and Stoughton.
Watson, Francis. 1991. "The Two Roman Congregations: Romans 14:1—15:13." Pages 203-15 in *The Romans Debate.* Rev. and expanded ed. Ed. Karl P. Donfried. Peabody, Mass.: Hendrickson.
Welch, Reuben R. 1988. *Our Freedom in Christ.* A Bible Study in Romans. Grand Rapids: Francis Asbury Press of Zondervan.
Wesley, John. 1931. *The Letters of the Rev. John Wesley, A.M.* 8 vols. Ed. John Telford. London: Epworth.
———. 1950. *Explanatory Notes upon the New Testament.* Reprint. London: Epworth.
———. 1979. *The Works of John Wesley.* 3rd ed. 10 vols. Ed. Thomas Jackson. Reprint Grand Rapids: Baker, 1872.
Wesley, John, and Charles Wesley. 1870. *The Poetical Works.* Ed. G. Osborn. London: Wesleyan-Methodist Conference Office.
Westerholm, Stephen. 2003. *Perspectives Old and New on Paul: The "Lutheran" Paul and His Critics.* Grand Rapids: Eerdmans.
———. 2004. "The Righteousness of the Law and the Righteousness of Faith in Romans." *Interpretation* 58, 3:253-64.
Wiles, Gordon P. 1974. *Paul's Intercessory Prayers: The Significance of the Intercessory Prayer Passages in the Letters of St. Paul.* Studiorum Novi Testamenti Societas Monograph Series, 24. Cambridge: Cambridge University Press.
Wiley, H. Orton. 1959. *The Epistle to the Hebrews.* Kansas City: Beacon Hill.
Williams, Colin. 1960. *John Wesley's Theology Today.* Nashville: Abingdon.
Winger, M. 1999. "From Grace to Sin: Names and Abstractions in Paul's Letters." *Novum Testamentum* 41, 2:145-75.
Wink, Walter. 1983. *Naming the Powers: The Language of Power in the New Testament.* Minneapolis: Augsburg/Fortress.
———. 1986. *Unmasking the Powers: The Invisible Forces That Determine Human Existence.* Minneapolis: Augsburg/Fortress.
———. 1992. *Engaging the Powers: Discernment and Resistance in a World of Domination.* Minneapolis: Augsburg/Fortress.
Witherington, Ben. 2004. *Paul's Letter to the Romans: A Socio-Rhetorical Commentary.* Grand Rapids: Eerdmans.
Wood, A. Skevington. 1963. *Life by the Spirit.* Grand Rapids: Eerdmans.
Wood, Lawrence W. 1996. "Third Wave of the Spirit in the Pentecostalization of American Christianity: A Wesleyan Critique." *Wesleyan Theological Journal* 31, 1:110-40.
Wright, J. Edward. 2003. *Early History of Heaven.* Oxford: Oxford University Press.
Wright, N. T. 1991. *The Climax of the Covenant: Christ and the Law in Pauline Theology.* Minneapolis: Fortress.
———. 1995. "Romans in the Theology of Paul." Pages 30-67 in *Pauline Theology.* Vol. 3: Romans. Ed. David M. Hay and E. Elizabeth Johnson. Society of Biblical Literature Symposium Series, 23. Minneapolis: Fortress.
———. 1999. *The Challenge of Jesus.* Downers Grove, Ill.: InterVarsity.
———. 2002. "The Letter to the Romans: Introduction, Commentary, and Reflections." Pages 393-770 in vol. 10 in *The New Interpreter's Bible.* Ed. Leander E. Keck. Nashville: Abingdon.
———. 2006. *Paul in Fresh Perspective.* Minneapolis: Fortress.
Wuest, Kenneth S. 1945. *Romans in the Greek New Testament.* Grand Rapids: Eerdmans.
Yoder, John Howard. 1972. *The Politics of Jesus.* Grand Rapids: Eerdmans.
Yoder, Perry B. 1987. *Shalom, the Bible's Word for Salvation, Justice, and Peace.* Newton, Kans.: Faith and Life.
Young, Richard A. 1994. *Intermediate New Testament Greek: A Linguistic and Exegetical Approach.* Nashville: Broadman and Holman.

INTRODUCTION

A. The Importance of Romans

Of Romans, Martin Luther wrote:

> This letter is the principal part of the New Testament and the purest gospel, which surely deserves the honor that a Christian man should not merely know it by heart word for word, but that he should be occupied with it daily as the daily bread of his soul. For it can never be read too often or too well. And the more it is used the more delicious it becomes and the better it tastes. (Quoted in Brunner 1959, 9)

Scholars have disputed the claim that Romans is "the principal part of the New Testament." There are strong reasons for maintaining that the Gospels hold this distinction since they constitute the primary historical witness to Christ, but we must agree with the judgment that "what the gospel is, what the content of the Christian faith is, one learns to know in the Epistle to the Romans as in no other place in the New Testament" (Nygren 1949, 3).

Throughout the centuries this Epistle has in a peculiar way been able to furnish an impulse for spiritual renewal. When the church had drifted away from the gospel, a deep study of Romans has repeatedly been the means by which the loss has been recovered. Who can estimate the far-reaching effects upon the church and the world of the conversion of Augustine through the prayers of his godly mother Monica, Bishop Ambrose of Milan, and his reading of Rom 13:11-14 (see From the Text on this passage).

In November 1515, Martin Luther, Augustinian monk and doctor of sacred theology at the University of Wittenberg, began his expositions of Romans. As he prepared his lectures he came to see more clearly the meaning of Paul's gospel of justification by faith. The phrase the "righteousness of God" he had once hated as demanding what he could not deliver. Now in his study he came to see righteousness as a gift of God by which a person came to live, by faith. And he felt himself reborn. The consequence of this new insight the world knows. The Protestant Reformation had been born.

Under the date of May 24, 1738, John Wesley noted in his *Journal:*

> In the evening I went very unwillingly to a society in Aldersgate Street, where one was reading Luther's preface to the Epistle to the Romans. About a quarter before nine, while he was describing the change which God works in the heart through faith in Christ, I felt my heart strangely warmed. I felt I did trust in Christ, Christ alone, for salvation: And an assurance was given me, that he had taken away *my* sins, even *mine,* and saved *me* from the law of sin and death. (1979, 1:103)

In that moment the Evangelical Revival of the eighteenth century was born.

In August 1918, Karl Barth, pastor of Safenwil in Canton Aargau, Switzerland, published an exposition of the Epistle to the Romans. "The reader," he said in the preface,

> will detect for himself that it has been written with a joyful sense of discovery. The mighty voice of Paul was new to me: and if to me, no doubt to many others also. And yet, now that my work is finished, I perceive that much remains which I have not yet heard. (1933, 2)

But what Barth heard he wrote down—and that first edition of his *Romerbrief* fell "like a bombshell on the theologians' playground" (Catholic theologian Karl Adam, in *Das Hochland,* June 1926, as quoted in J. McConnachie. 1926-27. "The Teaching of Karl Barth," *Hibbert Journal* 25:385). That bombshell exploded the liberal humanistic theology that prevailed in the early twentieth century and gave birth to the Evangelical movement that has subsequently revolutionized Protestantism (Collins 2005).

What happened to Augustine, Luther, Wesley, and Barth has turned the tide of Western civilization and culture. On a smaller scale similar things happen to us as we let the words of this Epistle come alive to our minds and hearts in the power of the Holy Spirit.

B. The Place and Date of Writing

In none of Paul's letters are the place and time of writing so clearly indicated in the letter itself as in the case of Romans. In 15:19-32 the apostle makes it clear that he is nearing the culmination of his ministry in the East. He had preached the gospel "from Jerusalem all the way around to Illyricum" (v 19). Curiously, Acts does not mention Paul's mission in Illyricum—including all or parts of today's Albania, Bosnia and Herzegovina, Croatia, Kosovo, Macedonia, Serbia and Montenegro, and Slovenia. It, like Spain, today's Spain and Portugal, was Latin-speaking territory in Paul's day (but see Jewett 2007, 75-77).

Paul felt that he had completed his mission in the East. As he wrote, he was making plans to go West—to barbarian Spain, and, since Rome was already evangelized, to visit the Roman church on the way. But first, he had to perform a special task in behalf of Jerusalem. For some time he has been engaged in gathering a collection among the churches of Macedonia and Greece "for the poor among the saints" (v 26) there. That offering now virtually complete, Paul awaited only the opportunity to deliver it.

Paul planned to end his work on the collection in Corinth and to depart from there for Jerusalem (1 Cor 16:3-4). While he wrote 2 Corinthians (see 2 Cor 9:3-5), Paul was carrying out that plan and was on his way to Corinth.

That the letter was delivered by the deacon Phoebe from Cenchrea, the eastern port of Corinth (Rom 16:1), adds plausibility to the supposition that he wrote Romans from Corinth. This was the apostle's final visit to Corinth, since soon after this in Jerusalem his long imprisonment began (Acts 20:2-3). The dating of this final visit to Corinth depends on which overall chronology of Paul's ministry one adopts. The earliest date suggested is January—March, A.D. 53, and the latest, January—March, A.D. 59, in either case barely a quarter century after the death and resurrection of Jesus (see Jewett 2007, 18-21).

C. The Occasion and Purpose for Romans

For a long time Paul had planned to visit the Roman church (Rom

1:8-15; 15:22). With this prospect in sight, Paul hopes to realize his plan as soon as he has delivered the collection to the mother church in Jerusalem. "So after I have completed this task and have made sure that they have received this fruit, I will go to Spain and visit you on the way" (15:28). This statement eloquently demonstrates that he conceived his work to be as an evangelist, not as a pastor. His calling was to plant, not to water. His mission was not to build on another's foundation but to lay his own (15:18-21). He hoped that the collection—so important that Paul intended to deliver it even in the face of threatened death (Acts 21:10-14)—would heal the breach between his Gentile converts and the Jewish believers in Jerusalem. With the presentation of this gift the work he began from Antioch (Acts 13:1-4) would be culminated and he would be free to move westward with his gospel.

The so-called *Romans Debate* (Donfried 1991, first edition published in 1977) is particularly concerned with answering the question: Why did Paul write this kind of letter to the Romans? Scholarly answers are inevitably circular, often telling more about their theology than their competence as historians. Beyond scholarly reconstructions of the alleged opponents and accusations Paul hoped to refute (Acts 28:21-22 denies that false rumors about Paul had reached Rome that he had to clarify), what Paul explicitly claims is that he hoped to recruit the assistance of the Roman church for his plan for evangelizing Spain (Rom 15:22-33). He prayed that the Romans would give him a warm welcome when he arrived and be in a mood to help him with his work in the western part of the empire.

Robert Jewett's recent commentary identifies Romans as "a unique fusion of the 'ambassadorial letter' with several of the other subtypes in the genre: the parenetic letter, the hortatory letter, and the philosophical diatribe" (2007, 44). Paul writes as a spokesman for the foreign policy of God. He writes to persuade the Roman Christian community to join him in a cooperative mission to evangelize Spain (for "The Cultural Situation in Spain," see Jewett 2007, 74-79). His theological arguments identify the message they would proclaim as the "power of God." His "ethical admonitions show how the gospel is to be lived out in a manner that would ensure the success of this mission" (Jewett 2007, 44; see 42-46).

> If the Roman house and tenement churches can overcome their conflicts and accept one another as honorable servants of the same master (14:4), they would be able to participate in a credible manner in the mission to extend the gospel to the end of the known world. (Jewett 2007, 88; see 79-90)

D. Christianity in Rome

We have no direct information about the origin of Christianity in Rome (see Jewett 2007, 59-74). Its beginnings are shrouded in obscurity. The tradition that Peter was its founder has no historical support. He was still in Jerusalem as late as A.D. 39 (see Gal 1:18), but there are no references in Acts or any of Paul's letters to Peter's presence in Rome. It is generally agreed, however, that Peter did eventually go to Rome and that he was martyred there (see Cullmann 1953).

Acts 2:10-11 refers to "visitors from Rome (both Jews and converts to Judaism)" present for the first Christian Pentecost. It is possible that these converts took the new faith back to the Eternal City. We know that travel was widespread at this time and that there was a steady migration to the capital from all over the empire. Romans 16 bears testimony to the fact that many of the Christians in the Roman congregations had come to the capital from other areas.

The fourth-century writer Ambrosiaster gives what is the most probable account of Christian beginnings in Rome.

> It is established that there were Jews living in Rome in the times of the apostles, and that those Jews who had believed passed on to the Romans the tradition that they ought to profess Christ and keep the law. . . . One ought not condemn the Romans, but to praise their faith; because without seeing any signs or miracles and without seeing any of the apostles, they nevertheless accepted faith in Christ, although according to a Jewish rite. (Knox 1951, 9:362)

This account accords well with a note in Suetonius' *Life of Claudius,* to the effect that Claudius "expelled Jews from Rome because they kept rioting at the instigation of Chrestus" (Knox 1951, 9:362). NT scholars widely assume that Suetonius confused the common Greek slave-name *Chrestus* with *Christos* (Fitzmyer 1993, 31). The riot Suetonius mentioned probably referred to trouble that arose in the synagogues of Rome when Christianity was introduced. In any event, Christian Jews as well as Jewish unbelievers would have been banished by Claudius's edict in A.D. 49. Acts 18:2 refers to that edict as the reason for the presence in Corinth of Priscilla and Aquila.

Therefore, by A.D. 49 Christianity had been introduced to the Jewish community of Rome. But by the time Paul wrote Romans the church was predominantly Gentile (Rom 1:4-6, 13; 11:13-24; 15:15-16). In the Jewish synagogues of Rome, there would have been, in addition to believing Jews, many "God-fearers," Gentile half-converts who had been attracted to the monotheism and ethical teachings of Judaism. This mixture of Jews and God-fearers (and perhaps some Gentile proselytes) would have made up the majority of Christians until Claudius's banishment of "Jews" in A.D. 49.

These Jewish Christians, on their return to Rome, apparently found a Christian situation quite different from the one they left. They were now in the minority in the church that they had shaped earlier (Fitzmyer 1993, 31). Both the returning Jewish Christians and the Gentile Christian majority found themselves under a prohibition against all quasi-political agitation (Stuhlmacher 1994, 7).

We should not be surprised that the central issue of Romans is the relationship of the Christian gospel to the Mosaic law. In its original setting, this letter to the Romans was Paul's attempt to address the problem created by the events sketched above and the resulting divisions between Jewish and Gentile Christians that threatened Roman Christianity ca. A.D. 57.

In getting at the historical "reasons" for Romans, these issues are important. From the wider canonical perspective, however, Romans stands as an ecumenical theology designed to show and insure the *true meaning* of the Torah in light of God's final word in Christ, and to liberate the message of Christ from its Jewish trappings in order "to win obedience from the Gentiles" (15:18 RSV; see also v 19; 1:1-6; 16:26). Romans does not simply address the Jewish problem—it addresses the *human* problem.

E. The Unifying Theology of Romans

Romans 1—8 constitute the heart of the letter. Leander E. Keck provides an intriguing analysis of these chapters as they address the human problem:

> Paul states the gospel in such a way that its scope reaches from Eden to the eschaton, from the "fall" to the redemption of the world. . . . The gospel is God's saving power for every being, albeit for the Jew first. There is one gospel and only one, for all. . . . But if the gospel is God's saving power for *all* who believe, the one gospel must bring one solution for the one condition in which all find themselves. However important are the election of Israel, the promise to Abraham, the gift of the Law, the Davidic ancestry of God's Son, in no way do these exempt "the Jews" from solidarity with the Gentiles in the human condition. It is the *human* problem that the gospel addresses.
>
> In developing the foregoing theme, Paul inevitably "goes back to Adam" and "unpacks the Adamic situation three times," with an argument that moves "in a spiral fashion, each time going deeper into

the human condition, each time finding the gospel the appropriate antidote." (Keck 1995, 3:24-26)

Paul's exposition of the human situation (1:18—4:25) indicts both Gentiles and Jews as guilty before God and under the power of sin (3:9). This indictment reaches its climax in 3:19-20. The indictment is followed by the good news of God's righteousness now manifest in Christ Jesus, which provides justification by faith (3:21-26). Keck prefers to call it rectification by faith. On the basis of ***the faithfulness of Christ*** (*pisteos Christou*, 3:22) as God's atoning sacrifice, a rectified relationship to God is now open to all people (3:30). Those who respond in faithfulness to God's free offer of participation in the saving benefits of what Christ has done not only enter into a right relationship with God but also are empowered to live in the way God considers right.

In 5:12-21, the human condition calls for more than a rectified relationship to God; humanity needs liberation from the sin that rules our Adamic condition. For Paul there are two, and only two, alternate realms: that of Adam (the rule of sin and death) and that of Christ (the rule of grace and eternal life through justification). As Paul develops this theme in 6:1—7:6, he argues that freedom from sin and death is possible only through *participation* in Christ's death and resurrection, which promises "newness of life" (6:4 KJV), that is, the "new life of the Spirit" (7:6 RSV).

In 7:7—8:17 we are taken deeper into the human situation. As fallen in Adam (7:7-25), Jew and Gentile alike discover that an alien power has so usurped control of their existence and enslaved them that they achieve the exact opposite of what they intend. This alien resident is the "sin that dwells in me" (7:17, 20 NKJV), against which the Law is powerless. But what the Law could not do, God has done through Christ—he has won a decisive victory over sin that sets "free from the law of sin and death" all those who "do not live according to the sinful nature but according to the Spirit" (8:2, 4) whom they have received through Christ (8:1-17).

To identify the unifying theology of Romans is more difficult than casual readers might suspect. Romans is, after all, a sent letter, not a systematic theology. Certainly, Paul writes with deep theological convictions, but he does not write here or elsewhere anything that might pass for a theological treatise. Even his theological convictions emerge indirectly, not as theoretical abstractions. His is pastoral and practical theology. Any truly biblical theology must be as timely and relevant as the biblical books it attempts to represent. And, thus, it must be redone in every generation. Romans comes closest to being "theology" of any book in the Bible. But it does not seem to be either the product or the presentation of a coherent theological system. It grew out of everyday life issues and is concerned with Christian living.

The discipline of "biblical theology" attempts to discern the theological convictions underlying, unifying, and arising from the anthology of books we call the Bible. It takes for granted that the community of faith that brought these diverse books together into the canon of Scripture found within them a coherent unity. Biblical theologians seek to discover and demonstrate the internal theo-logic that unifies the Bible's witness to the triune God—creator of the universe, redeemer of Israel, king of the mundane, incarnate Word, powerfully weak, mother and lord of the church, and grand designer of history's consummation (to be overly brief and deliberately provocative).

So what is the unique contribution to biblical theology of Paul's letter to the Romans? Romans does not stand as a monument to the genius of the Apostle Paul alone. As the heir of the OT traditions of Israel, Paul's thought was significantly shaped by first-century Pharisaism, apocalyptic Judaism, the cultural assumptions of the Mediterranean world of the Hellenistic age, the church's lived experience of the Christ event, and the universal gift of the Holy Spirit.

In turn, Romans has significantly influenced the Protestant tradition, which returned the complement and read Romans in ways that reflected its own emerging sense of identity. Careful research into Romans may help us distinguish which of our cherished theological convictions may actually be traced back to Romans and which arise from other sources.

The key concept of Romans is *the righteousness of God*—God's righteousness manifest in the death of Messiah Jesus, whom he put forward as an atoning sacrifice, to be received by faith—the eschatological (end time) salvation that irrupted into history with the death and resurrection of Jesus and the gift of the Spirit. This divine activity created a new humanity in the likeness of Jesus, which is destined to include chosen Israel. In the end, God's righteousness promises the renewal of creation itself.

The righteousness of God is his *saving activity* in Christ: "God was reconciling the world to himself in Christ" (2 Cor 5:19). In Christ we have a glimpse of God as Sovereign Love, who gives his creatures the freedom to receive or spurn his proffered love. As Creator of heaven and earth, he yearns to be worshipped by grateful creatures (Rom 1:18-21*a*).

In his foreknowledge he has in love predestined all humans—both Gentiles and Jews (1:21*b*—2:29)—"to be conformed to the image of his Son, in order that he might be the firstborn within a large family" (8:29

NRSV). Such is the gospel in a nutshell: the Creator's self-unveiling in his Son Jesus the Messiah.

This story Paul weaves in with that of the people Israel whom God had chosen as a witness to him as saving Lord of all nations. To this end God called Abraham, giving him the promise of Gen 12:1-3. Israel, however, inadequately understood and seldom faithfully pursued their mission, choosing to bask in their election (see Isa 40—53).

At a critical moment of salvation history Jesus was born, suffered, died, and arose—as the promised Servant of the Lord (see Gal 4:1-7; Isa 52:13—53:12). In retrospect the birth of the nation Israel was the birth of the church, destined to fulfill God's call to Abraham, to declare to the world the gospel as the "the power of God for the salvation of everyone who believes" (Rom 1:16).

The gospel proclamation created a "new Israel" primarily of Gentiles, with only a remnant of believing Jews, but with a hope firmly in view that finally "all Israel will be saved." This is the gospel Paul declares in Romans, but which we "see in a mirror, dimly" (1 Cor 13:12 NRSV). But what we see is true and trustworthy: that which God has made visible to human eyes in Christ.

This, however, is not the final story. In the end, Messiah Jesus will return, not only to save all Israel, but also to redeem the created order! This indeed is a mystery. "However, as it is written: 'No eye has seen, no ear has heard, no mind has conceived what God has prepared for those who love him'—but God has revealed it to us by the Spirit. The Spirit searches all things, even the deep things of God" (1 Cor 2:9-10).

Before going further, we must take account of another fundamental aspect of Paul's theology in Romans: the corporate nature of *"man."* The word must be italicized because "man" in Romans is the *'adam* of the OT—"humankind." Few biblical texts are more important for grasping the biblical understanding of humanity as moral beings than Gen 1:26-27:

> Then God said, "Let us make humankind in our image, according to our likeness; and let them have dominion over the fish of the sea, and over the birds of the air, and over the cattle, and over all the wild animals of the earth, and over every creeping thing that creeps upon the earth." So God created humankind in his image, in the image of God he created them; male and female he created them. (NRSV)

The Hebrew word for "humankind" is *'adam,* a generic term that embraces not only male and female but also all humanity. The transition from the generic *'adam* to the personal "Adam" does not occur until 4:25:

"Adam knew his wife again, and she bore a son and named him Seth" (NRSV). In ch 5 we find the corporate significance of the term: "This is the list of the descendants of [*'adam*]. When God created humankind, he made them in the likeness of God. Male and female he created them, and he blessed them and named them 'Humankind' when they were created" (vv 1-2 NRSV).

The dual sense of Adam is preserved in Rom 5:12-21. The first Adam is the *man* of Gen 3 who disobeyed his Creator and fell; but Adam was also the corporate *'adam* of Gen 1:26-27. In the fall of the first Adam, "humankind" became depraved and sinful. The last Adam is the *man* Jesus, conceived sinless by the Holy Spirit in the Virgin's womb, who in his own person coped with the power of the flesh and sin—not by some innate conditioning as divine Son of God but as a human whose Spirit-empowered obedience to God, even to death, "condemned sin in the flesh" (Rom 8:4 NRSV). "The first man Adam became a living being," whose disobedience set the race on the course of sin and death. "The last Adam, a life-giving spirit," whose obedience potentially sanctified all humankind (1 Cor 15:45; see 2 Cor 3:18). Romans 5:12-21, thus, offers us at least a partial glimpse of Paul's doctrines of sin and salvation.

Romans defines "sin" as *hē hamartia*—"the Sin" that entered the race at the fall, a personified power that tyrannizes all unbelievers, both "outside" and "under" the Law (5:13-14; 7:7-25), until the end. Sin and Death are vanquished at the Second Advent (see 1 Cor 15:22-27). "The sting of death is sin, and the power of sin is the law. But . . . God . . . gives us the victory through our Lord Jesus Christ" (1 Cor 15:56-57).

Romans further defines "flesh" (*sarx*) and "Spirit" (*pneuma*). *Pneuma* translates the Hebrew term *ruach*, used in the OT for the "power" and "presence" of God, who enabled Israel's champions to throw off the yoke of their oppressors. In Romans *pneuma* is the personal power of the Holy Spirit, who transforms sinners into saints (see 2 Cor 3:18).

Sarx is humanity in its weakness (see Rom 8:3 NRSV; see *basar* in Isa 31:3). *Sarx* is the humanity of Jesus (Rom 1:3), in which he by the power of the Spirit "condemned sin in the flesh" (8:4 NRSV). *Sarx* is unregenerate human nature (7:18). As believers, we were formerly "in the flesh," dependent on human resources alone.

But now we are "in the Spirit," liberated from the oppressive power of sin (8:9-10). As renewed believers we serve God in the spirit (*pneumati mou*, "my spirit," 1:9 NRSV). The Spirit of God = Spirit of Christ = Spirit imparts life to believers (8:2, 4, 5, 6, 10), frees them from the law, sin, and death (8:1-17), so that they possess "the new life of the Spirit" (7:6 NRSV); supplies directive power to "the sons [and daughters] of God" (8:14); intercedes for the children of God (8:26-27), is the sanctifying agent of believers (8:1-17), witnesses to their adoption, and pledges the certainty of their future glory (8:16-17, 22-25).

Romans also defines the Law (*nomos*). While the term *nomos* identifies the first division of the Hebrew canon (3:21), in salvation history it signifies the covenant that God made with Israel at Mount Sinai (Exod 19:4-6). But *nomos* can also mean "principle" (Rom 3:27; 7:21; 8:2). As covenant, by *nomos* Romans means the Law that was fulfilled by Christ (8:1-4). In yet another sense, by *nomos* Paul means the requirements of the moral law written on the human heart (2:14-15); in this sense it is also the requirements of the Law fulfilled by the Spirit in the heart, making one a true Jew (2:25-29).

Finally, Romans firmly defines the "works of the law" that nullify salvation for unbelievers. "Works of the law" are not "good deeds done to merit God's favor" (as Luther thought), nor are they the works of *individuals* seeking to *enter into* relationship with God. Such individualism is foreign to Paul's thought. Unbelieving Jews erroneously *presume* they are the Israel of God, even as they reject Jesus as Messiah. Their sin thus is a *corporate* refusal to acknowledge Christ as the "end" (*telos*) of the Law (10:4; see 9:24—10:4, with commentary).

Most recent interpreters have adopted E. P. Sanders' explanation of "covenantal nomism" concerning the relation between works and law in the Judaism of Paul's day. According to Sanders, the "pattern" or "structure" of covenantal nomism is this:

> (1) God has chosen Israel and (2) given the law. The law implies both (3) God's promise to maintain the election and (4) the requirement to obey. (5) God rewards obedience and punishes transgression. (6) The law provides the means of atonement, and atonement results in (7) maintenance of the covenantal relationship. (8) All those who are maintained in the covenant by obedience, atonement and God's mercy belong to the group which will be saved. An important interpretation of the first and last points is that election and ultimately salvation are considered to be by God's mercy rather than human achievement. (Sanders 1977, 130)

Throughout Romans, as in all Paul's letters, salvation's frame of reference is corporate. This corporate understanding governs both Israel and the church. The *old* Israel is the Israel of the law that rejects Jesus as the Christ. Those who believe—both Jews and Greeks—are the *new* Israel of God (until *all* Israel is saved, 11:25-32). Also, employing a different metaphor, Paul writes, "We were all baptized by one Spirit into one body—whether Jews or Greeks, slave of free—and we were all given the one Spirit to drink" (1 Cor 12:13). It is within these two images that the Pauline *kerygma* functions.

F. The Rhetorical Genre and Logical Organization of Romans

The use of a thesis statement to introduce the body of Paul's letter to the Romans (1:16-17) is unique among his letters. This gives it something of the character of a treatise within a letter frame (1:1-15 and 15:14—16:27). M. Luther Stirewalt overemphasizes this, identifying Romans as a "letter-essay" (1991). The almost systematic-theological character of Romans arises from its use of the demonstrative (epideictic) genre, here in praise of the gospel. Consistent with this rhetorical goal is Paul's repeated use of the diatribe style to advance his argument. Among the prominent features of diatribe is Paul's repeated use of imaginary interlocutors to clarify and solidify his presentation of the gospel (Stowers 1981).

Paul writes this letter not primarily as a theologian but as a missionary, with ambitious plans to evangelize Spain (15:22-29) with the good news that is "the power of God for the salvation of everyone who believes" (1:16). His exposition of the gospel is not ivory-tower theory but is intended to deepen the level of his readers' existing commitment to the implications of the righteousness of God revealed in the gospel. If he is to gain the support of a divided Roman audience for his missionary venture to the western, barbarian region of the Roman Empire, he must bring them together around their common gospel.

Romans begins much as Paul's earlier letters, with a salutation identifying its sender, intended recipients, and his characteristic greeting (1:1-7). It differs from the others primarily in being far more expansive in each of these three concerns.

The thanksgiving section customary in Pauline letters appears (1:8-15), distinguished here by the unusual circumstance of Paul writing to a Christian community he had neither founded nor previously visited. As in Paul's other letters, the thanksgiving doubles as a rhetorical exordium, formally introducing the purpose (*causa*) he intends to achieve in the body of the letter (1:16—15:13).

Within the thanksgiving, Paul announces his plans to visit Rome but delays divulging the details until the conclusion (*peroration*) of the letter (in 15:14—16:23). He does not postpone his "eagerness to proclaim the gospel to . . . Rome" (1:15 NRSV) until his arrival, however. The body of the letter preaches the message he identifies indiscriminately as "the gospel" (1:15, 16, 17; 11:28; 15:20), "the gospel of God" (1:1; 15:16), "the gospel of his Son" (1:9), "the gospel of Christ" (15:19), or "my gospel" (2:16; 16:25).

In the letter thesis (1:16-17), Paul insists that the gospel he preaches is the message of God's righteousness (see also 3:5, 21, 22, 25), which is "the power of God for the salvation of everyone who believes: first for the Jew, then for the [Greek]" (1:16). Throughout the letter, Paul will insist upon these themes: the universal scope of the gospel, the faithfulness of God and the necessity of the human response of faith, and the distinction within salvation history of Jews and non-Jews. The gospel recounts the powerfully transforming activity of God within communities of faith.

The message of God's righteousness is universally needed because all human beings without exception are hopeless slaves of sin (1:18—3:20). This is true whether that sin takes the baser form of Gentile idolatry and depravity (1:18-32) or the more sophisticated self-righteous delusion of Jews (2:1-29). But sinful humanity first encounters God's righteousness revealed as divine wrath (1:18). God abandons his rebellious creatures to suffer the consequences of their self-destructive refusal to honor God as God (1:19-23), which only leads them deeper and deeper into the darkness of moral depravity (1:24-32).

Paul is convinced that God is not indifferent about what humans do. The wrath that for the present expresses itself as divine abandonment (1:19-23) will only be confirmed in the final judgment, based on deeds—righteous or unrighteous (2:1-16). That is, apart from the gospel.

The gospel that came first to Jews (1:16) makes them first in judgment (2:9) and reward (2:10). Jews will not be exempt from judgment simply because of their privileges as God's people (2:17-24). To be truly a Jew is not a matter of name and ethnic identity, but "a matter of the heart" (2:29 NRSV; see 2:25-29).

Paul grants that Jews enjoy considerable advantages as God's people, particularly the gift of the Law. But their unfaithfulness only increases their accountability (3:1-8). Paul demonstrates that all humanity is under the power of sin (3:9) by appealing to scripture to show that what is true of Jews is all the more true of Gentiles (3:9-20). The Law points out sin but is powerless to prevent it (3:20).

In the new age inaugurated by the coming of Jesus Christ, God has revealed his righteousness apart from Law but not inconsistent with it (3:21). In the faithfulness of Christ God has provided the means of freeing enslaved humanity from sin and its consequences, while maintaining his integrity (3:21-26). He offers his righteousness as a gift to all who are not too proud to accept it (3:27-31).

The new thing God has done in Christ, offering justification by faith, is consistent with OT teaching. Paul presents Abraham as the prototype of all who are put right with God on the basis of faith in his promise (4:1-25).

The gospel that puts believers right with God has the power to enable them to live right through the sanctifying gift of the Holy Spirit (5:1—8:39). The power of grace brings with it the possibility of peace and reconciliation with God in this age and hope for final salvation in the age to come, even in the face of present suffering (5:1-11).

Contrary to how it has classically been used, Paul does not appeal to the original sin of Adam to account for human sinfulness (in 5:12-21). Instead, he shows how the obedience of Christ, which eventuated in his saving death, offers fallen humanity a new alternative. Adam and Christ are each the head of a human family. But human destiny depends on its lord, not on heredity alone. Grace more than compensates for the damage sin has done (5:20-21).

Thus, Paul urges believers to live out of the resources of grace under the lordship of Christ (6:1-14). By offering themselves freely as instruments of righteousness, Christians may be freed from the shame of sin to enjoy the gift of sanctification and its end, eternal life (6:15-23).

The same justifying act of God that sets believers free from slavery to the power of sin and its consequences frees them to live "in the new way of the Spirit" (7:6; see 7:1-6). Human strength alone is incapable of fulfilling the demands of Law, because Law itself has been victimized by sin (7:7-25).

Only by Christ's gift of the indwelling Holy Spirit are believers set free from sin and empowered to fulfill the Law (8:1-11). That same Spirit sustains believers as they await final redemption (8:12-17). He assists them to pray as they should and works in their lives to accomplish God's saving purpose for all humanity—"to be conformed to the likeness of his Son" (8:29; see 8:18-30).

Paul concludes his exposition of the provision of the gospel of righteousness with the confident assertion that nothing in the universe "will be able to separate [believers] from the love of God that is in Christ Jesus" (8:39; see 8:18-39). But this leads the Jewish apostle to the Gentiles to address a potential objection to this confidence—the current general lost state of most of God's historical people, Israel (9:1—11:36).

Paul approaches this delicate problem from several perspectives. He insists that ethnic descent alone was never sufficient to determine the identity of God's people. God acts with sovereign mercy, apart from human claims or supposed rights (9:1-29). Israel is presently resistant to the gospel because it refused to acknowledge Christ as its Messiah, although it should have known better (9:30—10:21).

Israel's present lost state is not an indication that God is done with them (11:1-32). A remnant of believing Israel is root and trunk of the new Israel, consisting of believing Jews and Gentiles (11:1-10). Israel's unbelief has provided the unexpected opportunity for the gospel to be proclaimed to the Gentiles, whose response of faith has made them to become honorary Israelites (11:11-24). They in turn will provoke Israel to come to faith.

Paul warns his mostly Gentile audience that if pride and unbelief excluded unbelieving Israel from the people of God, honorary members should not be presumptuous (11:13-14).

Paul is confident that within God's mysterious plan to have mercy on all people (11:32), "the full number of the Gentiles" (11:25) and "all Israel" (11:26) will come to faith in Christ and final salvation (11:15-32). He concludes his exposition of the gospel as the righteousness of God in history with a doxological praise for the incomprehensible wisdom of God (11:33-36).

The final section of the body of the letter to the Romans is an exposition of God's righteousness in practice (12:1—15:13). Repeating the sacrificial imagery of 6:13 and 19, Paul urges his readers to offer themselves collectively as a living sacrifice to God (12:1). This will allow God to transform them completely—through sanctification, renewing their corporate mind "to test and approve" God's will. This is the worship God expects of his holy church (12:2).

Among the dramatic changes that will mark the practice of the Christian community, Paul mentions the mutuality of humble believers who use their gifts for the benefit of the entire community (12:3-8). Such a church will put unpretentious love into practice, both inside and outside the community (12:9-21). They will not complicate the church's ability to preach the gospel by defying the government or refusing to pay taxes (13:1-7). Instead, by loving both fellow believers and unbelievers they will fulfill what the Law demands (13:8-10).

Aware that the full day of final salvation is rapidly approaching, Paul urges his audience to reject the evil done under cover of darkness and live already as people of the day. This they can do under the lordship of Jesus Christ (13:11-14).

If Paul's mission to Spain is to be successful, he will need the assistance of a united Roman church (15:14-33). Therefore, he urges Jewish and Gentile believers to put aside the petty differences that divide them (14:1-23). They must refuse to treat one another as competitors—strong vs. weak. Rather than judging and despising one another because of such differences, they are to accept one another as God in Christ accepted them (15:1-13).

Paul does not ask the Roman churches to agree on the cultural differences that divide them. But he does expect them to agree on this: "with one heart and mouth" to "glorify the God and Father of our Lord Jesus Christ" (15:6). This means they will join a universal chorus of praise for God's faithfulness to Jews and his mercy to Gentiles and "overflow with hope by the power of the Holy Spirit" (15:13; see 15:7-13).

Paul concludes his lengthy celebration of the gospel of the righteousness of God (1:16—15:13) with an account of his travel plans, including an intermediate stop in Jerusalem en route to Rome and, with the assistance of the Roman Christians, on to Spain (15:14-33).

In the process Paul demonstrates how intimately his self-understanding is tied to the gospel. He identifies himself as "a minister of Christ Jesus to the Gentiles with the priestly duty of proclaiming the gospel of God, so that the Gentiles might become an offering acceptable to God, sanctified by the Holy Spirit" (15:16).

The letter closes with an expanded version of the customary formalities of ancient letters. Paul recommends his patroness, Phoebe, who is delivering the letter to Rome in his behalf (16:1-2), sends greetings to significant known individuals in the churches of Rome (16:3-16*a*) and greeting from his companions (16:16*b*, 21-24).

Warnings against false teachers interrupt his greetings (16:17-20). The letter ends with a doxology "to God who is able to strengthen you according to my gospel" (16:25 NRSV; see 16:25-27).

G. The Different Text Forms of Romans

Robert Jewett notes that "text critics have discovered fifteen different forms of Romans, including one no longer extant that is described by the church fathers" (2007, 4). The church fathers report that in the second century Marcion "removed entirely" the last two chapters from his version of the letter.

The most troublesome feature of the different textual traditions of Romans concerns the so-called wandering doxology—16:25-27. In various manuscripts it appears after 14:23; 15:33; 16:20*b;* 16:23; 16:24; in other manuscripts it appears twice, after 14:23; 15:33, or 16:23; in others, it is absent entirely.

On this basis, many critical scholars speculated that Rom 16 was not an original part of Paul's letter to Rome. They conjectured that it originated as Paul sent a copy of the letter to Rome with greetings to his friends in Ephesus. Harry Gamble effectively exploded this theory with his 1979 *Textual History of the Letter to the Romans.*

Recent scholars have argued that the original Romans may have lacked the benediction, 16:25-27, and that 16:17-20 may have been "a very early interpolation inserted at the time of the publication of the letter corpus" (Jewett 2007, 6). Although a case may be made for such conjectures, this commentary interprets the canonical form of the letter, which includes both passages.

II. THE GOSPEL OF GOD'S RIGHTEOUSNESS: ROMANS 1:16—15:13 (continued)

C. God's Righteousness in History (9:1—11:36)

Introduction

In recent years the question of the relationship of the church to Israel has moved from the periphery to the center of theological dialogue. Representative of the dialogue is the 2003 volume *Jews and Christians: People of God,* edited by Carl E. Braaten and Robert W. Jenson. In addition to Braaten and Jenson, the list of Christian contributors includes Wolfhart Pannenberg, George Lindbeck, and David Novak. Jewish contributors include Peter Ochs, Jon D. Levenson, and Reidar Dittman. While neither group shies away from its definitive doctrines, the discussion is gracious and other-regarding. The Christian faith in the triune God and the Jewish experience of the Holocaust deeply color the dialogue.

This ongoing theological conversation means that Rom 9—11, the most sustained consideration of Israel and the gospel in the New Testament, is now receiving unprecedented attention. From being considered no more than a parenthesis in the letter, a peripheral passage of secondary importance, it has become the focus of deepening interest and enquiry.

Romans 9—11 clearly forms a self-contained unit within the letter. Dodd's idea that it was originally a sermon Paul had preached and later incorporated here (1932, 149) is now considered passé among serious students of Romans. It is even more difficult to sustain Barth's contention that it "cannot be simply a continuation of the argument in 1:18—8:39" (1959, 110). Such views have now given way to the almost universal recognition that Rom 9—11 forms an essential component of Paul's total project in Romans. The contemporary discussion gives almost no attention to the topic that occupied the exegesis of interpreters of a previous generation: the notion that Paul is here defending a doctrine of individual predestination. (For a survey of that doctrine, consult the commentary on Rom 8:28-30.)

Romans 9—11 is "a carefully composed and rounded unit with a clear beginning (9:1-5) and end (11:33-36), and with 9:6a giving the text or thesis to be expounded" (Dunn 2002b, 38B:518) much as 1:16-17 served as the thesis for chs 1—8. Paul's concern throughout is to prove that God's word had not failed (9:6).

Nonetheless, the theme of chs 9—11 continues to be "the righteousness of God" as Paul has developed it in 1:18—8:39 (see esp. 9:30—10:4). The theme is now "the righteousness of God *in history.*" Because this history is embedded in Israel's Scriptures, a midrashic interweaving of OT quotations makes up more than thirty percent of chs 9—11, more than half of the total quotations in the entire book; and forty percent of these are from Isaiah (Dunn 2002b, 38B:520).

Up to this point Paul has presented a truly inclusive account of the gospel. In negative terms, all of humanity—Jews and Gentiles alike—are considered under the power of sin and alienated from God; in this sense there is "no distinction" (3:22 NRSV; see 3:10) between them. In positive terms—through Israel's Messiah, Jesus—that common bond under sin has been victoriously overcome by God, bringing about a "much more" powerful solidarity of grace and righteousness, leading to eternal life "through Jesus Christ our Lord" (5:21; see 5:12-21). The consequence is the creation of a new community of faith, composed of Jews and Gentiles, waiting to inherit the ancient promises God made to Abraham. Now, all the privileges of Israel—election, calling, divine adoption, inheritance, and glory—

have been conferred without distinction upon a community that includes both Jewish and Gentile believers.

The extension to Gentile Christians of Israel's exclusive privileges and the inclusion of Gentiles within the eschatological (= end-times) people of God constitute a major problem. Exacerbating that problem and pressing for immediate attention is another: Not only have multitudes of Gentiles entered the church, but the vast majority of Israel, by rejecting the gospel, appears to be excluded from God's ongoing purpose. The gospel presented by Paul inclusively with regard to Gentiles has been overwhelmingly exclusive with regard to Israel. It appears that God has *included* Gentiles at the great expense of *excluding* God's ancient people to whom the promises were originally entrusted.

What Paul must address is not so much—as has sometimes been argued—the single issue of Israel's *unbelief* but the dual issue of the apparent failure of the gospel with respect to Israel *and* the paradoxical *belief* with respect to hosts of Gentiles. "The credibility of Paul's presentation of the gospel hangs upon a satisfactory resolution of this issue" (Byrne 1996, 282).

This paradox is a *theological* issue, in that it raises the question of God's appearing to have acted in a manner contrary to his original promises. Paul had allowed this aspect of the problem and offered a passing response to it earlier in 3:1-8 in connection with Israel's inclusion in the mass of sinful humanity. Now, following Paul's inclusion of the Gentiles positively in the promise of the gospel (4:1—8:39), the issue of *theodicy* becomes even more pressing. How, in the face of the present paradox, can the ways of God with his people be justified? How can God be trusted to allow nothing to separate his new people from his love, as Paul has asserted so eloquently in 8:31-39, if he cannot keep faith with his ancient people?

This is a *personal* issue for Paul (see 9:1-3; 10:1; 11:1, 13-14) in that so inclusive a presentation of the gospel with respect to the Gentiles risks appearing careless respecting the fate of Israel. Paul is, after all, a Jew himself. Is Paul indifferent to the salvation of the Jews? His future Jerusalem visit—intended as a sacramental gesture toward the Jews (15:25-27)—will be divisive and counterproductive unless the apostle can show that both his gospel and his personal attitude are equally inclusive with respect to Israel.

Romans 9—11, therefore, is no less a part of his inclusive presentation of the gospel than 1:18—8:39. There, Paul showed that God acted inclusively in Christ to bring non-Jews into the Christian community. The gospel of the God whose activity is always inclusive will be complete only when Paul shows that the same God who acted inclusively with respect to Gentiles acts equally inclusively with respect to Jews. (For Paul's defense of an inclusive ethical pattern that should characterize the Christian community, see the commentary on chs 12—15.)

That Gentiles would eventually have a share (in some limited degree) in Israel's end-time salvation had long been a part of Jewish eschatological expectation. In this sense Paul's gospel of inclusion was nothing new. What *is* new is a matter of timing. First, Paul was convinced that the eschaton had already arrived. Although the old age persisted, the new had dawned in Jesus of Nazareth, Israel's Messiah, tragically rejected by Israel. Second, the apostle reverses the expected order—not for Jews first, then for Gentiles, but for Gentiles first, then Jews—and that only after an extended period of the rejection of Israel.

Thus, Paul's task is to establish the foregoing pattern as the one truly intended by God from the beginning and presently being accomplished by his providential guidance. This explains why these chapters consist of scriptural exposition. Since it was in Holy Scripture that God had announced his plans for the "last days," it is in Holy Scripture that the justification of God's ways with Gentiles and Israel must be found. Just as he had turned to Scripture to account for the inclusion of the Gentiles (chs 3—4), so now he turns to it in his endeavor to justify the present rejection—and eventual inclusion—of Israel, in God's eternal purpose and plan (chs 9—11).

9:1—11:36 In pursuing the above task Paul first sets up the problem in 9:1-5, after which he proceeds to address the issues in three blocks:

- He presents a long scriptural argument to insist upon God's sovereign freedom to create an eschatological people according to his own will and purpose, without any tie to ethnic identity or human deserts (9:6-29).
- He examines the dual issue of Israel's rejection and the Gentile's inclusion from the standpoint of human response: Israel has been set aside for the present because it refused the righteousness of God and clung to its own legal righteousness (9:30—10:3).
- Having "vindicated" God from the charge of injustice, by way of both scripture and gospel (10:4-21), Paul directly addresses the fact of Israel's unbelief, and then in a remarkable tour de force, holds before Gentiles a "mystery," the final inclusion of those of his own race in the community of salvation, on the same basis as Gentiles (11:1-32): "For God has bound all men over to disobedience so that he may have mercy on them all" (v 32).

With this glorious vision before his eyes, Paul concludes with a hymn in praise of the unsearchable wisdom and fathomless mercy of God (11:33-36).

I. The Problem of Israel's Unbelief (9:1-5)

BEHIND THE TEXT

Paul is now about to broach a subject he shrinks from directly announcing. The strong protestation in these opening sentences indicates both the gravity of his convictions and the awareness that his fellow Jews may doubt his sincerity. With great tact, therefore, the apostle moves into his subject.

Having just triumphantly declared that *nothing* "will be able to separate us from the love of God that is in Christ Jesus our Lord" (8:39), Paul suddenly, and without a hint of what he was about to say, radically shifts his mood and affirms that he is willing to be separated from God's love in Christ—"cursed and cut off from Christ"—if forfeiting his own salvation would gain that of his own people. He declares he is telling them the truth "in Christ" and that "the Holy Spirit" confirms his clear conscience.

Paul does not linger with his agony, however, but turns the reference to his fellow Jews ("brothers [and sisters]") into a recital of Israel's privileged status as God's chosen people. He enumerates the God-given privileges they enjoy as the Israel of God: (1) their "adoption as sons," (2) the "divine glory" in their midst, (3) "the covenants," (4) "the receiving of the law," (5) "the temple worship," and (6) "the promises." After naming these, Paul begins afresh with the patriarchs and states their crowning privilege: (7) "Christ [the Messiah], who is God over all, forever praised!" This evokes an "Amen!" This seventh privilege, since nothing in the context requires a firm decision, raises a question that must be addressed: Did Paul call Jesus "God"?

Though never formulated explicitly, the question that lies behind every sentence in the passage sets in motion the whole argument of chs 9—11: that Israel, despite its great privileges and Paul's labors, has rejected the gospel the apostle preached.

IN THE TEXT

■ **1** Paul's avowal of truthfulness in vv 1-2 may have been intended to assure his Jewish hearers in the Roman church that he was by no means indifferent to the fate of his fellow Israelites. Or perhaps the vehemence of his assertion simply demonstrates the energy and seriousness with which he addresses the issue. Whatever the reason, he insists that what he is about to say as a Christian (**in Christ;** see 6:11) is **the truth,** that he is **not lying** (see 2 Cor 11:31; Gal 1:20), that his **conscience** is clear, that **the Holy Spirit** can confirm this (see 8:16).

■ **2** All this prepares for his assertion: **I have great sorrow and unceasing anguish** [see LXX Isa 35:10; 51:11] **in my heart** (Rom 9:2). He appeals to **Christ** and **the Holy Spirit** because it is impossible to validate what can only be proved by one who knows what is *within* his person (see 2:15). This gives what he is about to say the character of a solemn oath.

■ **3-4*a*** Paul was wracked with deep and chronic emotional pain (9:2), we only learn in vv 3 and 4, at the thought of Israel's unbelief. Like Moses (Exod 32:31-32), Paul swears that he would be willing to sacrifice himself for the sake of his people: **For I could wish** [*euchomēn,* lit. "pray"] **that I myself were cursed** [*anathema,* lit. "devoted to destruction"] **and cut off from Christ for the sake of my brothers, those of my own race, the people of Israel** (Rom 9:3-4*a*).

That Paul wished for a reversal of status suggests that he views Israel as currently **cursed** and **cut off** (v 3). The formulation of his oath indicates that he now realizes his repeated prayer that he might be eternally damned (see 1 Cor 16:22; Gal 1:8-9) **for the sake of** (*hyper*) his fellow Jews could not be granted.

The impossibility of fulfilling his wish is not because Paul imagines a justified and Spirit-filled person cannot by unfaithfulness to God be severed from Christ and eternally lost (see Rom 8:13; 1 Cor 9:27). Only the Holy One can become a curse for us and thereby effect our salvation (Gal 3:13-14). Paul's is certainly the language of love (see Rom 5:8), but it is a wish a mere human cannot achieve. His willingness to pray this way, "to stake everything, his own life included" on the truth of the gospel, makes clear how unshakable is his faith in the righteousness and faithfulness of God (Dunn 2002b, 38B:532).

Paul refers to his fellow Jews as **my brothers *and sisters,* those of my own race** [*tōn syngenōn mou kata sarka,* ***my relatives according to the flesh/humanly speaking***]. Normally, he reserves the term *adelphoi,* ***brothers and sisters,*** for his fellow Christians. Thus, he adds in effect: Sadly, our kinship is only skin deep.

It is also noteworthy that despite Paul's normal practice in Rom 1—8 (see 1:16; 2:9, 10, 17, 28, 29; 3:1, 9, 29), he uses the term "Jew" in chs 9—11 only in 9:24 and 10:12. Neither the name "Israel" (appears in the Greek of 9:6, 27, 31; 10:19, 21; 11:2, 7, 25, 26) nor the designation "Israelite" (see 9:4 and 11:1 in Greek) appears anywhere in chs 1—8. "Israel" was the people's preferred self-designation; "Jew" was the name by which others called them (Kuhn 1964, 3:360).

■ ***4b*** **Theirs,** Paul continues, referring to his fellow Israelites, are eight sacred and interrelated privileges he proceeds to list in vv 4*b*-5. First, because they had received **the adoption of sons** and daughters (*huiothesia;* v 4*b*), the people of Israel were considered children of God, a status conferred upon them at the Exodus (Exod 4:22; Isa 1:2; Jer 31:9; Hos 1:10; 11:1). Nonetheless, the term *huiothesia* never occurs in the LXX or other Jewish literature of the period (Dunn 2002b, 38B:526). Perhaps Paul uses anachronistically a term to designate the privilege he has already insisted now also belongs to Christians, whether Jews or Gentiles (Rom 8:12-17, 23; 2 Cor 6:18).

Israel's second privilege, **the divine glory** (simply *doxa,* "glory"), arises from the first (see Rom 8:17-18). It also seems to allude to the Exodus. It was manifested in the pillars of cloud and fire at the crossing of the Red Sea (Exod 16:10), which was a glorious act of deliverance (15:6, 11) and in the theophany at Mount Sinai and the gift of the Law, and the sanctifying of the Tabernacle in the wilderness (24:15-17; 33:18; 40:34-35; Lev 9:23; Num 14:10). Dunn (2002b, 38B:527) notes that Jews sometimes used "the glory" to refer to "the one God"—Israel's gift of monotheistic faith to the world. Paul may also have thought of Israel's hope for the eschatological manifestation of God's glory (see Isa 35:2; 40:5; 60:1-3; 66:18-19).

Paul does not go so far as he does in 1 Cor 3:7—4:6, where he claims that the new covenant, distinguished as it is by the coming of the Messiah and the gift of the Spirit, far outshines the glory of the old covenant (see John 1:14-18; 2 Cor 4:4). Nevertheless, we cannot forget what he wrote earlier in this letter—that all lack the glory of God (Rom 1:23; 3:23); that only through Christ can this glory be restored; or that as joint heirs with Christ, Christians, whether Jews or Gentiles, have the prospect of sharing this glory, once the exclusive property of Israel, in the future resurrection (5:2; 6:4; 8:17-18, 21, 30; see Phil 3:21).

Paul lists as Israel's third privilege **the covenants** (see the apocryphal Sir 44:12, 18; Wis 18:22; 2 Macc 8:15; 2 Esd 3:32; 5:29). He may have had in mind the covenant promises God made to Noah (Gen 9), Abraham (chs 15; 17), Isaac (26:24), Jacob (28; 32; 35:10-12; Lev 26:42-45), Moses (Exod 19:5; Deut 29:1), Joshua (Josh 8:30-35), David (2 Sam 23:5), Josiah (2 Kgs 23:3), and/or Nehemiah (Neh 9—10). Each initiated a unique mutual relationship of loyalty and blessing between God and a representative of Israel.

Following the precedent of Jer 31:31-34, Paul would have grouped all God's previous arrangements with his people together as *old* covenant in contrast to the *new* covenant Christ brought into existence (1 Cor 11:25; 2 Cor 3:6, 14; Gal 4:24). But, this new covenant is a renewal and expansion of the old covenant to include Gentiles, not a rejection of it.

The fourth and fifth preeminent privileges of Israel arose from the third. Both the Law and the temple cult accompanied the establishment of the Mosaic covenant. The bestowal of **the** Mosaic **law** (*nomothesia,* "lawgiving"; see 2 Macc 6:23) was considered one of Israel's greatest sources of confidence (Rom 2:17-24), but Paul would have shared Stephen's indictment of Israel: "You . . . have received the law . . . but have not obeyed it" (Acts 7:53). Despite the traditional Protestant misunderstanding of the Law as a failed experiment to be abandoned with the coming of Christ, Paul seems to think of this privilege of Israel as he does the others in his list—the possession of all believers, Jew and Gentile alike (see Rom 7:7, 12; 8:4; 13:8-10).

The NIV interpretively translates *hē latreia* (lit. ***the service***) as referring to the **temple worship** of Israel (see Heb 9). In Rom 1:9; 12:1; and 15:16 "Paul spiritualizes or secularizes the concept" of temple sacrifices (Dunn 2002b, 38B:527), using the term to refer to the acts of loving service Christians perform in everyday life.

9:4b-5 Sixth, **the promises** (*hai epangeliai;* see 2 Cor 6:18—7:1) certainly refer to God's covenantal (see **the covenants** above) assurances to Israel's ancestors, especially those to Abraham (see Rom 4:13 and the comments on the term there; 15:8) of land, progeny, and blessing (Gen 12:2-3; 18:18; 22:18; 26:4; 28:14). Unlike Gal 3—4, Paul does not in Romans even hint that God's **promises** and his giving of the Law might be at odds with one another.

■ **5** Seventh, **Theirs are the patriarchs** (Rom 9:5). Paul may refer in particular to the founding fathers of Israel—Abraham, Isaac, and Jacob (see Acts 3:13), his twelve sons, and other storied figures of prior generations (see Sir 44—49). But he often uses the term simply to refer to all of Israel's ancestors, famous or anonymous (see Rom 11:28; 15:8; 1 Cor 10:1; John 6:31).

Paul's Pharisaic contemporaries' interest in "the traditions of the elders" tended to expand the Law's dividing wall separating Jews and Gentiles. They assumed that "the merits of the fathers, mediated by physical descent" effectively blotted out the sins of their descendants and guaranteed them pardon at the final judgment (see Schrenk 1964, 5:977, for references to the primary sources). Paul was not the first to challenge such notions as presumption. Jesus (e.g., Matt 21:31-32; Luke 13:22-30; John 8:31-59) and John the Baptist (Matt 3:9) before him had done so.

Paul has made a special point of insisting that Jews are slaves to sin as surely as Gentiles and equally in need of justification (in Rom 1:18—3:26). Nonetheless, Paul insists that "the continuity between Christian believers and the ancestral faith of Israel has not been destroyed, even despite Israel's current resistance, for which Paul mourns" (Jewett 2007, 566).

Writing to a Gentile audience, he can refer to Israel's wilderness generation as *"our* ancestors" (1 Cor 10:1 NRSV, emphasis added). In Rom 15:8-9, he will claim that Christ became "a servant of the Jews on behalf of God's truth, to confirm the promises made to the patriarchs so that the Gentiles may glorify God for his mercy." It is the faithful God (3:27-31), not the patriarchs, who opens the possibility of including Gentiles among the children of *"our* father Abraham" (4:12, emphasis added; see vv 11-12, 16-17) and *"our* father Isaac" (9:10, emphasis added).

Israel's eighth and greatest privilege is that **from them is traced the human ancestry** [*kata sarka,* "according to flesh"; see 1:3-4; 9:3] **of Christ** [*ho Christos,* "the Christ"], **who is God over all, forever praised!** (v 5). Paul completes his list of the privileges of the Jewish people by stating that the Messiah himself is by natural descent a Jew. The Greek phrase translated "who is over all, God blessed forever!" (NRSV) allows for other plausible translations.

To put the matter simply, the scholarly debate concerns the interpretation of Paul's grammar: Does the phrase in whole or in part or not at all refer to **Christ;** or is it merely a disconnected doxology—***May God, who is over all, be forever praised***? (Cranfield [1985, 222] summarizes six major proposals; Moo [1996, 565] identifies eight options; Dunn [2002b, 38B:528-29] reduces these to two.)

The ultimate question is *theological:* Does Paul here call Jesus **God**? Some scholars argue that since he never applies that term explicitly to Jesus elsewhere in his letters, he must not have done so here (Dunn 2002b, 38B:529, 535). But Paul does confess him often as "Lord" (see e.g., 1 Cor 8:4-6; 12:3-5) (see Mark 12:35-37; Acts 2:32-36; see Jewett 2007, 567-68). New Testament authors, including Paul, do not hesitate to apply to Jesus OT references referring to the LORD—Yahweh, the personal name of Israel's God, the Creator of heaven and earth—to Jesus.

This in itself is remarkable, given the monotheistic commitments of early Christians and the fact that a fully nuanced doctrine of the Trinity would not be recognized as orthodox for centuries. Thus, it does not seem implausible that Paul should have confessed that *ho Christos*—the Messiah Jesus—is **God over all** (see Titus 2:13, where Christ is called "our great God and Savior").

Granted, the grammatical construction of Rom 9:5 is equivocal and might allow for an interpretation that makes a less exalted christological affirmation. Nonetheless, the NT witness to Jesus confirms the conclusion of Cranfield: "In v. 5 Paul is affirming that Christ, who, in so far as His human nature is concerned, is of Jewish race, is also Lord over all things and by nature God blessed forever" (1985, 224).

Such an understanding of v 5 paves the way for a Christian interpretation of Deut 30:14; Isa 28:16; and Joel 2:32, which Paul quotes in Rom 10:8-13: Jesus the Messiah embodies Israel's law; he is "the LORD" in these passages; and faith in him is the basis of salvation (see the commentary on 10:8-13). "If salvation results from calling on the 'name of the Lord' (10:13), then the salvation of 'all Israel' in 11:26 would entail their recognition that Jesus is 'really God over all things' (9:5)" (Jewett 2007, 568).

FROM THE TEXT

In Rom 1—8 Paul made a point of insisting *that* and explaining *how* through Christ Gentiles may experience privileges once reserved for Israel. But the good news of the gospel of free grace must now face the problem this creates:

> How is it that Gentiles are entering into the promises to Abraham so readily while most of his own people to whom the promises were given seem to be missing out? If God is not faithful to Israel, how can Paul proclaim his faithfulness to the Gentiles? (Dunn 2002b, 38B:530)

In Rom 9 Paul returns to the questions about Israel he left hanging in ch 3.

Romans 9:1-5 is an introduction to the apostle's theme in chs 9—11: "the righteousness of God *in history.*" More specifically, it is the hermeneutical key to understanding 10:4-13. There Paul will argue that Christ is the embodiment and goal of Israel's law. As the fulfillment of the OT, Christ is the saving Word of God, hidden deep in the human heart. More than anywhere in his letters, "Paul makes plain his fundamental conviction as to the continuity between Israel of old and the believer now, Jew first but also Gentile" (Dunn 2002b, 38B:535).

In these verses Paul claims that far from being a renegade and traitor to his people, it is his Jewish heritage that compels him to take the gospel to the Gentiles. Paul is in anguish because most of his fellow Jews misunderstand this truth, and in doing so "are failing to enter into their own heritage" (Dunn 2002b, 38B:531). This contention helps solve the conundrum of Israel's unbelief.

2. The First Answer: God's Promises Are Only to Believers (9:6-29)

In this section the apostle gives his first clear response to the thematic question raised in v 6: "'Has the word of God fallen to the ground?' 'No!' says Paul; 'God's word of promise from the very beginning meant only those elected by God's free grace'" (Goppelt 1964, 153). In vv 14-29 Paul's Jewish interlocutor returns to the stage as he resumes the diatribe style he often employed to advance his arguments in chs 1—8 (see ch 2). Although Paul's particular concern in chs 9—11 is with Israel, Gentiles are never out of sight (9:24-26).

a. The Children of Promise Are the Children of God (9:6-13)

BEHIND THE TEXT

Paul faces squarely the problem of Israel's unbelief. The fact that the majority of God's ancient people have rejected Jesus as their Messiah must *not* be construed to mean that the word of God has failed. Truth is, from the time of the call and faith of Abraham, God has always acted in ways hidden to a majority of Israelites but in a manner consistent with his divine character and purpose.

Understood in this way, God's unfolding plans are always in harmony with his merciful justice, even though at times it seems otherwise. What presently appears as something "new"—the inclusion of a bulk of believing Gentiles in God's people and the setting aside of the majority of the Jews—must be viewed as the faithfulness of God to his promise to have a people willing to "let God be God." *This* is the saving faith that opens the way to God's raising a people who are his true "children."

Romans 9:6-13 proceeds in two stages. The first is Paul's understanding of Abraham's faith as key to that of the "new Israel" as composed of believing Gentiles and Jews (vv 6-9); the second stage is his interpretation of the principle of election in the choice of Jacob and the rejection of Esau (vv 10-13).

This is the opening passage in an unfolding argument that will carry us through the OT story of God, where we must at all times keep steadily in view the character and purpose of the one true and living God, who—if we follow Paul's exposition—is holy, just, and good, in carrying out the plan of salvation history.

IN THE TEXT

(1) The True Israel (9:6-9)

■ **6** Although Paul does not ask the question directly, he implies it: "Has God's plan gone awry?" or, "Is Israel's unbelief God's fault?" He answers, **It is not as though God's word had failed** (*ekpeptōken,* v 6*a*).

In the NT **God's word** often refers to the Christian gospel (e.g., Luke 5:1; 1 Cor 14:36), but here it seems to refer to God's promise to Israel (Dunn 2002b, 38B:538). The implicit question of Rom 3:4 resurfaces: Has God been true to his word? The Greek verb translated **had failed** is in the perfect tense, referring to a state resulting from a prior event. The word had a broad range of application. It referred to flowers that had withered and fallen to the ground, ships that had drifted off course and run aground, and commercial ventures that had gone bankrupt (Bauer 1979, 243). Thus, Paul asks, "Is the gospel message unpersuasive?" or, "Is the gospel powerless to save Israel (see 1:16-17)?" (see Jewett 2007, 573-74).

Israel's present unbelief and unfaithfulness to God repeat tragic chapters from the earlier history of its relationship with God. Paul pointed out in 2:28-29 that the true Jew is one whose life praises God. Thus, racial identity and circumcision do not really matter. Now he points out in a similar vein that not all the biological descendants of Abraham are truly "children of Abraham," in the faith-sense he explained in ch 4.

Throughout the nation of Israel's history recounted in the OT, God's purposes were carried forward by an inner group, an elect minority, a saving remnant—a faithful subset of the whole. This is Paul's point here: **not all who are descended from Israel are Israel** (9:6*b*). That is, not all who claim the patriarch Jacob as their forefather are truly Israelites. Jewett explains:

> Since all believers in the messianic proclamation are part of the true Israel, the distinction is finally "between believing and physical Israel" as determined by their response to the "word of God." If the distinction between Israel and the true Israel can be sustained on the basis of the scriptural tradition on which Israel rests, the "word of God" cannot be held to have failed. (2007, 575)

■ **7** In v 7 Paul moves backward two generations to broaden the application to Abraham's descendants, which would include, not only Jacob, but also Ishmael, Isaac, Esau, and others. It is not **because they are his descendants** (*sperma, **seed;*** see 2 Chr 20:7; 2 Cor 11:22) that they are called **Abraham's children** (*tekna;* see John 8:31-59). God's covenant promises to Abraham did not apply to all of his children. Physical descent alone was not enough. Not *all* Israel is *true* Israel. His true children are not those who have Abraham's genes but those who share his faith (4:12; see Gal 3:7-9, 14).

Paul finds God's criterion in this matter in the account of the birth of Abraham's son Isaac. Thus, Genesis sets a pattern determinative of the future. Being Abraham's children is not a matter of human generation. **On the contrary, "It is through** [*en, **in***] **Isaac that your offspring** [*sperma, **seed***] **will be reckoned** [*klēthēsetai, **will be called***]," Paul rejoins (Rom 9:7*b;* citing LXX Gen 21:12). The words ***seed*** and "call" figure significantly in Paul's argument in Rom 9:8, 12, 24, 25, 26, and 29.

The Genesis Background

God had promised to bless Abraham's descendants (***seed***), and through them all nations of the earth (Gen 12:3). Since Abraham was unable to have a child by his wife, Sarah, he designated his servant Eliezer of Damascus his heir, but God rejected Abraham's culturally conditioned solution (15:2-4). Again, following cultural precedent, Sarah gave Abraham her Egyptian maid, Hagar, as a surrogate wife; and though her, his eldest son, Ishmael, was born (ch 16). But God rejected this humanly devised plan as well, insisting that Abraham's heir would be the offspring of his wife, Sarah, who was already in menopause (17:15-22).

Three heavenly visitors came to Abraham's tent in Mamre (ch 18) and assured him again that he would have a son by Sarah (v 10, quoted in Rom 9:9). After God had fulfilled his promise and Sarah had given birth to Isaac, she prevailed upon Abraham (with God's concurrence) to expel Hagar and her child Ishmael from the family (Gen 21). It was in Abraham's distress over sending away his firstborn that God assured him, **"It is through Isaac that your offspring will be reckoned"** (Rom 9:7, citing Gen 21:12). Although Abraham had still more children by another wife, Keturah, Isaac remained his sole heir (ch 25).

■ **8** Paul explains the Gen 21:12 quotation referring to Abraham's children in Rom 9:8: **In other words** [*tout' estin, **That is***], **it is not the natural children** [*ta tekna tēs sarkos, **children of the flesh***] **who are God's children** [*tekna tou theou;* see 8:21], **but it is the children of the promise** [*tēs epangelias;* see 4:13, 14, 16, 20, 21; 9:4, 9; 15:8 and the comments there] **who are regarded** [*logizetai*] **as Abraham's offspring** (*sperma, **seed***). By shifting from *sperma* to *tekna,* the terminology of 8:21, Paul implies "that Christians, Jewish and Gentile, are the true children of Abraham" (Fitzmyer 1993, 561). The neuter noun *tekna* not only eliminates ethnic particularity but also deonstrates that gender differences are inconsequential to God.

The echoes of ch 4 suggest that Paul has not forgotten his argument that **reckoning** (*logizomai* appears in vv 3, 4, 5, 6, 8, 9) is not a matter of getting one's due but of a gift freely given. Thus, Abraham became the father of all believers, both Jews and Gentiles. God's children are not defined by nor disqualified "by natural or ethnic criteria" (Dunn 2002b, 38B:540).

Curiously, Paul's logic moves from **God's children** to **Abraham's offspring,** and not vice versa. With the OT story echoing in the background, Paul does not consider Isaac Abraham's "natural child." Because the miracle-child was conceived on the basis of God's assurances to Abraham and Sarah, he is instead a "child of promise" (compare Gal 3:6-29). Paul's point is not merely to *narrow* the list of claimants to the status of being Abraham's children but also to *expand* it to include more than his physical descendants (as in Rom 4:13-18).

Paul distinguishes the ***children of the flesh*** from the **children of the promise.** The former are not ***the children of God;*** only the latter are. And only **God's children** are reckoned as descendants of Abraham. Paul views the limitation of Abraham's "descendants" to the line of Isaac (quoting LXX Gen 21:12), based on the distinction between Abraham's other **natural children** and Isaac, whose birth was the result of God's promise of "descendants." Paul concludes from this that Scripture reveals God's intention also to "reckon" nonethically defined "descendants of Abraham" who "will be called 'sons of the living God'" in the last days (see Hos 1:10, quoted in
9:8-9 Rom 9:6).

Paul's word for **descendants** here, *sperma* (***seed***), is a collective term. In Gal 3:16 he argues that the "seed" is focused on one descendant of Abraham, Christ. If Paul assumes the same here, the difficult theological reasoning of Rom 9:6-13 is fundamentally christological and soteriological. The true ***seed*** arose through **promise** (v 8), and accordingly the promise of Abraham belongs to the ***seed,*** i.e., to Christ alone (4:13; see Gal 3:16, 19, 29). But as in v 29, Paul also assumes that "If you belong to Christ, then you are Abraham's seed." Thus, his point here may be only to emphasize the collective or communal character of Abraham's seed, not its christological basis.

■ **9** In Rom 9:9 Paul finds the validation (*gar,* **For**) of his construal of the promise to Abraham in his rather loose quotation of LXX Gen 18:10 and 14: **For this was how the promise was stated**. God promises, **"At the appointed time** [*kata ton kairon touton,* ***at this time;*** see Gal 4:4 (*to plērōma tou chronou*), ***the fullness of time***] **I will return, and Sarah will have a son."** As in v 28, Isaac's birth is understood miraculously, typologically, and eschatologically. Paul may understand it as anticipating both the birth of Christ and the resulting family of those who in Christ are **children of promise.**

(2) The Election of the Unlikely (9:10-13)

Paul opens the second stage of his argument with an analysis of the Scriptures (Gen 25:23) referring to the next generation of patriarchs, the twin children of Isaac and his wife Rebecca—i.e., Esau the firstborn and his brother Jacob. Here also "the divine word rather than physical lineage determines the heir of the promise" (Jewett 2007, 577).

■ **10-11** **Not only that,** Paul begins, **but Rebekah's children had one and the same father** [*ex enos koitēn, **from one seminal emission;*** Bauer 1979, 440], **our father Isaac. Yet, before the twins were born** [*gennēthentōn, **be-gotten***] **or had done anything good** [*agathon*] **or bad** [*phalon;* see 2 Cor 5:10]**—in order that** [*hina*] **God's purpose in election** [*hē kat' eklogēn prothesis tou theou,* lit. ***according to the selective purpose of God***] **might stand** [*menēi, **remain in place***]: **not by works** [*ouk ex ergōn;* see 3:21-30; 11:6] **but by him who calls—she was told, "The older will serve the younger"** (Rom 9:10-12, citing LXX Gen 25:23).

Paul obviously writes presuming that his audience knows the Bible story. The words **the twins** (Rom 9:11) in the translation has no basis in the Greek text, which has only ***they*** as the implied subject of the verb ***were begotten.*** What this highly dense argument particularly brings out is the absolute freedom of the merciful God to pursue a creative purpose independent of human contribution. That the twins were conceived in one act of sexual intercourse and conceived as God's answer to one prayer by Isaac (Gen 25:21), and that both twins had the same father, the miraculous offspring of Abraham, had no effect on their standing with God. Natural descent is inconsequential to God.

■ **11-12** Paul seems concerned in Rom 9:11-12 to deny the contemporary Jewish notion that God's selection was based on foreknowledge of the future good works of Jacob and the evil of Esau (Dunn 2002b, 38B:543). Human merit is inconsequential to God. Birth order and the cultural expectations associated with it are equally of no concern to God. His choice of Jacob over Esau was made before they were even conceived.

Paul insists that God's choice was made **in order that** he might demonstrate the consistency of his *prothesis,* **purpose. Purpose** in v 11 should be understood in light of its use in regard to eschatological salvation and glorification in 8:29-30 (see the commentary there; see 11:5-6). The ***selective purpose of God remains*** unchanged to the present (see Isa 14:24).

■ **13** In Rom 9:13 Paul continues by citing Mal 1:2-3: **"Jacob I loved, but Esau I hated."** The first thing to note is the reference to the *descendants* of **Jacob** and **Esau:** the nations of Israel and Edom (see v 3), not the twin sons of Isaac and Rebecca (see the sidebar "The Original Context of Malachi 1:1-2"). "Loving" and "hating" in this context are Semitic ways of expressing a preference for one party and a rejection of another (see, e.g., Deut 21:15; see 2 Esd 3:16). There are no grounds here for erecting a doctrine of "double predestination" on the slender basis of this OT text.

The Original Context of Malachi 1:1-2

In its original context, this passage claims that God's love for Israel (= **Jacob**) is proven by his punishment of the nation Edom (= **Esau**), not only for failing to come to the aid of Jerusalem when the city was besieged by the Babylonians in 586 B.C. but for actually rejoicing in its fall (Ps 137:7; Lam 4:21-22). The figure of speech of metonymy uses the names **Jacob** and **Esau** to represent their descendants. Malachi assures Israel of God's preserving love by pointing to God's repression of Israel's adversary, Edom. Paul does not always quote the OT with the contextual sensitivities of a twenty-first-century exegete.

Importantly, nothing is said about the ultimate fate of either **Esau** or his Edomite descendants. Paul simply appeals to this text to demonstrate the workings of divine election—God remains sovereign and free to choose as he sees fit. Human qualities or actions cannot touch or determine his selections (Byrne 1996, 295). Since God elects the wholly undeserving, all grounds for presumption and ethnic pride are undermined (see Rom 3:27-31).

FROM THE TEXT

To understand Paul's doctrine of predestination, we must turn to 8:29-30 (see the commentary). The fundamental point is God's full self-disclosure in his Son. "The God and Father of our Lord Jesus Christ" is not a God who arbitrarily elects some individuals to salvation, passing over the rest to be damned. He is the God of holy love revealed in Jesus. Everything Paul says in these chapters must be seen as an unfolding disclosure of the God who has now unveiled himself in Jesus (see Heb 1:1-4). Further, Rom 9—11 are to be taken as declaring the apostle's faith in the *self-consistency* of the living God in carrying out his saving purpose and plans in Israel's Scriptures.

Paul's point in this passage is not to deny good works as the basis of salvation or to malign contemporary Judaism as legalistic. This Protestant reading tells more about the pre-Reformation Western church than about second-temple Judaism. E. P. Sanders (1977 and 1985) demonstrates that it is patently false to assume that most Jews of Paul's day were both legalists and hypocrites. Paul does not disparage doing good or obeying the Law (see 2:7, 10, 25; 7:18-19; 8:4). What Paul challenges is the notion of any kind of human merit as the basis for favorable standing before God. God's choice alone is decisive.

Paul's initial answer to his implied question in 9:6 is that God has not failed to keep his word. God has simply been misunderstood by those to whom the Scriptures belong. It is Israel according to the flesh, not God, who has failed (Dunn 2002b, 38B:549).

b. God Is Sovereign in Mercy and Wrath (9:14-29)

BEHIND THE TEXT

Paul emphasizes the absolute freedom of God, who chooses how he will act—whether "loving" or "hating"—in complete independence of any human conditioning. This understandably raises the objection that such a God is arbitrary and unfair. Rather than representing a difficulty posed by a real dialogue partner, the objection, stated in diatribe style, moves the apostle's argument to the next stage, where he continues his scriptural defense of God's sovereign freedom.

We would do well to remind ourselves of the hermeneutical principle first articulated by Augustine in his treatise *On Christian Doctrine.* Wesley appropriated it as his own: Biblical passages that are *difficult* to understand must be interpreted in light of the Bible's *clear* teaching. Wesley calls this "the general tenor of Scripture" (in light of God's final revelation in Christ). Scholars today insist on the necessity of placing the exegesis of a particular passage within its larger biblical-theological perspective. This principle, along with confidence in God's self-consistency, gives a solid basis for a positive, helpful understanding of this difficult passage.

IN THE TEXT

(1) In Defense of God's Justice (9:14-18)

Paul resumes his argument in the question-and-answer style of the diatribe. If the underlying assumptions—that Christ is the "seed" of Abraham and that humans are elect in him—are obscured, the assertions of vv

6-13 are open to objection. To distinguish between unborn twin infants, to love the one and hate the other, is patently unjust. Thus, it follows that, by Paul's argument, God is unjust. Since this is unthinkable, his imaginary objector will infer that the argument that leads to this conclusion is false.

■ **14** So Paul asks, **What then shall we say?** (v 14) [see 3:5; 4:1; 6:1; 7:7; 8:31; 9:30]. **Is God unjust** (*adikia*)? Paul's second question is clearly rhetorical and framed in such a way as to make clear that the expected answer is no: "There is no injustice with God, is there?" (NASB). Nevertheless, Paul responds as forcefully as possible, **Not at all!** (*mē genoito;* see the comment on 3:4). God is righteous (see v 5 and Deut 32:4), and his word has not failed (see Rom 1:18; 9:6).

■ **15-16** The apostle defends his position in vv 15-16—or, at least, reiterates it. To condemn divine election as unjust does God an injustice. Paul quotes LXX Exod 33:19*b:* **For he says in Moses, "I will have mercy** [*eleēsō*] **on whom I have mercy, and I will have compassion** [*oiktirēsō;* compare *oiktirmōn,* "mercy," in Rom 12:1] **on whom I have compassion"** (9:15). **For** (*gar*) indicates that the quotation explains the question in v 14. God's word to Moses explains divine fairness and impartiality in terms of God's sovereign freedom to act mercifully. **It does not, therefore, depend on man's desire or effort, but on God's mercy** (v 16).

This text emphasizes not only God's sovereign freedom but also preeminently his **mercy.** If God does anything at all for sinful humans, it is out of his **mercy.** If he does nothing, he is not unjust, for we deserve nothing. But **mercy** is the keynote of chs 9—11. The terminology of **mercy** will reappear in 9:16, 18, 23; 11:30, 31, and 32. Paul's argument insists "on the absolute freedom of divine mercy as the basis not only for understanding predestination but also for understanding the first eight chapters of the letter" (Jewett 2007, 582). **Mercy** provides the bookends enclosing chs 9—11 (see 9:15-18 and 11:32). The sovereign God is not an arbitrary tyrant; on the contrary, throughout Rom 9—11, "divine mercy is sovereign" (Jewett 2007, 583).

■ **17** Moses stands as "an example and representative of God's mercy—in contrast to Pharaoh in v 17" (Dunn 2002b, 38B:551). According to Exod 34:6-7, Yahweh reveals himself to Moses as first and foremost merciful and compassionate. This OT text is echoed elsewhere in the OT and intertestamental Judaism more perhaps than any other (Num 14:18; Deut 7:9-10; 2 Kgs 13:23; 2 Chr 30:9; Neh 9:17, 31; Pss 86:15; 103:8; 111:4; 112:4; 145:8; Isa 30:18; Jer 32:18; Joel 2:13; Jonah 4:2; Nah 1:3; Sir 2:11; Wis 3:9; 4:15; 15:1; 2 Esd 7:33; see 2 Cor 4:1; 1 Pet 2:10).

God's Mercy

One verb form (*eleēsō* and *eleō*, from *eleeō*) of the *ele-* cognate family first occurs here in Romans (9:15 [two times] and in 11:30, 31 [two times], 32). Yet another verb form appears in v 16 (*eleōntos*, from *eleaō*; and in 12:8). The noun form appears first in v 23 (*eleous*, from *eleos*; and in 11:31; 15:9).

In the Greek OT, both *eleos* and *charis* ("grace") translate the Hebrew word *chesed*, "loving kindness" or "covenant love." Romans 9—11 concludes on the theme of mercy: "God has bound all men over to disobedience so that he may have *mercy* on them all" (11:32, emphasis added). And ch 12 begins on the same note, but employs a different Greek noun (*oiktirmōn*, "mercies"). Although it appears only here in Romans, it is the verbal cognate of *oiktirēsō*, **I will have compassion,** used in synonymous parallelism with *eleēsō*, **I will have mercy,** in 9:15.

In Rom 1—8 Paul has dealt with the divine act of grace and redemption by virtue of which we may be justified, and finally saved, through faith alone. Behind this process is God's *agapē* ("love," 5:8), his saving **mercy.** Because God is love, he is merciful; and because God is merciful and compassionate, justification by faith is possible. God has determined to treat humans on the basis of mercy; otherwise none would be saved.

If God's dealings with us are to be governed by **mercy,** they cannot be 9:17
determined by human **desire or effort** (9:16; see 7:15, 16, 18, 19, 20, and 21; Ps 119:32). Paul insists that God's mercy does not depend on ***the one who wills or the one who runs.*** "Human willpower and effort . . . are set aside as irrelevant factors when compared with the merciful selection of God's children" (Jewett 2007, 582). God's election is not conditioned by anything humans can do (contrast Sir 15:15-17). Paul is not opposed to good intentions or concerted moral effort. He simply insists that they are of no avail for salvation. Everything depends, not upon us, but entirely upon the gracious, merciful God who calls all to accept his free offer of salvation.

Paul has not argued his case on the basis of absolute predestination by God conceived as timeless, arbitrary, and deterministic decrees. On the contrary, his dealings with humans rest solely upon his **mercy.** He presses his point further in a loose quotation in Rom 9:17 from Exod 9:16: **For the Scripture says to Pharaoh: "I raised you up for this very purpose** [*eis auto touto, **for this very thing;*** see Rom 13:6]**, that I might display my power** [*dynamin;* see Rom 1:16—a change from the LXX *ischys, **strength***] **in you and that my name might be proclaimed** [*diangelē*] **in all the earth."** While this quotation does not follow either the Hebrew or Greek of Exod

9:16 exactly, it faithfully gives its substance. The original context refers to these as the words of Yahweh (Rom 9:13-21); Paul's modification here assumes that for him **the Scripture** is the word of God. But it is the message, not the exact words, that matters.

Proclaiming God's Power

> The Jew could, of course, claim that the result of the Exodus had been to make known the redemptive power of God throughout the world; the centrality of the Exodus in Jewish thought, and their own dispersion throughout the world, meant that God's saving act in calling his people out of Egypt was celebrated wherever Jews of the Diaspora came together for prayer. And it was within that context that Pharaoh was remembered too, within the proclamation of God's electing grace, as part of the demonstration of God's purpose of mercy. Within that purpose, Pharaoh's obduracy served as the foil to set off God's redemptive power, the darker melody in a minor key which played counterpoint to the major key of God's powerful call of Israel. The sensitive reader might already recognize the implication that Israel's rejection of the gospel was to be explained in a similar way. (Dunn 2002b, 38B:563)

9:17 Paul scores two fresh points in this quotation. Pharaoh, the undisputed master in Egypt, imagines himself a god. He has in fact been brought on the scene by God, for two purposes: *First,* in order that God might manifest his power in Pharaoh (*en soi*). *Second,* so that God's name might be universally proclaimed.

Pharaoh exists not to further his political or personal ends, but God's. And God's ends are theological—to carry out a mighty act of salvation in order that this might be publicized throughout the world. On the stage of world history, Pharaoh provided the occasion for God's deliverance of his people Israel; if there were no Pharaoh, there would be no people of God; if there were no "Pharaoh of the oppression," there would have been no Exodus (or Passover observance).

Thus, Pharaoh's plans were overruled to God's ends—and his ends are merciful. Paul's application of his exposition reverses the roles, as contemporary Israel assumes Pharaoh's role in the original account. In the present, unbelieving Israel, like Pharaoh in his time, exists for a double purpose: *First,* Israel provides the occasion and context for an act of divine deliverance, in which believers are set free from the Law, and, thereby, from Sin and Death. *Second,* Israel acts so as to cause God's deliverance to be known worldwide. "This brings the Pharaoh incident into exact conformity with God's present behavior toward 'vessels' of wrath and mercy" in 9:22 (Jewett 2007, 884).

■ **18** Paul sums up his argument to this point: **Therefore God has mercy on whom he wants to have mercy, and he hardens** [*sklērynei*, "makes stubborn"] **whom he wants to harden** (v 18). The theme of Pharaoh's hardened heart figures prominently in the Exodus account (Exod 4:21; 7:3, 22; 8:15; 9:12, 35; 10:1, 20, 27; 11:10; 13:15; 14:4, 8, 17; see Rom 2:5, where Paul's Jewish interlocutor is condemned for his *sklērotēta*, "stubbornness"). The narrative at times says that Pharaoh hardens his own heart; at other times, God hardens it; at still other times, it states only that his heart was hardened, but Paul apparently senses no need to make such fine distinctions and merely assigns total responsibility to God.

Divine "hardening" has a harshness about it that grates against modern (esp. Wesleyan-Arminian theological) sensitivities, but it cannot be understood apart from 9:17, which emphasizes that God's saving purposes will not be thwarted. "Hardening" is not God's last word (11:7-12), nor does it necessarily imply final rejection. It rather calls attention to the way God has, in his unfathomable wisdom (see vv 33-36), chosen to carry out his purposes, all of which are governed by his **mercy.** If Paul fails here to qualify his emphasis upon the divine initiative in election, keep in mind that this is not the only biblical or Pauline passage that addresses the subject of human freedom and responsibility (see 1:4; 6:12-23; 8:13).

(2) In Defense of God's Right to Judge Sinners (9:19-24)

■ **19** Just the same, Paul recognizes that "hardening" is an offensive term and anticipates another objection: **One of you will say to me: "Then why does God still blame** [*memphetai*, "find fault with"] **us? For who resists his will** [*boulēma*, "intention," "purpose"; elsewhere in the NT only in Acts 27:43; 1 Pet 4:3]?" (v 19). Paul's imaginary interlocutor implies that God's moral government of the world is at fault. If God treats humans as Paul suggests, they have no moral responsibility: What right does God have to condemn sinners who sin because God has made them stubborn? Can we blame a ventriloquist's dummy for what the ventriloquist has it say? Paul apparently does not consider it necessary to repeat here the point he made in 2:1—3:20:

> Being outside the elect people of God is no guarantee of final condemnation, just as being inside the elect people of God is no guarantee of final justification—that . . . God's firm purpose in the broad sweep of salvation-history through the centuries does not exclude or

excuse any individual within that purpose from answering for his or her own deeds. (Dunn 2002b, 38B:564)

■ **20-21** Instead, Paul's reply appeals to still more OT imagery originating in Job 9:12; Isa 29:16; 41:25; 45:9; 64:8; Jer 18:1-6; Sir 33:13; Wis 12:12; 15:7. It may be influenced by the biblical understanding of human beings as creatures of clay (see Gen 2:7; Job 10:9; 33:6; Sir 33:10-13; 2 Cor 4:7). Within its present context, however, the analogy refers to God's sovereign freedom to elect Israel for purposes of his own deciding. **But who are you, O man** [*anthrōpe,* "O human"]**, to talk back to** [*antapodotēs,* "to counter-judge"] **God? "Shall what is formed say to him who formed it, 'Why did you make me like this?'" Does not the potter have the right to make out of the same lump of clay some pottery** [*skeuos*] **for noble purposes** [*timēn,* "honor" or "respect"] **and some for common use** [*atimian,* "dishonor" or "disrespect"; see 2 Tim 2:20]? (Rom 9:20-21).

Who do humans think they are, second-guessing God? Will the creature judge the Creator? Just as potters are not dictated by the clay they use and may fashion it as they please, so **God** has perfect liberty to make what he will of the humans he has created—and humans have no right to answer back. If God had not made them, they would not exist. Thus, they are to submit to the potter, to be made and remade as he sees fit. Paul seems to apply the familiar imagery of potter and clay ironically to challenge Israel's sense of national distinctiveness. With Wis 15:7 echoing in the background, he associates unbelieving Israel with dishonorable pottery, which it identifies as idols (Dunn 2002b, 38B:557).

How Odd!

William Norman Ewer apparently first penned the familiar anti-Semitic doggerel:

How odd
Of God
To choose
The Jews.

The reply by Cecil Browne is almost equally well known:

But not so odd
As those who choose
A Jewish God
But spurn the Jews.

(http://www.nybooks.com/articles/14176, accessed 7/27/06)

Dodd considers this illustration the weakest point in Paul's argument. But the argument is not as weak as it first appears. Of course, human beings and nations are not pots, and obstinate questions arise in our minds when we struggle with ultimate questions. Paul, in fact, wrote Romans because humans *do* raise such questions about the moral government of the universe. To stress this point, however, is to emphasize a detail of the imagery rather than to address the major comparison, which is between the final responsibility for what a potter does when he forms the clay *and the responsibility of God for what he does in history.* Everything depends not on human **desire or effort, but on God's mercy** (Rom 9:16).

In mercy God condescends to free a slave-people to make himself known as a God of mercy and compassion. In the same way God proves his love for willful rebels in the death of his Son (5:8). Who are we to second-guess his wisdom in such matters? The doctrine of divine predestination is not a crude numerical division within the human race, between the preordained elect and helpless reprobates; it is a profound definition of the living God and his merciful purpose for humankind. We are *all* predestined to *Christlikeness* (8:29; see v 17*b*). Those who refuse to be conformed to God's saving purposes have only themselves to blame for their eventual destruction (1:18-32).

Numerous problems emerge in translating, much less interpreting, 9:22-24. The NIV paraphrases freely, but it provides a starting point for discussing this difficult passage:

> **What if God, choosing to show his wrath and make his power known, bore with great patience the objects of his wrath—prepared for destruction? What if he did this to make the riches of his glory known to the objects of his mercy, whom he prepared in advance for glory—even us, whom he also called, not only from the Jews but also from the Gentiles?**

In Greek the entire passage consists of a conditional sentence, with no conclusion—technically speaking, a protasis without an apodosis; or simply, an "if" without a "then" clause. Since Greek sometimes uses if clauses to express what in English would be "What if?" this is not a serious problem. The rhetorical construction asks: "What if this is the case?" or, "Why should this not be so?" or even, "So what if . . . ?"

Paul's main affirmation is literally that ***with great patience God put up with the pottery of his wrath.*** The imagery of ***pottery*** (*skeuē*) is carried over from the OT allusions to the **potter** and his **pottery** (*skeuos*) in v 21. ***The pottery of his wrath*** here has its counterpart there in ***the dishonorable pottery*** there. Here, the ***pottery*** is used metaphorically to refer to people of a particular kind—**of his wrath** (see Wis 15:7-8).

■ **22** In light of Rom 1:18—3:20, this seems to refer to intransigent rebels against God—"Those who are lost" (Bauer 1979, 754). Thus, to paraphrase: ***God patiently withheld judgment against unrepentant sinners.*** This is a point Paul made previously of those unbelieving Jews who refuse to acknowledge their need of the gospel in 2:4-6. The participial phrase modifying ***pottery of his wrath***—*katērismena eis apōleian,* **prepared for destruction** (v 22; see Phil 3:19), might suggest that God created rebels merely for the purpose of eternally destroying them. But this seems totally inconsistent with Paul's emphasis on mercy throughout this passage.

■ **23** If Paul conceives of God as the one who **prepared** these pots awaiting judgment, we should recognize that the verbs translated **prepared** (from *katartizō*) in Rom 9:22 and **prepared in advance** (from *proētoimazō*) in v 23 are not the same. The former has to do with the reshaping of existing material for a new purpose; the latter, with a predetermined end (Dunn 2002b, 38B:559). **Glory** is God's predetermined goal for all (v 23; see 1:23; 2:10; 3:23; 5:2; 8:17-18, 28-30; 11:36; see Eph 2:10), but good clay may be used for unworthy purposes.

This is figurative language: These are people, not pots. Their status as stubborn rebels, which makes them subject to God's wrath, is not God's doing; it is due to their own refusal to repent (see Rom 11:17-24; 1 Pet 2:8). Thus, despite the imagery, in reality, they, not God, prepared themselves for their eventual judgment.

Another participial clause modifies Paul's main affirmation: **choosing to show his wrath and make his power known** (Rom 9:22; see 1:16, 18). The participle may indicate the cause of God's patience ("because he chose . . ."), or its means ("by choosing . . ."); or it may be concessive ("although he chose . . ."). Taking the participle as *causal* may help explain the conjunction *hína* in the parallel construction in 9:23 (most recent commentators; see Barrett 1957, 176-78), but how can God's patient withholding of judgment against the unrepentant be explained by his choice to display his wrath and power? And how can a display of wrath and power be the *means* of showing God's patience (but see 11:32)?

The *concessive* interpretation can be supported by appeal to 2:4-5, where Paul writes that God shows his "kindness" toward lost sinners to lead them to repent. According to 1:18—3:20, God's eschatological wrath is presently being revealed by his permissive approach to judgment for the present, i.e., giving sinners up to suffer the consequences of their own sin (esp. in 1:18-32). Through God's patience, judgment is mitigated so that sinners are not immediately consigned to destruction. "The ultimate purpose of divine wrath and power, as Rom 9:23 and 11:26-32 will show, is to change 'vessels of wrath' into 'vessels of mercy' through the power of the gospel" (Jewett 2007, 596).

The application of the imagery of the potter and his pottery from vv 20-21 to God's dealings with humanity continues in v 23. But here the focus shifts from the dishonorable pots to the honorable. The opening words of the translation—**What if he did this?**—have no explicit basis in the Greek text. They are necessitated, however, by the need to form an intelligible English sentence from a long and complicated Greek sentence. The *hina* clause that begins v 23 seems to explain the *purpose* for God's decision to delay his judgment of sinners. It was **to make the riches of his glory** [*doxēs*] **known to the *pottery* of his mercy** (*skeuē eleous*).

As in v 22, God's display of glory has people, not pots, in view. The honorable pottery (v 21) are such, not because of God's predestination, but because "by persistence in doing good [they] seek glory, honor and immortality" (2:7; see v 10). But, as Paul's exposition of the gospel in chs 1—8 makes perfectly clear, all who do good are onetime vessels of wrath—redeemed sinners, whose trust in God alone empowers them to obey him. They are honored because of God's **mercy.**

As 8:17-18 and 28-30 indicate, the manifestation of God's **glory** (*doxan*) is nothing less than the ultimate purpose (*eis,* **for**) of God. (See the sidebar "Glory" with the commentary on 8:17.) It is for the sake of accomplishing this one purpose that God also wills the fulfillment of the other two. ***What if, although he chose to show his wrath and make his power known, God patiently withheld judgment against unrepentant sinners destined to destruction in order to make the riches of his glory known to the recipients of his mercy with whom he plans to share his glory?*** (9:22-23).

■ **24** Verse 24 is only loosely attached to what precedes. Again, this is not a serious problem. The two relative clauses—**whom** [*ha*] **he prepared in advance for glory** (v 23) and **whom** [*hous*] **he also called** (v 24)—both explain to whom Paul applies the imagery of ***pottery of his mercy*** (v 23)—**even us**. It is the mixed Christian community, **not only from the Jews but also from the Gentiles,** whom God has called (*ekalesen,* see 1:6, 7; 8:28, 30) to share in his glory. (See the commentary on 8:28-30.)

In this light, the ***pottery of his wrath*** (9:22) applies to unbelieving humanity, particularly to rebellious Israel. Paul has reversed expected roles throughout, as Israel is recast as Ishmael, Esau, and Pharaoh (Dunn 2002b, 38B:558). This is the same approach Paul took in his allegory of Abraham's two wives in Gal 4:21-31, where Hagar represents unbelieving Jews; and Sarah, believing Gentiles. So also in Phil 3:2-4, unbelieving Jews are called "dogs"—a favorite Jewish epithet for Gentiles—and Christians are "the circumcision."

Paul invites the Christian community in Rome to share his understanding of God's patience: God endured Pharaoh (Rom 9:14-18), and he now endures rebellious Israel with much longsuffering for the sake of the ultimate manifestation of his glory on his faithful people (vv 19-24). Because of this, God has delayed the eschaton, both final judgment and final salvation—the full manifestation of **his wrath** and **his power** and **the riches of his glory**. All of these are necessary for accomplishing his ultimate *saving* purpose.

This truth will be further illuminated in 9:30—11:36. In these sections the ultimate purpose of God's patience toward rebellious Israel that is depicted in 10:21 includes the eventual salvation of rebellious Israel itself (11:25-32). But we will see how the divine patience must *first* show up the full seriousness of Israel's sin (9:30—10:21). In other words, God patiently withholds the full fury of his wrath—of judging humans' sin *in order that ultimately he may show mercy on all* (11:32).

Despite the analogy of the potter that initiates Paul's defense of God's right to hold sinners responsible for their sins, he writes of people, not pottery. It is clear that the status of being either **objects of his wrath** or **objects of his mercy** is not an immutable quantity. It is God's purpose that the **objects of his wrath** should become **objects of his mercy.** The showing of
9:24 God's wrath is necessary in order that it may be made known to the **objects of his mercy** that what is revealed in their case is indeed the riches of his glory—the glory of his boundless mercy—not any glory of their own deserving. Unbelieving Israel may still rejoin the elect community, "if they do not persist in unbelief" (11:23).

As often in Paul's letters, the conclusion of one thought introduces the next. Thus, 9:24 might be associated with the following thought unit (so Dunn 2002b, 38B:569). The thought of the final clause, **even us, whom he also called, not only from the Jews but also from the Gentiles** (v 24), should be compared with 8:28-30. Paul's point is that God has effectually called the **objects of mercy** not only **from the Jews** but also **from the Gentiles** (see 1:16; 3:29; 10:12). The presence of Gentiles within the church is the sign and pledge that the realm of rejection—of Ishmael, Esau, Pharaoh, and unbelieving Jews—is not yet shut out from the mercy of God. The presence of **even us** in effect gives this statement something of the character of Paul's personal confession of faith (Cranfield 1985, 241). It is no surprise, therefore, that when Paul announces, "And so all Israel shall be saved" (11:26) he breaks forth in doxology (v 33). But how so?

(3) Scriptural Precedent for God's Inclusion of Gentiles and Exclusion of Israel (9:25-29)

The identification of vv 25-29 as a discrete unit cannot be justified on the basis of grammar. The long sentence begun in v 22 continues through v 26, but the mention of Jews and Gentiles in v 24 allows Paul to address a new, but explicitly unstated, objection from his imaginary interlocutor. Paul defends God's right to include Gentiles and exclude Israel, with a catena of confirmatory OT quotations extending through v 29 (compare 3:10-18 and 15:9-12).

■ **25-26** In 9:25-26 Paul cites parts of Hos 2:23 and 1:10 as anticipating the inclusion of Gentiles. **As he says in Hosea: "I will call them 'my people' who are not my people; and I will call her 'my loved one' who is not my loved one," and "It will happen that in the very place where it was said to them, 'You are not my people,' they will be called 'sons of the living God'"** (amalgamated with LXX Isa 10:22-23; see Rom 4:17). Paul reapplies the original reference of Hosea to the northern kingdom of Israel to Gentiles (see 8:15, 23; 1 Pet 2:10).

■ **27-29** In Rom 9:27-29 Paul excerpts passages from Isa 10:22-23 and 1:9 that anticipate God's exclusion of unbelieving Israel from his people. **Isaiah cries out concerning Israel: "Though the number of the Israelites be like the sand of the sea, only the remnant will be saved. For the Lord will carry out his sentence** [*logon*, "word"; see Rom 9:6] **on earth with speed and finality." It is just as Isaiah said previously: "Unless the Lord Almighty had left us descendants** [*sperma*, "seed"; see 9:7, 8; see 1:3; 4:13, 16, 18; 11:1], **we would have become like Sodom, and we would have been like Gomorrah"** (9:27-29).

Having provided scriptural confirmation for **also from the Gentiles,** Paul now takes up **from the Jews** (in 9:24). All he has said so far, however, presupposes the fact that the great majority of Jews are unbelieving. Those called thus far from among them are few in number. So, in these verses Paul proceeds to show that this situation is foretold in Scripture. The burden of the passage quoted is that only a **remnant** will be saved. The patient withholding of judgment Paul puzzles over in 9:22-23 seems merciful in contrast to the speedy and final judgment threatened here.

But the hope of a **remnant** is a clear sign of mercy here (Gen 45:7; 2 Kgs 19:31; Mic 4:7; 5:7-8; Sir 44:17; 47:22), since **Sodom** and **Gomorrah** were totally destroyed (Gen 19). In pesher style, Paul regarded the words of Isaiah's oracle, as a reference to his time, anticipating the circumstances in which a small number of Jews was included in the church. But he thought of this as a condition through which Israel must pass rather than as God's last word concerning Israel (see Rom 10—11).

The Enigma of Israel

> The remnant and the seed alike were reduced to one—Jesus Christ; henceforth the elect people of God are elect in *him*. This fact reminds us that behind Paul's discussion here lies the historical background formed by the ministry of Jesus; his rejection and crucifixion by Israel, which thereby disavowed its own place in God's plan; and the election of a new Israel in Christ to take the place of the old. These were the events of the last age, which reflected the mind and character of God; but they were not the end itself, and the reflection in consequence remains something of a riddle (*ainigma,* 1 Cor. xiii. 12). The story of election is obscured by the brokenness of history, and God is hidden as well as revealed in its events. The time is still to come when men shall know as they have been known. The profoundest problem in history is the unbelief of Israel, God's elect people. In this chapter Paul has been talking round the problem in the light of God's freedom and mercy. He will now tackle it head on. (Barrett 1957, 178-79)

FROM THE TEXT

"The love of God that is in Christ Jesus our Lord" (8:39) is the foundational text of Rom 9—11. This is "mercy" expressed. The central fact to keep in mind is that Paul's exegesis of Scripture, and his eschatology, is here, as elsewhere in his letters, *governed* by this conviction (see Eph 1:9-10; 2:11—3:12).

This explains Paul's conviction that Scripture affirms the freedom of Israel's God to create for himself an eschatological people of both Jews and Gentiles—without any tie to ethnic identity or human deserving, supporting his argument by appeal to the Scriptures of Israel. This dense argumentation, as we are about to see, is based on Paul's understanding of "the righteousness of God" now unveiled in Jesus Christ our Lord.

3. The Second Answer: Israel Rejected for Unbelief (9:30—10:21)

In this section of the letter Paul resumes his emphasis on the key theological themes prominent in chs 3—8, which are almost entirely missing in chs 9 and 11. Righteousness and faith vs. law and works reemerge as crucial emphases in 9:30—10:21. Dunn suggests that this indicates the apostle's concern to hold together chs 1—8 and 9—11 and signals his intention that this section should be definitive in addressing the problem of Israel's unbelief (2002b, 38B:577).

a. Israel's "Stumbling" over Christ (9:30—10:4)

BEHIND THE TEXT

It had seemed essential to erect a wall around the Torah and to separate the returned Judean exiles in the restored nation of Israel from the paganizing influences of its neighbors during the time of Ezra (late fifth century B.C.), but by the first century A.D., many Pharisees had cultivated legalism and ethnocentrism into an art form. It was not that they imagined good works could save them. (To misunderstand legalism in this sense is to project the abuses of the Medieval Catholic Church on the Judaism of Paul's day, much as did Luther.) It was that they "confused the law and the righteousness it speaks of with works like circumcision which serve to make righteousness a function of Jewish identity rather than of God's gracious outreach to and through faith" (Dunn 2002b, 38B:576).

The Sadducees, Israel's priestly establishment, were more motivated by politics than faith, and the vast majority of the people of Israel were not really observant Jews at all. Thus, it is not surprising that Israel failed to understand its own Scriptures. Therefore, when Jesus came as Israel's Messiah—in fulfillment of its Scriptures—they "stumbled" over him. At least this is how Paul sees the situation of Israel from his Christian perspective. Of course, unbelieving Jews had their own quite different perspective. What Paul regarded as stumbling, they saw as steadfastness in the traditions of the elders.

The imagery of the race begins with the apostle's use of verbs from *diōkō*, "I run/pursue" (Phil 3:12; 1 Cor 9:24), as the basis for his contrast between Gentiles and Israel: **Gentiles . . . did not pursue righteousness** but **obtained it,** whereas **Israel . . . pursued a law of righteousness** but **has not attained it** (vv 30-31; see Isa 51:1). Paul similarly describes the reason for Israel's failure using the imagery of stumbling—borrowed from the missteps of athletes running in a race—elsewhere in his letters (see 1 Cor 9:24-27; Phil 3:12-16).

If the prize is righteousness, the Gentiles (outsiders to the covenant within which righteousness is defined) had not really entered the race. The righteousness conferred on Gentile believers came as a pure gift of God's grace, a prize "credited" to them as "ungodly" (NRSV) sinners (see Rom 4:5). Israel, on the other hand, was actively pursuing righteousness, but through the Law. In fact, Paul sees Israel's pursuit so closely tied up with Law that they *misread* the Law, which (in his view) was never intended to give the righteousness required for salvation.

Continuing the image of the race, Paul describes Israel's stumbling over the "stumbling stone." He cites an early Christian combination of two texts from Isaiah—8:14 and 28:16. The Messiah was not the triumphant leader expected by the Jews, but one "presented" as a *hilastērion* for sin (Rom 3:25)—the sins of Israel and of the entire world. Israel "stumbled" over such a Messiah, because to acknowledge him meant accepting their *need* for such a Messiah. This would entail the distasteful admission that Israel was as subject to sin as were the Gentiles—what Paul attempted to demonstrate as certain in 1:18—3:20. But those who trust in the shamefully crucified Messiah "will never be put to shame" (9:23). Faith in him will ultimately save them (see 1:16).

Paul concedes that Israel has a genuine, but misguided, ***zeal for God.*** They had confused it with "fervor for ethnic purity," regarding "righteousness as something peculiarly their own and not anyone else's" (Dunn 2002b, 38B:576). Such **zeal** was **not based on** the **knowledge** that true righteousness **comes from God,** because Christ is the **end/*goal* of the law**—the One through whom *God's* righteousness is given (10:1-4).

IN THE TEXT

■ **30** Paul resumes the diatribe style with a rhetorical question used frequently in Romans to begin a new section: **What then shall we say?** (v 30; see 3:5; 4:1; 6:1; 7:7; 8:31; 9:14). Paul's answer (as in 8:31) introduces a bold statement of truth flowing from and corroborating what he has just argued. ***Some Gentiles, who were not pursuing righteousness,*** **obtained** [*katelaben;* see 1 Cor 9:24; Phil 3:12, 13] . . . **a righteousness that . . . Israel . . . pursued** (*diōkōn;* see Phil 3:12, 14) but failed to attain (Rom 9:30-31). The **righteousness** (*dikaiosynēn*) in question is that required at the final judgment (2:13; 5:9), **a righteousness that is by faith** (*ek pisteōs,* v 30; see 1:17; 3:26, 30; 4:12, 16; 5:1; 9:32; 10:6). "To 'obtain righteousness' in this context is to find 'righteous status in God's sight,' that is, to respond positively to the gospel of grace and find a place among the remnant whom God has selected" (Jewett 2007, 609).

■ **31** According to 9:30-31, Israel's problem was not its pursuit but its misunderstanding of what it was after—the meaning of righteousness, of God's faithfulness, and of the appropriate human response to it. Thus, **Israel, who pursued** [*diōkonton;* see 9:16] **a law of righteousness** [*nomon dikaiosynēs, **a law defining righteousness*** or ***legal righteousness,*** see Isa 51:1; Wis 2:10-11; Sir 27:8], **has not attained** [*ephthasen;* see 2 Cor 10:14; Phil 3:16] ***the law*** (*eis nomon*). The fourfold repetition of **righteousness** and the contrast between **faith** and **works** suggests that Paul has resumed the theme of Rom 1—4 (see 1:16-17).

■ **32** In 9:32 Paul asks (continuing the diatribe style), **Why not?** His answer explains the irony of Israel's misunderstanding and missing of God's righteousness: **Because they pursued** [*diōkonton*] **it not by faith but as if it were by works.** Paul does not disparage either the active pursuit or the doing of Law. True, Paul insists upon the futility of Law as a means of achieving righteousness (see 3:20, 27-28; 4:2; and 8:3-4), but Israel's problem was its wrongheaded approach to both its pursuit and righteousness. The verb *diōkō* carries with it connotations of violent pursuit—even persecution (see Matt 10:23; 23:34; John 5:16; 15:20; Acts 7:52; 9:4; Gal 1:13, 23; Phil 3:5-6).

Basic to the entire section (and Rom 10:5-6) is the sustained contrast between two ways by which righteousness might conceivably be gained and sustained—through **works** of Law and through **faith** in the saving death of Jesus Christ (9:32). Israel's legal approach was based on a mistaken premise, "an erroneous subjective assessment" (Jewett 2007, 610)—**as if it were by works** (*hōs ex ergōn*). They rejected Jesus as the Christ because he was a Sabbath-breaker, a friend of tax gatherers and sinners, and apparently unconcerned with maintaining the distinction between Jews and Gentiles.

Paul is convinced that Israel's Scriptures testify that the **righteousness** of God comes "apart from law" (3:21) and "apart from works" (4:6); and that it is for all who believe, regardless of ethnicity (1:16). Because **Israel pursued** righteousness **not by faith** in Christ, it failed to obtain what it sought (9:31-32).

Continuing the imagery of the race, Paul concludes: **They stumbled** [*prosekopsan;* see 14:21; 2 Cor 6:3; and the OT echoes in Exod 23:33; Deut 28:25; Isa 8:14; 29:21; and Ps 91:12] **over the "stumbling stone."** In referring to Christ as the **"stumbling stone,"** he appeals to a widely held Christian conviction that applied to Jesus a collection of OT passages (*testimonia*) referring to the rejected cornerstone/headstone (see below).

Israel **stumbled** at Christ, because to accept him meant accepting their need of his redemption, i.e., accepting the verdict in Paul's sustained accusation in Rom 2:1—3:20—that Jews had not been and would never be a "righteous nation" on the basis of Law (see Gal 2:16)—"that Jews and Gentiles alike are all under sin" (Rom 3:9). The path to salvation opened up by God in Christ requires Israel's owning that she is bound up with the rest of humanity in a solidarity of sin that is now matched by a "much more" powerful solidarity of grace (5:12-21) (Byrne 1996, 310).

■ **33** Paul sees Israel's stumbling as a fulfillment of Scripture (citing a loose composite of Isa 8:14 and 28:16): **As it is written** [see 1:17]**: "See, I lay in Zion a stone** [*lithon*] **that causes men to stumble and a rock that makes them fall, and the one who trusts in him** [*ho pisteuōn ep' autō*] **will never be put to shame"** (9:33; partially repeated in 10:11). Israel, clinging to a pursuit of righteousness through "works of the law," which served only to set them apart from non-Jews, resisted this verdict of their guilt. And they **stumbled** in this way at the **stone,** which is Christ. "The very Christ for whom Israel yearned became its potential nemesis" (Jewett 2007, 613).

The parallel expressions, ***stone of stumbling*** and ***rock of offense*** (9:33) in the OT "often function as metaphors for moral, economic, or political ruin" (Jewett 2007, 614). By stumbling over the scandalous cross of Christ (see 1 Cor 1:23; Gal 5:11), Israel put itself in jeopardy, whereas—in the words of the second part of the Isaiah quotation—those who **trust in him will never be put to shame** [*kataischynthēsetai,* "dishonored," "disgraced," "humiliated," "disappointed"; see Rom 5:5; 2 Cor 7:14; 9:4] at the judgment. (See Behind the Text in the commentary on Rom 6.)

What holds together the two Isaiah texts is their mention of trusting in the **stone.** The synagogue practice of paraphrasing (targum) Isa 28:16 in an explicitly messianic sense antedated Paul. This reading allowed other OT **stone** references to cluster around it and also acquire a messianic interpretation. Christians, expanding upon Jewish precedents, following Jesus' lead (Mark 12:10-11), and sometimes adding the imagery of Ps 118:22, identified Jesus as the stumbling **stone** (see Matt 7:24; Luke 20:17-18; Acts 4:11; 1 Cor 1:23; 4:10; Gal 5:11; Eph 2:20; 1 Pet 2:4-8; *Barn.* 6:2-4). Since God laid the **stone,** Paul concludes that Israel's fall must have been by his design. They were tripped up by the crucified Messiah.

■ **1** Israel's failure provokes Paul's prayer in Rom 10:1: **Brothers** [and sisters], **my heart's desire** [*eudokia, **good pleasure***] **and prayer** [*deēsis*] **to God for the Israelites is that they may be saved** [*hyper autōn eis sōtērian, **for them for the purpose of salvation;*** see 1:16]. Paul directly addresses his Roman audience as his spiritual family, his Christian friends (see 1:13; 7:1, 4; 8:12, 29; 11:25; 12:1; 15:14, 30; 16:17; see 9:3).

Paul's reference to his **prayer** for Israel suggests the motif of the prophet as intercessor for the people (see Exod 32:9-14; Num 21:6-9;

Deut 9:18-20; 1 Sam 7:5-11; Pss 99:6; 106:23; Jer 15:1; 18:20; 42:2-4, 19-22; Ezek 11:13). His deep yearning for the salvation of his people clearly implies that he believes the majority of them are now lost, but not hopelessly so, as his prayer itself indicates.

■ **2-3** Perhaps speaking from his own pre-Christian experience (see Acts 22:3-4; Gal 1:14; Phil 3:6), Paul explains the basis for Israel's present standing outside the people of God. **For I can testify about them they are zealous for God, but their zeal is not based on knowledge** [*ou kat' epignōsin,* ***not according to knowledge***]. **Since they did not know** [*agnoountes,* ***acknowledge***] **the righteousness that comes from God** [*tēn tou Theou dikaiosynēn,* ***the righteousness of God***] **and sought to establish** [*stēsai,* ***validate***] **their own** [*tēn idian*], **they did not submit** [*hypertagēsan;* see Rom 8:7, 20; 13:1, 5] **to God's righteousness** (*tē dikaiosynē tou Theou,* ***the righteousness of God***) (10:2-3).

In Paul's usage **zeal** can be a good (see 2 Cor 7:7, 11; 9:2; 11:2) or a bad (= ***jealousy,*** in Rom 13:13; 1 Cor 3:3) thing. Israel's intense, passionate, consuming, even overwhelming dedication to their Law (see Acts 21:20), to their God, and to what they believed to be a righteous cause (see 1 Kgs 19:10, 14; 1 Macc 2:58)—a good thing—had become perverted and misdirected into violent persecution of violators of the Law, as Paul knew from personal experience (Gal 1:14; Phil 3:6). Israel defended its Law by killing rather than loving their neighbors (Rom 13:8; Dunn 2002b, 38B:587).

Israel's well-intentioned but delusional zeal took the form of ethnocentrism and a total intolerance of diversity. Zeal made them willing to protect their own uniqueness and prerogatives by the violent exclusion or elimination of others unlike themselves. Witness what was done to Jesus by the defenders of the Law! Witness Paul's pre-Christian persecution of believers in Jesus! And all in the name of God and right! Zeal for Law within the mentality of self-preservation caused Israel to become narrow-minded and nearsighted. Preoccupied with boundary markers distinguishing them from Gentiles (such as circumcision and food laws), they lost sight of the truly central concerns of the Law and their mission to the nations.

In 9:30-31 and 10:3, Paul seems to treat **righteousness**, **righteousness that is by faith, law of righteousness, righteousness that comes from God**, and **God's righteousness** as virtual synonyms. These equations show clearly the continuity Paul sees between God's covenant with Israel, the Law, and the faith that he proclaimed; they confirm that for Paul obedience—obedience to the Law (8:7), the "obedience of faith" (1:5 NRSV; see 16:26)—is fundamental to covenant righteousness, as much for him as for his fellow Jews. What he objected to was Israel's attempt to maintain a claim of national monopoly to that covenant righteousness and the consequent misunderstanding of "the righteousness of God" that that entailed (Dunn 2002b, 38B:588).

What Paul meant by Israel's attempt **to establish their own** righteousness (v 3) seems to be explained in 9:31-32 as its misguided pursuit of righteousness as if it were to be achieved by maintaining Israel's prerogatives. The apostle does not so much indict supposedly "self-achieved righteousness" as "self-centered righteousness"—i.e., a righteousness that belonged peculiarly to them to the exclusion of Gentiles (Dunn 2002b, 38B:587). Their **own** righteousness (see Phil 3:9) got in the way of **God's righteousness.** This subtle form of self-idolatry led them to imagine that God existed for Israel, not vice versa.

God's righteousness is a gift, not a human achievement. Establishing the terms for covenant relationships is God's prerogative (e.g., Gen 6:18; 9:11; 17:7, 19, 21). God as the divine Suzerain takes the initiative; his human subjects submit and remain loyal. To attain the **righteousness that is by faith** (Rom 9:30; see v 32) requires that we **submit to God's righteousness** (10:3). As in 6:18 (see vv 13, 16), Righteousness is personified as a power whose authority we must acknowledge. In reality, we must submit to the God who chooses to include all who believe among his people, not just Jews.

Israel's failure to "acknowledge" **the righteousness that comes from God** does not imply simply a lack of recognition in an intellectual sense but a failure to **submit** to the manifestation of God (see 1:21-23), i.e., a refusal to have faith. Christ crucified, proclaimed in the gospel, is the revelation of the righteousness of God (3:22-23; see 1 Cor 1:18-31). To "stumble" over Christ, therefore, is a failure to **submit to God's righteousness** and so to miss salvation (Rom 1:16-17).

■ **4** ***For*** [*gar*] **Christ is the end** [*telos*] **of the law so that there may be righteousness** [*eis dikaiosynēn, **for the purpose of righteousness***] **for everyone who believes** (10:4). This statement concludes and summarizes the extended passage that began at 9:6. *Telos* has two basic meanings: "end" in the sense of termination or conclusion (see Luke 1:33; Heb 6:11; 1 Pet 4:7) or in the sense of goal or purpose. The latter is Paul's usage in Rom 6:21-22 (see 2 Cor 11:15; Phil 3:19; 1 Tim 1:5; 1 Pet 1:9).

Although the term *telos,* like the English "end," is ambiguous, a number of considerations favor the second usage here. Paul does not seem to suggest that Christ terminates the Law, making it passé and irrelevant. Rather, Christ brings the Law to its God-intended purpose or fulfillment

(Rom 8:3-4). This usage is also consistent with the race imagery in 9:30-32. In such races the *telos* was the goal line, the destination (see Phil 3:12-16). "To specify the law's *telos* as Christ is to assert that its purpose, its intent, the goal toward which it is oriented, that in which its inherent character is actualized, is an event called Christ" (Keck 2005, 250).

In fairness to the first meaning of the word *telos,* we must acknowledge that when the race's goal is attained, the race is over. In Gal 3:19, 23-25 Paul seems to suggest that the Law was in force only "until" the coming of Christ. He adds, "Now that faith has come, we are no longer under . . . law" (v 25). In 2 Cor 3:13-14 Paul implies that "in Christ" the Law has been "set aside" (NRSV). So Dunn interprets Rom 10:4 to mean that "the epoch of Israel's exclusive prerogative is ended; the role of the law as a badge of election is over and done" (2002b, 38B:598). (For in-depth discussions of Paul's views on Law, see Räisänen [1986], Thielman [1994], Schreiner [1998], and Koperski [2001].)

FROM THE TEXT

Paul's understanding of Law is far more complicated than a simple either-or answer allows. In addition to the exegetical issues involved, salvation-historical and existential issues complicate matters. Thus, e.g., does the coming of Christ/faith refer to a specific date on the calendar during the first century A.D.? or, does it refer to a time that varies from person to person based on when one comes to personal faith in Christ?

Regardless of how we answer these questions, we must insist that Paul nowhere authorizes antinomianism. On the contrary, he assumes that faith upholds the Law (3:31), that the Law will be fulfilled in those who walk in the Spirit (8:4), that Christians are obligated to observe the love commandment and so fulfill the Law (13:8-10), and that our final justification is contingent upon actually doing the Law (2:13).

But Paul insists that our justification and fulfillment of the Law are not our own achievements. Through the power of the indwelling Holy Spirit, God enables those who trust in Christ to keep the law of love, no longer through external coercion, but through internal motivation. Thus, perhaps there is something to be said for living with the ambiguity of the word **end.**

Christ as the goal toward which the Law is oriented prepares the way for 10:5-13. It supports Paul's claim that the Mosaic law is a covenant of *grace,* a love command. It commands Israel to love God with all its heart and soul and strength (Deut 6:5) and their neighbors as themselves (Lev 19:18), including the aliens in their midst (vv 33-34). Jesus stands in continuity with Moses when he reaffirms the Mosaic love command in the "Great Commandment" of Mark 12:28-32.

In his declaration that through Christ "God has poured out his love into our hearts by the Holy Spirit, whom he has given us" (Rom 5:5), Paul claims that "the *Shema* is at last fulfilled" (Wright 1991, 45). Thus, 10:5-13 is only the logical conclusion that with reference to the gospel's relation to the Law, Christ is the **righteousness** of which Deut 30:11-14 speaks.

b. Scripture's Witness to Righteousness by Faith (10:5-13)

BEHIND THE TEXT

It is clear from Rom 2:27-29 that Paul knew Deut 30:1-11, although he quotes from only 30:11-14 within this section of the letter. In this Mosaic promise of Yahweh's covenant renewal for post-Exilic Israel Paul finds the promise of Christ.

To exonerate God of any responsibility for Israel's failure, Paul cites Moses against Moses, following the hermeneutical tradition of Israel's rabbis, who approached apparent contradictions in the Scriptures by comparing Scripture with Scripture. He quotes Lev 18:5 as a foil for his quotation of Deut 30:11-14, interpreted, following rabbinic precedents, both christologically and soteriologically. By this interpretation Paul "shows that the gospel of Christ is indeed 'the goal of the law,' thus substantiating Rom 10:4" (Jewett 2007, 623).

As in ch 4, Paul calls attention to the *protoevangelium* within the Law (see Gal 3:8). Faith does not overthrow the Law; it upholds it (Rom 3:31). Despite the antithetical relationship between **the righteousness that is by the law** (10:5) and **the righteousness that is by faith** (v 6), the Law itself anticipates the gospel.

Paul assumes that, properly understood, the Law is "not too difficult," and thus the occasion of Israel's failure (Deut 30:11, 14). God provides the necessary means of obedience (v 8), through the circumcision of the heart (v 6). This is good news to all who will trust in Christ and accept his gift of the Spirit (Ezek 36:25-27) as the fulfillment of this promise. God's word has not failed (Rom 9:6*a*). Israel's problem was and remains its lack of faith (11:20, 23).

IN THE TEXT

■ **5 Moses** [see 9:15; 10:19; 1 Cor 9:9] **describes** [*graphei, **writes***] **in this way the righteousness that is by law: "The man who does these things will live** [*zēsetai*] **by them"** (Rom 10:5). Paul presents **Moses** as the spokesman for the old covenant (see 5:14; 2 Cor 3:7-15) and the view of righteousness espoused by unbelieving Jews (see Rom 4:14, 16; 9:31-32; 10:3), citing Lev 18:5 (see Gal 3:12). Only inattentive hearers would not notice the dissonance between this quotation and the letter's thematic quotation of Hab 2:4 in Rom 1:17: "The righteous will live [*zēsetai*] by faith."

The Leviticus passage affirms a quite different approach to finding life—achieving **righteousness** by doing the **law** (so also Deut 4:1; 5:32-33; 8:1; 16:20; 30:15-20; Neh 9:29; Ezek 18; 33:15-19; Luke 10:28); i.e., "the law of life" (Sir 17:11; 45:5; 2 Esd 14:30; Bar 3:9). Paul has rejected such views in Rom 1:18—3:20 (even more so in Gal 3:21). To persist in the way of Law-righteousness is to refuse to acknowledge and submit to the "righteousness that comes from God" (Rom 10:3) and constitutes a rebuff of the grace of God, which renders Christ's death "for us" in vain (Gal 2:21) (Byrne 1996, 318).

The glaring tension between Hab 2:4 and Lev 18:5 about the source of life—faith vs. law—sends Paul to a third passage to resolve the contradiction. This was standard rabbinic practice in the tradition of pesher commentary (see Rom 4 and Gal 3:10-12, where Lev 18:5 is also cited). Thus, the Leviticus quotation serves only as a foil for Paul's main contention in Rom 10:5-13: true Torah observance is not a matter of works of Law but of heart obedience to God (see Exod 19:5-6; see Rom 1:5; 15:18; 16:26). To demonstrate this he appeals to Deut 30:12-14 (with vv 1-11 in the background).

■ **6** The phrase *tēn dikaiosynēn tēn ek* [*tou*] *nomou*, **the righteousness that is by law,** finds its counterpoint in *hē . . . ek pisteōs dikaiosynē*, **the righteousness that is by faith** (Rom 10:6). This is the understanding of the righteousness of God that Paul has championed throughout chs 1—8. He connects the preceding Leviticus quotation with **Moses** (10:5), but makes no such association with the Deut 30:12-14 quotation. That Paul knows the tradition of Mosaic authorship is evident in Rom 10:19, where he cites Deut 32:21 with the introductory formula, "Moses says." In Rom 10:6-9, however, Paul allows personified ***Righteousness by Faith*** (see 6:18) to speak for herself.

Paul prefaces his quotation from Deut 30 with a phrase borrowed from Deut 8:17 and 9:4 (LXX). Within their original contexts, both passages caution against presumptuously assuming that Israel's righteousness is the basis for the gift of the Promised Land. This is entirely Yahweh's doing (8:18; 9:5; see Rom 10:3).

Paul glosses his free quotation from Deut 30:12-14 with a series of pesher-style parenthetical explanations (see Bar 3:29-30), which give the passage a clear messianic and soteriological significance. Pesher commentaries among the Dead Sea Scrolls offer succinct (often arbitrary) contemporary applications of biblical texts (see Dunn 2002b, 38B:604 for examples).

Paul first quoted Deut 30:12—**Who will ascend into heaven?** Was Paul aware of the Jesus-tradition that no one can ascend into heaven except the Son of Man who came down from heaven (John 3:13; 6:62)? Perhaps the most characteristic feature of most nearly contemporary noncanonical Jewish apocalyptic works was their claim of divine authority based on their alleged authors' angel-escorted cosmic journeys—to heaven above or to hell below. Various Jewish sects in Paul's day sought to hasten the messianic age through self-serving religio-political programs associated with the Law (Jewett 2007, 626-27). But why? Christ has already come, Righteouness by Faith implies.

Paul introduces each of his parenthetical glosses with the explanatory words **that is.** His objective seems to be to connect the language of
10:6-7 Deut 30 with a summary of the gospel as he understands it. The entire
complex of these saving acts—the sending, death, resurrection, and exaltation of Jesus—amounts to the "revelation" of God's righteousness proclaimed in the gospel (Rom 3:21). The ordering of these salvation-historical events here is determined not by the historical sequence, but by the order of clauses in Deuteronomy. Paul explains the desire to ascend to heaven as **to bring Christ down.** Faith in Christ requires nothing so demanding or esoteric as a cosmic journey.

■ **7** In 10:7 Paul returns to Deut 30:13—**Who will descend into the deep** [abyss]? The MT has instead, ***Who will cross to the other side of the sea for us . . . ?*** The vertical contrast between *ouranos* and *abyssos* seems more logical (see Ps 107:26) than the shift to the horizontal notion of traversing the sea. Some surviving Aramaic paraphrases of Deut 30 have the same heaven-depths contrast as Paul. Thus, we cannot be certain, given the variety of text forms circulating prior to the medieval standardization of the Hebrew text, that the text Paul used did not already have this form (Dunn 2002b, 38B:604-5).

Again, Righteousness by Faith speaks for Paul, introducing a parenthetic comment with **that is.** She explains descent into the abyss as wanting **to bring Christ up from the dead** (see Ps 71:20; Wis 16:13). Why go down to the place of the dead, since the crucified and buried Christ has already been raised as "Lord of both the dead and the living" (Rom 14:9).

■ **8** Lady Righteousness warns the presumptuous *not* to ask for such esoteric revelations. **But what** then does she **say** positively? Paul asks in v 8. His answer quotes Deut 30:14: **"The word is near you; it is in your mouth** [*en tō stomati sou*] **and in your heart"** (*en tē kardia sou*). The **mouth** functions metonymously to represent one's oral confession. The three references to **heart** in Rom 10:8-10, in Hebraic usage point to "the motivating center of mind, emotion, experience, and purpose . . . [F]or Paul faith in the gospel about Christ crucified and resurrected involves a total reorientation of a person and his or her relationships" (Jewett 2007, 629).

Again, the pesher explanation begins with **that is.** This **word** Paul identifies as **the word of faith,** which is the subject of the Christian "proclamation." That is, the preaching of the Christian faith calls for a response of faith.

■ **9** What **we are proclaiming** (v 8) is this: **That if you confess** [*homologēsēs*] **with your mouth** [*en tō stomati sou*], **"Jesus is Lord," and believe in your heart** [*en tē kardia sou*] **that God raised him from the dead, you will be saved** (*sōthēsē*) (v 9). The word **confess** is comparatively rare in the Pauline corpus (vv 9 and 10; 1 Tim 6:12; Titus 1:16; *exomologeō* only within OT citations in Rom 14:11; 15:9; and Phil 2:11).

Paul's preaching rejects the possibility of achieving righteousness by preoccupation with maintaining Jewish particularity, scaling the heights or plumbing the depths. Righteousness by faith involves the simple announcement of what God has done in Christ and an affirmative inner response and outward public acknowledgment of its truth. Etymologically, *homologeō* is a compound of two Greek words meaning "I say the same thing"—i.e., here, I agree with God's assessment of Jesus.

Preserving the "heart" and "mouth" language of Deut 30:14, Paul defines more explicitly the appropriate heart response and verbal agreement that **Jesus is Lord** and that **God raised him from the dead.** The lordship of Jesus and his resurrection from the dead are closely correlated throughout the NT (see e.g., Rom 1:4; Acts 2:32-36). But to **confess . . . "Jesus is Lord"** was "not only to make a claim about his divine status but also to reveal one's own identity and commitment" of "final loyalty" to him (Jewett 2007, 630).

Those who confess the Shema (Deut 6:4) identify themselves as belonging to Israel. Those who confess the lordship of Jesus identify themselves as belonging to Jesus (see Rom 4:24; 14:14; Acts 2:36; 1 Cor 5:4;

8:5-6; 9:1; 11:23; 12:3; 15:28; 2 Cor 4:5, 14; Eph 1:15; Phil 2:9-11; Col 2:6; 1 Thess 2:15; 2 Thess 1:8). If this confession accompanied baptism, as widely assumed, it would "indicate a transfer of allegiance, a change in acknowledged ownership" (Dunn 2002b, 38B:607).

Not surprisingly, the verb **confess** is in the aorist tense, suggesting a completed act, perhaps a public profession of faith by means of a one-time experience of baptism. But Rom 10:9 offers one of the extremely rare instances of **believe** in the aorist tense in Paul's writings. This departure from his normal practice apparently refers to the initial act of Christian commitment (see vv 14-16; 13:11). The repetition of the heart language from the Deuteronomy text indicates that Paul understands conversion as necessarily involving human emotions and deep convictions, not merely the recitation of a creed (Dunn 2002b, 38B:608).

The acknowledgment of God's action (raising Jesus **from the dead**) and submission to its implications (the lordship of the risen Savior) are essential for conversion. But the risen Jesus does not need to remain bodily present on earth to render faith possible. Jewett claims, "Here as elsewhere in Romans it is clear that faith is primarily a matter of being persuaded by the gospel" (2007, 630).

Faith leads unerringly to salvation (*sōthēsē*), which is "eternal life." Law could not deliver the life it promised in Lev 18:5, because of the pervasive power of Sin (see Rom 7). But Jesus—who reigns as cosmic Lord—will save (see 10:13)! The future tense of salvation is not merely logical (this then that), but eschatological—the end of the process of justification, sanctification, and glorification (see 1:16; 5:9).

■ **10** In 10:10 Paul essentially repeats v 9, this time in the natural order: **You believe** the Christian proclamation to be **justified** [*eis dikaiosynēn, **for the purpose of justification/righteousness***] then you **confess** your faith publicly to be **saved** (*eis sōtērian, **for the purpose of salvation***). "Righteousness by Faith works its miracle first within the heart, convincing it of the love of God (5:5, 8) conveyed to the undeserving in the Christ event, and thereafter evokes the oral confession, 'Lord Jesus!'" (Jewett 2007, 631).

Here the verb **believe** is in the usual present tense. The present tense emphasizes the ongoing necessity of sustained trust in and obedience to the Lord. That the verb **confess** is also in the present suggests that Paul expects believers to live lives that continue to acknowledge their baptismal commitments (see ch 6).

Paul's point in appealing to Deut 30 is to emphasize the proximity and ease of the gospel way of righteousness compared to righteousness by Law.

> This response, while in essence "near" and "easy," is perhaps more difficult to wring from human beings than any commitment to a program of action no matter how arduous (see John 6:28-29). It is one which Israel, on Paul's analysis, failed to confront (see 9:32-33). (Byrne 1996, 319)

Paul has established the fundamental distinction between the two kinds of righteousness, providing scriptural support for the superiority of the way of faith. It remains for him to draw the conclusion. This has been in the interests of making justification available "for everyone who believes" (Rom 10:4*b*).

■ **11** In v 11 Paul appeals again to Isa 28:16 (as in Rom 9:33) to confirm his exposition of Deut 30, but he enlists personified **Scripture** as his spokesperson. **As the Scripture says, "Anyone** [*pas,* ***all;*** see Rom 1:16; 3:22, 30; 10:4] **who trusts in him will never be put to shame** [*kataischynthēsetai*]**."** The Greek present participle translated **trusts** is the same verb translated **believe** in vv 9 and 10. The antecedent of the pronoun **him** in Isa 28:16 is the "stone" Yahweh is laying in Zion, which Paul identifies as the crucified Messiah and the occasion of Israel's stumbling in Rom 9:32-33.

The verb *epaischynesthe,* "you are . . . ashamed," in 6:21 is from the same cognate family as **will . . . be put to shame** here. There shame describes how believers now feel about their preconversion lives as slaves to sin. Here Paul refers to future salvation from a negative perspective: Believers will not be humiliated at the Last Judgment.

■ **12** In 10:12 Paul clarifies (**For,** *gar*) the universal force of the word **Anyone** [*pas*] from his quotation in v 11: **There is no difference** [*diastolē*] **between Jew and Gentile—the same Lord is Lord of all** [*pantōn;* see Acts 10:36] **and richly blesses all** [*pantōn*] **who call on him.** Paul once again applies conclusions he reached in Rom 1—8 to the problem of Israel. "The gospel . . . is the power of God for the salvation of everyone who believes" (1:16). "Righteousness from God comes through faith in Jesus Christ to all who believe" (3:22).

Paul argues on the same monotheistic premise as in 3:27-31: Since there is only one God/Lord, he must be the God/Lord of Gentiles as well as of the Jews and will justify both on the same basis—faith alone. In ch 4 Abraham serves as the star witness for Paul's defense of **the righteousness that comes from God** alone and **is by faith** alone (10:3 and 6).

In v 12 Paul uses the metaphor of spiritual wealth (see 2:4; 9:23; 11:12, 33; 2 Cor 8:9; Eph 1:7; 2:7; 3:8, 16; Phil 4:19; Col 1:27): ***the Lord of all*** [*pantōn*] . . . ***is rich*** [*ploutōn,* **richly blesses**] ***to all*** [*pantes*] ***who call upon him.*** The parallelism between vv 12 and 13 suggests that endowment with spiritual riches is to be equated with the present experience of salvation yet in progress. To **call on** the Lord is simply to pray (Acts 9:14, 21; 1 Cor 1:2).

That there is **no difference between Jew and Gentile** implies that the "distinction" affirmed in Exod 8:23 and still maintained with religious fervor has been annulled in Christ (1 Cor 12:13; Gal 3:28; Eph 2:11-22; Col 3:11; see Acts 15:9). This seems an obvious corollary of the conviction that God shows no partiality/favoritism (Rom 2:11; Acts 10:34).

■ **13** Paul closes this section with 10:13 by quoting Joel 2:32—**"Everyone [*pas, all*] who calls on the name of the Lord will be saved"** (quoted in Peter's Pentecost sermon in Acts 2:21). Those who **call on him** (Rom 10:12), i.e., **on the name of the Lord** (v 13), are those who pray (see, e.g., Gen 4:26; 12:8; Deut 4:7; 1 Sam 12:17-18; Isa 55:6; Acts 2:21; 1 Cor 1:2). This is the fourth time in three verses that a form of the Greek word *pas, **all/every,*** appears, emphasizing the universal scope of the gospel invitation to future salvation (see Rom 10:9).

FROM THE TEXT

10:5-13

Taking Deut 30 as the Lord's promise for the church, John Wesley often quoted v 6 in support of his understanding of Christian perfection: "The LORD your God will circumcise your hearts and the hearts of your descendants, so that you may love him with all your heart and with all your soul, and live."

His reading of the passage fits well what Paul finds promised here: a Mosaic parallel to Ezekiel's prophecy to postexilic Israel:

> For I will take you out of the nations; I will gather you from all the countries and bring you back into your own land. I will sprinkle clean water on you, and you will be clean; I will cleanse you from all your impurities and from all your idols. I will give you a new heart and put a new spirit in you; I will remove from you your heart of stone and give you a heart of flesh. And I will put my Spirit in you and move you to follow my decrees and be careful to keep my laws. (Ezek 36:24-27)

A similar understanding apparently permits Paul to quote Lev 18:5 as a foil to the current Jewish view of salvation by law observance. It is not keeping the 613 laws that summarize Torah, but a *heart observance* that made both believing Jews and believing Gentiles the elect people God.

The emphasis here upon faith and simple confession as the appropriate human response to the offer of the righteousness of God has at times in history been played down as too "quietistic" (passive), minimizing the importance of active righteous behavior for such believers. But, Paul has already confronted this misunderstanding in Rom 6:1—8:13, where he insists that Christ's new era of grace involves an obedience no less demanding than that of the old dispensation.

But human desire and action (9:11, 16) are not the response God requires of human beings. Prior to any good works on our part, the response of faith requires acknowledging that we have no "good" to offer God, no "righteousness" that we can claim for ourselves; as sinful human beings we can only "submit to" (10:3) and humbly receive the "gift" of righteousness offered in overflowing abundance by the bountiful God (5:17). This response, although "near" and "easy," demands our *all.* It requires, Paul says, that we *die to sin and self* (6:1-13; see Gal 2:19-20). When the church fails to issue that clarion call, it betrays Christ and the apostolic gospel, paving the way toward cheap grace and a perverted evangel.

c. *Israel's Unbelief Is Inexcusable (10:14-21)*

BEHIND THE TEXT

Paul has taken pains to show in Scripture God's declared intention to make his salvation universally available on the basis of simple faith. Now he explores more deeply Israel's failure to place themselves in a position to receive salvation by joining those who "call on the name of the Lord" (10:13), which is for all and everyone.

How has this breakdown happened? Who is at fault—God and the preachers of the gospel or Israel? It is clear that it was Israel's rejection of God's word, but as Paul shows throughout Rom 9—11, Israel's failure is never to be considered apart from the Gentile's paradoxical widespread response. Paul quotes several OT scriptures to make the point of a causal, interactive relationship between the two groups.

Paul proceeds to outline a total process lying behind the "call[ing] on the name of the Lord" that leads to salvation (10:13, 14-15*a*). God has set the process in motion (sending preachers to whom Israel does not respond, v 15*b*). Failure cannot be attributed at the level of Israel's *hearing* (v 18) but at that of their *knowing* (vv 19-21). Israel is responsible because Scripture announced in advance both the inclusion of the Gentiles and Israel's difficulty with it; Israel knew but chose not to respond appropriately.

IN THE TEXT

(1) Overview

Before we deal with exegetical details in vv 14-21, let us clarify Paul's argumentative logic. Following up on v 13, the apostle raises a series of four methodological (*pōs,* **how**) questions: **How, then, can they call on the one they have not believed in? And how can they believe in the one of whom they have not heard? And how can they hear without someone preaching to them? And how can they preach unless they are sent?** (vv 14-15*a*). Paul sets up a chainlike pattern that operates backward—praying to the Lord presupposes hearing; hearing presupposes believing; believing presupposes preaching; and preaching presupposes a commissioning of preachers.

Each stage in the process is presented as a rhetorical question: **How** [*pōs syn/de*] **can** . . . [with a verb in the aorist subjunctive] . . . **not** [*ouk*]/**without** [*chōris*]/**unless** [*ean mē*] . . . [concluding with an aorist verb/present participle]? Rhetorical questions involving *pōs*—such as those in 3:6; 6:2; 8:32, and here—invite the response, "It is impossible" (Dunn 2002b, 38B:620).

Of course, one cannot pray to one he or she has not believed in, or believe in one he or she has never heard about, or hear without someone speaking, or speak without being authorized to do so. So the answer to the question of Israel's accountability finally depends on the initiative of God.

In vv 15-19 Paul dismisses one by one all possible excuses for Israel's failure to believe by appealing to Israel's Scriptures: Paul leaves the obvious unstated: Of course, God called preachers to take the gospel to Israel. In v 17, Paul adds an explanation, insisting upon the christological content and origin of the preaching in the chain of events leading to faith. Jewett identifies this as "the rhetorical centerpiece of the passage" (2007, 636).

Paul makes the point that the texts he cites from Israel's "Law" [Moses] and "Prophets" [Isaiah] (see 3:21) in 10:19-21 provided it with ample indication that God intended to include Gentiles within the community of faith and that this would **make** Israel **envious.** The only plausible answer to the question raised in v 19, **Did Israel not understand?** must be affirmative.

Israel cannot plead ignorance. It has no room to claim lack of "knowledge"—that is, knowledge of how things were to be at the time of God's eschatological intervention. If Israel balks at the gospel, which it to a large extent has, it cannot be due to divine revelation inadequate to **hear** or **un-**

derstand. The failure lies, rather, in the realm of response—it refused to submit in faith to the righteousness of God (Byrne 1996, 326).

(2) Details

■ **14** In v 14 as in vv 12 and 13, to **call on** is to pray. *Eis . . . ouk episteusan,* **they have not believed in,** is in the aorist tense (as in v 9; see the commentary), an indication that they have not yet come to faith; i.e., they are unconverted. In a primarily oral culture, the spoken word was the basic means of communication. This explains why Paul considered hearing and **preaching** (*kēryssontos*) essential; even written communication was read aloud.

Whether or not Paul would have regarded print, visual, and electronic media as acceptable substitutes for preaching in our day may be debated; but he certainly could not imagine a substitute for the personal dimension—**someone** communicates the message. This is, of course, not to deny God's ability to use other means of revelation, such as creation and conscience, which Paul concedes in chs 1 and 2.

Gospel preaching is not simply a message, but a person. Before the unconverted can pray, they must **hear** and **believe in** (*pisteuōsin*) the risen Christ—**the one** "who is really being heard in the gospel message" (see 10:17; Jewett 2007, 638).

Paul takes for granted that preachers do not speak for themselves; they are spokespersons for Christ (vv 15*a,* 17; see 1:5; 1 Cor 15:8-11; 2 Cor 4:5; 11:4; Gal 1:6-9, 15-16; 2:2). That is, **they are sent** (*apostalōsin*). The Greek verb here is from the same cognate family as the noun "apostle," which in Christian usage came to identify spokespersons commissioned by the risen Christ to serve as his ambassadors—"God . . . making his appeal through us" (2 Cor 5:20; see Isa 61:1; Mark 3:14; Luke 4:18, 43-44; Rom 1:5; 1 Cor 1:17; 1 Tim 2:7).

■ **15** The condensed OT quotation Paul cites in v 15 (see Jewett 2007, 639, for a discussion of the text form Paul adapts) as evidence that God has sent preachers is from Isa 52:7—**"How beautiful** [*hōraioi,* ***timely***] **are the feet of those who bring** [*euangelizomenōn*] **good news!"** The adjective *hōraioi* is from the same cognate family as the word *hōra,* the source of our word "hour." The coming of the traveling preachers happened at just the right time.

In this setting, **the feet** are used figuratively (by metonymy) as one part of the entire process of coming on foot. Thus: *"How timely is the arrival of those who bring joyful tidings, who proclaim salvation"* (Bauer 1979, 896 s.v. *hōraios*). In 2:24, Paul quoted Isa 52:5 as part of his collection of biblical evidence that Jews were as guilty of sin as Gentiles—"God's name is blasphemed among the Gentiles because of you." Because Israel was desperately in need of salvation, and God sent Israel preachers of salvation. The Dead Sea Scrolls (11QMelch 15-19) indicate that Isa 52:7 was already understood within Jewish circles well before Paul's time as messianic prophecy. Thus, Paul sees the preaching of the gospel "as one of sharing and completing that of the Messiah" (Dunn 2002b, 38B:622).

■ **16** The use of **not all** in Rom 10:16—**But not all** [*ou pantes*] **the Israelites accepted** [*hypēkousan, **obeyed***] **the good news**—is an example of deliberate understatement for rhetorical effect (technically meiosis or litotes). "Most" would be more accurate. But Paul uses *pas,* **all,** to call attention to the stark contrast between the universal availability of salvation (emphasized by the fourfold use of *pas* in vv 11-13) and Israel's almost complete disobedience.

Paul uses a play on words to indicate that although Israel repeatedly **heard** (vv 14—*ēkousan,* 17—*akoē,* and 18—*ēkousan*), it failed to ***heed*** (v 16—*hypēkousan*) the gospel **message.** The Greek word translated **message** is from the same root as ***obeyed*** (compare the English "hear" and "hearken"). Israel's unresponsiveness is not due to any lack of effort to evangelize them.

As evidence for his claim, Paul cites Isaiah (53:1, LXX): **Isaiah says, "Lord, who has believed** [*episteusen*] **our message** [*akoē,* lit. "hearing"]?" The rhetorical question is an implicit complaint that few Israelites have put their faith in the gospel. That this quotation validates Paul's claim demonstrates that faith and obedience are complementary (see Rom 1:5; 5:19; 6:12-17; 15:18; 16:26) in his understanding; one is impossible without the other. Paul presents the present situation with that in Isaiah's day. Israel's problem is not the gospel but its refusal to believe/obey God.

■ **17** In v 17, Paul twice repeats a form of the word *akoē*—***Consequently, faith is from hearing, and hearing is through the word*** [*rhēmatos,* as in v 8] ***of Christ.*** Preaching occasions faith, as hearers believe and respond in obedience to the message (see Gal 3:2-5). It is unlikely that Paul carefully distinguished between the subjective and objective genitives here; he probably thought of **the word of Christ** as both the message Christ preached and the christological content of Christian preaching.

■ **18** Paul interjects himself (I) into the argument in Rom 10:18—**But I ask: Did they not hear** [*ēkousan*]?—as he does several times in chs 9—11 (9:1-3, 19; 10:1-2, 18-19; 11:1, 11, 13-14). The wordplay on hearing and hearkening to the message begun in v 16 continues. The formulation of his question is rhetorical and presumes that Israel has heard, despite its failure to heed the message. A literal translation of his rhetorical question sounds convoluted in English: ***They have not not heard, have they?*** His answer verifies the obvious: **Of course they did.**

He cites Ps 19:4 (LXX) as scriptural evidence—**"Their voice has gone out into all the earth, their words [*rhēmata*] to the ends of the world"** (Rom 10:18). Paul engages in self-conscious exaggeration for literary effect (hyperbole) to indicate the remarkable geographical reach of apostolic preaching within the few years since the Messiah's coming (consider Paul's mission as described in 15:19). From Paul's perspective, only the remote western region of the Roman Empire remained unevangelized (vv 20-24, 28). Israel's unbelief is not for lack of opportunity.

■ **19** In v 19 Paul (I) poses another rhetorical question—**Did Israel not understand?** i.e., ***Israel has not not known, has it?*** In this context hearing and knowing may be synonymous; or, Paul may imply that Israel not only heard but also understood the message of Christian preachers, making their disobedience to their own Scriptures a fully responsible act of rebellion.

Again, the apostle cites scriptural evidence for his claim, this time appealing to Deut 32:21 (LXX), cited as the words of **Moses** (see Rom 10:5, 6). The MT of this verse reads, "They made me jealous by what is no god and angered me with their worthless idols. I will make them envious by those who are not a people; I will make them angry by a nation that has no understanding."

Yahweh's complaint in this text form is about Israel's *idolatry* ("what is no god"). Because of this, God threatens to provoke Israel to jealousy with what is a "not a people," with what is a ***non-understanding nation.*** Paul, however, cites the LXX text form, which announces God's intention to make Israel "jealous" of the Gentiles—a motif he develops in 11:11, 13-14.

The preceding verse, Deut 32:20, is the only instance in the LXX Pentateuch to use the word *pistis,* "faith." Thus, Paul seems to understand the contrasting words in v 21—**make . . . envious** and **make . . . angry** (Rom 10:19)—to imply Israel's lack of faith and God's complicity in it (Dunn 2002b, 38B:625). **"I will make you envious by those who are not a nation [*ouk ethnei*]; I will make you angry by a nation [*ethnei*] that has no understanding [*asynetō*]."**

Despite Paul's verbatim citation of the LXX verse otherwise, he twice substitutes the pronoun **you** (*hymas*) for "them" (*autous*). The **I** within the quotation, of course, refers to God, whom Paul conceives as charging Israel directly. The Greek word normally translated "Gentiles" in the NT is merely the plural form of the word "nation." "Israel ought to have seen in the positive response of the Gentiles to the gospel of the Messiah a fulfillment of Deut 32:21" (see Rom 9:25-26; Dunn 2002b, 38B:631). Here, Paul correlates for the first time God's intentions to call the Gentiles (v 25) and Israel's rejection of the gospel.

Moses says that God intends to bring Israel to faith by provoking them to *parazēlōsō*. Traditional translations take the expression to mean **make . . . envious** or "jealous" (NASB, NRSV). But Jewett argues that the parallelism with **make . . . angry** suggests the meaning "make zealous" (as in Gal 1:13-14; Phil 3:4-11).

> In the context of this pericope, the words from Moses explain the behavior of Jews rejecting the gospel as deriving from divinely provoked zeal and anger against the Gentile world. . . . Israel angrily rejected any gospel that accepted Gentiles as equals. (Jewett 2007, 646)

■ **20-21** After citing the Law in Rom 10:19, in vv 20 and 21 Paul cites two verses from the Prophets: **And Isaiah boldly says, "I was found by those who did not seek me; I revealed myself to those who did not ask for me." But concerning** [*pros, to*] **Israel he says, "All day long I have held out my hands to a disobedient and obstinate people"** (quoting Isa 65:1-2).

Because of Israel's inattention to its own Scriptures, God **revealed** himself to Gentiles, contrary to Israel's expectations. Gentiles **found** him without seeking or asking for him. **Israel** can only be described as **a disobedient and obstinate people** (see Rom 2:8), constantly resisting God's overtures and rejecting the gospel (see 9:30-31). The verbs **seek** and **ask** are in the present tense.

Jews stereotyped Gentiles as uninterested in God, but here it is Israel who is characterized as rebels, despite God's remarkable continual pleading for them to come to him. Clearly, Paul has demonstrated his thematic claim in 9:6—"It is not as though God's word had failed." On the contrary, Israel is **disobedient** (*apeithounta*)—not submissive (10:3) and not obedient (*ou . . . hypēkousan*, v 16)—and **obstinate** (*antilegonta*)—far from faithful (*ouk episteusan*, v 14).

> Within the wider context of the scriptures and "intertestamental" literature as a whole, the expectation was fairly well established that in the end time the Gentiles would recognize Yahweh to be the only God. . . . Israel ought to have recognized the perfect match between . . . scripture and the situation now resulting from the Gentile mission of the believers in Jesus Messiah. Those who rejoice in the scriptures cannot put forward the excuse that they never knew what is so plainly prophesied therein. (Dunn 2002b, 38B:631)

FROM THE TEXT

Paul brings his analysis of the present situation to a conclusion—wide acceptance of the gospel by the Gentiles and rejection by most of Israel. He explains this situation as due, not to divine predestination, but to human response or lack thereof. Israel has failed to heed its own Scriptures. But why? Paul's exposition of Scriptures hints that, within the mysterious interplay between God's free grace and human free will, the present paradoxical situation was anticipated by God and even divinely intended. It is precisely this incorporation of Israel's failure within the wider purpose of God for its future salvation that Paul will unfold in ch 11.

4. The Third Answer: Israel's Rejection Not Final (11:1-32)

Paul continues to address the problem: *Has God cast away his ancient people Israel* (9:1-6)? In chs 9 and 10 the apostle has dealt with the problem of Israel's apparent rejection by God from two points of view. First, because God is sovereign, he chooses whom he will, and whom he will he hardens; and humans can present no claims to God. God's people are freely chosen by his grace.

Although Gentiles have accepted God's offer of mercy, God's historic people, Israel, paradoxically, has rejected it (9:6-29). Paul demonstrates that God's rejection of Israel is her own fault. God's promises depend upon faith; but Israel seeks her own righteousness by Law. Israel's rejection, therefore, is the consequence of her unbelief (9:30—10:21).

If Paul had said no more, it would seem to imply that Israel's rejection is final: God intended it to be so, and Israel deserved it. But this is not the last word. "Of what use was all God's procedure with His peculiar people, if, when the fullness of times has come, they are simply to be rejected? That is a question which absolutely demands an answer" (Nygren 1949, 390). Has God rejected that people, which as a whole had received the special benefits enumerated in 9:4-6? The answer is a resounding **By no means!** (11:1).

The rejection of Israel, Paul now shows, is not final, for several reasons: (1) Even now there is a faithful remnant in Israel (11:1-10). (2) The fall of Israel opened the door of opportunity for the salvation of the Gentiles; and here we see a hint of her eventual acceptance (vv 11-24). Finally (3), ethnic Israel is destined to receive salvation in connection with the return of Messiah Jesus (vv 25-32). The hardening of Israel that arose with the Gentile mission will continue until its purpose is complete, but when it is all complete, "all Israel will be saved"—not only all believing Gentiles but also all believing Jews (v 26).

a. A Remnant of Israel Is Already in the Church (11:1-10)

BEHIND THE TEXT

Romans 11:1-10 summarizes chs 9 and 10, providing a smooth transition and introduction to the conclusion of Paul's argument in 11:11-32. Jewett describes it as "a brilliant fusion of diatribe and midrash" (2007, 651), in which Paul raises a series of rhetorical questions followed by scriptural evidence.

Romans 11 expresses one purpose throughout: Paul's argument that the divine plan—from God's promise to Abraham until its fulfillment in Christ—must be viewed as moving steadily forward toward *one* end: the salvation of Israel. As the plan unfolds, we see that this entails, *first,* the inclusion of the Gentiles and, *finally,* the end-time salvation of "all Israel." Both Gentiles and Jews will be saved *by grace alone, through faith alone, in Christ alone.* But this is a reversal of the previous divine order (1:16-17): "first for the Jew, then for the Gentile." Romans 9—11 must be seen throughout as targeting the ultimate salvation of Israel (11:25-32).

Paul now moves beyond this paradoxical situation. In advancing the argument in vv 1-10, denying the rejection of Israel, he in essence repeats his first answer in 9:6-13: God has not rejected his people, for they are present in the elect remnant. Yet there is a difference in tone here. "There the word was: only a remnant. Here it is: *already a remnant!*" (Goppelt 1964, 158). There the remnant was only those elected by God's free grace; here it is the firstfruits of Israel's rejection (see 16:25-27).

IN THE TEXT

■ **1** **I ask then** (*legō oun*) emphatically marks a new stage in Paul's argument: **Did God reject** [*apōsato, **push aside/repudiate;*** see Acts 7:27, 39; 1 Tim 1:19] **his people** [*ton laon autou*]? (Rom 11:1). The rhetorical form of the Greek question (introduced with *me*) implies a negative answer: ***God has not rejected*** [*apōsato*] ***his people, has he?*** This is reinforced by the juxtaposition of **God** (*ho theos*) and **his people** (*ton laon autou*). Paul refers to Israel as God's **people** (*laos*) only within OT quotations (9:25-26; 10:21; 11:1-2; 15:10-11; 1 Cor 10:7; 14:21; 2 Cor 6:16; Dunn 2002b, 38B:634). Here he quotes the OT (1 Sam 12:22; see Ps 94:14) promise, "The Lord will not forsake his people" (*ouk apōsetai Kyrios ton laon,* LXX). These words remind Paul's readers of the promise and reinforce his negative answer (Sanday and Headlam 1929, 309). Admittedly, some OT passages consider the possibility that their unfaithfulness might lead God to disown them (e.g., Judg 6:13; 2 Kgs 21:14; 23:27; Pss 44:9, 23; 60:1, 10; Jer 7:29; 31:36-37; Hos 9:17).

Perhaps this biblical ambivalence made implicit denials seem insufficient, so Paul adds an explicit **By no means!** (see the comments on Rom 6:1) to repudiate the horrifying thought of Israel's rejection. As evidence, Paul presents himself as a case in point: **I am an Israelite myself, a descendant** [*ek spermatos;* see 4:13-18; 9:7, 8] **of Abraham, from the tribe of Benjamin** [see Phil 3:5] (Rom 11:1). We might paraphrase Paul's claim, "How can anyone think that God has rejected his people? Consider the evidence: I, Paul, am an Israelite [see 2 Cor 11:22] and a Christian. More than most of my fellow Israelites, I was a victim of the same zeal [Gal 1:13; 1 Thess 2:16] that blinds them to Christ. The grace that rescued me can save anyone."

Dunn rejects such readings as "ludicrous," "egotistical," self-aggrandizing, and "almost surely not what Paul meant":

> It is not because he is a Christian that Paul can dismiss the suggestion that God has repudiated his people (by implication, in favor of the Gentiles), but because he is an Israelite, because he is so conscious that he belongs to God's people. It is precisely as a Jew that Paul reaffirms God's faithfulness to the Jews. (Dunn 2002b, 38B:644)

■ **2*a*** Nevertheless, we maintain that the very existence of Jewish Christians like Paul (see Rom 11:5) offered proof that **God did not reject** [*apōsato;* see 9:29] **his people, whom he foreknew** (v 2*a*). Without acknowledgment, Paul's question echoes 1 Sam 12:22 and Ps 94:14.

Divine foreknowledge (see Rom 8:29) has to do with God's promises made to Israel's ancestors, which are unaffected by contemporary developments; they concern the nation as a whole. Rabbis (m. Sanh. 10.1) claimed that "all Israelites have a share in the world to come." Paul agrees, provided he can redefine the meaning of Israelite. Paul rejects the typical "Jewish idea of God's people as an ethnic or national entity" and attempts to redraw Israel's boundaries (Dunn 2002b, 38B:635-36). Israel is both smaller and larger than most Jews imagined.

Paul might have cited any one of numerous OT passages that speak of the election of Israel as God's special people (see on 9:4) to validate his claim that God had not reneged on his ancient choice of **Israel,** but he appeals to the story of Elijah, perhaps because he conceives of himself as a latter-day Elijah (Munck 1967, 109).

■ **2*b*-3 Don't you know** [see 6:3; 7:1] **what the Scripture says in the passage about Elijah—how he appealed to** [*entynchanei*] **God against** [*kata;* see the sidebar "Prepositions" with the commentary on 8:4] **Israel: "Lord, they have killed** [*apekteinan*] **your prophets and torn down your altars; I am the only one left, and they are trying to kill me"** [*zētousin tēn psychēn mou, **they are seeking my life***]**?** (vv 2*b*-3; 1 Kgs 19:10, 14). The addition of chapter and verse divisions to the Bible during the late medieval period has certainly facilitated specifying biblical references.

■ **4 And what was God's answer** [*ho chrēmatismos, **the divine answer***—only here in the NT] **to** [Elijah]**? "I have reserved** [*katelipon,* "have left behind"] **for myself seven thousand** [***men,*** *andras*] **who have not bowed the knee to Baal"** (Rom 11:4; 1 Kgs 19:18; see 2 Kgs 19:4). Paul's modification at the beginning of the quotation emphasizes the divine initiative in preserving the faithfulness of the elect minority. Their number—7,000—may be symbolic, "representing the completeness of Israel" (Dunn 2002b, 38B:637). That the righteous remnant has **not bowed the knee to Baal** indicates that they have resisted idolatry and continue to worship Yahweh alone. "As God sustained and carried out his covenant purpose through such a minority then, so now" (Dunn 2002b, 38B:645).

■ **5** Paul applies the Elijah story in Rom 11:5: **So too, at the present time** [3:26] **there is** [*gegonen, **there has come to exist,*** to reflect the perfect tense] **a remnant** [*leimma,* "remainder," "leftovers"; from the same cognate family as *katelipon* in 11:4; see 9:27, citing Isa 10:22] **chosen by grace** [*kata eklogēn charitos, **according to election of grace;*** see 9:11].

This 1 Kings passage, which is one of the seminal remnant passages in the OT (see Isa 6:13; 10:20-22; see Jewett 2007, 659 for more), suits Paul's purpose admirably, with its contrast between the apparently hopeless state of Israel and God's assurance of his continuing care for the people through his preservation of a remnant of true believers. But God's preservation of an elect **remnant** chosen on the basis of **grace** is not only evidence of his present faithfulness to Israel but also a pledge of hope for the future of the people (Moo 1996, 677).

■ **6** Paul continues, clarifying his point: **And if** the remnant has been chosen **by grace** [*chariti*], **then it is no longer by works** [*ouketi ex ergōn;* see Rom 3:20, 27-28; 4:2, 6; 9:12, 32]**; if it were, grace** [*hē charis*] **would no longer be grace** (11:6; see ch 4). ***The* grace** of God revealed definitively in Christ (see 5:15, 21; 16:20) demands that God be perfectly free to bestow grace on whomever he chooses (see 9:15-16).

But, if God's election were based on what human beings do, his freedom would be violated and he would no longer be acting out of sheer generosity. For Paul, the gracious character of God's free activity is a theological axiom, automatically ruling out anything that would control it. The KJV, following a gloss found in some late mss, adds to 11:6: "But if it be of works, then is it no more grace: otherwise work is no more work."

That Israel's election is on the basis of grace contributes to Paul's emerging redefinition of Israel (see 9:6, 27-28). His point is that the remnant is not defined as a subset within Israel by their faithfulness to the Law but by their absolute dependence on God's grace.

Paul is not "objecting to a belief that justification can be earned by good works" (see 3:20; 9:32; Dunn 2002b, 38B:639). He objects to the assumption that election is defined by racial descent, circumcision, kosher laws, and other merely human identifying marks. Grace is not about what humans can do without God. Gentiles do not have to become Jews or adopt their customs or rituals to be a part of the grace-defined elect community. This is the first time in the entire letter to the Romans in which Paul explicitly presents **grace** and **works** as antitheses.

■ **7** The rhetorical **What then?** [*ti oyn,* see 3:1, 9; 4:1; 6:1, 15; 7:7; 8:31; 9:14, 19, 30] is the result of this principle: **What Israel sought so earnestly** [*epizētei, **wished for***—only here in Romans] **it did not obtain** [*epetychen,* see Heb 6:15; 11:33; Jas 4:2], **but the elect did** (Rom 11:7; see 9:30-33).

So who are **the elect**? In 9:30-31 and 10:20 Paul insisted that Israel as a whole, through seeking righteousness by means of Law, failed to achieve it; whereas Gentiles, who could reach it by faith alone, had achieved it. This might limit **the elect** to Gentile Christians. But 11:5 seems to require that this group must also include Jewish Christians. In 8:33, "those whom God has chosen" (*eklektoi theou, **the elect of God***) clearly refers to justified believers, i.e., the elect are Christians. In 9:24 Paul similarly refers to Christians as "us, whom [God] also called [*hous kai ekalesen, **whom he elected***], not only from the Jews but also from the Gentiles." Thus, **the elect** here must refer to Christ-believing Gentiles and Jews. This new reality came to exist through an act of grace by which they were constituted **the elect** (Barrett 1957, 210).

In contrast to **the elect** stand **the others** [*hoi lopoi, **the rest***], who **were hardened.** Israel, apart from the remnant, stood outside the relation of grace and consequently were **hardened** (*epōrōthēsan;* see Mark 6:52; 8:17; John 12:40; 2 Cor 3:14; in Rom 9:18 *sklērynei* means "hardens"; see the synonym *pauchynomai* in Matt 13:15; Acts 28:27 following Isa 6:9-10). "Their religious enthusiasm was turned to sin" (Barrett 1957, 210). Who has caused Israel's obtuse stubbornness? Jewett cites the findings of

Marie-Irma Seewann suggesting that not only was Israel "'hardened by God (11:7-10) but also that on its own responsibility it chose the wrong path (9:30—10:3)'" (2007, 662).

Early Christians followed the LXX in using a variety of terms for the metaphor of hardening "to explain the puzzling obtuseness of most Jews' response to the gospel." Dunn cautions against presuming prematurely that Paul considers **the others** as hopelessly lost (2002b, 38B:640).

■ **8** Paul sees the current state of affairs as fully in accord with Scripture (**as it is written;** see Rom 1:17; 2:24; 3:4, 10; 4:17; 8:36; 9:13, 33; 11:8, 26; 15:3, 21) in all of its canonical divisions—Law, Prophets, and Writings: **God gave them a spirit of stupor** (*pneuma katanyxeōs*) (11:8). That is, God caused them to be dull and insensible to everything spiritual, as if they were in a drunken **stupor** (alluding to Isa 29:10 and 6:9-10).

Without interruption Paul continues (echoing Deut 29:4), God blinded their **eyes so that they could not see and** deafened their **ears so that they could not hear, to this very day.** With this conflation of texts Paul concludes that Israel's present unbelief (as in the past—**to this very day;** see 2 Cor 3:14-15) is God's doing. Israel's failure was foreseen, intended, and effected by God (Dunn 2002b, 38B:647). But Paul does not say why. In Rom 11:11 and 25-27 he will say that God did this to give the Gentiles an opportunity to come to him through faith in Christ.

■ **9-10** In vv 9-10, Paul paraphrases Ps 69:22-23 (alluding to Ps 35:8; LXX): **And David says** [see Rom 4:6; 10:5]**: "May their table become a snare and a trap, a stumbling block** [see 9:33] **and a retribution for them. May their eyes be darkened** [see 1:21; 2:19] **so they cannot see, and their backs be bent forever** [*dia pantos,* ***continually***]." (See Dunn 2002b, 38B:642 for a table of other NT quotations of Ps 69.)

> Their table is their table-fellowship: their unity, and interrelatedness created by the law and so highly valued in Judaism were no more than a delusion since they were in union with sin (iii. 20), not righteousness. The bent back is a symbol of bondage; compare Gal. iv. 25. (Barrett 1957, 210)

Speculations differ widely among commentators as to the particular relevance Paul saw within these Psalm verses to unbelieving Israel or to relations between Jewish and Gentile believers in Rome (see Cranfield 1979, 2:551-52; Dunn 2002b, 38B:642-43; and Jewett 2007, 663, for recent opinion).

The maintenance of ritual purity through the enforcement of kosher laws related to table fellowship was one of the central features of the Jewish particularism of Paul's day. For example, in Acts 10 Peter claims never to have eaten anything other than kosher food and makes a point of calling Cornelius's attention to the exception he made as an observant Jew by even entering his house. Jewish refusal to associate with Gentiles included the half-Israelite Samaritans as well (see John 4:9).

In the minds of pious Jews there was a correlation between what they ate at **their table** and who they were. Partly because Gentiles consumed "unclean" foods, Gentiles themselves were considered "unclean" (Blue 1997). This zealously maintained religious-cultural work of Law built a wall of separation between Jews and Gentiles that complicated community relations within mixed Jewish and Gentile Christian congregations (see e.g., Gal 2:11-21; Rom 14 and 15).

Paul apparently sees the words of Ps 69:22-23, a curse paradoxically originally invoked on Israel's enemies, as an inspired curse pronounced on Israel as punishment for excluding believing Gentiles from their communities. This would provide yet another reason for seeing Israel's continuing stubborn refusal to accept the gospel as somehow ordained by God.

b. Israel's Fall and Gentiles' Salvation (11:11-24)

BEHIND THE TEXT

The exclusion of the bulk of Israel is not permanent. God's punishment for its rebellion is remedial, not final. Paul expects the inclusion of the Gentiles to effect an awakening of unbelieving Israel, bringing it to a realization of what it has been missing and so to lead it to repent. Paul hopes the success of the Gentile mission will contribute in this way to the saving of some of his fellow Jews.

And, if the present exclusion of the majority of Israel has made available such a rich benefit for Gentiles, what glory shall accompany Israel's final restoration? In the meantime the existence of those Israelites who already believe in Christ serves to sanctify the unbelieving majority. What Paul says here and in the following subsection is addressed explicitly to the Gentiles in the Roman Christian community (see 11:13*a*). He is clearly concerned to warn them against the pride of imagining themselves superior to the unbelieving Jews. For the sake of directness and forcefulness Paul uses the second person singular in vv 17-24, singling out individual Gentile believers more effectively than the collective plural "you."

IN THE TEXT

(1) From Rejection to Riches to Resurrection (11:11-16)

(a) Stumbling into Riches (11:11-12)

■ **11** A rhetorical question introduces this subsection as it does v 1. Perhaps the imagery of the stumbling stone (*skandalon*), mentioned in 9:32-33 and 11:9, prompts Paul's question: ***Therefore*** [*oun*], ***I say, They did not stumble so as*** [*hina*] ***to fall, did they? By no means!*** (v 11; see 10:19; 11:14).

The inferential conjunction *oun* refers back to the catena of scriptural accusations against Israel in 11:7-10. The rhetorical question is formulated so as to demand a negative answer, but Paul denies it nonetheless (using *mē genoito* for the tenth and last time in the letter; see 6:1). The point of the passage is the contrast between **stumble** (*eptaisan*) and **fall beyond recovery** (*pesōsin*). The conjunction *hina*, which connects the two verbs, indicates either the purpose or potential result of the prior action. One who stumbles may fall and recover or may fall never to rise again (see Isa 24:20; Heb 4:11).

There is no question that "a portion of Israel had stumbled and fallen" (see Rom 11:17 and 22). "While the result of Jewish rejection of the gospel was clear, the divine intention was not." This "gave rise to the rhetorical question" (Jewett 2007, 673). Paul's question implies that God did not intend Israel's misstep over Christ to be a fatal fall, an act of apostasy leading to its destruction (see 1 Cor 10:12; Rom 11:22; 14:4).

Contrary (*alla*, ***But***) to the conclusion readers of Rom 9—11 up to this point might have drawn, the unbelief of the majority of Israel is not beyond remedy. Paul describes Israel's **stumble** as **their transgression** (see 4:25; 5:11-12), from which restoration was possible (see Gal 6:1; Rom 11:24). But more than this, ***the result of their false step*** [*paraptōmati*] is bringing **salvation** [see 1:16; 10:1, 10] . . . **to the Gentiles.**

How so? Israel's rejection of Christ led to his saving death. Its hostility to early Christian preaching drove the church to preach the good news to Gentiles (Acts 11:19-21; 13:45-48; 18:6; 28:24-28; Dunn 2002b, 38B:653). They believed the message and confessed their faith in Christ (Rom 10:10). Finally, Israel's resistance to God's saving purposes (11:26) "provides time for the Gentile mission" (Jewett 2007, 674).

God wastes nothing; he intends to use the conversion of the Gentiles to achieve his saving purpose for Israel—**to make Israel envious** or ***jealous/zealous*** (*eis to parazēlōsai autous;* see 10:19, citing Deut 32:21). Jewett finds it extremely improbable that such an unworthy motivation as envy or jealousy could lead unbelieving Israel to salvation. Since "Jewish legalists viewed the early Christian proclamation as heretical, no satisfactory explanation has ever been given to explain why they would have been 'jealous' when Gentiles accepted this allegedly mistaken doctrine" (Jewett 2007, 675). Perhaps Paul had in mind envy of a community whose Messiah had already come. Or, perhaps, it was not the beliefs but the quality of community life within the Christian church that Paul thought would make Israel envious. Cranfield suggests:

> When Israel, the people whom God had made peculiarly His own, His special possession, see others the recipients of the mercy and goodness of their God, they will begin to understand what they are missing and to desire that salvation which they have rejected. Thus the hardening of which v. 7 spoke has for its ultimate purpose the salvation of those who are hardened. (1985, 274)

Jewett prefers an interpretation of *parazēlōsai* that is consistent with its use earlier in Romans (esp. 10:2, 19)—***zealous.*** But is it not at least as puzzling that Paul would think that zeal—religious fanaticism and hostility—should lead Israel to salvation (11:14)? Jewett answers:

> Perhaps he has the model of his own conversion in mind, namely, that when his zeal reached its violent climax in the persecution of the believers in Damascus, the risen Christ was revealed to him and his desire to destroy alleged evildoers turned into its opposite, a desire for coexistence with those whom the Messiah had chosen to accept. Zeal to exclude hated Gentiles turned into a comparable zeal to include them as part of the people of God. It appears that Paul hoped for a similar process of conversion for current Jewish critics of the gospel. (2007, 675)

■ **12** With v 12 Paul begins a series of conditional sentences, reasoning from the lesser to the greater (Hebrew: *qal waḥomer;* Latin: *a minore ad maius*). **But if** [*ei de;* see 11:16, 17, 18] **their transgression** [*paraptōma*] **means riches** [*ploutos;* see 2:4; 9:23; 10:12; 11:33] **for the world, and their loss** [*hēttēma*] **means riches** [*ploutos*] **for the Gentiles, how much greater riches will their fullness** [*plērōma*] **bring!** (see 11:24—"how much more"; 5:9, 10, 15, 17).

Romans 11:11 could leave the impression that the only importance of Gentile salvation is instrumental—to make unbelieving Jews ***jealous/ zealous*** so as to lead them to salvation. Here Paul stresses that **much greater riches** will accrue to **the Gentiles** from the **fullness** of Israel. Since God's grace is in unlimited supply, the gain for Israel is not a loss for the Gentiles.

The imagery of **riches for the world** depends on a reversal of the prophetic expectation of an eschatological pilgrimage to Jerusalem of Gentile converts taking "the riches [*ploutos*] of the nations" with them (see 9:26; see Isa 60:5 LXX; see Ps 22:27; Isa 2:2-3; 56:6-8; 60:2; Mic 4:2; Zeph 3:9; Zech 2:11; 14:16). Perhaps Paul envisioned that his planned trip to Jerusalem to deliver the collection from his Gentile churches would fulfill this (see Rom 15:22-29). And he was confident that his trip to Rome after that would be "in the fullness [*plērōmati*] of the blessing of Christ" (v 29 NRSV). Thus, Paul's thinking seems to shift from material to spiritual **riches.**

But what does the ambiguous **fullness** of Israel mean? Some interpreters take it to refer to "the predestined number of the saved" (see *4 Ezra* 4:35-37; so Jewett 2007, 676). Paul's terminology in Rom 11:12 seems to be influenced by rhetorical considerations. Note the succession of neuter nouns ending in *-ma* (a suffix indicating the results of an action): *paraptōma*, *hēttēma*, and *plērōma*.

The word **fullness** is used as a virtual antonym of **transgression** and **loss** in Paul's parallel construction. Thus, he seems to expect Israel finally to fulfill God's demands (see 13:10; Bauer 1979, 672, s.v. *plērōma* 4), to achieve the purposes for which he originally called it to be his people. Thus, "obedience" and "recovery" would seem to be far more suitable antitheses to **transgression** and **loss** than something like "all Israel destined to salvation." This is true whether "all" includes every Israelite or only an elite subset.

Israel's stumbling and the surrender of its privileges as God's unique people showered spiritual benefits on the Gentiles. Just so Israel's repentance and restoration will rain down even greater spiritual benefits on them. Paul will shed more light on the reality behind his imagery in 11:15.

By *to plērōma autōn*, the **fullness** of Israel, in v 12 Paul must have in mind something comparable to what he means by *to plērōma tōn ethnōn*, ***the fullness of the Gentiles*** in v 25. With the future prospect of the salvation of "all Israel" in view in v 26, the present small remnant of Jewish believers stands in marked contrast to such **fullness.** "Paul cannot rest content in the thought of only a remnant saved" (Dunn 2002b, 38B:655). He assumes that the number of believing Jews will increase, but he cannot mean to suggest that every single Israelite will come to faith any more than he imagines that all Gentiles will certainly become Christians. That is, unless 11:32 is taken to imply universal salvation, contrary to all Paul writes elsewhere.

Perhaps Paul envisions the uniting of the two groups—believing Jews and Gentiles—into one messianic community as the **fullness** of Israel. Since Paul seems unwilling to engage in speculative eschatological calculus, we might do well to follow his lead and allow the ambiguity of **fullness** to stand.

(b) An Aside to Gentiles (11:13-14)

■ **13*a*** In v 13 Paul addresses his non-Jewish Roman readers directly, using the first person singular (**I**). He refers to them in the second person plural (**you**). Although he speaks of Jews throughout chs 9—11 in the third person (they), his audience probably includes Jews as well, but they are Jewish Christians. Here he narrows his audience: **I am talking to you Gentiles** (11:13*a*). This is not the beginning of a new paragraph but only a parenthesis. The thought of the previous verses resumes in vv 15-24.

■ **13*b*** In vv 13-14 Paul prods the **Gentiles** to weigh his words in vv 11-12 and to appreciate why (*eph' hoson*, **Inasmuch as**) he writes as he does: **Inasmuch as I am** [*eimi egō*] **the apostle to the Gentiles, I make much of** [*doxazō, **I glorify***] **my ministry in hope that** [*ei pōs*, "if perhaps, if somehow" (Bauer 1979, 220)] **I may somehow arouse** [*parazēlōsō, **I may make jealous/zealous;*** see v 11; 10:19] **my own people** [*mou tēn sarka, **my flesh***] **to envy and save** [*sōsō, **I will save***] **some of them** (11:13*b*-14).

Despite the emphatic *egō*, Paul does not call himself **the** (there is no definite article in the Greek) only **apostle to the Gentiles;** but his identity is intimately tied to this special calling (see Gal 1:16; 2:2, 7-9). He identifies his role as an **apostle** (see 1:1, 5), as **my ministry** (*diakonian, **service;*** see 12:7; 13:4; 15:8, 25, 31; 16:1; 2 Cor 4:1; 11:23). Paul glorifies his **ministry** by giving himself wholeheartedly to it, as an expression of praise to God for the grace that empowered him to serve (Rom 1:5; see 1 Cor 1:4; 15:9-11; 1 Thess 2:13). And he makes a public issue of his ministry, advocating for the inclusion of Gentiles within the people of God, deliberately provoking his fellow Jews **to envy** or ***zeal,*** to fulfill the Scriptures (Deut 32:21, quoted in Rom 10:19).

■ **14** In 11:14 the Hebrew idiom referring to blood relatives as one's ***flesh*** (see 9:3) explains Paul's designation for his fellow Jews—**my own people.** Some Gentile Christians might mistakenly have supposed that by turning to the Gentiles Paul had no interest in Jewish evangelism. On the contrary, he hopes that his success as apostle to the Gentiles might **somehow** provoke Israel **to envy/*jealousy/zeal*** (see 10:19; 11:11).

Bringing Gentiles to faith would enable him to **save some of** his fellow Israelites (see 11:11). Of course, Paul does not imagine himself a savior, but he is confident that God will use his missionary preaching as an instrument of God's power to save (see 1:16; 1 Cor 7:16; 9:22; 2 Cor 5:16-21; 1 Thess 1:4-5; 2:1-4, 16). There is no reason to think that Paul imagines Israel's salvation by any other means than that outlined in Rom 10:8-10; that is, by preaching the gospel, confession of Jesus as the Christ, and faith in him. Whatever Paul means by **fullness** in 11:12 and by "all" in v 26 must be balanced by his modest aspiration here, to **save some of** his fellow Israelites.

(c) From Zeal to Salvation (11:15-16)

■ **15** In v 15 Paul resumes his "how much more" argument from v 12. He explains (*gar,* **For**) his imagery as follows: **For if** [*ei gar;* see vv 21, 24] **their rejection** [*apobolē, **loss***] **is the reconciliation** [*katallagē*] **of the world, what will their acceptance** [*proslēmpsis, **gain,*** only here in the NT] **be but life from the dead?**

Whether the genitive pronoun **their** has an objective (i.e., God rejected them) or subjective (i.e., they rejected God) force affects our understanding of Paul's emphasis but does not affect his point. It was Israel's active **rejection** of Jesus as their Messiah that led to his death at the hands of the Gentiles. As a result, Israel's present, temporary state might be described as **rejection** by God, something Paul explicitly denies in v 1. Rather, Israel's "transgression" (vv 11, 12) led to their temporary ***loss*** of standing within the people of God.

By **their acceptance** Paul might mean that God will eventually include Israel within his eschatological (end-times) people, despite their continuing unbelief in Christ. But Paul more likely refers to the hope that unbelieving Israel will finally give a favorable response to the gospel (see 10:8-10), to their ***gain.***

Regardless of his emphasis, Paul insists that Israel's **rejection** has already resulted in **the reconciliation of the world** (see 5:10-11; 2 Cor 5:18). Through the death of Christ, God proved himself the friend of all humanity. Paul uses **world** in the more typically Johannine sense of humanity at odds with God, whom God loves nonetheless and gave his Son to save (e.g., John 3:16-17).

In Christ, God was in the process of creating a reconciled community of believing Jews and Gentiles, former mutual enemies (see Eph 2:16). In Rom 14 and 15 Paul will urge the church in Rome to realize what Christ made possible. No one may experience reconciliation—God's overture of all-inclusive friendship through participation in the new humanity in Christ—who refuses to accept God's friendship or who fails to welcome his friends (2 Cor 5:18-20).

Jewett notes the grandiose character of Paul's claim that the conversion of Gentiles to Christ had already meant **the reconciliation of the world.** Paul's language suggests that the gospel was fulfilling

Greco-Roman and Jewish visions of global peace under the rule of a single sovereign. This formulation reveals the breathtaking vision that is embodied in Paul's project of extending the circle of Christ's reconciling sovereignty to the end of the known world in Spain. (Jewett 2007, 681)

If Israel's **rejection/*loss*** has already yielded these "riches" (Rom 11:12), Paul is confident that their **acceptance** (*proslēmpsis, **welcome;*** compare *proslambanō* in 14:1, 3; 15:7) can mean nothing less than **life from the dead.** Paul uses the final resurrection as a metonym for all the events accompanying the eschaton (end times). The consummation of the age will come only when God is satisfied that his purposes for humanity have been fully achieved. Paul takes for granted that Israel plays a decisive role in these purposes.

■ **16** In 11:16 Paul mixes metaphors to make his point. His first image would be fully intelligible only to Jews in his audience. He alludes to Num 15:17-21, which required Israel to offer to God the first portion of its grain or dough. The holiness of the **firstfruits** (*aparchē;* see the commentary on Rom 8:23) insured that ***the entire batch*** would be **holy.** God blessed both the remaining bread and those making the sacrifice. "A holy relationship between supplicants and God is renewed through the offering that removes sins that distort that relationship" (Jewett 2007, 682).

The second image has no cultic significance but may adapt agricultural idioms of Jesus (see Matt 7:17-19; 12:33; Luke 6:43-44; John 15): **if the root is holy, so are the branches.** Regardless, it clearly anticipates the image of the olive tree Paul will develop in Rom 11:17-24.

Leviticus 19:23-25 regards the fruit of trees as "uncircumcised" until an offering from them has been made to God. A tree that has been dedicated to God would then bear branches and fruit that belonged to him. On this basis, a Jew might also think of the offering of the **firstfruits** of the dough as purifying the rest of the **dough,** i.e., setting it apart for sacred use alone.

Paul uses **holy** here, not in a moral but in a cultic/ritual sense. The sacrificial offering is **holy** because it is dedicated to God for exclusive use at the altar within Israel's temple rituals. Exodus 29:37 (cited in Matt 23:19) indicates that "the altar"—by metonymy the entire sacrificial process—makes the gift offered on it holy (compare 1 Cor 7:14-16).

Paul no longer shares the typical Pharisaic interest in ritual purity, "but the idea of a 'holiness' which pervades all of life by virtue of an act and attitude of dedication is certainly fundamental to his thought (1:7; 6:19, 22; 12:1; see 1 Cor 6:11; 1 Thess 4:3-4, 7)" (Dunn 2002b, 38B:671).

Paul seems to apply this double figure to suggest that Jewish Christian converts somehow "sanctify" the unbelieving majority of Israel. This is consistent with his use of *aparchē,* **firstfruits,** to refer to the first Christian converts in a particular geographical area (Rom 16:5; 1 Cor 16:5 [see Rom 1:16]; 2 Thess 2:13). Here he includes the holy remnant—both Jewish and Gentile Christ-believers (Rom 11:2-15)—among the **firstfruits.** Just as the risen Christ is the firstfruits of the resurrection from the dead (1 Cor 15:20, 23), so current believers anticipate and guarantee the full harvest of believers yet to come (see Rom 1:13).

Most commentators, however, take **the root** to refer to the "patriarchs" (see 11:28; 15:8), particularly Abraham (see ch 4). The patriarchs are **holy** by no merit of their own but because of God's election of grace. The "holiness" of Israel's fathers benefits not only their physical descendants but also the entire believing community. Paul's expansion on the metaphor of the **root** and **branches** in 11:17-24 draws on the imagery of "Israel as God's planting" (Dunn 2002b, 38B:659; see Dunn and Jewett [2007, 682] for OT and apocryphal parallels).

(2) The Olive Tree Israel (11:17-24)

Here Paul resumes the diatribe style, with its second person singular (**you**) address, appealing to a Gentile Christian conversation partner as in vv 13-14. His third person plural (**they**) refers to unbelieving Israel. He ex-
11:16-17 pands the second metaphor from v 16, specifically identifying Israel as an olive tree, following OT imagery (Jer 11:16; Hos 14:6). Paul's audience would have known that one of the synagogues in Rome was called the "Synagogue of the Olive" (Jewett 2007, 684-85).

The omnipresent olive tree for most educated Greco-Romans in the Mediterranean world symbolized Athens as the source of the pervasive influence of Hellenistic culture. But here, the tables are turned. Paul regards the Jewish spiritual heritage as superior to the non-Jewish (Dunn 2002b, 38B:661). It was normal practice in the Mediterranean world to graft domesticated olive branches into the sturdier wild olive trees, but wild branches were sometimes grafted into unproductive domestic trees to rejuvenate them and make them more productive (Jewett 2007, 684).

■ **17** In Rom 11:17-18*a* Paul's imagery takes the form of a conditional sentence, although the situation he describes refers to the current situation. **If** [*Ei,* ***Since***] **some of the branches have been broken off** [*exeklasthēsan*], **and you, though a wild olive shoot, have been grafted in among the others and now share in the nourishing sap from the olive root, do not boast over these branches.**

The aorist passive verb, **have been broken off,** presumes that God is somehow responsible for unbelieving Israel's stubborn refusal of the gospel (see vv 7-10). Remarkably, Paul refers to the vast majority of Israel, which remains in unbelief, as **some** [*tines*] **of the branches** (recall the surprising use of *tinas* in v 14). Unlike Matt 3:10 and John 15:6, "Paul, of course, does not pursue the usual corollary—discarded branches are burnt" (Dunn 2002b, 38B:660). Instead, he looks forward to their being grafted in again (Rom 11:23).

Within the allegorical imagery, the **wild olive shoot** refers to Gentile believers. These Gentiles **have been grafted in among the others** (*en autois, **among them***). The aorist passive verb **have been grafted in** presumes that God has made their inclusion in the cultivated tree possible. **The others** represent Jewish Christians, who might have been expected to have shared in the heritage of Abraham and "the patriarchs" (11:28; 15:8)—**the olive root.** At best, Gentile believers only share with Jews in the virtues of the **root,** which is not Gentile but Jewish. But given the unbelief of the majority of Israel, both Jewish and Gentile believers must be "a remnant according to the election of grace" (see 8:29-30; Murray 1959, 2:86). "By grace, believers from different ethnic groups now enjoy a 'shared lineage' as God's people" (Jewett 2007, 685).

Building on the holiness premise established in 11:16, Paul presumes that both Jewish and Gentile believers mutually **share in** (*synkoinōnos, **are partners;*** see 12:13; 15:26, 27; 1 Cor 1:9; 9:23; 10:16; 2 Cor 1:7; 6:14; 8:4, 23; 9:13; Gal 2:9; 6:6; Eph 5:11; Phil 1:5, 7; 2:1; 3:10; 4:14-15; Phlm 6, 17) the extraordinary privilege of being nourished by the graced heritage of Israel. Both partake in the holiness of the patriarchs, the one historical **root** of the people of God, and in the blessings attached to it. "Salvation is to be found only in historical continuity by inheriting promises given to the fathers: The Gentile Christians are what they are only because they have become 'Abraham's seed.' Consequently there is still hope for unbelieving Israel" (Goppelt 1964, 160).

■ **18** In Rom 11:18 the conclusion of Paul's conditional sentence takes the form of an exhortation to the Gentile Christians in his audience: **do not boast over those branches** (v 18*a*). He warns them to avoid claims of comparative superiority to the broken-off branches—unbelieving Jews, but he also rejects unfavorable comparisons based on the Gentile-Christian majority's superior numbers or status compared to the natural branches—Jewish Christians—within the Roman church (see chs 14 and 15).

Paul echoes and reverses "the earlier rebukes of Jewish presumption [in chs 2 and 3], . . . since the danger is the same—of assuming that a portion within the people of God (the same tree!) is a matter for which the 'haves' can boast over the 'have-nots'" (Dunn 2002b, 38B:652). In both instances, the prohibition of boasting is based on "the believer's experience of grace, unearned and undeserved" (Jewett 2007, 686).

Paul's warning suggests that there was a temptation in Rome for Gentile Christians, who had lived independently of Jewish Christians for years following their eviction by Claudius (see the Introduction to the commentary), to imagine that the church had moved beyond its Jewish roots. That "this is clear evidence of residual anti-Semitism within the Roman churches" (Jewett 2007, 686) is debatable.

The apostle's point is that the church is not entirely new, nor a replacement of Israel. It is instead the continuation of God's ancient people. Thus, he insists that the church is no place for competition and innovation but for community and continuity. Believers—both Jews and Gentiles—live by dependence on God and the ancient traditions of the people of God (see 15:27).

The purpose of the olive tree illustration is to prevent any false sense of security on the part of the Gentiles. Keep in mind that Paul's interlocutor is imaginary. We cannot be certain that the views Paul places on his lips were actually held by Gentile believers in Rome. Nevertheless, Paul must have known enough about the situation there to fear some might hold such views. Thus, he wrote to prevent (if not correct) destructive conceptions of Jewish-Gentile relations within the church.

■ **19** In 11:19 Paul places an alibi for anti-Jewish sentiments on the lips of his Gentile-Christian interlocutor (Godet 1883, 407): **You will say then, "Branches were broken off** [see v 17] **so that I** [*egō*] **could be grafted in."** The emphatic first person singular pronoun **I** presents him as a braggart. Paul challenges the egotism and presumption of this self-assured **I,** who imagines that unbelieving Jewish **branches** were broken off just to make room for him. This suggests that Gentile arrogance and presumption were Paul's real targets, not latent anti-Semitism. He assumes that "there is no salvation apart from the history of Israel" (see John 4:22; Käsemann 1980, 309-10).

It seems unlikely that early Gentile-Christian converts cherished strong anti-Semitic feelings, given the synagogue roots of the Roman house and tenement churches, but there is no question that later "Christians" have been guilty of such attitudes. There was a widespread dislike, if not contempt, for Jews common among the socially elite in the contemporary Roman world. Given the human temptation to arrogance and boastfulness—whether Jewish (see Rom 2:1-3; 3:9, 27-31) or Gentile, as here, Paul's caution was definitely in order.

■ **20** Paul concedes his objector's point, **Granted,** God did break off the unbelieving branches. **But,** he quickly adds, **they were broken off because of unbelief** [*tēi apistia;* see 3:3], **and you stand by faith** (*tēi pistei*) (11:20; see 4:20; 5:2). God did not arbitrarily lop off Jewish branches as an act of sovereign power. Paul presumes that **God did not spare** (11:21) Jewish unbelievers as a consequence of their rejection of the gospel. **They were broken off**—excluded from the ranks of his people—**because of unbelief.**

Paul assures his Gentile Christian readers, **you stand** [*estēkas*] **by faith.** The perfect tense of the verb **stand** presumes a past event resulting in a present state sustained **by faith.** "As . . . throughout Romans, the test of faith is not doctrinal but behavioral. When social or cultural competition remains dominant, faith in Christ crucified has not yet achieved its transforming purpose" (Jewett 2007, 688).

The Jewish apostle to the Gentiles assumes that descent from Abraham has nothing to do with one's current standing within the people of God. He knows nothing of salvation based on ethnicity nor of once-saved-always-saved security. He warns Gentile believers that their present security within the people of God is entirely contingent upon continued faithfulness. They, too, will not be spared but broken off, if they turn from reverent dependence on God to arrogance and presumption.

> If even the promises to Israel could not prevent such an outcome, then gentile Christians should not assume that they were exempt from a similar outcome. The possibility of believers "falling away" (. . . v 20), apostatizing, is one which Paul certainly did not exclude . . . [8:13, 17; 9:3; 11:22; 14:15, 20; see 1 Cor 3:17; 8:11; 9:27; 10:1-12; 15:1-2; 2 Cor 13:5; Gal 5:4; Col 1:22-23; Heb 3:14; 6:4-8; 10:29]. A doctrine of "perseverance of the saints" which does not include the lessons of salvation-history has lost its biblical perspective. (Dunn 2002b, 38B:664)

Thus, Paul warns, **Do not be arrogant** [*hypsēla*], **but be afraid** (*phobou*). The fear he calls for is not terror in the face of a capricious god but reverent respect for God's right to act as Judge and Savior (see Prov 24:21; Eccl 12:13). Since his warning, **be afraid,** has no object, his point may simply call for caution, lest the boastful lose their gracious privileges.

■ **21** The preceding warning is supported by its rationale in Rom 11:21: **For** [*gar*] **if** [*ei, **since***] **God did not spare** [*epheisato;* see 8:32] **the natural branches, he will not spare** [*pheisetai*] **you either** (see 1 Cor 10:12). The favored birth status (*kata physin,* **natural;** Bauer 1979, 869) of Israel was not unconditional. The "greater to lesser" logic of **how much more** (see Rom 5:10, 15, 17; 11:12, 15-16, 24) reminds Gentile Christians that they have no claim before God. The continuity between Israel and Gentile believers is not intrinsic; it rests solely on God's faithfulness and their sustained faith.

■ **22** In 11:22 Paul admonishes: **Consider therefore the kindness** [*chrēstotēta, **goodness***] **and sternness** [*apotomian, **severity;*** only here in the NT] **of God: sternness** [*apotomia*] **to those who fell, but kindness** [*chrēstotēs*] **to you, provided that you continue** [*epimenēs,* "stay, remain, persist, persevere"] **in his kindness** [*chrēstotēta*]**. Otherwise, you also will be cut off** (*ekkopēsē*). Unlike the traditional contrast between divine mercy and justice, nowhere else in Jewish literature are God's **kindness** and **severity** employed antithetically, as here.

As in 2:4 **the kindness** of God seems to characterize his patient willingness to give sinners time to repent. Paul's threefold mention of **kindness** in 11:22 strongly emphasizes this aspect of God's nature (compare "mercy" in 9:15, 16, 18, 23; 11:30-32), but he also insists that God is capable of **sternness,** i.e., strict judgment toward the unrepentant who misunderstand his **kindness** as indifference to human rebellion (see 2:12).

Although Paul describes Israel's unbelief as stumbling in contrast with falling (*pesōsin*) in 11:11, in v 22 he refers to unbelieving Israel as **those who fell** (*tous pesontas;* see vv 17, 19). Here the contrast, as in 14:4 (see Heb 4:11; Rev 2:5), is between those who **stand** [*stēkas*] **by faith** (Rom 11:20) and **those who fell** (v 22) from gracious inclusion in the people of God **because of unbelief** (v 20). Those who **stand** are faithful believers, both Jews and Gentiles. Those who "are standing firm, [must] be careful that [they] don't fall" (1 Cor 10:12).

One's standing with God is provisional (*ean,* **provided;** *epei,* **otherwise**). Continuing to live **by faith** (Rom 11:20) requires persevering in God's **kindness** (see Col 1:21-23). If Gentile (and Jewish) believers do not, they, too, **will be cut off,** i.e., God will judge, excommunicate, and break them off (see Rom 11:17, 19, 20) from the olive tree that is the Israel of God. Believers must abandon themselves to God's **kindness** or face his judgment. "Paul's whole point is that presumption is fatal, whether of Jew or of Gentile" (Dunn 2002b, 38B:665).

■ **23** In v 23 Paul draws an even more significant lesson: The fall of unbelieving Israel is not final; it, too, is provisional (*ean,* **if**). **And if they do not persist** [*epimenēs;* see v 22] **in unbelief** [see v 20]**, they will be grafted in, for God is able** [*dynatos, **powerful***] **to graft them in again.** Obviously, the olive tree imagery does not control Paul's understanding of what **God is able** (see 1:4, 16-17; 4:21; 9:17, 22; 14:4; 15:13, 19) to do.

Of course, dead and withered branches cannot be grafted again into the tree from which they were removed. But God is not limited by the rules of horticulture; and people are not branches. Just as the grafted-in Gentile branches remain secure in the olive tree only through perseverance in faith, so the cropped-off Jewish branches may be **grafted in** again, **if they do not persist in** their **unbelief.**

Despite what God *can* do, the human response of faith/unbelief is decisive in determining what he *will* do. God does not overpower human unbelief unilaterally, making faith inevitable, but "God is powerful enough to break through the resistance against grace, which is as formidable a barrier for Gentiles as for Jews" (Jewett 2007, 692).

The faith of Christians demonstrates their relationship with God. Gentile believers **stand by faith** (11:20) only as they confess that the God who graciously saved *them* can save those most hopelessly lost; therefore, above all, the severed branches of the people of Israel (see 10:1). Christian faith trusts God in spite of the apparent hopelessness of death (see 4:17, 23-25; 11:15). "The God who gives life to the dead and calls things that are not as though they were" (4:17) **is able to graft** unbelieving Israel back into the olive tree they abandoned once **again,** by bringing them back to faith.

■ **24** Once again in 11:24, Paul appeals to the "greater to lesser" argument (see similar **how much more** logic in 5:10, 15, 17; 11:12, 15-16, 21). The salvation of Israel is possible, because, **After all, if you were cut out of** [*exekopēs*] **an olive tree that is wild by nature, and contrary to nature were grafted into a cultivated olive tree, how much more readily will these, the natural branches, be grafted into their own olive tree!**

The strength of Paul's argument lies in the fact that the process he describes is **contrary to nature.** It is a process unexpected in horticulture. Paul disarms his critics by acknowledging that he is aware of the unnaturalness of this particular kind of grafting, but this is what God has done (and will do), **contrary to nature** or not. "Ethnic identity has no bearing on membership of the people of God" (Dunn 2002b, 38B:666). **God** has grafted wild olive branches into his cultivated tree, and he is certainly able to graft the **natural branches** in again.

Paul does not envision the church as a replacement for Israel, nor of separate Jewish and Gentile churches, "but rather a church of Jews and Gentiles" (Jewett 2007, 693). The God who was able to bring Gentiles to faith is able to restore unbelieving Israel into the one people of God. If the incorporation of Gentiles into Israel is possible, **how much more** is the restoration of unbelieving ethnic Israel to the people of God a divine possibility. **God is able** (v 23)!

FROM THE TEXT

The sovereignty of God paradoxically exists side-by-side with human freedom and responsibility. Somehow—Paul does not explain how—Israel's self-chosen rebellion against God and the gospel have nevertheless served God's purposes, opening the way for believing Gentiles to be included within his ancient people Israel. And God will use this gracious inclusion of Gentiles to serve his purpose of making unbelieving Jews jealous/zealous, so as to recover their squandered privileges by coming to faith in Christ. Their return will not squeeze out the newcomers to the enlarged and redefined Israel. On the contrary, Paul sees this scenario as bringing about the final and complete fulfillment of God's redemptive purposes for humanity and the created order.

The interplay of divine sovereignty and human responsibility challenges simplistic either-or thinking. God is able to work with all things to achieve his ultimate purposes without violating human freedom to persist in unbelief, come to faith, or persist in faith. Therefore, God has every right to judge with severity those who insist upon maintaining their presumptuous autonomy.

Paul's optimism of grace knows no bounds. He sees in the now comparatively small and insignificant Christian church, comprised of believing Jews and Gentiles, the basis for hope not only for a revitalized Israel but also for reconciliation of the entire world to the Creator and the consummation of all of human history in the resurrection of the dead.

Paul emphasizes God's power to restore unbelieving Israel to the original "olive tree" from which it was severed because of unbelief through the success of the Gentile mission. By God's grace, believing Gentiles had been grafted unnaturally into the "olive tree" Israel. Surveying their privileged status among the few remaining branches of believing Israel, Gentiles might be tempted to boast over what they perceived to be their superiority over the disqualified majority of unbelieving Jews. The danger of Gentile pride and anti-Semitism provides the transition to the climactic passage that follows—the final mystery of God's merciful plan to accomplish in the end the salvation of all Israel.

What is ethnic Israel's role in Pauline eschatology? Did Paul expect that the success of his Gentile mission would bring Jews to their senses and cause them to come to faith in Christ en masse (11:12, 25-32)? Did he imagine that their conversion, in turn, would persuade God to bring a final end to the present age? Did Paul claim for himself such a significant supporting role in history's final drama? If so, the apostle was apparently mistaken. Are we then to abandon this reading of Rom 9—11? If so, should we concede that Paul might also be mistaken in his hope for the future salvation of Israel as well?

Everything we can say with biblical authority about Israel's eschatological role must apparently be based on Rom 9—11 alone. Israel does not play even a bit part in Paul's apocalyptic schema in 1 Cor 15:20-28, unless it is among the various anonymous enemies resistant to God's rule that Christ brings into subjection between his two advents. The same silence about Israel marks Paul's discussions of the second coming and resurrection from the dead in 1 Thess 4:13—5:11 and in 2 Thess 1:5—2:12.

Noncanonical apocalyptic and rabbinic literature treats Israel's redemption as "the decisive event leading to the eschatological scenario that would climax with the resurrection of deceased saints" (Jewett 2007, 681; see n 151). Perhaps Paul takes such scenarios for granted, but within the canon, only Romans assigns Israel a starring role in the final drama. But even here, God is the leading actor, sovereignly bringing about his saving purposes as and when he sees fit.

c. The Mystery of Salvation (11:25-27)

BEHIND THE TEXT

In 11:25-32 Paul resumes the second person plural address dropped in vv 17-24. He proceeds to identify as a three-part "mystery" views he has already mentioned more briefly in 9:18 and 11:7—the partial hardening of Israel. He also refers again to the fullness (v 12), now of the Gentiles, rather than of Israel. And he predicts that the gospel will achieve its intention announced in the theme of the letter in 1:16—the salvation of all.

He gives as the purpose for imparting this mystery to be in order that his Gentile audience within the Roman church might not be conceited. The substance of the mystery is developed in three successive stages of the fulfillment of God's plan of salvation: *first,* the unbelief of the greater part of Israel, because of their divine hardening; *second,* the completion of the coming in of the Gentiles, and *finally,* the salvation of "all Israel." This order of salvation history is the reverse of the expected order according to 1:16: "salvation . . . first for the Jew, then for the Gentile."

Romans 11:26*b* and 27 provide scriptural confirmation of Paul's claim, "And so all Israel will be saved" (v 26*a*). The concentration on the composite OT quotation for the "taking away" of Israel's sins is striking. Verses 28-32 draw out the implications of vv 25-27 and summarize the main points of the entire letter succinctly. First, vv 28-29 depict Israel subjected to the wrath of God for the sake of the Gentiles, while at the same time "loved on account of the patriarchs" (v 28), who were faithful to God. The balancing sentence, v 30—"Just as you who were at one time disobedient to God have now received mercy as a result of their disobedience," with its temporal framework, prepares for Paul's bold conclusion in v 32: "For God has bound all men over to disobedience so that he may have mercy on them all." Verses 25-32 gather together the substance of the whole argument of 9:1—11:24. This prepares for the concluding doxology in 11:33-36, a paean of praise combining texts from Isaiah and Job

IN THE TEXT

■ **25** ***For*** [*gar*] **I do not want you** [*hymas*—plural] **to be ignorant of this mystery, brothers** [***and sisters***]**, so that** [*hina*] **you may not be conceited** [*phronimoi, **wise;*** see 1 Cor 4:10; 2 Cor 11:19] (Rom 11:25*a*). The explanatory *gar* connects vv 25-32 with Paul's reasoning in vv 11-24. Paul's reason [***For***] for disclosing the mystery summarizes his concern already expressed in vv 18-24.

The negatively stated disclosure formula, **I do not want you to be ignorant** (*agnoein*), customarily marks the beginning of a new section of a letter. Such epistolary formulas call attention to crucial information readers need to know (see 1:13; 1 Cor 10:1; 12:1; 2 Cor 1:8; 1 Thess 4:13; compare the positively formulated 1 Cor 12:3; 15:1; 2 Cor 8:1; Gal 1:11).

Paul directly addresses his audience as fellow believers—**brothers *and sisters,*** no longer in the guise of an imaginary interlocutor. He wants to prevent these Christian friends—both Jews and Gentiles—from becoming **conceited**—self-important, boastful, and presumptuous (echoing Prov 3:7; see Rom 12:16) about their privileged status as God's people, as Israel had about theirs (see 2:17-24).

The most common use of the word *mysterion*, **mystery,** in Greco-Roman antiquity was within the mystery cults as a designation for their closely guarded secret instruction and initiation rituals, which were disclosed only to their members. Paul, however, uses the term with the sense it had acquired in Jewish apocalyptic literature (see Dan 2:18-19, 27-30; 4:9; Dunn 2002b, 38B:678 offers an extensive list of references). There it was a technical term referring to divinely *revealed* secrets, previously hidden, but now *publicly* disclosed (see 1 Cor 2:9-10). In such writings, "mystery" refers most often (but not always) to end-time events (Moo 1996, 714). "The revelation given in apocalyptic writing was . . . often in response to . . . the puzzle of Israel's defeat or failure or chastisement" (see Isa 6:10-13; Zech 1:12-17; Rev 6:10-11; 2 Esd 4:33-37; Dunn 2002b, 38B:678), which seems to be the case here as well.

The **mystery** Paul discloses concerns God's saving intention to include Gentiles along with Jews among his end-times people (see Rom 16:25-26), to unite both believing Jews and Gentiles in one saved community (see Eph 1:9-10; 3:3-6; Col 1:26-27; 2:2; 4:3; Dunn 2002b, 38B:678). God had disclosed **this mystery** to Paul, so that he might make it known as the solution to the agonizing problem of Israel's present hardened state (see Rom 9:1-3; 10:1; 11:7). Paul does not say whether the mystery was revealed to him in a stroke of charismatic inspiration (see Luke 2:25-26) or as an insight derived from his study of the Scriptures (as often in the Dead Sea Scrolls).

The **mystery** is: **Israel has experienced a hardening in part** (Rom 11:25; see 9:27; 11:7, 14, 17). That is, ***a hardening has come*** [*gegonen*—perfect tense] ***in part to Israel.*** In v 7, Paul implies (by his use of the passive voice—"The others were hardened") that Israel's spiritual insensitivity and obstinacy was divinely anticipated, if not ordained. Here, he merely asserts *that* the **hardening** was an existing state, not *how* it came about.

In v 7, Paul suggested that a hardening of part of Israel, i.e., of "the others," had occurred. Believing Jews, like himself, made up a faithful remnant. Here, the adverbial prepositional phrase **in part** (*apo merous*) might suggest that the **hardening** was partial, not that only part of Israel was stubbornly resistant to God's intentions for them. "Paul still retains a concept of Israel as a unified whole: the people suffering partial blindness, rather than only part of the people suffering blindness" (Dunn 2002b, 38B:679). Paul himself had been a zealous persecutor of Christians before he became a believer.

Paul indicates that this partial **hardening** will persist **until** [*achri hou*] **the full number of the Gentiles** [*to plērōma tōn ethnōn;* see v 12] **has come in** (*eiselthē*)**. Until** anticipates an unspecified future time when the hardening of Israel will end. Paul makes no predictions as to how this expectation relates to other eschatological events. In v 15 he implies that Israel's "acceptance" will trigger the resurrection from the dead. Elsewhere, he identifies the Parousia as the decisive event that will effect the final resurrection (1 Cor 15:20-28; 1 Thess 4:15-16), but none of his other apocalyptic scenarios mention within them a mass conversion of Israel.

The translation of the phrase **the full number of the Gentiles**—literally ***the fullness of the Gentiles***—would seem to imply that a predestined number of the elect **Gentiles** were needed to fill up the total. Did Paul share the apocalyptic assumption that the completion of a divinely predetermined number of the elect would signal the end of the present order (see, e.g., *2 Bar.* 23:4; 30:2; 75:6; 2 Esd 2:40-41; 4:36-37; *Apoc. Ab.* 29:17; Rev 6:11; 7:4; 14:1; *1 Clem.* 2:4; 59:2)?

By using the same term to refer to the *plērōma*, "fullness," of both Israel (Rom 11:12) and the Gentiles, "Paul presumably intended to indicate that the incoming of the Gentiles would be equivalent to that of Israel. . . . This is not necessarily an exact numerical equivalence" (Dunn 2002b, 38B:680). Even the 144,000 redeemed in Rev 14:3 is clearly a symbolic number (see the commentaries). "The 'full number [*plērōma*] of the Gentiles' does not mean 'all Gentiles, without exception,' nor Gentiles predestined to be saved, but rather that multitude of Gentiles comparable to the riches of the grace of God" (Goppelt 1964, 160). But the ambiguity of the word *plērōma* makes it difficult to be certain precisely what Paul means.

Within the Gospels, there are frequent references to *coming into* "the kingdom of God" or "life," which employ the verb *eiserchomai* (e.g., Matt 5:20; 7:21; 19:17; Mark 9:43, 45, 47; 10:15, 23-25; John 3:5). But of its four instances within Paul's letters (Rom 5:12; 11:25; 1 Cor 14:23, 24), on-
11:25-26 ly this one (***until the fullness of the Gentiles <u>has come in</u>*** [emphasis added]) has an eschatological setting. Dunn follows a number of interpreters in suggesting that it is

> likely that Paul is drawing here on pre-Pauline tradition which stems from Jesus. . . . Paul has used the spatial imagery of Jesus' formulation to transform the traditional Jewish expectation that the final acceptance of Gentiles would be a physical pilgrimage to Jerusalem . . . so that in an important sense Israel's restoration is on Gentiles' terms (that is, in terms of grace alone). (2002b, 38B:680)

■ **26 And so all Israel will be saved** (Rom 11:26*a*). Jewett insists that Paul expected that "all members of the house of Israel . . . without exception, would be saved. . . . There is also little doubt that the verb *sōthēsetai* ("they shall be saved") refers to evangelical conversion, as in 5:9-10; 10:9-13; and 11:14." Thus, Paul believed that "all the peoples of the earth [would] accept the gospel," but his magnificent hope remains so far unfulfilled (2007, 702).

If this view were correct, Paul's anguished prayer for Israel's salvation in 10:1 remains inexplicable. Although the expression **all** [*pas*] **Israel** might mean every individual Israelite, in many biblical passages (e.g., 1

Sam 25:1; 2 Sam 5:1; 1 Kgs 12:1; 2 Chr 12:1; Matt 3:5; 4:24; Acts 13:24) the word **all** is clearly hyperbolic, referring to a large, representative number, but definitely not **all** in a strict, literal sense. Thus, most recent interpreters take **all Israel** to be representative of the whole community, but not the entire nation (see Jewett 2007, 701 n. 74).

Nevertheless, Paul's **all** here must be more inclusive than "some" (Rom 11:17), the present "remnant" (v 5) of Israelites numbered among the saved community. The parallelism between **all Israel** and the ***fullness*** of Israel (v 12) has its natural counterpart in the ***fullness of the Gentiles*** (v 25; see Dunn 2002b, 38B:681 and Goppelt 1964, 160). Thus, whatever portion of Israel Paul foresaw would be saved, he apparently expected a comparable portion of the Gentiles to be saved.

What is the point of the little word **so** in Paul's claim, **And so** [*houtōs*] **all Israel will be saved?** The Greek adverb *houtōs* does not, like **so** in English, sometimes mean "therefore" or "consequently." This is not simply a conclusion Paul has reached. Nor does **so** have the same purposive force it does in the English expression **so that** (*hina*) in v 25. *Houtōs* describes the manner in which the action of the verb it modifies occurs—***in this way;*** here *how* **all Israel will be saved.** *Houtōs*—may refer back to a preceding thought or forward to the following.

If *houtōs* has a backward reference (as in 11:5; 1:15; 6:11; 9:20), Paul's point is that **all Israel**'s salvation will come after ***the fullness of the Gentiles.*** This is a three-part **mystery:** (1) Israel's present partial **hardening,** (2) **the full number of the Gentiles** in the future, (3) **and *in this manner* all Israel will be saved** (Cranfield 1985, 282).

On this interpretation the "core" of the **mystery** is its *newness.* In 11:25*b*-26*a* Paul reverses the normal *sequence* of the Jewish expectation by which **all Israel will be saved**: Israel will remain hardened and resistant to the gospel *until* the Gentiles come in and *in this way* all Israel will be saved. The Gentiles will be saved first, then the Jews.

Did Paul extrapolate **this mystery** from Jesus' repeated sayings about the first being last and the last first (Matt 19:30; 20:8, 16; Mark 9:35; 10:31; Luke 13:30)? Numerous OT passages predict that Gentiles will join in the worship of Israel's God, their interest piqued by the salvation of Israel (e.g., Isa 2:4; 27:13; 66:18-21; Zech 8:20-23). But wholly novel is the idea that the inauguration of the eschatological era will involve setting aside the majority of ethnic Israel, while Gentiles enjoy the blessings of salvation promised Israel.

The adverb *houtōs* may instead have a forward reference (as in Rom 5:12, 18, 19, 21; 6:4, 19; 10:6; 11:31; 12:5; 15:20). The following expression *kathōs gegraptai,* **as it is written,** suggests a correlative (***thus . . . as***) use of *houtōs,* which definitely favors a forward reference (as in Luke 24:24; Phil 3:17; Bauer 1979, 597)—Israel's salvation fulfills Scripture.

On this interpretation, Paul's concern is less *when* **all Israel will be saved,** than with *how* this will occur. His point is that **Israel will be saved** in the way Scripture predicts: **"The deliverer will come from Zion; he will turn godlessness away from Jacob. And this is my covenant with them when I take away their sins"** (Rom 11:26*b*-27). If this is so, his point is that all-Israel-that-will-be-saved **will be saved** in this way. If Paul does not predict how many Israelites will be saved, the importance of the adjective **all** is minimized.

As Paul has done in the conclusions of each of the other main sections of Rom 9—11 (9:25-29; 10:21-22; 11:8-10), he makes his point by citing a pastiche of OT quotations. Here he cites part of Isa 59:20-21*a* in Rom 11:26*b*-27*a* and a clause from Isa 27:9 in Rom 11:26*b*. The quotation follows the LXX translation, with one notable departure in Isa 59:20. The LXX says, "the redeemer will come *for the sake of* [*heneken*] Zion." And the MT says, "the redeemer will come *to* Zion." But Paul writes, ***"the redeemer will come out of*** [*ek*] ***Zion"*** (emphasis added).

The form of the text Paul quotes differs from every known pre-
Pauline text or version. Did he cite a now lost textual tradition? Did he
11:26 quote from fallible memory? Or, did he deliberately accommodate the
quotation to fit his Christian understanding of it? Both Ps 14:7 and Isa
53:6 refer to deliverance coming *from* (*ek*) Zion (see Rom 1:3; 9:5, 33).
The change from ***for Zion*** to ***from Zion*** reflects Paul's transformation of
the typical Jewish expectation of an eschatological pilgrimage of Gentiles
to Zion (as noted above). "He does not wish to rekindle the idea of Israel's
national primacy in the last days [with] Zion either the physical focus of
or sole reason for the redeemer's coming" (Dunn 2002b, 38B:682).

Zion, one of the seven hills of the city of Jerusalem, appears frequently in the OT as a metonymy for the nation, its capital, its people, or its temple (Mare 1992). After considering a full range of possibilities, Douglas Moo concludes that Paul here seems to assume the tradition that surfaces in Heb 12:22. Thus, **Zion** refers to the heavenly Jerusalem (see Gal 4:26; Rev 3:12; 21:2), where Christ now reigns as Lord and intercedes for believers, and from which he was expected to descend at the Parousia (see 1 Thess 4:16). If so, Paul probably changed the text to make clear that Israel's final salvation will be accomplished by Christ at the eschaton (Moo 1996, 729).

While the "redeemer" in Isa 59:20 is the LORD, in Rom 11:26 Paul casts Christ in the role earlier assigned to Yahweh: Christ is **the deliverer** (*ho rhyomenos;* see 7:24; 1 Thess 1:10). When Christ comes **from** [*ek, **out of***] **Zion** [= heaven], **he will turn godlessness away** [*apostrepsei asebeias, **remove impiety***] **from Jacob.** As often within OT poetic parallelism, **Jacob** is merely an alternative way of referring to Israel.

■ **27** Consistent with the rules of Jewish exegesis (Jewett 2007, 705), in Rom 11:27 Paul turns to Isa 27:9 to identify the **covenant** with God's intention to **take away** [*aphelōmai;* only here in Paul's letters] Israel's **sins.** This connects the coming **deliverer** (Rom 11:26) with the "new covenant" of Jer 31:31-34, in which Yahweh promises, "I will forgive their wickedness and will remember their sins no more" (Jer 31:34). None of these expressions describing Israel's salvation employ the soteriological language Paul prefers when he is not quoting Scripture.

"Jacob's *asebeias* ('impious deeds') . . . must refer to Israel's 'stumbling,' 'trespass,' and 'unfaith' in relation to the gospel message" (Jewett 2007, 704). Thus, the elimination of **godlessness** (see Rom 1:18; 5:6-10) and **sins** from Israel here surely implies that Israel's salvation will come **when** (*hotan*) they put their faith in God's Messiah. For Jews, coming to faith cannot be described as conversion from one religion to another but coming to the ***fullness*** (see 11:12) of their covenant with Israel's God—a reconfiguration of "the religion they already have" (Keck 2005, 286).

Paul seems to have in mind a renewal of the promise-**covenant** God entered into with Abraham (see vv 28-29). Some interpreters take this as a reference to the first advent of Christ, i.e., his incarnation from heaven. This covenant was fulfilled in the life and ministry of Christ, allowing both Jews and Gentiles to enter, by faith, into the people of God (Gal 3; Rom 4). But, many other interpreters take it as reference to his second advent, i.e., his Parousia.

Paul ties this deliverance to the Cross, where God in Christ suffered and died for the sins of all, including Israel's sin. With the quotations from Isaiah, then, he indicates *when* their deliverance will take place—at the second coming. He also makes clear *how* it will occur—by Israel's acceptance of the gospel message offering forgiveness of sins in Jesus Christ.

> Paul trusts the power of evangelical persuasion, because when it becomes evident to all that the Crucified One is the designated Messiah, zealous violence to ensure his coming will no longer seem appropriate. Repentance and forgiveness will only be possible when the self-righteous madness of zealous rage is broken by divine power. (Jewett 2007, 706)

This interpretation of **And so all Israel will be saved** does not solve all of the problems of reconciling it with Paul's teaching elsewhere, but it does move Christ and saving faith into their more typically Pauline position of prominence. Considerable aspects of the **mystery** remain enigmatic, but we are not left with an interpretation that runs contrary to central NT theological convictions.

d. Mercy for All (11:28-32)

A break in Paul's argument is signaled by the lack of any conjunction connecting 11:27 and 28. With this obvious shift in thought, vv 28-32 become a discreet paragraph, providing the grounds for vv 25-27, while elaborating on his prediction of Israel's final salvation. He does this by highlighting *God's purpose* in showing mercy to Israel (the central theme of vv 28-32 and the climactic point in each of these arguments, in vv 28*b*, 31*b*, and 32*b*). This paragraph rounds off Rom 11.

Paul's assertion of Israel's **election** in v 28*b* brings the argument back to where he began in vv 1-2, while vv 30-31 summarize the process of interaction between Gentiles and Jews that Paul had asserted throughout vv 11-27. This interaction is highlighted as the vehicle by which God manifests his election of Israel in Christ.

Finally, these verses recapitulate and summarize the argument of chs 9—11 as a whole: the Israel now at enmity with God because of the

gospel is nevertheless the Israel to whom God has made irrevocable promises of blessing (Moo 1996, 729). But vv 30-32 also serve as a fitting conclusion to the entire letter to this point.

(1) Enemies and Beloved (11:28-29)

■ **28** In v 28 Paul refers to unbelieving Israel as God's **enemies** (*echthroi;* see 5:10). It is not that God actively hated them. On the contrary, their active hostility against **the gospel** put them at odds with God (see 5:10; 8:7; 1 Thess 2:14-16). "The reason that zealous Jews rejected the gospel was precisely because it placed Gentiles and Jews on the same footing before God" (Jewett 2007, 707). But Jewish opposition benefited the Gentiles (*di' hymas,* **on your account;** see Rom 11:15, 17, 19-21) by opening **election**'s door for the Gentile mission. God facilitated Israel's present **hardening** (v 25; see 9:18; 11:7-10) in order to give Gentiles opportunity to enter the people of God (vv 11-12, 15, 17-24).

Thus, Israel's status as God's **enemies** is instrumental, not final. They are **enemies** only **as far as** [*kata*] **the gospel is concerned.** Israel's hostility to **the gospel** is part of the "mystery" Paul discloses (v 25). **But as far as** [*kata*] **election is concerned, they are loved** [*agapētoi, **beloved***] **on account of the patriarchs** (see 9:5; Deut 7:7-13; 10:15; Isa 41:8). Despite present appearances, God loves his people Israel. God relates to all humanity in terms of grace. Even Israel's ancestors were chosen graciously, not out of intrinsic merit (see Rom 9:11), but because of God's faithfulness (see 3:3-4).

In saying that God's love for Israel is **on account of the patriarchs,** Paul does not suggest that they did anything to deserve God's favor for themselves or their descendants. As Gal 3 and Rom 4 make clear, the significance of Abraham and **the patriarchs** is based solely on the promises God made them. The response of faith on their part is not meritorious but merely receptiveness to God's grace. Israel is destined to salvation, as they are delivered from sin by accepting God's gracious terms (11:28-29). This is not blatant favoritism; God extends the same **mercy** to all (v 32).

■ **29** Paul explains (*gar,* **for**) God's faithfulness to his gracious promises to Israel's ancestors in v 29: **for God's gifts** [*charismata;* see 1:11; 9:4-5] **and his call** [*klēsis;* see 9:7, 12, 24-26; Phil 3:14; 2 Thess 1:11] **are irrevocable** [*ametamelētai,* ***not to be regretted;*** elsewhere only in 2 Cor 7:10]. That the word **irrevocable** stands as the first word in the sentence gives it an unmistakable emphasis. This clinches Paul's argument in Rom 11:1—God has by no means rejected his people.

The OT refers to God's character as holy love and his gracious purpose to save all humanity as constant and unchanging. God is neither fickle nor forgetful, as humans are (Num 23:19; 1 Sam 15:29; Ps 110:4; Jer 4:28; Ezek 24:14; Zech 8:14). But the OT also often refers to God's willingness to change his mind by withdrawing threatened judgment in response to human repentance, intercession in behalf of others, or merely because he is compassionate (see Exod 32:14; Deut 32:36; 2 Sam 24:16; 1 Chr 21:15; Ps 106:45; Jer 15:6; 18:8; 26:3, 13, 19; 42:10; Joel 2:13; Amos 7:3, 6; Jonah 3:9-10; 4:2).

Paul makes no concession here to Greek notions of divine immutability. His concern is to stress the unchanging character of God's purpose and promises and the impossibility that he should lie (as in Heb 6:17-18). God can always be trusted to be gracious and faithful (see Rom 9:4-6). God's saving purpose for his stubborn people "stands firm no matter what enmity Israel currently expresses against God's Messiah and his people" (Jewett 2007, 708).

(2) Disobedience and Mercy (11:30-32)

■ **30** In vv 30-32 Paul applies the preceding theological insights to the practical situations of his largely Gentile audience, to unbelieving Israel, and, in fact, to all humanity. Paul's rhetorically shaped comparison and contrast between the Gentiles and Israel bring the two peoples into total parity, as an overly literal translation of vv 30-31 demonstrates:

For just as [*hōsper*] ***you*** [*hymeis*]
formerly [*pote*] ***disobeyed God,***
but now [*nyn*] ***you have received mercy***
by their disobedience;
so [*houtōs;* see 11:26] ***also they*** [*houtoi*] ***now*** [*nyn*]
have disobeyed by your mercy,
in order that [*hina*] ***they*** [*autoi*] ***too now*** [*nyn*]
may receive mercy.

Just as Gentile believers were converted from their former disobedience (see 2:8, 15; 5:19) to receive God's **mercy** (see 9:15-18), so disobedient Israel will be graciously converted. God's once mysterious plan is to make all human disobedience an opportunity for showing mercy—first to Gentile believers, then to Israel. "God's mercy is absolutely sovereign, which means that salvation is entirely a matter of grace rather than any form of human achievement" (Jewett 2007, 710).

It should be noted that the only temporal contrasts here are between ***formerly*** (*pote*) and **now** (*nyn*). Paul has nothing to say here about the future salvation of Israel. This might support a reading of **And so all Israel will be saved** in 11:26 as a logical, not necessarily an eschatological future.

Paul employed this same **just as . . . so** formulation in 5:12, 19-21 to
compare and contrast Adam and Christ and the two humanities they repre-
11:30-31 sent. In both passages **disobedience** (*apeitheia* in 11:30; *parakoēs,* in 5:19)
describes the natural human response to God. Only one man, Christ, is described in terms of "obedience" (*hypakoēs,* 5:19). In response to persistent
human disobedience, instead of judgment, God offers **mercy** so that the disobedient may become obedient (see 1:5; 6:15-17; 15:9, 18; 16:26).

Consistent with the mysterious timing of God, the expected order of salvation history is reversed, but God also reverses even human perversity, causing it to serve God's saving purposes in Christ, as witnessed best at the Cross. Paul's claims in his rhetorically crafted comparison-contrast are fully intelligible only in light of what he has said earlier (esp. 11:11-12, 15).

■ **31** Israel's disobedience—their rejection of the gospel—became the occasion for God to extend his **mercy** to the notoriously **disobedient** Gentiles. This, in turn, hardened Israel in its unbelief—**they too have now become disobedient . . . as a result of God's mercy to you** [Gentiles] (v 31). But **God's mercy** to Gentiles has a deeper purpose (*hina*)—to make Israel jealous/zealous (vv 11, 14), **in order that they too may now receive mercy.**

Just as **mercy** defined God's covenant with Israel (see the commentary on 9:15; see Exod 34:6), so it defines his relationship with Gentiles. It is this consistency in God's essential character that occasioned Paul's assertion in Rom 11:29. "Israel will receive salvation in exactly the form that the Gentiles have already received, as 'mercy' that they will not have earned but which places all humans on an appropriately equal level before God" (Jewett 2007, 710).

■ **32** In v 32 Paul offers a summary of his summary (Dunn 2002b, 38B:695): ***God has imprisoned all people in disobedience, in order that he might have mercy on all people.*** Paul makes a similar point in Gal 3:22-23. Because God has determined that humans will relate to him in terms of his grace, not their achievements, Paul is not reluctant to acknowledge God's ultimate responsibility for their sin as well. Paul is not unaware of intermediate causes, thus he leaves room for human responsibility. But he recognizes God as the ultimate cause of everything; he is, after all, the Creator.

Perhaps Wis 11:23 is relevant here: "But you are merciful to all, for you can do all things, and you overlook people's sins, so that they may repent" (NRSV). If so, Paul recognizes the universal scope of God's mercy, not as a guarantee of universal salvation, but of universal opportunity. "Paul not only expresses the essence of the gospel but also makes clear that no remnant of claims of cultural superiority or personal entitlement through piety, social status, or other achievement can remain legitimate" (Jewett 2007, 711).

Paul's claim that God shows mercy only to the disobedient seems to echo Jesus' definition of his mission—that he came not to call the (supposedly) righteous but sinners to repentance (Luke 5:32; 15:7) or that only those who acknowledge they are sick need a physician (Matt 9:12; Mark 2:17; Luke 5:31; see John 9:40-41). We must realize our need for salvation before we are willing to let God save us.

"Double Predestination?"

> Here at length the full meaning of Paul's "double predestination" is revealed. God has predestinated *all men* to wrath and he is predestined *all men* to mercy. If they were not predestined to the former, they could not be predestinated to the latter. . . . Paul does not intend to make a definite pronouncement about the ultimate destiny of each individual man. But the hope of mankind is more, not less, secure because it is rooted in the truth about God, rather than that about man himself. (Barrett 1957, 227)

Compare C. K. Barrett's analysis with that of John Wesley, written nearly two centuries earlier:

> I believe election means . . . a divine appointment of some men to eternal

> happiness. But I believe this election to be conditional, as well as the reprobation opposite thereto. I believe the eternal decree concerning both is expressed in these words: 'He that believeth shall be saved; he that believeth not shall be damned.' . . . According to this, all true believers are in Scripture termed elect, and all who continue in unbelief are so properly called reprobates, that is, unapproved of God, and without discernment touching the things of the Spirit. (1979, 10:210)

In this, Wesley proved himself a faithful interpreter of James Arminius, who objected stridently to Calvin's doctrine of absolute double predestination, some two centuries before Wesley's time. In his exposition of Rom 9, Arminius had expounded "the predestination of the class of believers. . . . But the class is not a mere aggregate; it is the body of those who believe in Christ" (Bangs 1971, 350, 351). On Rom 9, Arminius had written: "The question, 'Why do some believe and others not . . . is not here discussed by the apostle, nor has it even the least connection with his design." Bangs comments: "This is to say that there is a predestination of *classes* which has priority over (or takes the place of) the predestination of individuals" (1971, 196; emphasis added).

Dunn suggests that **election** (see Rom 9:11; 11:5, 7)/**call** (see 9:7, 12, 24-26) and **mercy** (see 9:15-16, 18, 23) in 11:28-32 recapitulate the key themes of chs 9—11. But these verses also provide a fitting conclusion to all of chs 1—11. The sharp contrast between **disobedience** and **mercy**
11:32 might summarize 1:18—3:20 and 3:21—5:11, only with added clarity concerning Israel's place in the grand scheme of salvation history. The tension between the two ages and the two humanities represented by Adam and Christ in 5:12—8:39 is also reflected in Israel in chs 9—11. All humanity must finally choose between **disobedience** and accepting God's **mercy.** Only the resurrection from dead (8:19-23) and the salvation of Israel (11:15) can resolve this tension (Dunn 2002b, 38B:677).

FROM THE TEXT

Paul's claims in 11:25-27 have led some interpreters to conclude that he was a universalist. Did he expect all humanity eventually to be saved? It is not merely to protect Paul's reputation as a prophet that we maintain that his claim that **all Israel** [and, by implication, all Gentiles] **will be saved** may allow for many exceptions.

Although Christ freely offers "life for all," Paul speaks of those who accept it as "many" (5:18-19). Throughout Romans, Paul refers to the potentially universal scope of salvation. He describes the purpose of his vocation as "to call people from among all [*pasin*] the Gentiles to the obedience that comes from faith" (1:5). The gospel is God's power to save "everyone [*panti*] who believes" (v 16). God's promise to Abraham "comes by faith, so that it may be by grace and may be guaranteed to all [*panti*] Abraham's offspring" (4:16). Paul concludes, "God has bound all men [*tous pantas*] over to disobedience so that he may have mercy on them all [*tous pantas*]" (11:32).

If Paul expects universal salvation here, he certainly does not hold out this hope elsewhere in his letters. Does he here use **saved** in the fullest possible sense—being spared from God's wrath (5:9) to share in his eschatological gift of eternal life? Or does salvation here have some lesser, temporal sense? The OT speaks of the return of scattered Israel from the exile as salvation (e.g., Deut 30:1-5; Neh 1:9; Jer 23:3-6; 29:14; Ezek 11:17; 36:24; Mic 2:12; 4:6-7; Zeph 3:19-20; Zech 10:8-10; Bar 4:37; 2 Macc 2:18). And the Gospels and Acts describe healing miracles as salvation (e.g., Matt 8:25; 9:21-22; 14:30; Mark 3:4; 5:23; 6:56; 10:52; Luke 1:79; 17:19; John 11:12; Acts 4:9; 14:9; 27:34). Is it likely that Paul merely anticipated more Diaspora Jews returning to the land of Israel? Did he expect more than a deliverance of Israel from their divinely imposed stubbornness, so they could decide for or against the gospel without blinders? Or does he have final salvation in view?

How is Paul's claim here about the salvation of **all Israel,** however inclusive, to be reconciled with Jesus' assertion that the number to be saved would be few (e.g., Matt 7:14) and that many of the children of Israel would be excluded from the kingdom of God (Luke 13:22-30)? And, how is Paul's claim to be aligned with what he writes elsewhere?

There is nothing in Rom 11:25-32 to suggest that Paul considered faith for salvation unnecessary for Israel. Thus, he must not assume that **all Israel will be saved** by divine fiat, despite its unbelief. God will not show favoritism based on ethnicity after all, will he? God will not coerce Israel to believe, withdrawing his gift of responsible freedom, will he? Thus, Paul must allow for the possibility that some individual Israelites may persist in unbelief (v 23).

If Paul had in mind a mass conversion of Israel at the end of the age, what will be the fate of the generations of unbelieving Israelites who lived and died before the eschaton? Will they be disadvantaged by not living at the time of the final denouement (see 1 Thess 4:13-18)? Or will they be resurrected and given a second chance to change their minds about Christ? And, what about unbelieving Gentiles; will they have the same opportunity as Jews?

Is faith in Christ decisive for salvation or not? Will all be saved by accepting the same gospel? Or, will observant Jews be saved by obeying the law of Moses or by some other means than Christ? Will God simply decide to have mercy on all—Jews and Gentiles alike (Rom 11:32)—whether or not they have faith? If so, on what basis might we expect someone *not* to be saved? Paul's revealed **mystery** remains mysterious. His remarkable claim raises far more theological questions than it answers. Only the historical unfolding of the future events he expects will allow us to move from speculation to certainty.

Significantly, there is no trace of encouragement in 11:26-28 for the hopes entertained by Paul's Jewish contemporaries for the reestablishment of a national state of Israel (see Acts 1:6-8) in independence and political power, nor—incidentally—anything that could feasibly be interpreted as a scriptural endorsement of a modern state of Israel as Christ's base for his millennial reign and the evangelization of the Gentile world subsequent to the Parousia.

Preachers especially may still find useful what I wrote in 1975 on Rom 9—11 in *Beacon Bible Expositions* (149-70).

5. Concluding Doxology (11:33-36)

IN THE TEXT

■ **33** The mystery of God's eternal purpose (11:25-32) leaves Paul lost in wonder: **Oh, the depth** [*bathos;* see 1 Cor 2:10] **of the riches** [*ploutou;* see Rom 2:4; 9:23; 11:12, 17 (see NRSV note)] **of the wisdom** [*sophia*] **and knowledge** [*gnosis*] **of God! How unsearchable** [*anexeraunēta,* ***unfathomable;*** only here in the NT] **his judgments, and his paths beyond tracing out** [*anexichniastoi,* ***incomprehensible***]! (v 33). Paul's doxology glorifies God as God and gives him the thanks sinful humanity denies him (1:21). It also "prepares the way for the climactic vision of 15:9-12, in which all nations join in the chorus of glorifying God" (Jewett 2007, 722).

Riches are the first attribute of God Paul praises. "The combination of the two metaphors (depth and riches) jars at first, but increases the force of the imagery (a treasury which has no bottom)" (see Eph 2:7; 3:8; Dunn 2002b, 38B:698). God's resources are inexhaustible and infinite.

The second and third attributes, God's **wisdom and knowledge,** refer here to the "mystery" of God's universal saving purposes in Christ (Rom 11:25-32). Although Paul does not identify Christ as the embodiment of God's **wisdom,** as he does in 1 Cor 1:24, a christological allusion here is not impossible. Divine **knowledge** here probably refers to God's foreknowledge—he knows fully how to accomplish his saving purposes (see Rom 8:29-30; 11:2). (See Dunn 2002b, 38B:699 for the OT background of the terms **wisdom** and **knowledge.**)

Paul praises God's **judgments** as beyond human comprehension. "In the context of Romans, the 'judgments' of God are concentrated in the sphere of establishing righteousness through grace alone" (Jewett 2007, 717). Paul was convinced that God always acts justly and does what is right, even when we cannot understand what he is doing or why (see Gen 18:25; Deut 32:4; Job 40:8; Pss 10:5; 36:6; 111:7; 119:75; Isa 30:18; 40:14; Wis 17:1).

God's **paths, *his ways*** (*hai hodoi autou*), refer to his inscrutable behavior (see e.g., Exod 33:13; Ps 103:7; Ezek 18:25-29). Only unreserved trust in God allows us to accept what he does, as and when he does it, trusting that ***his ways*** are always wise and just. Mere creatures must depend on a Creator who is finally ***unfathomable*** and ***incomprehensible.***

In the context of Rom 9—11, God's ***ways*** refer to his mysterious dealings with Israel and the Gentiles and their unexpected responses to the gospel. God's "reversal of traditional expectations . . . remains incomprehensible, except for the revelation of divine righteousness in the Christ event" (Jewett 2007, 718).

■ **34** In 11:34-36 two OT quotations pose rhetorical questions. The first cites LXX Isa 40:13: **"Who has known the mind of the Lord? Or who has been his counselor?"** (Rom 11:34; see Job 15:8; Isa 55:8-9; Jer 23:18; 1 Cor 2:16). The implicit answer is, of course, No one! God needs no advice from mere creatures as to how and when to accomplish his saving purposes. 11:33-36

■ **35** The second quotation in Rom 11:35 loosely paraphrases Job 41:11: **"Who has ever given [first] to God, that God should repay him?"** (compare Job 35:7). Again, the implied answer is No one! God always takes the initiative. We can only respond to his gifts with gratitude (Rom 1:21), which is the receptivity of faith. God bestows his riches graciously. It is impossible to put him in our debt or deserve his reward.

■ **36** God is the source and destination of all that exists: **For from him and through him and to him are all things. To him be the glory forever! Amen** (11:36). Numerous NT parallels may be cited for Paul's doxology (see, e.g., 1:25; 9:5; 16:27; Matt 11:25-26; John 1:3; Acts 17:28; 1 Cor 8:6; Eph 3:21; 4:6; Phil 4:20; Col 1:16-17; 1 Tim 1:17; 2 Tim 4:18; Heb 1:2; 2:10; and Rev 1:6; 4:9; 5:13). In the context of Rom 9—11,

> that "all things" will return to God, despite their current distance from the gospel, reinforces the claim that Israel's sins will be "re-

> moved" (11:27), that the full number of Jews as well as Gentiles will come into the realm of grace (11:12, 25), and that all humans will thereby be shown "mercy" (11:30-32). (Jewett 2007, 722)

In this "universe of grace . . . , the common salvation of Jew and Gentile . . . is of God and through God and to God" (Denney 1970, 686). "The *sola gratia* and the *sola fide* of these eleven chapters can issue only this *soli Deo Gloria"* (Barrett 1957, 227).

D. God's Righteousness in Practice (12:1—15:13)

A vital relationship exists between the earlier divisions of the letter to the Romans (1:18—3:20; 3:21—8:39, and 9.1—11:36) and this final division (12:1—15:13). Paul is convinced that the Christian ethic is grounded in the righteousness of God—provided by grace and received through faith.

The apostle's repeated emphasis on "the obedience of faith" (1:5; 16:26 NRSV; see 15:18) demonstrates that ethics is not a dispensable appendix to his exposition of the gospel; it is its practical and necessary expression. Moo rightly insists, "The 'imperative' of a transformed life is therefore not an optional 'second step' after we embrace the gospel: it is rooted in our initial response to the gospel itself" (1996, 745).

Nowhere does Paul attempt to define the Christian *summum bonum* [= supreme good] and deduce from this a hierarchy of virtues. Just as foreign would be a Christian adaptation of the Pharisaic *Halakah*, or Rule of Conduct, derived from a fixed code of commandments regarded as divine and unalterable. Paul's ethic arises from the apocalyptic conviction that in the death and resurrection of Jesus Christ the righteousness of God has invaded this present evil age, which lingers still, to inaugurate already the new age. This final section, like all of Romans, is written from this eschatological perspective.

The apocalyptic revelation of God's righteousness in this final section of the letter has general and specific ethical consequences. These consequences are not "virtues" of some ethical system; they are what Paul elsewhere calls "the fruit of the Spirit" (Gal 5:22-23). Here, as usual, in Paul's letters, "love" is expected to be the all-embracing expression of the Spirit's presence in the Christian community. These are "none other than the virtues of Christ" (Schleiermacher 1956, 576).

In the theological sections just concluded Paul announced the way of righteousness through Christ. All humans without exception are sinners, desperately in need of the righteousness only God can provide (Rom 1:18—3:20). Through what God has done in Christ, he has graciously provided righteousness by faith (3:21—9:39)—sinners are reconciled to God by faith (3:21—4:25), put into a right relationship with God (5:1-21), sanctified in Christ and prepared to share God's glory by the gift of the Holy Spirit (6:1—8:39). Israel's refusal of God's righteousness has opened the way for the inclusion of believing Gentiles among the people of God, which will bring unbelieving Israel to accept Christ and the salvation he mercifully offers all (9:1—11:36).

What are the ethical consequences of God's righteousness? Paul sketches his answer in this final section—for the house and tenement churches of Rome with their heterogeneous mix of Jews and Gentiles. What is the *way* of salvation for the church? That is, what lifestyle should come to practical expression in communities of justified believers? What does God's righteousness look like in the lives of those who participate in the new humanity inaugurated by Christ and in the realm of the eschatological Spirit? Paul summarizes an answer to these questions in this practical section of the letter.

The life of the Spirit is communal—life in the body of Christ. In chs 12 and 13 the apostle makes a general application of love (*agapē*) as the distinguishing mark of the Christian life. Paul points to the ways in which Christians should put love in practice in their mutual relations within the Christian community and in the ways they relate to unbelievers outside the church. Paul's answers reveal his indebtedness to the Jesus traditions, subsequently preserved in the Gospels. An impressive array of parallels may be drawn between Jesus' teachings and Paul's. In chs 14 and 15, Paul applies the love ethic to the tensions created by the divisions within the Jewish and Gentile house and tenement churches in Rome. Since Christ has accepted each, they must all, therefore, accept one another.

Paul's apocalyptic perspective presumes that while the church stands in "this present time between the times," it eagerly awaits the consummation of the resurrection and a new cosmic order. The present age is marked by an anomalous interval in which the "already" and the "not yet" of redemption exist simultaneously in dialectical tension (see 5:1-6). The presence of the Holy Spirit in the church is an eschatological sign that the end has already dawned. He is for believers a foretaste of the glory that will be revealed at Christ's return (8:18-27).

What is God doing in the world in the interval between the resurrection of Jesus and the end?

> According to Paul, God is at work through the Spirit to create communities that prefigure and embody the reconciliation and healing of the world. The fruit of God's love is the formation of commu-

nities that confess, worship, and pray together in a way that glorifies God (see e.g., Rom. 15:7-13). (Hays 1996, 32)

1. The Basis of Christian Ethics (12:1-2)

BEHIND THE TEXT

In 12:1-2, Paul's argument moves from the redemptive work of God in Christ (3:21-31) and the power of the resurrection in baptized believers (6:1-11), to its logical conclusion. H. A. W. Meyer calls the opening verses of the "practical part of the epistle" a "general exhortation to sanctification" (1889, 467). Paul urges Christians to **offer** their **bodies** [*sōmata,* plural] ***as a living sacrifice*** [*thysian,* singular] . . . ***to God.*** He conceives of this voluntary presentation of themselves as an act of reasonable worship. It is the expected exhibition of "the obedience that comes from faith" (1:5) in righteousness and holiness (6:15-22).

By refusing to conform to the ways of the old Adamic age and instead "walking in newness of life," Christians' minds may be continually transformed according to the pattern of the risen Christ (7:4, 6; 8:1-17). Believers must steadfastly resist the pressures of this present age to conform them to the pattern of this world, which is already "passing away" (1 Cor 7:31). As the firstborn of ***many brothers and sisters,*** God's Son is the predestined model to which all believers may be conformed (Rom 8:29), the destination of the new age, the shape of things to come.

Paul's application of this apocalyptic ethic leads him in several different directions. He begins with general exhortations about the nature of the Christ-conformed life in community and the discernment of God's will to which those whose minds are being renewed in Christ are called.

IN THE TEXT

■ **1 Therefore** [*oun*], Paul begins, **I urge** [*parakalō*] **you, brothers** ["and sisters," NRSV], **to offer your bodies as *a living sacrifice*** (*thysian*). The Greek word translated **urge** refers less to moral harangue than to ethical encouragement. Paul urges his audience to act for the benefit of all (12:8; see 1 Thess 5:11). The word *adelphoi,* ***brothers and sisters,*** is both a philophronetic and filial expression (see 1:13). Paul addresses the members of the community collectively as ***friends*** and a part of his ***Christian family.*** Those he addresses with this plural vocative and the second person plural pronoun, **you, offer** a singular ***sacrifice.*** This suggests the corporate nature of Christian consecration and transformation. They present themselves to God as individuals, but their sacrificial offering is a community project.

This "most important 'therefore' in the epistle" (Grieb 2002, 117) marks the beginning of Paul's urgent request (= moral exhortation). "The earlier argument of Romans provides the basis and force of the ethical appeal" (Jewett 2007, 726). The appeal is made **in view of God's mercy.** It is not made on the basis of Paul's apostolic authority alone. He invites Christians **to offer** themselves **to God** as the appropriate response to (*dia,* ***through***) **God's** prior demonstration of **mercy.**

Some interpreters take the plural noun ***mercies*** (*oiktirmōn*) to refer back to the verb "mercy" in 11:32 (e.g., Meyer 1889, 467), but the terminological connection is more apparent in English than in Greek, for there Paul refers to God's purpose to "have mercy" (*eleēsē*) on all people. Elsewhere in Romans, words from the cognate family of *oiktirmōn* appear only in 9:15 within a quotation of Exod 33:19, "I will have mercy [*eleēsō*] on whom I have mercy [*eleō*], and I will have compassion [*oiktirēsō*] on whom I have compassion [*oiktirō*]." The plural form, ***mercies,*** reflects Hebrew and LXX usage (see, e.g., 2 Sam 24:14; Pss 25:6; 51:1; Isa 63:15).

But if Paul is thinking of concepts rather than catchwords, "the appeal on the basis of the 'mercies of God' links this passage not only with 9:15-23; 11:30-32, but also with the entire earlier argument of Romans concerning the mercy/grace of God that comes to those who do not deserve it" (Jewett 2007, 724; see also 726). Thus, it is supremely Christ's "sacrifice of atonement" (*hilastērion*) (Rom 3:25) that serves as the basis and rationale for Paul's appeal for *Christians'* metaphorical **sacrifice** (*thysian*) of their bodies to him.

The entire letter to the Romans emphasizes God's initiative, providing all that is necessary for salvation. Thus, **Therefore** introduces the practical implications of the whole of the theological argument of Romans, beginning with the thematic 1:16 (so Calvin, Bengel, and Dunn 2002b, 38B:708).

Paul's appeal urges his readers to respond to the **mercy** of their divine benefactor with gratitude. They are to honor God as God and give him thanks (see 1:21), not merely with words, but with their redeemed lives. In grateful recognition of God's self-sacrificing love, Paul exhorted his Roman audience to present their bodies to him as a ***living sacrifice.*** This is Paul's primary concern.

Roman Christians are **to offer** (*parastēsai*—an aorist infinitive) their

bodies . . . to God. Sanday and Headlam insist that this offering of their bodily existence is to be taken literally, as were "the parts of your body" (*ta melē hymōn*) mentioned in 6:13. There Paul had commanded, ***Do not keep offering*** [*paristanete*—a present imperative] ***your bodily members as instruments of unrighteousness to Sin, but offer yourselves once-and-for-all*** [*parastēsate*—an aorist imperative] ***to God.*** God literally desires to be the sovereign of Christian bodily existence (see 1 Cor 6:13, 20).

A merely **spiritual** or intellectual (see the reference to the **mind** in Rom 12:2) sanctification is insufficiently comprehensive (see 1 Thess 5:23). Nevertheless, the call to a decisive act of self-sacrifice is not to be taken literally, as if Paul urges suicide. The oxymoron of **living sacrifices** demonstrates the figurative character of the apostle's plea. Christians were not to kill themselves but to make themselves—all of their bodily parts (*ta melē*)—unreservedly available to serve God ***as instruments/weapons*** [see Rom 13:12] ***of righteousness*** (*hopla dikaiosynēs*) to be used for his sanctifying purposes (see 6:13-19; 15:16). "Surely an element of communal risk is envisioned when one speaks of placing the entire membership of house churches on the altar" (Jewett 2007, 728).

J. D. G. Dunn notes that "it is as part of the world and within the world that Christian worship is to be offered by the Christian" (2002b, 38B:709). Unlike both Jews and pagans, early Christian worship had no need for literal sacrifices, priests, or temples. "Their use of sacrificial imagery implies a *replacement* of ritual sacrifice and indicates an assumption that the death of Jesus had been a *final* sacrifice to end all sacrifices" (Dunn 2002b, 38B:710), but Jesus' self-sacrifice is not merely vicarious; it is exemplary. "The boundary of cultic ritual is transposed from actual cultic practices to the life of every day and transformed into nonritual expression, into the much more demanding work of human relationships in an everyday world" (Dunn 2002b, 38B:717).

The authoritative basis for Paul's appeal in 6:13 was that his readers owed their Christian existence to God, who had brought them "from death to life." Because the bodies of Christians are "members of Christ [*melē Christou*]" (1 Cor 6:15), they are to "be holy in body and spirit" (7:34 NRSV) (see Sanday and Headlam 1929, 352). "In contrast to 8:23 where the singular *sōma* refers to the collective body of believers, here the plural *ta sōmata hymōn* clearly refers to 'your bodies,' each of which is to be sacrificed individually" (Jewett 2007, 729).

The infinitive **to offer** (*parastēsai*) is not a sacrificial term per se, although it may have this force within sacrificial contexts (Meyer 1889, 467; Moo 1996, 751; Dunn 2002b, 38B:709). Within the present hortatory context (following **I urge you**) the infinitive has the same imperatival force explicit in Rom 6:13. This is a veiled command: "offer [*parastēsate*] yourselves to God."

In 6:13, 16, and 19, **offer** expresses the idea of putting our bodies at the disposal of God as opposed to Sin (see the comments on 6:13). Christians in 12:1 are urged to **offer** their **bodies** (*ta sōmata*) to God as an act of worship, as members of the Christian community. Such consecration is an *activity,* "a crisis and a process . . . a gift and a life" (Erdman 1925, 131). Believers are to act decisively, making themselves totally available for ongoing service as God's weapons in the apocalyptic struggle against the entrenched forces of evil still resistant to his rule.

Three attributes distinguish the communal sacrifice (*thysian*) Paul calls for. It is to **living, holy,** and **pleasing to God.** It is to be **living** (*zōsan*) in contrast to the bloody OT sacrifices, which were slain animals. We die to nothing but Sin and Self so that we may live wholly to him who died for us and rose again (see 6:11).

To live sacrificially is not heroic. In fact, we will all die sometime, whether or not we give ourselves courageously as weapons of righteousness. Our choice is not between heroism and cowardice. It is the choice of for what and for whom we will live, and die. Paul calls for us to offer ourselves in the service of a cause that is greater than we are. We offer ourselves as a living sacrifice (see 1 Cor 9:19-27) so that even our dying may be living in the deep *theological* sense—**living** in the "newness of life" of the Spirit.

This sacrifice is to be **holy** (*hagian*). That is, those whom Paul exhorts to consecration are not their own, but already God's property in some sense—they belong to God. As such, **holy** here has no ethical content (Dunn 2002b, 38B:710). By consecrating ourselves to God, Cranfield correctly observes, Paul

> implies that we are no longer in our own power, but have passed entirely into the power of God. . . . The Christian, already God's by act of creation and by right of redemption, has yet again to become God's by virtue of his own free surrender of himself. (Cranfield 1979, 2:599-600, following Calvin)

But there is no evidence favoring Cranfield's additional comment: "This self-surrender has, of course, to be continually repeated" (1979, 2:600; similarly Moo 1996, 750). The aorist tense of the infinitive **to offer** and the logic of sacrificial imagery, on the contrary, call for a decisive, once-for-all consecration that is to be perpetually sustained, not repeatedly retracted and returned.

This sacrifice, moreover, is **pleasing to God.** That is, it is the kind of sacrifice God accepts as satisfying his expectations (see Rom 12:2; 14:18; John 16:2; 2 Cor 5:9; Eph 5:10; Phil 4:18; Col 3:20; Titus 2:9; Heb 12:28; 13:15, 21).

Paul explains that such a sacrifice is not literal, but metaphorical, or better ***rational*** (*logikēn;* see 1 Pet 2:2 and 5, which refer to "pure spiritual [*logikon*] milk" and "spiritual sacrifices" [*pneumatikas thysias*]). As rational, **spiritual worship** (*latreian;* contrast Rom 1:9 and 9:4) is the "true worship" (TEV) God desires to embrace the whole of our daily lives, not just the interruptions in our routine set apart for cultic activities at the place of worship.

Etymologically, *logikē* means "pertaining to the *logos*, or reason," and therefore implies a worship befitting a rational creature, as opposed to merely somatic, bodily compliance—"going through the motions"—or pneumatic, irrational emotionalism—"worship experiences" (see 1 Cor 14:15; 13:1-3). *Latreia* refers not simply to worship in the sense of religious activities confined to the sanctuary—it is service. In fact, the verbal form of the word (*latreuō*) is often translated "serve" elsewhere in the NT (see Rom 1:9, 25; Matt 4:10; Luke 1:74; Acts 7:7; 24:14 [NASB]; 27:23; Phil 3:3 [HCSB]; 2 Tim 1:3; Heb 12:28 [KJV]). True worship "is nothing less than the offering of one's whole self in the course of one's concrete living, in one's inward thoughts, feelings and aspirations, *but* also in one's words and deeds" (Cranfield 1979, 2:604).

Spiritual worship/reasonable service is not simply what Christians say or do at church in praise of God but also what he does for them, enabling them to praise him through their lives in the world. The ministry of God to his people, as he brings Good News and grace into their lives, is his service to the church. Divine resourcing, enabled by mutual edification, comes as Christians assemble for what is called "worship" (see Rom 14:19; 15:2; 1 Cor 3:9; 8:1, 10; 10:23; 14:3-5, 12, 17, 26).

In one sense worship is God's saving action for us, which we cannot do for ourselves. All that takes place when the Christian community gathers is God's service to us. Our response of worship of God, our service to God, takes place in the world and takes the form of service to our brothers and sisters—believers and unbelievers. These two understandings of worship are not contradictory but complementary. Worship is the service of God to the church and the church's service before God.

Worship that is "reasonable" involves more than cultic ritual or emotional awe. "True worship means agreement with God's will to his praise in thought, will, and act" (Käsemann 1980, 328). It occurs not only when the church is gathered but also when it is scattered as salt and light in the world. It is not primarily a religious activity, but a response of the whole person to God's mercy.

> Christian worship does not consist [only] of what is practiced at sacred sites, at sacred times, and with sacred acts (Adolf Schlatter). It is the offering of bodily existence in the otherwise [worldly] sphere. As something constantly demanded [worship] takes place in daily life, whereby every Christian is simultaneously sacrifice and priest. (Käsemann 1980, 329)

To talk about worship in this broad New Testament sense requires attention to ethics as much as to the "etiquette" of congregational gatherings—liturgical style. Worship is not merely a matter of taste; it is the true test of whether we understand the difference between right and wrong.

God's expectations of Christians extends to the supposedly "secular" as well as the "sacred" dimensions of life. God longs to guide every day of our lives, not simply our special days. "Either the whole of Christian life is worship, and the gatherings and sacramental acts of the community provide equipment and instruction for this, or these gatherings and acts lead in fact to absurdity" (Käsemann 1980, 327-29). To talk about worship in this broad biblical sense requires attention to personal and social ethics as much as to corporate and private spiritual disciplines.

■ **2** Paul's appeal to self-surrender is elaborated in his explicit commands in Rom 12:2*a:* ***Do not be conformed*** [*mē syschēmatizesthe*] ***to this age*** [*tōi aiōni toutōi;* see 1 Cor 1:20; 2:6, 8; 3:18, 19; 5:10; 7:31; 2 Cor 4:4; Gal 1:4; Eph 1:21], ***but be transformed*** [*metamorphousthe*] ***by the renewal of the mind.*** Both verbs in this exhortation are in the second person plural, passive voice, and imperative mood (see the sidebar "Greek Verbs"). Despite the NIV translation, Paul does not say, **Do not conform!** any more than he says, "Transform!" He commands his Christian readers collectively to refuse the negative option and accept the positive.

Apparently, communal cooperation is called for. This is not a call for rugged individualism—you all are involved. Sanctification is not a solo performance; it demands a choir, an orchestra, a community of saints. This was John Wesley's point when he wrote:

> "Holy solitaries" is a phrase no more consistent with the gospel than "holy adulterers." The gospel of Christ knows no religion but social, no holiness but social holiness. Faith working by love is the length and breadth and depth and height of Christian perfection. (1870, 1:xxiii)

One cannot be holy alone. Holiness is experienced only within the context of a holy church, more specifically a particular local community of believers.

Greek Verbs

Few English speakers understand any other language than their own. Fewer still have studied Koine, the colloquial Greek of the NT. Even speakers of modern Greek must use a translation of the NT because of changes in the language across two millennia. The neglect of English grammar instruction in recent decades has resulted in a generation that is ill equipped to understand how English works, much less understand an explanation of the functioning of biblical Greek. The following is an overly brief and simplistic attempt to remedy this deficiency, at least as applied to Greek verbs. We begin with some definitions.

A *verb* is a word that describes an action or a state of being or becoming. In the sentences, "God *created* the heavens and the earth" and "The earth *was* formless and empty," the italicized words are *verbs*. The first describes an action; the second, a state of being. In English, the form of the verb *created* would be unchanged, even if its subject, "God," were replaced by another noun or pronoun. But the verb "to be" would be changed in the sentence "The heavens *were* cloudless."

In Greek, verb forms change much more than in English to agree with the *person* and *number* of their subjects. Subjects are either first, second, or third person. The *first person* is either "I" in the *singular* or "we" in the *plural number*. The *second person* is "you" in both singular and plural. Modern English no longer distinguishes these two pronouns; only from the context can we tell whether an author or speaker refers to and addresses a single person or a group of persons. In the Elizabethan English of the KJV, "thou" was the second person singular pronoun and "you" the second person plural. *Third person* pronouns include "he," "she," and "it" in the singular and "they" in the plural.

Greek verbs require different endings to *agree* with the person and number (but not the gender) of their subjects (compare I *am;* we *are;* thou *art;* you *are;* he *is;* she *is;* it *is;* they *are*). Even if Greek subject pronouns are not explicitly expressed, they are implied by verb endings (e.g., English-speakers know instinctively the subject of the verb *am*).

The forms of Greek verbs vary as their *tenses* change, somewhat like English (see I *am;* I *was;* I *have been;* I *will be*). But the tenses are different; and their concern is less with the time of an action (as past, present, or future) than with the kind of action described.

The Greek *present* tense describes actions that are continuous or repeated (e.g., I run; I am running). The Gospels often use the present tense to describe past events, much as we do in telling a joke (e.g., There is this absent-minded professor and he . . .). This practice probably arose as a result of the oral origins of the story, which was told before it was written down. The *imperfect* tense describes customary or repeated actions in the past (e.g., I ran; I was running). The *aorist* tense describes actions as complete, stressing only the "happenedness" of an event (e.g., I ran). The *perfect* tense emphasizes the present state resulting from a past event (e.g., Christ has been raised; i.e., Christ is risen). The *pluperfect* tense describes past states resulting from prior past actions (e.g., He *had lived* 33 years before his crucifixion).

Greek verbs also change forms based on their *voice*. Voice refers to the relationship between the subject and its verb. If the verb's subject does the action described, the verb takes the *active* voice (e.g., The mother *bathed* her baby). If the subject receives the action of the verb, the verb is in the *passive* voice (e.g., The baby *was bathed* [by its mother]). Unlike English, Greek has a third voice. If the subject is both the doer and the receiver of the action, it's said to be in the *middle* voice (e.g., The mother bathed [herself]). Nevertheless, most Greek verbs in the middle voice are not reflexive but actually *deponent*. That is, they lack an active form and take a middle form to express an active meaning. Changes in voice are reflected in changed endings attached to Greek verb forms (see English verb changes: He bathes; They bathe).

Some features of verbs are not reflected in changed forms (*morphology*) but
only by their meaning and usage (*semantics* and *syntax*). Verbs that may take direct
objects are *transitive;* those that may not are *intransitive* (e.g., we may say, "He
drives a car" but not, *"He goes a car"). Verbs that involve the action of a doer on
a receiver are transitive. Those that merely describe a state of being are intransitive (e.g., to be, become, sit). Only transitive verbs may have a passive form (e.g., 12:2
we may say, "A car is driven" but never, *"A car is issed.")

Verb forms also change based on the relationship between the verb's action and reality, a dimension of its meaning called *mood*. A verb in the *indicative* mood describes something that actually exists, as opposed to something that only may or might be. That is, indicative verbs make statements or ask questions about what authors consider factual. (This reflects an author's or speaker's perception of reality, not reality itself.)

A verb in the *imperative* mood gives a command or makes a request—what authors want to be true. In English, all imperative verbs have implied second person subjects (e.g., "Study Greek" means "You are hereby ordered to study Greek"). But Greek also has third person imperatives. Lacking this form in English complicates translating such commands (e.g., "Let them marry" in 1 Cor 7:9 [KJV] means something like "They ought to get married" or "They should marry" [NIV and NRSV]).

A verb in the *subjunctive* mood indicates uncertainty or only potential reality (e.g., If you *were to study* Greek, you *might understand* this more easily. This lengthy explanation of Greek verbs *would be* unnecessary, if this *were* a reality. But it is not.) Verbs in the *optative* mood express wishes or prayers (e.g., "*May* God himself . . . *sanctify* you through and through" [1 Thess 5:23, emphasis added]).

Since the voice of both verbs is passive, Paul's readers are not the agents ultimately responsible for either action. Some unnamed, external force is responsible for the pressure to conform and another for the possibility of their transformation. Because the verbs are in the imperative mood, these are orders; Paul expects those addressed to cooperate or refuse to cooperate with these forces. The actions he calls for may occur only as they are allowed or encouraged. Doing so will prevent conformity and promote transformation. These are not accomplished facts, but possibilities open only to those who heed the exhortation. Apart from the anonymous actors offstage, neither could take place. But these actions are not magical or automatic either.

Who are these anonymous actors? Who pressures Christians to allow themselves to be conformed to this age? J. B. Phillips interpretively paraphrased: "Don't let the world around you squeeze you into its own mould." The dualistic imagery of the present evil age and the coming new age points to Paul's contrastive parallels between the two humanities headed by Adam and Christ set out programmatically in Rom 5:12-21. Thus, we might identify the pressure as coming from Adam and all of his personified cohorts—Sin, Death, Flesh, and Law. Christians must not "be conformed" to the **world,** i.e., to the reigning *fashion* of the present evil age.

Paul's apocalyptic worldview persuaded him that "the time [was]
12:2 short" (1 Cor 7:29), that "this world [*kosmou*] in its present form [was]
passing away" (v 31). Christians were, therefore, to refuse to become engrossed in a world order that was doomed to destruction. They were to resist the old humanity that would pressure them to accept the discredited values and patterns of living championed by the age that was fading away. Set free from Sin, they were never again to allow Sin to exercise its rule over their lives. They were no longer to pursue sinful passions; never again to be slaves of Unrighteousness, Rebellion, and Impurity. Instead, they were to offer themselves as slaves to righteousness for the purpose of sanctification (see Rom 6:12-23). Since the night of the present age would soon give way to the dawning day of salvation, Christians were already to "put aside the deeds of darkness" and "behave decently, as in the daytime" (13:12-14, see vv 11-14; Eph 2:7 refers to "the coming ages"; see Matt 12:32; Mark 10:30; Luke 20:34-35). The competing allegiances of the two ages almost certainly account for Paul's appeal, ***Do not be conformed to this age.***

The present tense of Paul's plea is a reminder that this unbending refusal to be deceived by the illusory pleasures of Sin must continue uninterrupted so long as this age persists. The implicit second person plural subject is a reminder that this is not a plea to stand alone in valiant, but solitary, resistance. It is a call to stand together, "encouraging one another, and all the more as you see the Day approaching" (Heb 10:25 NRSV).

Positively, Paul exhorts his Christian audience: ***Instead*** [*alla*, **but**] ***be progressively transformed by the constant renewing*** [*tē anakainōsei*] ***of your mind*** [*noos* (singular)]. Clearly, the agent of their ongoing transformation is not single-mindedness, a communally shared understanding, or their collective powers of moral perception. Just as the old humanity and its discredited cronies must be rejected, Christians must allow God—in Christ, by his indwelling Holy Spirit—to transform them. Their communal **mind** is the means God employs to effect this continuous participation in the mind of Christ (see Rom 8:5-6; 1 Cor 2:16; Phil 2:5-11). The **mind** is more than the human thinking capacity; it is the character, the inner disposition, the motivating center of our personal and communal lives (see 2 Cor 3:17-18; 4:6-7, 16; Eph 4:23-24; Col 3:10; Titus 3:3-7). Thus, "the transformation Paul has in view here is shaped by the recovery of a realistic appraisal of ethical choices in the light of the converted community's experience of the 'new creation' brought by Christ" (Jewett 2007, 733).

Several Greek words in the NT may be translated "transform" or "change." One of these is the exact opposite of the negative verb here—"be not conformed" (from *syschēmatizō*). In 2 Cor 11:14 the verb *metaschēmatizō* refers to Satan's transformation of himself into an angel of light. He's still Satan, he only looks different. Transformation of this kind is really only a disguise, a masquerade, an outward change of appearance and behavior. It is by this notion of change that legalism parades itself as an inferior imitation of holiness. Another NT word for change, *allassō* in 1 Cor 15:51-52 describes the bodily alteration from mortality to immortality that awaits living believers at the second coming (see Heb 1:12).

The word for **be transformed** Paul uses in Rom 12, *metamorphousthe*, is the source of the English word "metamorphosis." What Paul urges is not merely a change of appearance and behavior, but a change of essence. This is not a matter of *acting* a part, but of *being* completely different. The indwelling Spirit of Christ is God's agent in effecting this inside-out transformation, reproducing Jesus in the lives of committed Christians (see Rom 8:29; 2 Cor 3:17-18; 2 Thess 2:13). The transformation of believers Jewish apocalypses (*2 Bar.* 51:5; *1 En.* 71:11) expected only in the eschaton, Paul claimed was a present possibility.

Since *schēma* and *homoiōma* are used synonymously in Phil 2:7, the contrast between conform and transform, in Greek as in English, may finally depend more on their prepositional prefixes, *syn-* ["together"] and *meta-* ["change"] than on their verbal roots (Meyer 1889, 468; Moo 1996, 755-56). If we recognize that "conformity to this age is no superficial matter" (Barrett 1957, 214), the difference between the two imperatives is not merely a contrast between external and essential change. What matters most is the change-agent. To be conformed is to fit comfortably within the present age. To be transformed is to be fitted by God for the age to come. Consequently, Christians are often misfits in the world's eyes.

Christians are not to be crammed into the mold of the present **world;** they are to seek a new model to be realized by a power within them, the power of the transforming Spirit. The **mind,** freed from the power of the flesh (Rom 8:1-4) is refocused "on things above, where Christ is seated at the right hand of God" (Col 3:1). The Greek word translated **be transformed** in Matt 17:2 and Mark 9:2 describes the "transfiguration" of Jesus. The only other NT example of this verb is in 2 Cor 3:18: "And we, who with unveiled faces all reflect the Lord's glory, are being *transformed* into his likeness with ever-increasing glory, which comes from the Lord, who is the Spirit" (emphasis added). Transformation means that "the Christian's concrete living is henceforth to be marked by the continuing process of sanctification (*hagiasmos*): it is to be moulded and shaped ever more and more into conformity with God's righteous will" (Cranfield 1979, 2:601).

12:2 Christians cannot go on contentedly and complacently, allowing themselves to be stamped afresh by the whimsical fashions of the dominant culture. They must now yield themselves to a different pressure, to the direction of the Spirit of God. We are to allow ourselves to **be transformed**—continually remolded, remade, progressively sanctified. By this means our lives here and now may more and more clearly exhibit signs and tokens of the coming age of God, the new order that has already come in Christ. The ongoing transformation Paul calls for prepares us to fulfill our destiny "to be conformed [*synmorphous*] to the likeness" of Christ (Rom 8:29).

Then [*eis to,* ***So that***] **you will be able to test and approve what God's will is—his good, pleasing and perfect will** (12:2*c*). **Then** in English does not represent the time marker *epeita* (as in Gal 1:18, 21; 2:1). The final clause beginning with *eis to,* followed by the infinitive *dokimazein,* indicates the *purpose* (or the *result* [**Then**]) of the renewed **mind.**

Paul uses **mind** (*nous*) to refer to a person's "moral consciousness" (Moo 1996, 756). The *nous* is not an unfallen element of human nature; it is not a higher self in contrast to a debased body. The **mind** needs radical renewal (see Eph 4:23; Titus 3:5), if it is to recognize and do **God's will.**

The whole point of moral renewal is to enable Christians to live ethically responsible lives. This singular **mind** belongs to the community.

Apart from God the **mind** of the old humanity is depraved (Rom 1:28; 1 Tim 6:5), corrupt (Titus 1:15), enslaved to Sin (Rom 7:23, 25) and the Flesh (Col 2:18), purposeless (Eph 4:17). It is an illusion to imagine that unaided human intellect or an individual's conscience may be a reliable "guide" to moral conduct. But a Christ-shaped community mind "made new" may be "created to be like God in true righteousness and holiness" (v 24).

Thus, Paul invites his Christian audience to exercise responsible freedom by offering themselves wholly to God. Only in this way may they be thoroughly renovated, entirely sanctified in body and mind, so as to come increasingly to prefer and practice what God wants (see 1 Thess 5:23). "This 're-programming' of the mind does not take place overnight but is a life-long process by which our way of thinking is more the way God wants us to think" (Moo 1996, 756-57). And it does not take place alone. We are changed within holy communities marked by mutual love and accountability.

A single Greek infinitive, *dokimazein*, is translated **to test and approve** (see Phil 1:10; 1 Thess 5:21). The *dokim-* cognate group appears more than 30 times in the Pauline corpus (and about 20 times elsewhere in the NT). Paul assumes that **God's will** (Matt 6:10; Eph 5:17; 6:6; Col 1:9; 1 Thess 4:3) may be empirically known, examined, heeded, and validated. "The righteous requirements of the law [may] be fully met" in those who live "according to the Spirit" (Rom 8:4). Through loving one another, the law of God may actually be fulfilled (13:8-10). Doing what God wants proves itself in the practical test of everyday experience. Those who pursue, do, and approve **God's will** demonstrate by their lives that it is the **good** [*to agathon*], **pleasing** [*euareston*], **and perfect** [*teleion*]. These terms combine Greco-Roman and Jewish ethical ideals (Jewett 2007, 734).

The delicate process of moral renewal demands a continual perfecting, even of the transformed mind. Paul describes the **will** of God with three adjectives: God's will is **good** in that its directions are free from all connivance with evil, in any form whatever. It is **pleasing,** referring to the impression made upon us when his will is realized in our lives, finding it beautiful as well as good. God's will is **perfect,** in that through doing it we realize the *end* for which our lives were designed, experiencing its completeness in Christ (from *telos,* "end," "goal," "complete").

FROM THE TEXT

Unlike some of his Holiness-tradition followers, John Wesley was not guilty of the error of diminishing justification so as to maximize the need for and consequences of a subsequent experience of sanctification. He understood justification as a truly, although not entirely, sanctifying work. Theologians sometimes refer to regeneration as initial sanctification. In Wesley's classic sermon "On Sin in Believers" (1979, 5:146 paraphrased) he said:

> We consider the state of justified persons to be inexpressibly great and glorious. They are born again. They are children of God, members of Christ, heirs of the kingdom of heaven. They enjoy the peace of God. Their bodies are temples of the Holy Spirit. They are new creatures in Christ Jesus. They are washed and sanctified. Their hearts are purified by faith. They are cleansed from the corruption that is in the world. The love of God is poured out in their hearts. And as long as they walk in love, which they may always do, they worship God in spirit and in truth. They keep the commandments of God, and do what pleases him, so as to have consciences void of offense toward God and toward men. And from the moment they are justified they have power over both outward and inward sin.

12:1-2 But Wesley continues. Although believers have been set free from the power of sin, sin "remains, though it does not reign." Sin, in the guise of pride, self-centeredness, self-will, and self-trust remain, but do not govern the converted person's life. Christ cannot reign where sin remains. Freed from the slavery of sin, justified persons are called to consecrate themselves unreservedly to God. This total surrender to God is the necessary human condition for entire sanctification (1 Thess 5:23-24).

In the first two sentences of Rom 12 Paul solemnly addresses the house and tenement churches of Rome—and all who have read them since, looking over their shoulders. He urges Christians to pursue a pattern of life responsive to a faithful hearing of the gospel. Believers are to offer their bodily existence as "lived-out-sacrifices" as the "rational worship" they owe God. "Bodily life" embraces our entire existence, with particular stress on the interrelatedness within Christ's body as well as interaction with the surrounding culture.

Like James, Paul's concern is for practical, everyday religion. Religion that helps the helpless and empowers the powerless (see Matt 25:31-46; Jas 1:27). Religion that puts fine talk about love into action (see 2:14-17; 1 John 3:17-18). Ritual can never replace doing right. Just seeking God is no substitute for seeking justice in the street (see Amos 5:21-24). Worship and prayer are not means of bribing God to give us security, justification, or emotional release. Sacrificial offerings, worship services, and private devotions are meaningful only in the context of a life of wholehearted obedience (see 1 Sam 15:22; Jer 7:21-26; 14:12; Hos 6:6; Mic 6:6-8).

Worship in this sense is indeed **spiritual worship.** In such worship God is glorified and the church is edified. Such **spiritual worship** is not an opportunity of isolated individuals to have a collective "worship experience." It is, rather, the opportunity to exalt God *together.* The worshipping community consists not merely of gathered believers. It includes the heavenly host saying, "Amen! Praise and glory and wisdom and thanks and honor and power and strength be to our God for ever and ever. . . . For the Lamb at the center of the throne will be their shepherd; he will lead them to springs of living water" (Rev 7:12, 17). This communal setting contributes to the transformation of the entire community into Christlikeness, not just isolated pious individuals.

Positively, Paul calls for a *lived-out* sacrificial consecration to God that entails spiritual discernment as members of the new age, inaugurated by the resurrection of Christ. The new age has become obvious in the experience of the Spirit, attesting to a new relationship with God (see Rom 5:5; 8:23). Negatively, the conditions of the old era still endure for the time being and will continue to be so until Christ's victory is complete (see 1 Cor 15:23-28).

The fundamental issue in Paul's apocalyptic worldview was, "To whom does the sovereignty of the world belong?" (Käsemann 1969a, 135). This explains his concern for connecting bodily existence and ethics. The human body is "that piece of the world which we ourselves are and for which we bear responsibility" (Käsemann 1969a, 135). Thus, the bodily obedience of Christians was for Paul the essential expression of worship to God the Creator in the world of everyday.

Christ's heavenly lordship finds visible expression only when it takes personal shape in us in this present world and thereby makes the gospel credible. The bodily obedience of Christians is an expression of the power of the resurrection. But resurrection is not just about the future reanimation of the dead, but about the present reign of Christ. The risen Christ already reigns as Lord. "His own are already engaged today in delivering over to Christ by their bodily obedience the piece of the world which they themselves are" (Käsemann 1969a, 135). In so doing Christians bear witness to his lordship over the entire world and anticipate the future reality of the resurrection of the dead and the uncontested reign of Christ.

Believers are all ready to participate in Christ's destiny as representatives of the new age that is coming. Thus, "membership in the Church *is* membership in this divine new world" (Käsemann 1969a, 128). Paul does not conceive of humans as solitary individuals. As specific pieces of the world, they are always determined from the outside, by the lordship to which they surrender themselves. They will either be conformed or be transformed. Human life is "a stake in the confrontation between God and the principalities of this world," and thus, "mirrors the cosmic contention for the lordship of the world" (Käsemann 1969a, 136).

Paul's appeal to self-surrender for sanctification was not simply an optional matter of personal piety for an elite minority of believers. More is at stake than the individual holiness of isolated exceptions. The life of holiness can never be experienced in isolation from the world, whether in a monastic conventicle or separatist sect. Refusal to be conformed to this world must not be confused with reluctance to engage the world on its turf. Paul considered the holiness of the church the necessary validation of the lordship of Christ in this present world. It cannot await the world to come, for then his lordship will be obvious to all.

Paul appeals for moral discernment before he spells out its communal expression in Rom 12:3-21. Holy living involves a constant quest for God's will in the confusing and trying circumstances of the present "over-
12:1-2 lap" time. The perpetually "renewed mind" creates in believers the capacity to discern and then do what is required to live according to God's will. The bodily existence flowing out of that discernment makes our lives a continual "sacrifice" pleasing to God. True worship takes place in the world and in behalf of the world.

Ethical Discernment

These two sentences contain a spirituality and a theory of ethical discernment that is both suggestive and open-ended. Granted the vast cultural and historical gap between the ancient world and our own, scripture provides little concrete guidance for the ethical dilemmas of modern life. The abiding values of the gospel have to be discerned and lived out in totally different circumstances, with science and technology, in particular, throwing up ethical challenges unimaginable in the biblical world. In these circumstances, Paul's stress upon the capacity of the "renewed mind" to discern, his sense of the need to test (allowing for some measure of trial and error), his readiness to speak in the language of the surrounding secular world . . . offer contemporary moral theology an important biblical charter as it confronts the issues of our time. (Byrne 1996, 365)

At the heart of life in this "present evil age" is authentic Christian worship. Such worship is fundamentally communal, but it requires individual participation of mind and spirit. It is offering our bodily existence to God in a profane world. John Chrysostom commented sixteen centuries ago:

> And how is the body, it may be said, to become a sacrifice? Let the eye look on no evil thing, and it hath become a sacrifice; let the tongue speak nothing filthy, and it hath become an offering; let thine hand do no lawless deed, and it hath become a whole burnt offering. (Quoted in Moo 1996, 754)

The special times of corporate worship are only one aspect of the continual worship that each of us must offer to God in the sacrifice of our bodies day by day. Paul calls for worship that fills the whole of our Christian lives, not just our formal corporate gatherings and sacred acts. The latter must give us strength and guidance for perpetual worship in the world, or these gatherings are essentially useless (Käsemann 1980, 327).

2. Love Expresses the Righteousness of God (12:3—13:10)

a. Humility and Mutual Service (12:3-8)

BEHIND THE TEXT

Paul has communicated his vision of Christian bodily life through the imagery of a sustained "sacrifice" to God (v 1). He has summoned the community to activate its capacity to discern and do the will of God. Now he begins to sketch out the remarkable scope of God's will. He insists that what God wants of believers comprehends far more than the supposedly sacred dimensions of life; God's will extends to the secular as well.

Verses 3-8 fill out the picture of the shape of Christian "worship" with more detailed directions as to how relationships within the Christian community should proceed. Remarkably, in view of his sacrificial imagery, Paul has nothing to say about what most people (then and now) think about as "worship." He says nothing at all about cultic activities—rites, rituals, liturgies, sacramental acts, Scripture-reading, singing, etc.

Paul takes up and clarifies what he means by his appeal for "rational" worship by those whose minds are being "renewed." Paul considers foundational the adoption of a modest attitude of mind as the key factor in establishing right intercommunal relationships (v 3; see chs 2—4, where he warns against Jewish arrogance, and 11:7-24, where he warns against Gentile presumption). The basis for this appropriately humble mental attitude is a right assessment of one's distinctive grace-gifts (*charismata*) and their proper exercise. Then he sets out the image of the community as one "body" in Christ (12:4-8).

Paul envisions ministry within the body of Christ as *charismatic.* That is, he expects that the work of the church will be accomplished through the mutual benefits of God's gracious gifts distributed throughout the Christian community, not merely through ecclesiastical hierarchs and formally trained and paid full-time professional "ministers." He makes his appeal in virtue of the grace-gift (*charis*) he personally has been given (v 3). Tactfully, he holds back any explicit definition of the gift, but clearly alludes to his God-given and empowered calling to be an apostle responsible for establishing and overseeing Gentile churches (see 1:5; 11:13; 15:15).

On this basis, Paul makes his appeal in strongly personal and authoritative terms. Employing a wordplay on the Greek root *phron-*, he formulates the appeal first in negative (12:3*b*), then in positive (v 3*c*) terms. He urges his audience to refrain from presuming a "higher" sense of self-importance than appropriate. Rather, each is to "think" (*phronein*) in a way that leads to a sensible understanding (*sōphronein,* **sober**). Paul presupposes that each believer has a special *charis* (gift). He insists that one's self-assessment as a Christian rests entirely on an appropriate perception of one's gifts. All are to exercise their gifts for the common good of the community. "The 'measure' is always the faith which all can exercise" (Dunn 2002b, 38B:719).

Paul's use of "body language" to describe the Christian community seems to depend on widely shared imagery in the ancient world, used to illustrate the interrelatedness and mutual working of social groups such as cities or states. Misguided scholarly attempts to prove Paul's theological indebtedness to supposed Hebrew notions of corporate personality or Hellenistic Greek (especially Stoic) or Hellenistic Jewish (especially Philo of Alexandria) religious ideology or incipient Gnosticism should be abandoned. (For a survey of the proposed origins of the imagery of body as applied to the church, see Jewett 1971, 210-50; or Lincoln 2002, 70-72, and Dunn 2002b, 38B:722-24.) Scholars have given far too little attention to the appropriateness of this imagery in light of Paul's earlier contrastive comparison of the two humanities—in Adam and in Christ—presented in 5:12-21 (see the commentary) and his appeal in 12:1 for Christians to present their bodies to God.

The apostle may have been no more self-conscious about applying body imagery to the community of Christ than we are when we refer to businesses as diverse as Microsoft and McDonalds as *corporations,* using the same imagery. This English term is, after all, derived from the Latin *corpus,* which means "body" (see 1 Cor 12:12-27; Eph 1:22-23; 4:15-16; 5:23; Col 1:18; 2:19).

Paul's imagery is not simile, but metaphor. Believers are not *like* a body, they *are* Christ's "body." But this is imagery; it should not be taken to suggest that the church is somehow a literal continuation of the Incarnation (against Robinson 1952, 51, 58; Cerfaux 1959, 262 n. 1, 263, 282, 323, 330, 347, 349, 357; Schnackenburg 1965, 175; Benoit 1973, 53-58). "Body language . . . is primarily for Paul an ecclesiological rather than Christological concept" (Dunn 2002b, 38B:724). Dunn's caution should be taken seriously. The Christian

> community can certainly claim to be a focal point of Christ's earthly presence, but as soon as a church thinks it has an exclusive claim to represent Christ . . . that church is making the same mistake as Israel [according to the flesh]—the very mistake against which Paul pits himself in this very letter. (2002b, 38B:724)

Paul's body imagery serves only to illustrate the diversity of gifts operative within the unity of the Christian community. Within the overall oneness constituted by life "in Christ," "many" believers make up one "body." Each member represents a body part that functions in relation to others (*to de kath' eis allēlon melē,* **each member belongs to all the others,** v 5). In vv 6-8 Paul develops this basic description of the Christian community, pointing to a number of functions exercised by *charismata*—**gifts** (v 6).

Diverse Gifts

Evidently Paul is neither identifying the gifts so that the Romans may know what they are, nor ranking them so that the readers know their respective standing in the community, but rather is using the variety of gifts to make concrete what it means to be "members of one another" precisely because, like the body, "not all the members have the same function." "In Christ" this diversity is not something to be overcome but to be treasured and actualized rightly. (Keck 2005, 298)

IN THE TEXT

■ **3** Paul addresses individually **every one of** the members of the Jewish and Gentile house and tenement churches in Rome (v 3*a*). His opening words in Greek, **For . . . I say,** have the force of an imperative (Dunn 2002b, 38B:720). Speaking with the authority of an apostle, he urges his readers to adopt a self-concept appropriate for members of Christ's body.

The apostle claims that his recommendation is more than simply his personal opinion on the matter. He speaks **by the grace** of God **given** to him (see 15:15; 1 Cor 3:10; Gal 2:9; Eph 3:2, 7). "Paul speaks as a charismatic to charismatics" (Dunn 2002b, 38B:720). That is, he addresses his readers as fellow recipients of grace (**grace given us,** Rom 12:6; see 1:11-12), but also as one specially commissioned as an apostle of Christ. His grace-gift authorizes him to admonish them (1:5-6, 11-12; 15:14-16)—i.e., to issue orders with divine authority.

Within this hortatory context begun in 12:1, the four infinitives in v 3 (*hyperphronein,* "to think too highly of oneself"; *phronein,* "to think"; *phronein,* "to think"; and *sōphronein,* "to think sensibly") assume the force of imperative verbs. **Do not think of yourself more highly than you ought** [to think], **but rather think of yourself with sober judgment** (v 3*bc*). Paul plays with the meanings of words derived from the Greek word describing the activity of the mind (*phronēsis;* see 11:20, 25).

Thought (*phronein,* "to think"), the energy of the mind, that is excessive, overdone (*hyper-,* like our English "hyper-" or "super-" prefix [+ *phronein*]), and self-preoccupied becomes haughty and arrogant. Thought that is "safe and sound" (*sōs* [+ *phronein*]) recognizes and respects its limits. Sober-mindedness (*sōphronismos,* "sanity," "seriousness," "moderation") was ranked by Aristotle next to "courage" in his *Nichomachaean Ethics.* "In popular Hellenistic philosophy . . . [it was] the golden mean between license and stupidity" and "the antonym of *hybris* [pride]" (Dunn 2002b, 38B:721). Paul probably came to esteem this cardinal Greek virtue through the filter of Hellenistic Judaism (see Wis 8:7; 4 Macc 5:22-24). "Christian humility and unity is . . . one important manifestation of the transformation in thinking" (Moo 1996, 759) the apostle expects of believers who have offered themselves as living sacrifices to God.

For Paul, even sober-mindedness is determined by a different frame of reference than the world's. Believers' opinions of themselves should be in proportion not to their natural capacities, but to God's gifts—**in accordance with the measure of faith God has given you** (v 3*d*). If they do this, they will never (even though God may call them to be apostles) be boastful, for they will remember they have nothing they have not received (1 Cor 4:7; see 15:10—"by the grace of God I am what I am"). Our gifts are not an occasion for selfish pride because they are a community asset, not a private hoard.

That ***God has measured*** [*emerisen*] ***to each*** [*hekastōi*] ***a measure of faith*** does not imply that all have the same amount. Elsewhere (7:17; 2 Cor 10:13-15) Paul uses the verb m*erizō* to emphasize the differences between the ministries of the various members of the church. He recognizes that there are some "whose faith is weak" (Rom 14:1) and others whose faith is "strong" (15:1). Even the same individual may at times have weaker or stronger faith (4:19-20). Not all Christians are equally mature (see 1 Cor 2:6; 3:1; Phil 3:15) or equally competent to lead.

Nevertheless, **the measure** [*metron*, compare "meter"] is the standard by which Christians should estimate their contribution to the church. Because all members of the body belong to Christ by virtue of **faith,** all are equally important, despite their differences (Cranfield 1979, 2:613-15).

In 1 Cor 12:9, Paul lists "faith" among the spiritual gifts God distributes as he sees fit (vv 7-11). He assumes that each Christian contributes some indispensable gift to the body (see v 7; 1 Pet 4:10) (Dunn 2002b, 38B:721). He does not take for granted the modern Western ideals of democracy and equality and apply them to the church.

The Christian standard of self-measurement is not that of fluctuating subjectivity used by those who have been conformed to (Rom 12:2) "the present evil age" (Gal 1:4). Self-deceptive evaluations are based on conceit, competition, envy, and individualism (see 5:26—6:5)—*hyperphronein*. Christians should assess themselves based on the **measure of faith God has given** (Rom 12:3; see 2 Cor 5:16-17; 10:12).

In the present context, **faith** does not mean "saving faith" but "the measure of reliance on God which enables *charis* [grace] to come to expression in *charisma* [giftedness]" (Dunn 2002b, 38B:722). Paul cautions against delusions of superiority, without minimizing the reality that some lead, others follow. That not all members of the body are the same and yet exist in mutual interdependence is, in part, what makes it a **body** (Rom 12:4). "The point is that the body is *one* not despite its diversity, but is *one body* only by virtue of its diversity; without that diversity the body would be a monstrosity (1 Cor 12:17-20)" (Dunn 2002b, 38B:724).

Paul simply takes for granted that Christians collectively constitute the singular body of Christ; he does not defend this presupposition. That he did not develop a theological argument for this within the body of the letter (chs 1—11) suggests that he assumes his readers also presuppose the corporate nature of the church. Here Paul merely spells out the implications of this community consciousness. The Christian life is not simply about my personal relationship with Christ but about my mutual relations with other Christians.

■ **4-5** The assumed similarity between body and church provides the basis for Paul's analogy: **Just as** [*kathaper*] **each of us has one body with many members, and these members do not all have the same function, so** [*houtōs*] **in Christ we who are many form one body, and each member belongs to all the others** (vv 4-5; emphasis added). This explains why we must **think of** ourselves **with sober judgment** (v 3). We must realistically assess our assets and deficits, our gifts and graces, our privileges and responsibilities within the community of faith.

"Countering the divisive forces within and between the Roman house and tenement churches and the refugees returning from the exile of the Edict of Claudius," Paul stresses that Christian unity may be found only **in Christ,** because **each of us** is interdependent upon **all the others.** "Christ is the larger reality within which the various congregations and individual members are to find their unity" (Jewett 2007, 744).

In 6:13, 19; 7:5, 23, Paul mentions **members** (*melē*) of the **body,** appealing for Christians to offer (*parastēsate* in 6:13, 19) themselves unreservedly to God. Their body parts were to serve as instruments/weapons of righteousness. Paul identified this act of corporate consecration as the necessary condition for holy living and bearing fruit for God. Social holiness is not competitive; it is cooperative, empowered as it is by God's gifts to the community as a whole.

The reference to **members** in 12:4 follows a similar appeal for believers "to offer" (*parastēsai*) their bodies to God as a living sacrifice in v 1. Paul expects Christians to offer God bodily expressions of worship within the community, "ways of acting" (*praxin*, **function**) as diverse as the **many members** constituting the body (v 4). Because the **many form one body, and each member** is indispensable to the whole; none are competitors with **the others** (see 1 Cor 12:14-26). On the contrary, they complement one another and are interdependent on one another, since **each member belongs to all the others** (Rom 12:5).

■ **6** As members of Christ's body, **we have different gifts, according to the grace given us** (v 6). God's **grace** enabling service within the community assumes multiple forms of expression and empowers in varying degrees different individuals to use their unique endowments for God's diverse purposes. Of course, **grace** is an abstract noun, personifying an action as if it were a thing. Grace is what God does to empower members of Christ's body to serve the community effectively.

Although the gifts God gives are popularly labeled "spiritual gifts," appealing to 1 Cor 12—14, Paul nowhere explicitly refers to the Spirit in

Rom 12. His only reference to "spirit" in v 11 (NRSV) concerns the human spirit. Nonetheless, the passive voice of the adjectival participle **given** clearly implies that God is the source of these grace-gifts (see 1 Cor 12:4-6).

This acknowledgment of divine giftedness undercuts pride and unhealthy comparisons (see Gal 5:26; 6:3-4). It enables one to "take a sane view of [one]self" (Rom 12:3 MOFFATT). The Christian context of Paul's teaching gives a deeper meaning to the precept indebted to Delphi, "Know thyself," while also pointing the way to put it into practice (see 1 Cor 4:7; 15:10; Jas 1:17).

In Christ, we are a corporate body (1 Cor 12:13). Believers have varied and essential functions within this body. There is no place for anyone to think too highly of himself or herself. Apart from the collective body and its other essential parts, individual members exist as dissected, grotesque, dead, and worthless body parts (see vv 12-27).

Our gifts assign us a particular line of service. Clearly, they bring with them responsibilities to the body as a whole. Those who have gifts should ***use them.*** Although this seems clear enough from the context, there are no explicit imperative verbs in the Greek text of Rom 12:6-8. The expression **let him . . . ,** repeated with each of the seven gifts, has no Greek equivalent. Nor does Paul imply that these gifts are given only to males; there are no references to **a man's gift** or to the masculine pronoun **him** or **his** (eight times in the NIV) anywhere in the Greek text. The **gifts** that make up the body are actually given in what resembles a bullet-list entirely lacking verbs and pronouns. The passage might be literally translated:

- ***whether prophecy*** — ***according to the analogy of faith***
- ***whether service*** — ***in service***
- ***whether the one teaching*** — ***in teaching***
- ***whether the one encouraging*** — ***in encouragement***
- ***the one sharing*** — ***in generosity***
- ***the one leading*** — ***in eagerness***
- ***the one showing mercy*** — ***in cheerfulness*** (vv 6*b*-8)

Most translations resort to a paraphrase that is more explicitly *prescriptive* than Paul (esp. the RSV and NIV). What he writes could be taken as merely *descriptive* of the diverse functioning of the one body of Christ. In either case, his list is miscellaneous, not exhaustive. The mention of seven gifts is not accidental. The perfect number in Hebrew thought emphasizes comprehensiveness—what is true of these seven representative gifts is true of all.

This overly literal translation also calls attention to the variations in Paul's formulation of the list, concealed in the English translations. In vv 6 and 7, "prophecy" and "service" (RSV) or "ministry" (KJV, NRSV) are nouns; the other gifts are substantive present active participles (= verbs used as nouns). The first four gifts in the list are preceded by the term "whether" (*eite*); the last three are not. Each of the qualifiers, identifying how the specific gifts are to be used, are introduced with the preposition "in" (*en*, or "with"), except for the gift of "prophecy," which has the preposition "according to" (*kata*). (See the sidebar "Prepositions" with Rom 8:1-8.) Paul uses the prepositional phrase concluding gifts one, four, six, and seven to define the manner with which those endowed with these gifts utilize them. He concludes the second half of his list of gifts using a participle with gift three and by means of a cognate noun in the conclusion of gifts two and five.

It is not surprising that "prophecy" (**prophesying**) appears at the head of Paul's list of gifts, in light of his discussion in 1 Cor 14. There, he defines prophecy as divinely inspired speech—even "a revelation" (1 Cor 14:30), spoken in conscious possession of one's mind and in fully intelligible words. God enables some within the community to discern and declare with clarity and conviction what God is doing among them (vv 13-19, 29-33). As a result, others in the church are strengthened, encouraged, comforted, edified, and instructed (vv 3-4, 31). Simultaneously, unbelievers present are convinced by such prophecy that they are sinners and that God is present in the community (vv 24-25).

From Paul's description in 1 Cor 14, we might characterize such **prophesying** as much more like what we call preaching than the prediction of the future popularly associated with the term. He recognizes that certain individuals possess a latent giftedness and calling that causes them to have the regular status of "prophets" (v 29). Nevertheless, unlike our usual understanding of preaching, the apostle assumes that every believer—both men and women (11:5)—may be enabled on occasion to prophesy (14:22-25, 31).

Dunn's claim that "prophecy as inspired speech," refers to words given "by the Spirit" and "not consciously formulated by the mind" (2002b, 38B:727), defends an inappropriate either-or alternative. In vv 13-19 Paul implies that it is possible to have Spirit-inspired speech *and* use one's mind. Furthermore, he insists that speech alleging to be prophecy should not be accepted uncritically as divinely inspired. He urges prophets to "weigh carefully what is said" by other prophets in God's behalf (v 29). Are we to imagine that such weighing was to be done unconsciously apart from their mental faculties?

Paul expected believers to listen carefully, refusing to "treat prophecies with contempt." But they were also to listen critically, to "test everything" to discriminate the good from the evil (1 Thess 5:20-22). Contrary to Dunn, ecstatic prophecy—"spontaneous and unstructured . . . inspiration" (2002b, 38B:727)—does not appear to have been distinctive or characteristic of Christian prophecy, but rather the exception.

Paul was certainly open to ecstatic spontaneity, but his regulations in 1 Cor 14:24-33 indicate that prophecy need not preclude intellectual formulation. Furthermore, "the usual scope of early Christian oracles was pastoral rather than esoteric" (Jewett 2007, 746).

The second half of Paul's reference to the gift of ***prophecy*** characterizes its use as ***according to the analogy of faith.*** Commentators dispute the meaning of this expression. In mathematics and logic *analogia* referred to something that was "in right relationship to, in agreement [with], or in proportion to" an objective standard of measurement (Bauer 1979, 57). If this is Paul's usage here, he implies that the community's **faith** serves as the norm for testing the truth-claims of allegedly prophetic utterances. Thus, **faith** "is not our act of believing but that which we believe: Christian teaching" (Moo 1996, 765, who rejects this interpretation).

This meaning of **faith** is rare in Paul (see Gal 1:23; 1 Tim 1:4, 19; 3:9; 4:1, 6; 6:21) and occurs nowhere else in Romans. Furthermore, Paul refers explicitly here only to prophets, not to others in the community. If ***according to the analogy of faith*** is parallel to **the measure of faith** in Rom 12:3, as seems plausible, his point may be that prophets speak prophetically only in proportion to their faith. That is, their preaching is inspired only to the extent that they depend on God as the source of their inspiration (Dunn 2002b, 38B:728).

■ **7** The remaining six gifts describe other ways in which God empowers the work of the church. Those whose gift is ***service*** give themselves to ***service*** (v 7*a*). In 1 Cor 12:4-5 Paul virtually equates ***service*** and the full range of charismatic gifts. The Greek nouns *diakonia* ("service" or "ministry") and *diakonos* ("servant" or "minister") are the source of the English term "deacon." Despite modern American usage, however, the term "ministry" has no strictly religious connotations, even in English. In parliamentary governments, the leaders responsible for various departments (e.g., defense, treasury, etc.) are "ministers," who answer to the "prime minister."

Paul uses "service"/"ministry" to refer to a variety of tasks or offices—both sacred and secular—associated with the practical work of the church and its leaders (see 1 Cor 3:5; 12:5; 16:15; Eph 4:12; Col 4:17). Such "service" can identify the mundane tasks of entertaining dinner guests (Luke 10:40), distributing food, and waiting on tables (see Acts 6:1-4), charitable assistance to the poor in Jerusalem (Rom 15:31; 2 Cor 8:4; 9:1, 12). But it also characterizes the work of apostles and others (Rom 11:13; 2 Cor 4:1; 6:3; 1 Tim 1:12; 2 Tim 4:11)—e.g., reconciliation/evangelism (2 Cor 5:18; 2 Tim 4:5).

Since Paul knows nothing of the later ecclesial distinction between clergy and laity, the gift of ministry/service might belong to any member of the community who provides a range of services on behalf of others. It seems unnecessary to follow Dunn in assuming that Paul refers here only to "*ad hoc* service" of various kinds and not to lifelong, vocational ministry (2002b, 38B:728). The clearly defined diaconal office may have emerged only in the second century, but well before Paul's time church ministries were called *diakonia*. This was based on the acts performed, not on the calling of those who performed them.

Although Paul knows the Greek nouns for "teacher" (*didaskalos;* see
Rom 2:19-20; 1 Cor 12:28-29; Eph 4:11; 2 Tim 1:11) and "teaching" (*didachē;* Rom 6:17; 16:17; 1 Cor 14:6, 26; 2 Tim 4:2; Titus 1:9), here he
refers to the third gift using the substantive participle, ***the one who teaches***
(*ho didaskōn;* Rom 12:7*b*). Paul's shift from nouns identifying the function-
al tasks of ***prophecy*** and ***ministry*** to participles specifying particular agents
of the task—here, ***the one who teaches***—was probably for the sake of stylis-
tic variety alone. The regular ministry of the ***teacher*** emerged early in the
12:7 church's history alongside that of the ***prophet*** (Acts 13:1; 1 Cor 12:28; Gal
6:6; Heb 5:12; Jas 3:1; despite Matt 23:8). Paul's terminology offers no indication that he preferred charismatic functions to official functionaries.

That Paul recognizes **teaching** among the charismatic gifts suggests that he assumes teachers depend on divine inspiration, and not their intellects and education alone, as surely as prophets. Thus, there is only a fine line separating **teaching** and prophecy—the latter offers "new insight into God's will"; the former, "new insight into old revelation" (Dunn 2002b, 38B:729). That is, **teaching** interprets and applies in ever new settings the will of God revealed in the past, preserved and passed on in the church's Scripture and tradition.

Paul uses **teaching** to refer to ethical guidance (1 Cor 4:17; 11:14; 1 Tim 4:11; 6:2), practical admonition (Col 3:16), doctrinal instruction (Gal 1:12), and the passing on of Christian tradition (2 Thess 2:15). **Teaching** here may identify the divinely enabled task of providing effective catechetical instruction for the newly converted. Those so gifted engage ***in teaching*** (*didaskalia;* see Rom 15:4; Eph 4:14; Col 2:22; 1 Tim 1:10; 4:6, 13, 16; 5:17; 6:1, 3; 2 Tim 3:10, 16; 4:3; Titus 1:9, 10; 2:1, 7, 10). Despite the warning of Jas 3:1 against assuming the responsibilities of teaching,

Paul seems to share with Hebrews (5:11) the conviction that this is not an assignment reserved for a professionally trained elite, but might be fulfilled by any gifted, mature believer (see 5:11—6:2).

■ **8** In v 8*a* Paul identifies the fourth gift using another substantive participle rather than either the noun *paraklēsis* ("encouragement," "exhortation," "appeal," "comfort"; see Rom 15:4; 1 Cor 14:3; 2 Cor 1:3-7; 7:4, 7, 13; 8:4, 17; Phil 2:1; 1 Thess 2:3; 2 Thess 2:16; 1 Tim 4:13; Phlm 7) or *paraklētos* ("counselor," "helper," "intercessor"; reserved in the NT for the Holy Spirit [John 14:16, 26; 15:26; 16:7] and the heavenly Christ [1 John 2:1]). The person whose gift **is encouraging** [*ho parakalōn*, "the one who encourages"] others applies the teaching of the gospel to everyday life.

Paul uses the verb *parakaleō* to refer to activities of pleading, urging, exhorting, and encouraging others to live as God wants (2 Cor 10:1; 1 Thess 2:12; 5:11; 1 Tim 5:1). He uses the verb to introduce the practical—usually ethical—implications of his theological reasoning (Rom 12:1; 1 Cor 4:16; 2 Cor 5:20; 6:1; Eph 4:1; Phil 4:2; 2 Thess 3:12; 1 Tim 2:1). But encouraging is not restricted to letters or to church leaders. Any believer may encourage others to lead lives of faithfulness to God—by precept or example (Rom 15:30; 16:17; 1 Cor 4:13; 14:31; 2 Cor 7:6, 7, 13; 13:11; Eph 6:22; Col 2:2; 4:8; 1 Thess 2:12; 3:2, 7; 4:18; 5:11, 14; 2 Thess 2:17; 1 Tim 6:2; 2 Tim 4:2; Titus 1:9; 2:6, 15). The gift of encouragement may be simply the God-given capacity to empathize with others and to motivate them to perseverance. Paul presumes that those who have been encouraged by the comfort God gives, pass it on by similarly encouraging others (2 Cor 1:4, 6; 2:8; 1 Thess 4:18).

The fifth gift in Paul's list refers to ***the one who shares*** [*ho metadidous*], once again by means of a substantive participle. The prepositional prefix (*meta-*; ***with***) with the verb "give" (*didōmi*) suggests that Paul refers to the sharing with others a part of one's resources (Rom 1:11; 1 Thess 2:8). As he uses the term, sharing may refer to intangible assets (like a spiritual gift [Rom 1:11] or the gospel [1 Thess 2:8]) as well as to financial resources (Eph 4:28). Thus, the one who **is contributing to the needs of others** need not be imagined to be among the more well-to-do in the community. If Paul refers to sharing of economic means, the appropriate translation of *en haplotēti* would be ***with generosity/liberality*** (see 2 Cor 8:2; 9:11, 13). If the sharing involves intangible assets, the expression might be translated ***with sincerity/simplicity***—i.e., "without ulterior motives or secondary purposes" (Cranfield 1979, 2:625).

The person whose gift is **leadership** (*ho proistamenos;* see 1 Thess 5:12; 1 Tim 3:4-5; 5:17; Titus 3:8, 14) guides others ***with eagerness, zeal-***

ously,* diligently. *The one who leads not only "stands in front" of others to offer direction but also provides a model for those who follow. It is unlikely that Paul thinks of such leaders as duly elected church officials, but as those whose giftedness allows them to arise to the needs of a given occasion. It is not clear whether their giftedness consists in an unexpected divine "thumb in the back," so-called natural endowments, or wealth or social status. *Spoudē,* the Greek noun describing *how* gifted leaders should administer, is the source of the English "speed." However, Paul's concern is not to urge hasty decisions but that those who lead exercise zeal for and devotion to their managerial tasks (Rom 12:11; 2 Cor 7:11, 12; 8:7, 8, 16).

Those who have the gift of **showing mercy** (*ho eleōn,* ***the one who shows mercy***) **serve cheerfully,** as a privilege, not as a burden. The Greek noun in the phrase ***with cheerfulness,*** *hilarotēti,* is the source of the English "hilarity" (see LXX Prov 22:8*a:* ***God blesses a merry [hilaron] and generous man;*** 2 Cor 9:7). It is not that compassionate care should be frivolously given; but neither should it be performed with drudgery. Cranfield speculates that this **mercy** took the form of tending the sick, relieving the poor, and caring for the aged and disabled (1979, 2:626). We are all beneficiaries of God's mercy (Rom 9:15-16; 11:30-31; 1 Cor 7:25; 2 Cor 4:1; Phil 2:27; 1 Tim 1:13, 16). In fact, "this is the only occasion in the Pauline literature in which *eleeō* is used of human rather than divine mercy" (Dunn 2002b, 38B:731). Because we have received mercy, we minister with gladness to the needs of others, not with gloom.

FROM THE TEXT

The meaning of both **the measure of faith** (*metron pisteōs;* Rom 12:3) and ***the analogy of faith*** (*analogian tēs pisteōs;* v 6) are disputed. Wesley defends the Medieval and classical Protestant concept of "the analogy of faith" as "the general tenor of 'the oracles of God.'" More recent interpreters have referred to what Wesley calls the "grand scheme of doctrine which is delivered therein, touching original sin, justification by faith, and present, inward salvation" (1950, 569; on 12:6) as an aspect of "biblical theology." It is certainly a sound hermeneutical principle to avoid proof-texting and to balance the Bible's teaching in one context with that in other canonical contexts. But this is not Paul's point here.

If **the measure of faith** in v 3 is closely related to ***the analogy of faith*** in v 6, both describe the ability God gives us to see ourselves as he sees us. We do not idealize ourselves as members of the first Adam but properly assess ourselves "in Christ," as those who have received "the gift" that came through the last Adam (see 5:12, 15; 1 Cor 15:45). Both phrases imply that the effectiveness of our gifts depends on how completely we depend on God, not on our own human resources for the performing of our ministry, whatever it may be.

Christian self-assessment does not mean evaluating ourselves according to our fluctuating subjective feelings and greater or lesser degrees of self-confidence, but according to our God-given relation to Christ. The most important and indeed the controlling, determinative, element in faith is not faith in oneself, or even faith in faith, but faith in God. Thus, we measure ourselves according to the standard of faith—Christ himself. In Christ God's judgment and mercy are revealed. He is, in fact, the true measure of all things.

Like Abraham (Rom 4:19-21), we grow strong in faith as we acknowledge our inadequacy and assign all the glory to God. Paradoxically, the essential prerequisite for effective ministry—regardless of our specific gifts—is to depend not on ourselves but on the power of God (2 Cor 12:8-10). Our competence to serve as ministers of a new covenant is from God (3:4-6).

Paul's reservations about the potential abuse of the gift of (so-called) **prophesying** should be taken seriously. Not everyone who claims to speak for God actually does so. Jesus urged his disciples not to expect the Spirit to fill their mouths with the right words to speak, except when they were on trial (Mark 13:11). Thus, under ordinary circumstances, pastoral education, regular study, and diligent sermon preparation may be reconciled with Paul's charismatic understanding of **prophesying.** It is surely not only when preachers fail to study or feel compelled to depart from their notes and speak extemporaneously that they prophesy. God can inspire pastors in their studies as surely as he can in the pulpit. Preachers are well advised to "listen" to responsible commentators as they weigh what to say in God's behalf to their gathered congregations.

But if we take Paul seriously, we must also be open to the possibility that God may choose to speak through ordinary believers endowed with the gift of prophecy. Preachers must learn to value thoughtful critiques of their sermonizing as not necessarily uninformed and unwelcome faultfinding. After all, "the spirits of prophets are subject to the control of prophets" (1 Cor 14:32). Not all that claims to be **prophesying** truly is. Even faithful expositional preachers must recognize that the whole of divine revelation is not found within a single biblical text. Too often, we depend too much on our ingenuity and not enough on divine empowering.

Paul does not imagine that God's gifts to the community are limited to preachers or full-time, professional ministers. He assumes that the entire church is divinely gifted. He could not conceive of the church's ministry as confined to what happens in the pulpit at 11:30 A.M. on Sunday morning. At least four of the seven ministries he lists here might be expected to be fulfilled outside the time when the church gathers. Only God's gifts enable the community to fulfill its calling to offer real worship in the world (see Rom 12:2).

"At a time when in many churches the need for the renewal of [compassionate ministry] is beginning to be felt and recognized," a careful study of this passage is particularly important. Of course, it affords "interesting glimpses of the [practical labors] of the early Church." But it also opens "up vistas into the future, suggesting varied tasks which a renewed diaconate . . . might undertake" (Cranfield 1979, 2:628). Paul's discussion also offers invaluable guidance as to the truly Christian spirit in which these ministries ought to be undertaken.

The earliest church—poor, powerless, and relatively uneducated—humbly and effectively ministered to the human needs of its day in the strength of an alien power they knew was not their own. Do we imagine that the affluent, powerful, and privileged Western church of today can minister effectively through human resources and programs alone? Do we imagine that these gifts—affluence, power, and privilege—are of our own creation or given only to make us comfortable in a suffering world? Or, do we imagine that a church can fulfill its ministry through the labors of just one "minister"? Ministry must be the corporate task of the entire body of Christ, gifted to serve in his behalf.

b. Christian Love in Practice (12:9—13:10)

BEHIND THE TEXT

Most English translations gloss over the difficulties of Paul's Greek in 12:9-21. Of the twenty-eight commands in the NIV, only nine translate Greek imperative verbs. The three in v 14 and one in both vv 16 and 19 are second person plural ("you all") commands. The two commands in both vv 20 and 21 are second person singular ("you"), because they are Scripture quotations. In three instances, the instructions translate verbless clauses (vv 9*a*, 10*a*, and 11*a*). Paul's two orders in v 15 are actually infinitives (lit. ***to rejoice; to weep***). The other commands translate adverbial participles (e.g., in v 9, lit. ***hating the evil, clinging to the good***). Because all of the participles in vv 9-19 are nominative plurals, their presumed implicit "subjects" must also be "you" plural.

Romans 12:3-8 provides a bullet-list indicating how committed Christians, who are being progressively transformed (vv 1-2), use their sevenfold giftedness for the benefit of the entire community. Verses 9-21, with similar brevity, sketch out how the holy community tests, approves, and does the "good, pleasing and perfect will" (v 2) of God—with ***sincere love.*** The renewed mind Paul expects in those who have offered themselves to God for sanctification (v 2) should express itself in the way Christians think. A form of the verb *phroneō,* which appears four times in v 3, appears twice in v 16 along with a warning against depending on human thought (*phronimoi*).

In 1 Cor 12—14 Paul supplements his discussion of the utilization of gifts within the community (chs 12 and 14) with an emphasis upon the decisive importance of love and what those who love do and do not do (ch 13). This same logical connection appears in Rom 12. The opening words of v 9*a*—literally ***unhypocritical love*** (*hē agapē anypokritos*)—function much like a heading for the remaining verses. These verses outline what such unpretentious love should look like in practice; this is definitely not a fully developed ethical discourse. Within the hortatory context initiated by the opening appeal in vv 1-2 and under the influence of the imperative main verbs in vv 14, 16, 19, 20, and 21, the paraphrase, **Love must be sincere,** adequately does justice to Paul's point.

Verses 9-21 may be divided into three subsections: 9-13, 14-16, and 17-21. Verse 9*a* sets the theme for the entire passage, ***sincere love,*** which v 9*bc* elaborates negatively and positively. Verses 10-13 offer a series of ten stylistically similar implicit exhortations, clarifying how ***real love*** should be expressed inside the Christian community. Verses 17-21 are thematically unified in rejecting vengeance as an appropriate response to "evil" (twice in both vv 17 and 21) outside the community. Between these two subsections, vv 14-16 offer guidance on living wisely by way of three contrasts—blessing vs. cursing; rejoicing vs. mourning; haughty vs. humble.

Paul presupposes that ***unpretentious love*** is the ethical quality most distinctive of believers. His earlier treatment of love within the letter to the Romans, most notably 5:1-11 and 8:31-39, uses the Greek term *agapē* to characterize God's saving action in Christ. Here he identifies love as a totally unmerited act of condescension and reconciliation offered to those who treated God as their "enemy" because of their sin (see 5:6-10; 8:32). The *agapē* expected of believers represents the *outflow* of God's love from their own lives.

(1) Sincere Love (12:9-13)

IN THE TEXT

■ **9** The sentence opening this important ethical passage serves as a heading introducing all that follows. Literally, Paul writes, ***unhypocritical love*** (*hē agapē anypokritos;* see 2 Cor 6:6). Apart from its hortatory context, Greek usage would allow the translation, ***Love is unhypocritical.*** But within Rom 12, the translation **Love must be sincere** is justified. The words that follow explain what **love** that is **sincere** should and should not do (v 9). "To remain 'genuine' in love requires a disciplined commitment to honesty and the respect of limits, as the rest of this passage will demonstrate" (Jewett 2007, 759).

In 1 Cor 12 Paul's enumeration of the gifts of the Spirit leads up to the conclusion in ch 13 that "love" (*agapē*) is greater than all gifts. In fact, gifts are useless and worthless unless motivated by love as expressions of love. Here the train of thought is the same, although the link is not expressed.

Paul would agree with 1 John 4:7-21 that love (*agapē*) best characterizes the essential nature of God; God's love comes to express his redemptive goodness concretely in the cross (Rom 5:8; 1 John 3:16). Paul thinks of love in metaphorical terms as something poured out into believers' hearts by the Holy Spirit (Rom 5:5). Love, of course, is not a "thing" at all; it is an abstract verbal noun describing behavior and attitudes of a particular kind. It is the supreme and all-inclusive gift of the Spirit to the Christian community, superior to all *charismata* (1 Cor 12:1—13:13). It is not by chance that love is here, as elsewhere in Paul's writings, mentioned first among the virtues of the Christian life. When he enumerates "the fruit of the Spirit," it is *agapē he* names first (Gal 5:22). This is not because love is simply the first in a series of comparable virtues but because it is the comprehensive manifestation of the Spirit (see 5:6; Col 3:12-14; 1 Tim 1:5). If **love** is **sincere,** all that follows in this passage will be manifested.

As abstract nouns, both the English "love" and its Greek equivalent *agapē* must come to concrete expression. Love should not be confused with either vapid sentimentality or self-indulgent passion; it is a vigorous moral quality. When they genuinely love, believers **hate what is evil; cling to what is good** (v 9; see Amos 5:15). Jewett (2007, 759) proposes that hating evil is elaborated in Rom 12:17-21; clinging to good, in vv 10-16. Paul's sense of love's passionate commitments goes "far beyond the mild 'live and let live' stance of Greco-Roman humanitarian ideals" (Jewett 2007, 760).

Of Christ, who incarnated God's *agapē,* it is written, "You have loved righteousness and hated wickedness" (Heb 1:9). There is something inexorable about divine love; it never condones evil: *agapē* is *holy* love. Thus, Christian love must never evaporate into mere pretense, merely an outward display or emotion that does not conform to the God who is love and who has loved us in Christ (see Rom 5:8; 1 John 4:7-9). While such *agapē* should be universal (see Matt 5:43-48), it has a special manifestation within the Christian fellowship.

The comprehensive nature of the noun *agapē* in Rom 12:9 is reinforced by participles that *modify* it. In fact, unless we grasp the significance of these participles (which also dominate vv 17-21), we tend to chop up the remainder of ch 12 into a series of disjointed exhortations. But seeing the participles as modifiers of *agapē* gives integrity to the passage as well as divine support to those who will their love to be **sincere.**

Love that is **sincere** (*anypokritos*) literally refers to love ***without hypocrisy,*** i.e., that does not play the part of an actor onstage (v 9*a*). The paraphrasing NIV translation (as **sincere**) disguises the figure of speech known as litotes, which negates the opposite of Paul's positive point. Unpretentious love calls for love that is not a ruse, but real. The apostle uses the same adjective to describe love in 2 Cor 6:6 (see Matt 6:2; 1 Tim 1:5; 2 Tim 1:5; Jas 3:17; 1 Pet 1:22).

Different explanations have been offered as to how modifying participles came to acquire the force of imperatives. But they are probably best seen as "a natural development within the Greek language" (see Moo, 776 n. 27). The translation that follows reflects this understanding of the imperatival force of these participles, flowing from their dependence on the noun *agapē* within the parenetic section of the letter. Although these participles clarify the meaning of "sincere love," their nominative plural forms agree with the pronominal subject of these implied commands—*hymeis,* "you" (plural). This is not about love in the abstract; it is a description of what you do when you love.

The following woodenly literal translation of the Greek of Rom 12:9-13 attempts to illustrate Paul's bullet-list approach. Note the striking absence of main verbs and conjunctions. Neither idiomatic nor interpretive, this translation graphically illustrates the structural organization of the passage.

Sincere love.

- Hating the evil,

- clinging to the good,
  - by sibling love to one another devoted,
  - by honor one another preferring,
  - by diligence never [being] indolent,
  - by spirit burning,
  - by the Lord serving,
  - by hope rejoicing,
  - by tribulation enduring,
  - by prayer persisting,
  - by needs the saints sharing,
  - hospitality pursuing.

Genuine love requires believers to **Hate what is evil; cling to what is good** (v 9*bc;* see 1 Thess 5:21-22). Both verbs are strong. The prepositional prefix *apo-* merely intensifies the force of the verb *stygeō* (not used in the NT), which means "hate" or "abhor." Thus, *apostygountes* (only here in the NT) could be translated ***hating exceedingly*** or ***totally abhorring*** **what is evil** (*to ponēron;* only here in Romans).

The antithesis, ***clinging*** [*kollōmenoi*] ***to the good,*** elsewhere in the NT refers to the intimate sexual union of marriage (Matt 19:5) or prostitution (1 Cor 6:16), to the adherence of dust to one's sandals (Luke 10:11), to committing oneself to a community (Luke 15:15; Acts 5:13; 9:26; 10:28; 17:34), or to traveling together (Acts 8:29). Real *agapē* is not directionless emotion or unexpressed feelings. Love is not genuine when it leads a person to do wrong or to refuse to do right. Genuine love is "the real thing" that will lead the Christian to do what is **good** as a result of a transformed life and renewed mind (Rom 12:2).

Paul narrows his focus, reminding Christians *how* sincere *agapē* expresses hatred for evil and commitment to good. A series of nine dative nouns specify the *means* by which Christians should intentionally express authentic love. Only the first phrase in the sequence does not also utilize an adverbial participle.

■ **10** Various attempts have been made to distinguish different kinds of love based on supposed shades of differences between the meanings of the various Greek terms for **love.** Paul, however, seems content to clarify the meaning of *agapē* by using two of these synonyms in v 10*a:* **Be devoted** [*philostorgoi;* the vice-lists in 1:31 and 2 Tim 3:3 include *astorgos,* "unloving"] **to one another** [*allēlous*] **in brotherly love** [*philadelphiai*]. If *agapē* is Christian love in its highest form, it does not supplant but fulfills all other loves. As genuine love is expressed in a church, it acquires something of the character of an extended family or a community of close friends. Its members are bound together in deep fellowship, exhibiting toward one another a heartfelt and consistent mutual concern.

In v 10*b* Paul urges Roman Christians to outdo one another in bestowing honor on one another or to take the initiative in showing honor (Dunn 2002b, 38B:741). They were to recognize and praise one another's accomplishments and defer to one another. This merely makes explicit the implications of Paul's call for the mutuality of community life within the body of Christ in vv 3-5. To **Honor one another** [*allēlous*] **above yourselves** is the obvious expression of unselfish humility. Because *allēlous* (**one another**) is a reciprocal pronoun, everyone should be able to expect to give *and receive* **honor** (*tēi timēi*)—one of the most prized commodities in Mediterranean society, while avoiding the offensiveness of self-praise.

■ **11** Bauer translates the verbless negative clause that begins v 11 "when earnestness is needed, never be indolent" (1979, 563). The positive second part of the verse uses the metaphor of boiling or bubbling to recommend spiritual **fervor** and intensity instead of laziness. By means of their proximity to v 10, the exhortations of v 11*ab* serve as a reminder of the urgency and enthusiasm required in the ongoing responsibility of mutual love and respect within the community. Christians were not to take one another for granted.

ROMANS

Far from nonchalance, Paul expected Spirit-filled Christians to be distinguished by ***fiery intensity.*** The metaphorical connection between fire and Spirit is common in Jewish and Christian thought (Isa 4:4; 30:27-28; Matt 3:11; Luke 3:16; Acts 2:3; 18:25; 1 Thess 5:9; Rev 3:15; 2 Esd [*4 Ezra*] 13:10-11; Dunn 2002b, 38B:742). Although Paul does not specify the object of unflagging zeal, we should probably think of "the rational worship" demanded in Rom 12:1. 12:10-11

> The temptation to "lose steam" in our lifelong responsibility to reverence God in every aspect of our lives, to become lazy and complacent in our pursuit of what is "good, well pleasing to God, and perfect," is a natural one—but must be strenuously resisted. (Moo 1996, 778)

True worship requires not only words of praise to God but more importantly words and deeds that affirm and edify others within the community.

Serving the Lord (v 11*c*) might seem anticlimactic here, but the witness of church history is that so often "when stone walls rise up, fire dies down." Keeping ablaze in the Spirit is, therefore, an important aspect of **serving the Lord.** Of course, Christians can become so "charismatic" that they lose sight of those objective standards of Christian behavior essential to Christian witness and unity.

The Lord is served best when we serve one another in his behalf; **spiritual fervor** is of no value for its own sake. This would seem to be Paul's concern. He seeks to preclude such abuse by reminding us that ***burning in the Spirit*** (see Acts 18:25) must lead to and be directed by our service to the Lord. "For Paul the Spirit was the Lord's presence in believers, evoking obedience." The gift of the Spirit "is not an end in itself, aiming at an emotional peak experience . . . , but rather extends the Lord's rule over a formerly disobedient creation" (Jewett 2007, 763). It is not the "spiritual enthusiasm" of self-centered display, but of the humble service of the Christ who creates the fire of the Spirit, and other members of the body of Christ.

■ **12** The next three implicit exhortations in Rom 12:12 are interrelated in both style and content, since ***hoping, persevering,*** and ***persistent praying*** are natural partners. Love is spurred on and sustained by **hope.** Christian **hope** does not mortgage the present by preoccupation with the future. Although Paul uses the Greek term for **hope** (*elpis*), it has the force of the Hebrew it translates in the LXX. Thus, it was not "tentative expectation" of a better future, but "confident trust" in God (Dunn 2002b, 38B:742). Such hope becomes an occasion for joy already, even as the present age persists and the consummation of the new age is delayed (see 15:13; 1 Thess 2:19).

Paul is convinced that ***rejoicing*** and **hope** belong inseparably together (see Rom 5:1-5; 8:24-27). Trials, far from crushing early Christian **hope** for the dawning of the eschaton, only fueled it. This was not based on naive optimism; they believed matters would only get far worse before they finally got better. The trials of the last days were actually the birth pangs of the coming messianic age (see 1 Thess 3:3-5; 5:1-11; see Matt 24, esp. v 8). The experience of persecution was not an unexpected problem that believers had to reconcile with their faith. It merely confirmed that they were living as followers of their crucified Lord (Rom 8:17-25). And so, regardless of their circumstances, "joy" was a characteristic feature of earliest Christianity (14:17; 15:13; 2 Cor 6:10; Gal 5:22; Phil 1:4, 25; 2:17-18; 3:1; 4:1; 1 Thess 3:9; 5:16; see Acts 2:46; 13:52; 1 Pet 1:8; 1 John 1:4; Dunn 2002b, 38B:742), not to be confused with "happy moods or victorious exultations" (Jewett 2007, 763).

Knowing the "down side" of hope, Paul, ever the realist, here as elsewhere, quickly moves from ***hope*** to the need for ***endurance*** (see Mark 13:13; 1 Cor 13:7; Jas 1:12). In this age, Paul accepts suffering as inevitable. At the same time, he knows that our ability to remain faithful under **affliction** (see Rom 5:3) demanded persistence ***in prayer.*** Early Christians did not pray as a last-minute gesture of desperation when all else failed. ***Persisting in prayer*** was their lifestyle (Luke 18:1; Acts 1:14; 2:42; 6:4; Eph 6:18; Col 1:9; 4:2; 1 Thess 5:17). They prayed even when they did not know what to say (Rom 8:26-27). Genuine love could not be postponed until some uncertain future date when it became convenient and comfortable.

■ **13** Paul concludes his bullet-list of implicit imperatives with the reminder that *agapē,* when it is sincere, ***participates*** (*koinōnountes*) in ***meeting the needs of the saints.*** In the present context, these needs are surely material necessities, such as food, clothing, and shelter (see 15:26-27; Acts 2:45; 4:35; 6:3; 20:34; 28:10; 2 Cor 8:4; Gal 6:6; Eph 4:28; Phil 2:25; 4:14-16; Titus 3:14; 1 John 3:17; Rev 3:17), not merely spiritual resources (Eph 4:29). Therefore, when *agapē* is sincere, it outflows in generosity toward those less well off.

The *koin-* cognate word group, from which the participle translated **share** is derived (*koinōnountes*), appears 30 times in the Pauline letters. The basis for sharing (*koinōnikos*) is the conviction that what we own is not ours alone; we hold it in common (*koinos*) with others in the community (*koinōnia*). Our most obvious partners (*koinōnoi*), ***the saints*** (*hoi hagioi*), "the holy ones," are God's people, fellow Christians (see Rom 1:7).

Another aspect of Christian *agapē* is ***pursuing*** [*diōkontes*] ***hospitality*** [*philoxenian*]. This active expression of love invites us to run after (used figuratively, to *"pursue, strive for, seek after, aspire to"* [Bauer 1979, 201]; see 9:30, 31; 14:19; 1 Cor 14:1; 1 Thess 5:15; 1 Tim 6:11; 2 Tim 2:22) "friendship" (*philia*) with "strangers" (*xenoi*). There were very few hostels in the ancient world, and most of them had an unsavory reputation. Thus, the necessity of offering food and shelter to traveling Christians was great.

The unstinting practice of hospitality in the Mediterranean world was costly; families denied themselves to fulfill their obligations to others. Among Christians the need for hospitality was regularly exacerbated by the many traveling missionaries and Christian workers. It seems likely that many among the recently returned Jewish-Christian minority, deported because of the Edict of Claudius, were destitute and in desperate need of hospitality. Paul urged the Roman house and tenement churches to share the economic burden this imposed on the entire community, not just Jewish Christians.

As he wrote, Paul expected soon to be the beneficiary of Roman hospitality himself (Rom 15:28). But he requests no special favors for Christian leaders alone. The NT frequently urges Christians to offer hospitality to ordinary fellow believers (see 1 Tim 3:2; Titus 1:8; Heb 13:2; 1 Pet 4:9).

Paul, however, does more; he urges the community not merely to **practice** but to ***pursue* hospitality** (see Dunn 2002b, 38B:743-44, 754 for a fuller discussion of the role of hospitality in ancient Mediterranean society).

FROM THE TEXT

Romans 12:9-16 offers a précis of 1 Cor 12:1—13:8, which Paul had penned a few years earlier. Believers have been "baptized" into the one body of Christ, where "we were all given the one Spirit to drink" (1 Cor 12:13). That one Spirit is the Spirit of Christ, whose essence is love, which Paul says must govern all gifts (*charismata*) bestowed on the church.

It is easy for those who emphasize spiritual gifts to fall victim to spiritual excesses, while neglecting Paul's reminder that the *definitive* mark of Christian spirituality is love. Without it all else Christians say and do is an irrelevant (13:1) caricature of the Christian ethic. Paul calls all "charismatic Christians," all Christians who claim to live out of the resources of divine grace (*charis*), to ***genuine love.***

Paul calls for the church of Jesus Christ to demonstrate "perfect love." For the eighteenth-century apostle of holiness, John Wesley, this was a call to express love within the body of Christ. If such "social holiness" is to characterize Christianity, it demands that *individual* Christians take with utmost seriousness Jesus' call to godlike perfection in Matt 5:48. This call to all-inclusive love drove Wesley's ministry, which sparked the eighteenth-century Revival that transformed England.

In this connection Wesley asks:

> But what is perfection? The word has various senses: here it means perfect love. It is love excluding sin; love filling the heart, taking up the whole capacity of the soul. . . . How clearly does this express the being perfected in love! How strongly imply being saved from all sin! For as long as love takes up the whole heart, what room is there for sin therein?

Here the sin problem is resolved at its deepest level, the level of self.

"But what is that faith wherewith we are sanctified, — saved from sin, and perfected in love?" Wesley asks.

> It is a divine evidence and conviction, first, that God hath promised it in the Holy Scripture [Deut 30:6; Ezek 36:25-27]. . . . Secondly, that what God hath promised he is able to perform. . . . Thirdly, . . . that he is able and willing to do it now. . . .
>
> To this conviction, that God is both able and willing to sanctify

us now, there needs to be added one thing more, — a divine evidence and conviction that he doeth it. . . .

He is at the door! Let your inmost soul cry out,
Come in, come in, thou heavenly Guest!
Nor hence again remove;
But sup with me, and let the feast
Be everlasting love. (1979, 6:52-54; sermon on "The Scripture Way of Salvation")

Wesley defended his preaching of Christian perfection by quoting the Anglican Collect to the Holy Eucharist:

> Almighty God, unto whom all hearts are open, all desires known, and from whom no secrets are hid: Cleanse the thoughts of our hearts by the inspiration of thy Holy Spirit, that we may perfectly love thee, and worthily magnify thy holy Name; through Christ our Lord. (*Book of Common Prayer* 1945, 323)

When Wesley explained to Edmund Gibson, Anglican bishop of London, his preaching of perfection, the bishop's response was, "Mr. Wesley, if this be what you mean, publish it in all the world" (Heitzenrater 1995, 121). Wesley and Paul were certainly on the same page in their conviction that the practical expression of love is central to Christian identity.

(2) Love Under Pressure (12:14-16)

IN THE TEXT

■ **14** The second person plural imperative verb *eulogeite* (**Bless**), used twice in v 14, is the first finite verb since v 5. The antithesis, **do not curse,** is another second person plural imperative (*mē katarasthe*). The next finite verb in v 16*d* is also a second person plural imperative (*mē ginesthe, **do not become***). These imperatives and the parenetic context begun in 12:1 provide the basis for translating all of the adverbial participles and infinitives here as imperative verbs.

The command to **bless** and **not curse** are the first explicit imperatives since Paul's exhortation to "be transformed by the renewing of your mind" in v 2. To **bless** in response to persecution allows Christians, thoroughly transformed and renewed in mind, to demonstrate that "God's will is . . . good, pleasing and perfect" (v 2). This unexpected response is at the same time an obvious expression of ***sincere love*** (v 9).

The verb translated **persecute** (*diōkontas*) in v 14 is the same as that translated ***pursue*** in v 13. It is striking that Paul should use the same verb with such different senses in such proximity. To **bless those who persecute you** (v 14) for his Roman readers may have meant to *"speak well, praise, extol"* (Bauer 1979, 322) those who pursued them with the intention of doing them harm (see Matt 5:44; Luke 6:28; 1 Cor 4:9, 12; 15:9; Gal 1:13, 23; 4:29; 5:11; 6:12; Phil 3:6; 2 Tim 3:12; 1 Pet 3:9; *Did.* 1:3). Some important early manuscripts of Rom 12:14 omit the pronoun **you** (*hymas;* see the sidebar "Bless Those Who Persecute"). If Paul used the word **bless** with the distinctive force it has in the LXX, he was calling the Romans to pray that God might grant persecutors grace, peace, and well-being (Beyer 1964, 2:754-63). Only a God-given love can do that.

Bless Those Who Persecute

The generic formulation "bless the persecutors" implies that all persecutors are to be blessed, whether they have persecuted you or not. This has a direct bearing on the Roman situation after 54 C.E., because it extends the scope of the reference to include those in the Roman church situation who had not experienced the deportation under Claudius. . . . [With] the deletion of "you/your," . . . a possible squabble between the persecuted and those whose inclination may have been to sympathize with the persecutors is avoided. For the Gentile Christians who remained in Rome, to "bless and not curse" was not to condone the deportation, but to convey divine aid and concern for the well-being of the authorities. For the Jewish Christians who had been deported, it means refraining from the natural desire to place their adversaries under divine wrath. (Jewett 2007, 766)

Persecutors are to be blessed and not cursed. The verb translated **curse** (*katarasthe*) is derived from a verb, not used in the NT, meaning "pray" (*araomai;* see Liddell, Scott, Jones, and McKenzie 1996, 223) with a prepositional prefix meaning "against" (*kata-*). Both blessings and curses involve more than merely human words of encouragement and condemnation. They presume that these human words are implicit prayers for God to intervene for the well-being of those blessed or to bring disaster on those cursed. Jesus had called his followers to bless, love, and do good to their enemies—those who hated and abused them (Luke 6:27-28). Paul's reference to persecutors suggests that he has shifted his focus from practical expressions of love within the Christian community (Rom 12:9-13) to love's expression in the world outside, which is clearly the focus in vv 17-21.

■ **15** That vv 15 and 16 are directed again toward inter-community relations is no organizational failure on Paul's part. He refuses to compartmentalize Christian living, to treat as discrete the supposed sacred and secular dimensions of life (see the commentary on 12:1-2).

> Paul did not see a Christian's life as divided neatly into two sets of attitudes and obligations—one to fellow believers, the other to non-believers. The same sympathetic concern and positive outgoing love should be the rule in all cases—a love which does not reckon or depend on receiving a positive response in turn. For this not only Jesus' words but Jesus' example provided the model. (5:1-11; 8:18-39; Dunn 2002b, 38B:755)

The Greek words translated as imperative verbs in v 15—**Rejoice** (*chairein, **to rejoice***) and **mourn** (*klaiein, **to weep***)—are actually infinitives. Although familiar in secular Greek, imperatival infinitives are infrequent in the NT and appear only within parenetic contexts (i.e., ethical admonitions; see Eph 4:21-24; Phil 3:16; 2 Thess 3:14; Titus 2:2, 6, 9; see Moulton 1978, 179).

Community-consciousness—"one body with many members . . . and each member belongs to all the others" (Rom 12:4-5)—provides the basis for Paul's appeal. Christians have no reason to resent the good fortune of their fellow believers or to take satisfaction in their misfortunes. On the contrary, they ought ***to rejoice with those who rejoice, to weep with those who weep*** (see Sir 7:34; *T. Jos.* 17:7-8; Luke 6:21, 25; John 16:20; 1 Cor 7:30; 12:26; Phil 2:17-18; 3:18; Jas 5:1). Of course, weeping (*klaiontōn*) is not merely the shedding of tears, but "an expression of any feeling of sadness, care, or anxiety" (Bauer 1979, 433).

> In the Roman church situation the burden of sharing sorrow would fall on those who had not suffered persecution and exile. . . . The returnees would need to rejoice with the reports of successful expansion of the house and tenement churches in their absence, while those who had remained in Rome would need to share in the joy of those returning. (Jewett 2007, 768)

■ **16** The first three imperative verbs in the translation of v 16 are actually adverbial participles (as in vv 9-13). Only the fourth is a second person plural imperative in Greek.

The translation of v 16*a*—**Live in harmony with one another**—is actually a paraphrase. This obscures Paul's use of the language of the renewed mind (v 2), employed earlier in v 3 and again in v 17. The NASB stays closer to the Greek original: "Be of the same mind [*phronountes*] toward one another." Unanimity of thought calls for agreement in essentials, harmonious relationships despite differences of opinion, not mindless uniformity (see 15:5; 2 Cor 13:11; Phil 2:2; 3:15-16; 4:2). We might say, "Be on the same page with one another."

The reciprocal pronoun **one another** (*allēlous*) reminds us again that to live in love calls for accommodations from everyone; reciprocity requires that the same ones do not always get things their way. And if we genuinely love, we will not constantly ask, "Why is it my turn to give in again?"

Do not be proud, but be willing to associate with people of low position (Rom 12:16*bc*) is another paraphrasing translation. It similarly obscures Paul's use of mind-imagery. What he says in the negative half of this two-part exhortation urges ***not thinking*** [*phronountes*] ***high things.*** The NIV correctly captures Paul's insistence that sincere love cannot be expressed by those who are **proud** in the sense of haughty, high and mighty, or self-exalted (see 11:18-20; 1 Tim 6:17)—a point made earlier in Rom 12:3.

Genuine love calls for true "humility" (*tapeinophronēsis, **humble-mindedness***). Thus, to refuse to imagine oneself "a cut above" the rest, positively requires ***being carried away*** [*synapagomenoi;* see Gal 2:13; 2 Pet 3:17] ***by low things*** [*tois tapeinois;* see *Did.* 3:9]. Paul's imagery could be taken as a call for believers to accommodate themselves to humble ways and menial tasks or to associate with humble people (Bauer 1979, 784 s.v. *synapagō*). The model of Jesus routinely calls Christians to pursue the countercultural
12:16 ideal of *downward* mobility (Phil 2:5-11). But the OT also provides numerous examples of God's choice to favor the lowly (Judg 6:15; Job 5:11; Pss 18:27; 82:3; 138:6; Zeph 3:12; see Luke 1:52).

The fourth exhortation in Rom 12:16*d,* **Do not be conceited,** translates a true imperative verb, but again periphrastically. What Paul urges is literally: ***Do not become wise minded*** [*phronimoi*] ***before yourselves.*** This is certainly no recommendation of ignorance or folly. The expression ***before yourselves*** is an idiom that means ***in your own eyes, in your opinion*** (see 11:25; Prov 3:7; Bauer 1979, 610 s.v. *para*). Thus, to be *"wise in your own estimation"* means *"relying on your own wisdom"* (Bauer 1979, 866 s.v. *phronimos*). "The plural formulation suggests that Paul had a corporate self-esteem in mind" (Dunn 2002b, 38B:747). Paul's call for equality, solidarity, and cooperation undercut the claims of superiority any of the Roman congregations or ethnic groups might make (Jewett 2007, 769-70).

Believers know that a renewed mind (Rom 12:2) is theirs only as the result of the ongoing transformation effected by God's sanctifying work in their wholly consecrated lives (see v 3). Elsewhere Paul reminds believers, "We have the mind [*noun*] of Christ" (1 Cor 2:16). Therefore, "Let the same mind [*phroneite*] be in you that was in Christ Jesus" (Phil 2:5

NRSV). He refused to humiliate the lowly, instead humbling himself to the lowest place (vv 6-8).

(3) Love Expressed in the World (12:17-21)

BEHIND THE TEXT

Once again, Paul formulates his appeal to the Roman house and tenement churches in terms of the imagery of the renewed mind of v 2. As in previous sections (see vv 3 and 16), in v 17 he does this by means of the *phron*-stem. His discussion of the obligations of love toward those outside the church, in the world, in vv 17-21 includes a double reference to "evil" (*kakon*) at the beginning (v 17*a*) and end (v 21). As in vv 9-13 and 14-16, Paul begins this section with a series of Greek participles to clarify the meaning and implications of ***sincere love*** (the heading in v 9).

In contrast to the rapid movement from one theme to another in the preceding sections, here Paul focuses on the single theme of nonretaliation. This theme, stated negatively in v 17, is restated more positively and hopefully in v 21. Also in contrast to previous sections, Paul reinforces his appeal by explicitly citing scripture (Deut 32:35 and Prov 25:21-22*a*) in Rom 12:19*b*-20.

IN THE TEXT

Continuing the grammatical structure of vv 9-16, consisting of a series of four participles (underlined) explicating *agapē* in vv 17-19 Paul succinctly writes (translated literally):

Giving back [*apodidontes*] ***evil for evil to no one,***
minding [*phronooumenoi*] ***what is morally good before all people,***
　　　　if possible, so far as it depends on you,
　　living peaceably with all people,
　　not avenging yourselves, beloved,
but give [*dote*] ***place to the wrath*** [of God]***;***
　　for it is written:
　　　　"Vengeance is mine,
　　　　I will repay,
　　　　　　says the Lord."
On the contrary,
　　　　"If your enemies are hungry,
　　feed them;

if they are thirsty,
give them drink;
for in so doing
you will heap coals of fire on their heads."
Do not be overcome by evil,
but overcome evil with good.

■ **17** The passage opens in v 17 with a blunt negative statement of its theme: Christians must *not* repay evil for evil, in response to the hostility of the surrounding world. This contradiction of the *lex talionis* (= law of the talon; i.e., eye-for-eye, tooth-for-tooth retaliation) seems to represent Paul's version of Jesus' teaching in Matt 5:38-42 and Luke 6:27-36 (see 1 Thess 5:15; 1 Pet 3:9; *Jos. Asen.* 23:9; 28:14).

As a positive counterpart, Christians should use their renewed mind (*noos;* Rom 12:2), by ***giving forethought to*** [*pronooumenoi;* see 2 Cor 8:21] ***what is honorable*** [*kala*]. Paul conceives of the Christian life as a drama played out on a world stage before a basically hostile, uncomprehending audience (see 1 Cor 4:9; 2 Cor 2:14-15), which is nonetheless a field for conversion (see Phil 2:15-16). In such situations, the temptation is always present to give way to resentment. Instead, motivated by love, Christians should make calculated plans to give their renewed mind to ***what is morally good*** (*kala*). Paul sums up the Hellenistic world's idea of all that is noble, admirable, and worthy of aspiration and praise (Bauer 1979, 400 s.v. *kalos*).

Thus, when Paul adds *enōpion pantōn anthrōpōn,* ***in the opinion of all people*** (see 2 Cor 8:21; echoing Prov 3:4), he certainly implies that Christians should accommodate the tastes of other Christians. But he also suggests that Christian moral ideals cannot be entirely countercultural (see Rom 12:16). Believers may find common ground with unbelievers sometimes. But when disagreement remains, tolerance is possible. ***Giving forethought*** does not require agreeing with the opinions or practices of fellow Christians or our pagan neighbors. It does require us to give consideration to what they consider good and to try to understand their motives (Jewett 2007, 772-73).

Paul urged the Philippians: "Whatever is true, whatever is noble, whatever is right, whatever is pure, whatever is lovely, whatever is admirable—if anything is excellent or praiseworthy—think about such things" (Phil 4:8; see 1 Thess 4:12). This is not a list of uniquely Christian values. In fact, it seems to represent the best of the virtues urged by pagan ethicists of Paul's day. Christian morality cannot be defined simplistically as the antithesis of the world's values.

■ **18** Sincere love finds a way of affirming positively the worthy ideals and aspirations even of non-Christians in the interests of the widely shared Christian ideal of ***living peaceably with all people*** (v 18; see Ps 34:14; Matt 5:9; Mark 9:50; 2 Cor 13:11; 1 Thess 5:13; Heb 12:14). Paul realizes that this will not always be possible, however, since peace requires the cooperation of both parties involved. Paul's qualification brings a note of realism into the picture: **If it is possible** [see Mark 13:22; 14:35; Gal 4:15], **as far as it depends on you.**

■ **19** Verse 19 essentially repeats the appeal in v 17, now specified as ***not avenging*** [*ekdikountes*] ***yourselves*** for an injury received (see Prov 20:22; Sir 28:1). At this point, Paul again directly addresses his Roman audience (see *adelphoi* in Rom 1:13; 7:1, 4; 8:12; 10:1; 11:25; 12:1; 15:14, [30]; 16:17), but here, for the only time in the letter, as *agapētoi*, ***loved ones;*** i.e., **friends** (see 1:7; 16:5, 8, 9, 12). This seems unexpected in a letter addressed to members of Roman churches, most of whom he had never met. It is, however, coherent with his appeals to demonstrate genuine love even to strangers (12:13). And, it is, perhaps, noteworthy that Paul will later identify returned Jewish-Christian refugees he has met in his travels as "loved ones" (16:5, 8, 9, 12; Jewett 2007, 774-75). ROMANS

Denying injured Christians the right to avenge themselves, Paul explicitly exhorts them (using a second person plural imperative): ***Instead*** [*alla*], ***give*** [*dote*] ***place to wrath. Wrath*** here must refer to the judgment God will inflict on the unrighteous, whether in the end or already in this present age (see 1:18; 2:5, 8). Paul does not suggest that Christians should refrain from seeking to punish their adversaries so that they will receive more severe punishment from God. 12:18-19

Instead, to ***give God room*** to act is to refuse to usurp his role (see Wis 12:10, 20; Sir 4:5; 16:14; 38:12; Eph 4:27; 2 Thess 1:6; Heb 12:17)—to let God be God (see Rom 1:18-23). Paul's appeal arises from the biblical prohibition of humans taking vengeance in their own hands. Vengeance is the sole prerogative of the Judge of the universe. In the classic statement of this tradition in Deut 32:35 (see Heb 10:30), echoed in Rom 12:19*b,* humans are urged to entrust justice to God, to allow him to right the wrongs inflicted unjustly. (For the quotation formula, **it is written,** see 1:17.)

Paul's addition of **says the Lord,** gives the quotation from the Law the prophetic character of a warning (see Jer 5:9; 23:2; Rom 14:11; 1 Cor 14:21; 2 Cor 6:17-18). Such a warning may seem unnecessary. After all, what could politically powerless Roman Christians do to avenge themselves against their oppressors? Nevertheless, a decade after Paul wrote this letter desperate and vastly outnumbered Jewish Zealots in Palestine futilely attempted to do just that (Dunn 2002b, 38B:749).

■ **20** Genuine love calls for more than doing no harm. Beyond simple abstention from taking vengeance against one's enemies, in Rom 12:20 Paul quotes LXX Prov 25:21-22*a*. Apparently because the passage offers its advice in the second person singular ("you") imperative, Paul abandons the community perspective (second person plural) he has followed up to this point in Rom 12. With ch 13, his perspective will shift again, this time to the third person singular imperative ("he"/"she").

The Wisdom tradition advises reviving hungry and thirsty enemies with food and drink. Greek often uses definite articles "to distinguish one particular class from other classes," whereas customary English usage indicates such generic use with plural or indefinite nouns (Young 1994, 56). Thus, *ho echthros sou* (lit. ***the enemy your***) should be translated ***your enemies.*** Did Paul urge the Roman believers to invite their hostile neighbors to share in their common meals (so Jewett 2007, 778)?

Paul quotes Proverbs' rationale (*gar,* ***for***) for **doing this:** ***You will heap coals of fire on their heads.*** Taking this last clause literally seems utterly inconsistent with love as the operative term for this passage. The meaning of pouring ***fiery coals*** on the heads of your adversaries is as obscure in Proverbs as in Paul's quotation. The phrase has been variously interpreted.

The Eastern Church Father Chrysostom thought that by refusing to take vengeance, Christians made their enemies more deserving of divine judgment. But the majority of church fathers—Origen, Augustine, Pelagius, Jerome, and others—thought the expression meant that Christian nonretaliation might make their enemies ashamed enough to repent and be spared judgment (Dunn 2002b, 38B:750). Perhaps the imagery in Proverbs originated from an ancient Egyptian penitential ritual involving carrying a pan of blazing coals as a symbol of sorrow for one's misdeeds (see Fitzmyer 1993, 657-58).

Whatever the precise significance of the rationale in Proverbs, it is noteworthy that Paul does not quote the conclusion of the saying: "and the LORD will reward you" (Prov 25:22*b*). Christlike love is not motivated by concern for one's own well-being but pursues the good of others (see Rom 12:21). Whatever heaping coals originally symbolized, we can be certain that Paul's rationale was consistent with such *agapē*. Paul, no less than Jesus, expects believers to love their enemies by actively seeking their good (Matt 5:44; Luke 7:27).

■ **21** Paul's final admonition, **Do not be overcome** [*nikō,* ***be conquered***]

by evil [*kakou*], **but overcome** [*nika, **conquer***] **evil** [*kakon*] **with good** [*agathōi*] (Rom 12:21; see 2:10; 12:9) is clearly consonant with this understanding of *agapē* within vv 9-21.

Paul's point in this context is not that the cause of good always triumphs over evil in battle. It is not that good people ultimately win, and bad people lose. This is not a tactic for victory at all. This is advice for suffering believers: Treating your enemies well may turn them into friends, bringing an end to their evil. Paul emphasizes the converting power of love. Whereas vengeance simply intensifies hostility, answering enmity and injury with love and kindness can effect reconciliation.

FROM THE TEXT

The mission and destiny of the body of Christ is to be fulfilled through his holy church living out the genuine love described in vv 9-21. Jesus' High Priestly Prayer may be answered: "that all of them may be one, Father, just as you are in me and I am in you. . . . that the world may believe that you have sent me. . . . that the love you have for me may be in them and that I myself may be in them" (John 17:21-22, 26).

(4) Love Applied to Government (13:1-7)

BEHIND THE TEXT

This is the most controversial passage in the letter. Paul appears to interrupt the flow of his argument, which continues quite smoothly from 12:21 (omitting 13:1-7) in 13:8-10, with the "eschatological" conclusion in vv 11-14 reinforcing the ethical appeal. But does 13:1-7 actually disrupt Paul's call to give tangible expression to genuine love in 12:9—13:10? How does his abrupt rejoinder, **Everyone must submit himself to the governing authorities,** cohere with its context? Traditionally, Paul has been understood in this passage to address the Christian's civic responsibilities to worldly power and the state (Stein 1989). What does this have to do with Christian love?

Paul uses a variety of expressions to describe the **authorities** to whom his Roman audience is to subordinate itself: **governing authorities** (*exousiais hyperechousias,* v 1), **rulers** (*archontes,* v 3), **God's servant** (*Theou . . . diakonos,* v 4), **agent of wrath** (*ekdikos eis orgēn,* v 4), and ***God's ministers*** (*leitourgoi . . . Theou,* v 6). Elsewhere in the NT the Greek word translated **authorities** in vv 1-7 is apparently used sometimes to designate worldly "princes," "authorities," and "powers"; and sometimes to refer to supernatural powers opposed to God (see 8:38, where *archai* is translated "demons"; see 1 Cor 2:8; Eph 1:21; Col 1:16; 2:15). Walter Wink's trilogy (1983, 1986, 1992) exposes the "demonic" potential of earthly powers.

What are we to make of early Christian claims that these **authorities** are *now* subject to Christ, having been "disarmed" and publicly humiliated by God's triumph "over them by the cross" (Col 2:15; see Eph 1:18-23)? And how are such exultant claims to be reconciled with Paul's still *future* hope for the destruction of "all dominion, authority and power" accompanying the Parousia at "the end" (1 Cor 15:23-24)?

What are the practical, political implications of the lordship of Christ? Does it leave any place for other dominions? Must Christians, as far as possible, separate themselves from worldly "authorities"? Since their citizenship is in heaven (Phil 3:20), are they free from earthly allegiances? Or, are those who confess "Jesus is Lord" (Rom 10:9) yet obliged to obey worldly "authorities"? How is their subjection to Christ manifested in the mundane realm of everyday political realities?

Tension exists for the church because its life must be lived out in "the present evil age" (Gal 1:4). "This age" indeed has "authorities," quite apart from those of the "new age." It is precisely in this "present time," when the two ages overlap (Rom 8:18-25), that the church participates, despite its heavenly citizenship. It is in this world that the church lives as the present people of God. How then should the church shape its life in relation to **the governing authorities** of this world?

Synagogue Authorities?

Mark Nanos (1996, 289-336) has made a plausible case for an alternative reading of the passage. He contends

> that Paul's instructions in 13:1-7 are not concerned with the state, empire, or any other such organization of secular government. His concern was rather to address the obligation of . . . Christian gentiles associating with the synagogues of Rome . . . to subordinate themselves to the leaders of the synagogues and to the customary "rules of behavior" . . . developed in Diaspora synagogues for . . . "righteous gentiles" seeking association with Jews and their God. (291)

Nanos takes for granted that both Paul and the Christians in Rome did not understand themselves as a new religion in competition with Judaism (1996, 166-238). Thus, Paul expected Gentile converts to recognize their responsibility to operate within the definitions of righteousness operative within the synagogue community (293; see Matt 23:3).

If the issue Paul addresses in Rom 13:1-7 outlines the Christian's responsibilities to the state, how does this topic make sense within its surrounding context? Käsemann (1980, 352) is typical of many interpreters, who identify it as "an independent block," "an alien body in Paul's exhortation," if not a later "interpolation" (Kallas 1964).

But vv 1-7 are more closely related to its context than first appears. Relations with the **governing authorities** fits neatly into Paul's overall appeal from 12:3 onward to "work outward" from responsibilities and demands of love within the Christian community (vv 3-16), to those affecting the world around the church (vv 17-21). In effect, 13:1-7 extends and specifies the command to "live at peace with everyone" (12:18). Herman Ridderbos (1975, 321) suggests that beginning with 12:1 Paul defines "the Christian life as 'liturgy,' the service of God in everyday life." That is, "spiritual sacrificial service" involves "obedience to earthly authorities" (Ridderbos 1975, 321).

There are thematic links connecting both the preceding (see *orgē*—**wrath** in 12:19 and 13:4, 5 (NRSV); *apodidōmi*—**repay** (lit. "give back") in 12:17 and 13:7; *ekdikeō*—**take revenge** in 12:19 and *ekdikos*—***avenger*** in 13:4; *proskartereō*—***be devoted to*** in 12:12 and 13:6) and following (see *opheilas*—***debts*** in 13:7 and *opheilō*—***be indebted*** in 13:8) contexts of vv 1-7. The contrast between "good" (*agathon*) and "bad" (*kakon*) appears throughout (12:2, 9, 17, 21; 13:3*a*, 3*c*, 4*a*, 4*b*, 4*d*, 10; see Dunn 2002b, 38B:758 on 2:7-11 and 13:3-4).

A sufficient explanation for the presence of 13:1-7 in its present context may be found in the unfortunate consequences of infighting between Jews and Christians a decade earlier that led to Claudius's eviction of Jews from the city (see the commentary Introduction). Paul would almost certainly have favored a course of action that would prevent the recurrence of such a public display of the failure of the people of God to settle their differences respectably (see 1 Cor 6:1-8). Renewed civil unrest among the Roman populace that came to a head in the 50s concerning abuses in the collection of taxes (for the details, see Dunn 2002b, 38B:766) may offer another plausible historical explanation for Paul's instructions here.

It seems likely that Paul was aware of the history of civil disturbances in the capital of the empire. And he must have suspected, or known, that the Christian community there was divided on the matter of taxes. He must have been anxious to prevent the highly vulnerable house and tenement churches of Rome from adopting policies sure to bring them into conflict with government officials (compare 1 Tim 2:1-3; Titus 3:1-3; and 1 Pet 2:13-17). Paul's ambitious plans to evangelize Spain would be severely compromised if Christians in Rome did not make reasonable accommodations to political realities.

Romans 13:1-7 serve as a corrective to any impression that the gospel's proclamation of the in-breaking of the new age implies freedom from obligations to rule and authority belonging to the present, passing age. Paul's overall presentation of the gospel involves maintaining a delicate balance between the realities of the present and coming ages (see 5:1-11). His repeated use of words from the *tass-* cognate family (see below) suggests that his major concern is preserving ***order*** in the face of the threat of anarchy. This concern arose not simply out of pragmatic expedience but out of theological conviction: "For God is not a God of disorder [*akatassias*] but of peace" (1 Cor 14:33). Thus, the civil order Paul calls for in Rom 13:1-7 is an apt expression of the ***genuine love*** he describes in 12:17-19.

Paul was willing to accept the inevitability of the persecution of Christians (8:17-25; 1 Thess 3:3-4), but he certainly was no masochist and did not recommend provoking it (see 1 Pet 2:19-25; 3:13-17; 4:12-19). In 1 Thessalonians, he similarly follows his reminder of the necessity of mutual love (4:9-10) with a call for prudent political quietism (vv 11-12). He urged his persecuted converts to maintain a low profile, refusing to tolerate ***disorderly*** (*ataktous* [from *a-tassō-ōs*], 1 Thess 5:14; 2 Thess 3:6-7) believers. Christians must not give their opponents reason to believe they are social subversives. On the contrary, from his earliest correspondence, Paul recommended: "Make it your ambition to lead a quiet life, to mind your own business and to work with your hands, just as we told you, so that your daily life may win the respect of outsiders and so that you will not be dependent on anybody" (1 Thess 4:11-12).

The structural organization of Rom 13:1-7 is clear. A blunt opening statement states the basic instruction: **submit** (*hypotassesthō;* v 1*a;* from *hypotassō,* ***sub-ordered***). Verses 1*b-2a* provide the theological underpinning for this command: Behind earthly **authorities** (*exousiais*) lies the **authority** (*exousiais*) of God, who **established** (from *tassō,* ***ordered***) them. Verse 2*b* states the theme of a second supporting argument, developed in vv 3-4. By not **rebelling against** (v 2, from *antitassō,* ***ordering against***) **the one in authority** (v 3, *tēn exousian*) **God has instituted** (v 2, *diatagēi,* from *tassō*), one avoids the **punishment** they inflict as agents of God. Verse 5 restates the initial instruction: **submit** (*hypotassesthai*), introducing the further notion of **conscience.** Verses 6-7 make the point toward which Paul was driving all along—**This is . . . why you pay taxes.**

IN THE TEXT

■ **1** Paul's basic command is: **Everyone must submit himself to the governing authorities** (v 1). **Submit** in Greek (*hypotassesthō*) is to be distinguished from the "obedience" (*hypakoē, hypakouō*) or "offer" of oneself (*paristēmi*) to God alone, which Paul calls for in ch 6. By voluntarily submitting to the **authorities** (*exousiais*) ***placed over*** (*hypotassesthō*) them, Christians recognize their subordinate status in the social pecking order and acknowledge their readiness to act accordingly. One may submit to governmental authority and refuse to be conformed to this world; both actions express the will of God (12:2).

Everyone correctly translates the Semitic idiom *Pasa psychē*, ***every soul.*** Clearly, Paul is not seeking merely inward, spiritual submission, referring in Platonic fashion to some hidden, eternal dimension of the human person. ***Every soul*** simply refers to all humanity (see *pantōn anthrōpōn* in 12:17, 18).

Paul's rationale [*gar*, **For**] for universal submission is that **there is no authority except that which God has established** [*hypo Theou*, ***by God***]. **The authorities that exist have been established** [*tetagmenai* from *tassō*] **by God** (v 1*bc*). This Jewish view of submission to existing political realities finds its first expression in the exilic prophecy of Jeremiah: "Seek the welfare of the city where I have sent you . . . , for in its welfare you will find your welfare" (29:7 NRSV). It appears also in the narratives of the first half of Daniel (2:21, 37-38; 4:14, 26; see *Let. Aris.* 15), and in later apocryphal works (see Wis 6:1-3; Sir 10:4; 17:17; elaborating on Prov 8:15-16).

Jewett calls attention to a neglected question: Precisely who is this **God** who orders worldly authority? He is not Mars or Jupiter or any of the others in the pantheon of Greco-Roman deities. Nor is he the "divine" Emperor Nero. He is the Judeo-Christian **God** proclaimed in the preceding twelve chapters of Romans. He is the **God** incarnate in the Christ, crucified by Rome.

> If the Roman authorities had understood this argument, it would have been viewed as thoroughly subversive. That the Roman authorities were appointed by the God and Father of Jesus Christ turns the entire Roman civic cult on its head, exposing its suppression of the truth. (Jewett 2007, 790)

Nanos notes a striking omission in Paul's call for subordination to the **authorities.** Typically, Jewish calls for submission include "an implicit, if not always explicit, judgment of . . . foreign governments, even if God was somehow using their evil intentions to accomplish his ultimate goals" (1996, 299). This is missing in Rom 13:1-7.

■ **2** Refusal to submit to the **governing authorities** is futile and potentially fatal: **Consequently** [*hōste*], **he who rebels against the authority is rebelling against what God has *appointed*** [*diatagēi*, ***ordered/lined up***]**, and those who do so will bring judgment** [*krima*] **on themselves** (v 2). John Howard Yoder notes that in vv 1-7 "God is not said to *create* or *institute* or *ordain* the powers that be, but only to *order* them, to put them in their place." This is not tacit approval of what worldly authorities do, nor for their existence; God merely "lines them up with his purpose" (Yoder 1972, 203).

The perfect participle underlying **rebelling** suggests that Paul rejects a fixed disposition toward disorder. This does not prohibit any protest against injustice (see Paul's own practice in Acts 16:35-40). Rebels who oppose God are bound to be punished. Since *krima* here is punishment that comes through the human instrumentality of the state, it is temporal rather than eternal. Nevertheless, it is punishment authorized by the **wrath** of God by his **agent** (Rom 13:4; see 2:2-3).

■ **3** The role of government is here portrayed in almost entirely negative terms; it punishes those who resist its orders. **Rulers hold . . . terror . . . for those who do wrong** (v 3*b*). Paul assumes that government exists primarily to maintain order; thus, to prevent anarchy.

On the other hand, **Rulers hold no terror for those who do right** (*tōi agathōi*, v 3*a;* see 2:7; 12:9, 21), which in the present context means those who submit to government authority. Paul refers to lower-echelon **rulers,** such as local magistrates, rather than the emperor, whom few average citizens encountered.

Paul reinforces his call for Christians to do ***good*** (*agathos*), by asking and answering a rhetorical question: **Do you** [singular] **want to be free from fear** [*phobos*] **of the one in authority? Then do what is right** [*to agathon*] **and he will commend** [*epainon*, ***praise***] **you** [singular; v 3*bc;* see 12:17*b;* Phil 4:8; 1 Pet 2:14]. Does the rhetorical question and the shift to the second person singular ("you") address suggest that Paul has resumed the diatribe style (Jewett 2007, 792) or does it merely reflect his concern for the individual responsibilities of his audience? And does Paul refer to **the one in authority** or to God as **he** who **will commend** them?

Although government-honoring good citizenship is seldom rewarded, Jewett (2007, 793) calls attention to notable exceptions during the period when Paul wrote Romans. Since government's primary purpose is to restrain the irresponsible exercise of freedom, it naturally comes into collision with lawless persons. Those who exercise self-restraint should find no reason to fear the state. Paul advised his readers to promote the goodwill of the imperial bureaucracy, whose cooperation was essential to the success of his prospective mission to Spain.

■ **4** Since the state exists by divine ordination, submission to its authority is the responsibility of every individual. In v 4 Paul declares that the civil authority **is God's servant to do you** [*soi,* **you** (singular)] **good** [*agathon*]. The magistrate is God's ***minister*** (*diakonos,* **servant**) for **good** (in Wis 6:4 foreign rulers are called "servants of his [God's] kingdom" NRSV; in Isa 45:1 and Jer 25:9 Cyrus and Nebuchadnezzar are called servants of Yahweh). The fact that ***minister*** designates Paul's office (in Rom 11:13), that of other church leaders (in 12:7), and even of Christ (in 15:8) may explain his choice of this term, rather than the title of a more prestigious Roman official.

But if you [singular] **do wrong** [*kakon,* ***bad;*** see 7:19]**, be afraid, for he does not bear the sword for nothing. He is God's servant, an agent** [*ekdikos,* ***avenger;*** see 1 Thess 4:6] **of wrath** [*orgē n;* see Rom 12:19] **to bring punishment on the wrongdoer** [*to kakon prassonti,* v 4]. Clearly, Paul's broader understanding of what counts as service acceptable to God (12:7) does not limit ministry (*diakonia*) to the sacred realm of religious service (Dunn 2002b, 38B:764).

ROMANS

13:3-4

"The sword was carried, if not by, then before the magistrates, and symbolized the power of life and death" (Leenhardt 1957, 330), or at least "police powers and governmental coercion in a broader sense" (Jewett 2007, 795). The **sword** (see 8:35) was used by metonymy as "more a symbol of authority than a weapon" (Yoder 1972, 66). God has authorized his servants, the magistrates, to punish those who do wrong in his behalf, even to the exacting of capital punishment. Paul considered the government to have been assigned by God with the responsibility denied individual believers in 12:17 and 19—the right to take revenge on wrongdoers.

The Danger of Overgeneralization

Within a few years after writing this letter a fateful travesty occurred. Tacitus reports what happened to the audience receiving Paul's letter after the terrible Roman fire in the summer of 64 C.E.: "Nero substituted as culprits . . . , and punished with the utmost refinements of cruelty, a class of men, loathed for their vices, whom the crowd called Christians. . . . First, then, the confessed members of the sect were arrested; next, on their disclosures, vast numbers were convicted, not so much on the count of arson as for hatred of the human race. . . . And derision accompanied their end: they were

> covered with wild beasts' skins and torn to death by dogs; or they were fastened on crosses, and, when daylight failed were burned to serve as lamps by night. Nero had offered his Gardens for the spectacle, and gave an exhibition in his Circus" [Tacitus *Annales* 15.44]. It is obvious from Paul's formulation of 13:4 that no such travesty of law enforcement was envisioned as even remotely possible. (Jewett 2007, 796)

If anarchy is to be prevented, governing authorities must be invested with powers of repression and punishment. Paul's reasons (*gar,* **For**) for not resisting the government is that **Rulers hold . . . terror . . . for those who do wrong** [*tōi kakōi,* ***bad things;*** v 3]. But **those who do right** [*tōi agathōi ergōi,* ***good works;*** v 3] have no reason to **be afraid** (v 4).

> The citizen whose intention is to live in his sphere and play his part, without trespassing on the rights of his neighbour, is acting in the same sense as state authority and has nothing to fear from the latter; he is performing a good work for which he will be praised by the authority of the state. (Leenhardt 1957, 330)

Of course, our notions of citizenship did not apply to most of Paul's original readers, few of whom were Roman citizens, a right limited to an elite few. And not only wrongdoers were victims of Roman power.

Paul's own experience with government officials often contradicted
13:4-5 his common-sense observations here. Here he articulates the way things ought to be ideally. In actual practice, at times both the secular government and the synagogue were guilty of sponsoring or tolerating what can only be called injustices against Christians, punishing the good and rewarding the evil. Paul may be concerned that if Christians are to be persecuted, their suffering, like that of Christ, should be innocent and unjustified (see 1 Pet 2:19-25; 3:13-17; 4:12-19). Since Paul writes to the Romans with their specific political context in mind, we should be cautious about how we apply his advice to other situations.

> The rhetorical force of Paul's argument was clear for the original audience: the Spanish mission will not encourage illegal subversion against the empire. . . . The missional motivation of Paul's discourse may be commendable, but one cannot say the same of his assessment of the evil potential of totalitarian regimes, including the Neronian government then in power. (Jewett 2007, 796)

■ **5** Whether or not government officials properly execute their divinely sanctioned responsibilities, **Therefore** (*dio;* see 1:24; 2:1; 4:22), Paul calls upon the members of the Roman house and tenement churches **to submit to authorities** (v 5). They were to do this, **not only because of possible**

punishment for rebellion, **but also because of conscience.** Official sanctions were not to be treated lightly, but submission is a ***necessity*** (*anankē*) **because** (*dia*) Christians were not to violate their **conscience** (*syneidēsin;* see 2:15).

This statement seems to be Paul's conclusion (*dio*): An informed **conscience** (see 2:15; 9:1; 1 Cor 10:25, 27) recognizes the right of the state as ordered by God to command submission. Thus, Paul reminds his Roman audience that they are obliged to make responsible moral choices in the realm of government that will not violate their sense of what is right.

■ **6** The payment of **taxes** emphasized in v 6 is not just an illustration of what submissive subjects of the state do. It is the point Paul was preparing for in vv 1-5. **This is also why** [*dia touto gar*] **you** [plural] **pay taxes** [*phorous,* ***tribute***], **for the authorities are God's servants** [*leitourgoi*], **who give their full time to governing.** ***Tribute taxes*** (Latin: *tributum*) exacted of noncitizens—most of Paul's audience—occasioned a major tax-protest in A.D. 58 (reported in Tacitus *Annales* 13.50-51).

The shift in words for **servants** here reflects the change to a more particular issue, here taxation—officials charged with the collection of **taxes.** The *leitourg-* word group often involves cultic service (an argument for Nanos's position). In 15:16 Paul will describe himself as "a minister [*leitourgon*] of Christ Jesus to the Gentiles with the priestly duty of proclaiming the gospel of God." Elsewhere, he refers to other church workers using the same title (2 Cor 9:12; Phil 2:17, 25, 30). But in Rom 13:6 the term ***ministers*** is used with the secular force it has in the British parliamentary system.

Paul claims for tax collectors the same divine authority as other public officials (*diakonoi,* see v 4) wielded. The overall sense of v 6 requires an implied imperative: ***You ought to keep paying taxes!*** By making tax-paying a legitimate and necessary expression of worship in everyday life (12:1), "the division between sacred and secular for Paul has been broken down" (Dunn 2002b, 38B:767).

■ **7** In v 7 Paul generalizes: **Give** [*apodote;* see 15:27] **everyone what you owe him** (*tas opheilas*). That is, ***Pay your debts to everyone!*** The second person plural aorist imperative Greek verb conveys the timeless gnomic force: The community should always give back what it owes. The same verb in the same form appears in the Gospels in Jesus' saying concerning paying taxes (compare Matt 17:24-25; 22:21; Mark 12:13-17, 28-34; Luke 20:25).

The two lines of Rom 13:7*bc* offer neatly balanced rhyming couplets in Greek: **If you owe taxes** [*phoron*], **pay taxes** [*phoron*]**; if revenue** [*telos*], **then revenue** [*telos*]. *Phoros* is technically ***tribute*** [see v 6]; *telos,* ***direct tax***. Roman citizens were exempt from paying ***tribute*** (Latin: *tributum*) in

Rome. Everyone paid **revenue** (Latin: *vectigalia*)—sales taxes, revenues from rents, customs duty, and scores more (Byrne 1996, 392).

Paul continues: **if respect** [*phobon*, ***fear***], **then respect** [*phobon*]; **if honor** [*timēn*], **then honor** [*timēn*] (v 7*de*). There may be an allusion here to the saying of Jesus about rendering to Caesar his due—taxes; and, to God his due. If so, it is God, rather than earthly rulers, one should "fear" (Yoder 1972, 211). Scripture rarely has earthly rulers as the objects of "fear," whereas references to "fearing God"—in the sense of giving him reverence and respect—are regular (see 3:18; 11:20; Prov 24:21; Luke 1:50; 12:5; 18:2, 4; 23:40; 2 Cor 5:11; 7:1, 11; Phil 2:12; 1 Pet 2:17).

To interpret Rom 13:7*e* as an injunction to "fear" the "governing authorities" seems to contradict vv 3-4, where they are a terror only to wrongdoers. But the "theological" interpretation suggests an unexpected parity between God and human rulers. Formal considerations—constructing a rhetorically pleasing couplet—might have overridden theological sensitivities here.

FROM THE TEXT

Anabaptist communities of the radical Reformation took so seriously
13:1-7 the political implications of their baptismal confession that they effectively eliminated Rom 13:1-7 from their Bibles. They thought that Jesus' admonition, "You know that the rulers of the Gentiles lord it over them, and their high officials exercise authority over them. Not so with you" (Matt 20:25-26), exempted them from earthly obligations. Accordingly, Anabaptists refused to recognize civil authorities or to participate in civil government.

Popular interpretations of Paul's injunction to be submissive to earthly authorities, along with the rationale supporting it, has made Rom 13:1-7 one of the favorite passages for the ruling classes through the centuries. Theologies of divine rights of kings and of church-state relations have been built upon it. Worse still, autocratic, even demonic, governments have been defended by employing it. Believers who have found it obligatory to resist or seek to overthrow civic power in certain of its historical manifestations—most notably Nazi Germany—have found it an embarrassment, at best; at worst, something to be rejected in the name of Christ and the gospel. For some, it has been the most "hateful" passage in the Bible.

Modern sensibilities about the extraordinary measure of divine guarantee attributed to human rulers here have been reason enough to reject it as naive and simplistic to the extreme. In vv 1-7, Paul makes no explicit allowance for the abuse of power by human authorities, nor does he recognize that it may be good to protest on occasion in behalf of those who have felt the brunt of penal sanctions through either mistakes or overt miscarriages of justice. Paul's silence seems all the more remarkable in light of the known excesses of Nero, the Roman emperor when Paul wrote this letter. Did Paul live to regret his own advice when Nero unjustly ordered his execution by beheading? In cases where just government does not exist, does this passage still have any relevance?

Would Paul have agreed with Peter and John: "We must obey God rather than men!" (Acts 5:29; see 4:18-21)? Would he have granted that those who conscientiously object to unjust human laws should be prepared to accept the punishment the state dictates, since anarchy is contrary to the character of God (1 Cor 14:33)? Paul was convinced that the lords of this age would eventually answer to the Lord of all for their abuse of power (2 Thess 1:4-10; see Dan 4:13-17, 23-25; 5:20-21; Wis 6:4-5).

Paul's repeated concern in Rom 13:1-7 to avoid anarchy and to maintain public order should not be taken to endorse divinely tolerated injustice. It seems unlikely that he anticipated that believers beyond his first readers in Rome would be reading his letter centuries later, much less assumed that his advice to them would be considered timelessly applicable to all Christians everywhere.

We cannot ignore the unintended consequences of the application of traditional, mainstream Protestant interpretation of this passage. It has been mistakenly used to encourage, for example, silent consent to the evil and destructive politics of Hitler and the Nazi regime. Have the holocaust and weapons of mass destruction, for example, made vv 1-7 irrelevant?

In the United States, where Evangelical Christianity represents the dominant religious community, would Paul advise the same kind of pragmatic political quietism he recommended in the very different context of early Roman Christianity? Or would the same theo-logic applied to the American context lead Paul to call for a kind of activism that would make most socially conservative believers uncomfortable? Would he have urged that the same socially conservative Evangelical rationale supporting pro-life activism calls Christians to a similar concern to address the problem of global hunger?

Paul's advice in vv 1-7 is meaningless if it has no political implications. Nevertheless, the specificity of his advice that called for tangible expressions of genuine, self-sacrificial love within the life of the mid-first century house and tenement churches of Rome makes it impossible to apply all he says without thoughtfully reflecting on our specific situation vis-à-vis the government. If his proposed mission to Spain motivated his advice here, what missional considerations would dictate his advice in our setting?

> Romans 13:1-7 was not intended to create the foundation of a political ethic for all times and places in succeeding generations—a task for which it has proven to be singularly ill-suited. . . . [Paul's] goal was to appeal to the Roman audience as he conceived it, addressing their concerns in a manner that fit the occasion of his forthcoming visit. (Jewett 2007, 786-87)

Verses 1-7 do not address the situation of believers within the modern democratic state whose authority derives from the governed through a vote of the people. In such situations the theological rationale for the assertion that all authority, including civic authority, ultimately derives from God, must be nuanced, to say the least. Otherwise, we may be tempted to confuse the results of the latest opinion poll and political demagoguery with the will of God. Modern developments challenge the continuing relevance of the classical "theological" doctrine of church and state constructed on this passage.

What would Paul say to Christians in increasingly secular, post-Christian, Western Europe? or to Christians in the recently democratized Eastern European nations, many still facing the temptations of ethnic cleansing? or to the rapidly growing churches of South America and Africa? or to the underground churches of China? or to the churches in parts of the world confronted with increasingly intolerant Islamic theocracies? Verses 1-7 do not provide a simple one-size-fits-all answer to the question of the Christian's responsibility to government.

The text's reminder that no government is a law entirely unto itself would seem to be a timeless principle. From the perspective of believers, all rule, all exercise of human authority, is accountable to God, the supreme authority. Likewise, the conviction that civic responsibility forms part of the worship owed by "rational beings" (see 12:1) also remains.

In the present age in which the church finds itself, until the Parousia of the Lord, believers cannot withdraw from public responsibility and participation in civil government on the plea that their "citizenship is in heaven" (Phil 3:20). All is drawn before the bar of conscience and final accountability to God.

The irony of the history of interpretation of Rom 13:1-7 is noteworthy. Paul arrived in Rome much later than he anticipated, and as a prisoner, not as a missionary. It is unclear whether he was ever released to achieve his ambitious plans to evangelize Spain. We can be certain that in

Rome he was eventually tried and executed during Nero's reign (see Acts 28:16 and *1 Clem.* 5).

The political realism of Rom 13:1-7 reminds us that Paul was not unaware that worldly rulers and powers, far from facilitating the church's mission, might mean persecution, danger, and death (see 8:35-39). But he was convinced that none of these things could separate believers from the love of God in Christ. Paul himself was taken as a "sheep to be slaughtered" (v 36) at the hands of the civil authority. Thus, it is ironic that the warning that the authority "does not bear the sword for nothing" (13:4) should have served as the warrant for so many centuries for the unquestioning obedience of Christians to the state (Grieb 2002, 125).

(5) Love Fulfills the Law (13:8-10)

BEHIND THE TEXT

Within the pervasive patronage system of first-century Mediterranean society, it was taken for granted that reciprocity between patrons and clients should be carefully maintained. By accepting favors, clients implicitly promised to repay their patrons whenever and however they saw fit. Repayment might take the form of loyalty, service, and honor rendered to benefactors. By granting favors, patrons implicitly promised openness to future requests from their beneficiaries.

Mutual obligations such as these reflected and maintained social stability within a highly stratified society. Even among friends and social equals, similar mutual hospitality "debts"/expectations existed, obliging hosts and guests to return favors in equal or higher measure—to maintain reciprocity. Not surprisingly, patronage and hospitality arrangements sometimes "degenerated into petty favor seeking and manipulation . . . in an often desperate struggle to gain economic and political advantage" (Malina and Pilch 2006, 383).

Paul first uses the imagery of indebtedness in Romans to explain his eagerness to preach in Rome: "I am obligated [*opheiletēs*]" (1:14). He was, after all, called by his divine Patron to be an apostle to the Gentiles. The imagery appears again in his insistence that justification by faith is a gift rather than "an obligation" (*opheilēma;* 4:4). All believers are indebted to God, but God owes no one anything.

Because believers have received the gift of the Spirit, they "have an obligation" (*opheiletai*) not to live according to the Flesh (8:12). "God is the ultimate patron whose resources are graciously given" (Malina and Pilch 2006,

384). But God expects a return on his investment. In 15:1, Paul will insist that the "strong ought [*opheilomen*] to bear with the failings of the weak." The strong, who might normally expect to be patronized, were themselves clients of a divine Patron, who became weak that they might become strong (see 1 Cor 1:26-31). As his clients, they were to fulfill their obligations by serving their clients, the weak, as God had graciously served them in Christ through the Spirit.

Paul lists representative commandments from the Torah—**"Do not commit adultery," "Do not murder," "Do not steal," "Do not covet."** Undoubtedly, these four were not arbitrarily selected; they were critical to the life of the community. He insists that all the commandments are summarized and fulfilled in one from Lev 19:18*b*, **"Love your neighbor as yourself"** (v 9).

Leviticus 19:18*a*, which Paul does not quote (but see Rom 12:17-21), calls for the avoidance of vengeance: "Do not seek revenge or bear a grudge against one of your people, but love your neighbor as yourself. I am the LORD." John Howard Yoder insists that Rom 12 and 13 should be read together. This, he claims, suggests that the people of God, who are enjoined not to take vengeance, are deliberately contrasted with the citizens and administrators of the empire. The empire does not bear the sword in vain but is the servant of God to execute wrath on wrongdoers (1972, 198). It seems difficult, however, to sustain Yoder's claim that Paul's emphasis is to be found in the part of the quotation he omits.

Finally, the explicit focus in this passage on "love" resumes and completes the exhortation begun in 12:9 with the words "Love must be sincere." Thus the theme of "love" brackets the entire section from 12:9 to 13:10, including the otherwise intrusive passage on obedience to civil authorities. Paul does not mean to suggest that paying taxes ought to be inspired by love! But the bracketing does enfold all obligations, even the most mundane, within the one central response of love. No part of Christian life stands apart from the core command to love.

IN THE TEXT

■ **8** Paul uses the catchword "owe" to bridge 13:7—"Give everyone what you owe [*tas opheilas*] him"—and v 8—**Let no debt** [*opheilete*] **remain outstanding.** This suggests that it was his particular concern that Christians should pay their taxes to avoid unwanted attention from the government that motivated vv 1-7. In v 8, Paul contrasts owing **no debt** such as taxes, revenue, respect, and honor (v 7) to continuing **debt to love one another,** which ***fulfills*** [*peplērōken*] **the law.** "All other obligations are to be met, taken care of, paid off, so that believers are free to devote themselves to their new obligations" (Jewett 2007, 806).

The NASB translates the opening command literally: "Owe nothing to anyone." It would be anachronistic to understand Paul so literally as to forbid mortgages and other modern finance-purchase arrangements. His experience with **debt** undoubtedly reflects first-century expectations and pitfalls of reciprocity obligations.

It seems unlikely that Paul warns his Roman audience to avoid patronage entanglements entirely. If (as seems likely) most early Roman Christians came from the poorer strata of society, they could no more avoid being low-status clients than most of us can imagine quitting our day jobs to become self-employed. "Their former social obligations are to be replaced by a single new obligation to meet the needs of fellow members in the church" (Jewett 2007, 806).

Paul recommended **love** (*agapē*) rather than obligation alone as the basis for Christian community life (see Gal 5:13; 1 Thess 3:12; 4:9; 2 Thess 1:3). Once again, Paul's parenesis reminds his audience of the practical implications of ***genuine love*** (Rom 12:9). The obligation to love one another—their fellow believers—is a "never-ending debt" (Moo 1996, 810; following
Johannes Bengel). 13:8

Both loving **one another** (*allēlous;* v 8) and neighbor-love (v 10) might be taken to include only fellow believers (see 14:13, 19; 15:5, 7, 14; 16:16). Certainly, Jesus' parable of the Good Samaritan (Luke 10:29-37) challenged his Jewish audience's assumption that only fellow Israelites were their neighbors. The exhortations in the second person plural in Rom 13:8-9 refer to mutual love within the community as a whole. But the expression *ton heteron,* ***the other,*** in v 8 must refer to outsiders (see 7:3-4; 12:13, 14, 18, 20; Gal 6:10; 1 Thess 3:12; 5:15). Love must embrace everyone, not just the members of the particular Roman house or tenement church to which each belonged.

A few commentators read *ton heteron* with *nomon.* This allows the translation: ***For the one who loves has fulfilled the other law.*** But most recognize *ton heteron* as the direct object of *agapōn.* In Rom 13:8 Paul supports his commendation of love by speaking of it as **the fulfillment** [*plērōma*] **of the law** (v 10).

Greek uses singular nouns generically whereas English uses plurals for the same purpose. Thus, Paul's rationale (*gar,* **for**) should be translated: ***for those who love others have fulfilled the Law.*** His primary concern was not to challenge legal righteousness (see 3:31), nor to insist upon the mere compatibility of **love** and Law. His point was not simply to remind the Romans that the Law was the source of the love-command, thus, justifying his commendation of it. His claim is not that the imperative in Lev 19:18*b* is a timeless demand. It is that carrying out the love-command somehow *fulfills* the Law. No theory or theology of love could do that; love was to be put into practice.

The question as to what **fulfillment of the law** (v 10) might mean was raised earlier in the commentary on 8:4. There Paul claimed that God sent his Son ***in order that the just requirement of the Law might be fulfilled*** [*plērōthēi*] ***in us, who walk . . . according to the Spirit.*** In 8:4 Paul insisted that the Law is fulfilled but did not say *by whom*. His claim was that the Law is fulfilled ***in us*** (*en hēmin*), not "by us" (*hyp' hēmōn*).

But, of course, Spirit-filled Christians are the ones Paul expects to live according to the Spirit and actually to love others. Thus, no sharp distinction between "in" and "by" can be maintained. Paul's theological conviction seems to be that the wherewithal to love is actually the achievement of Christ through the power of the Holy Spirit. But this does not prevent him from claiming that ***those who love others have fulfilled the Law*** in 13:8.

If the perfect tense of Paul's verb ***have fulfilled*** is significant, the im-
13:8 perative to remain debt-free except for **the continuing debt to love one another,** gives the perfect tense a timeless, gnomic quality. If so, Paul insists that all who love others always fulfill the Law by doing so. The Greek verb *pleroō* literally refers to the filling of an empty container. But what does this mean as applied to the Law? In what figurative sense have ***those who love others*** filled the Law?

Does Paul claim that those who obey the love-command completely and essentially observe all that the Law really requires? Does loving others make attention to other legal requirements unnecessary? Or is loving others simply the entry point for observing the rest of the Law with undiminished rigor? Paul does not seem to be saying the reverse of Jas 2:10—"whoever keeps [*tērēsēi*] the whole law and yet stumbles at just one point is guilty of breaking all of it."

In Gal 5:14 Paul maintained: "The entire law is summed up [*peplērōtai*] in a single command: 'Love your neighbor as yourself.'" But there fulfillment of ***all the Law*** seems to be distinguished from obeying (*poiēsai*, ***doing***) "the whole law," which Paul characterizes negatively in Gal 5:3. Thus, he does not seem to claim in Galatians "that one fulfills/performs the many requirements of the Law by fulfilling/performing the one requirement of neighbor love" (Martyn 1997, 488). But this does not determine what Paul means here.

■ **9** In v 9 Paul refers to the commandment to love our neighbors as ourselves as summarizing (*anakephalaioutai*) all the other commandments. Does the proximity of this statement with those referring to **the fulfillment of the law** on either side of it (vv 8 and 10) suggest that loving others **fulfilled the law** by simplifying its 613 specific requirements into one comprehensive task? Several modern translations of Gal 5:14 translate *pleroō* on this assumption: "For the whole law is summed up in a single commandment" (NRSV).

Does love fulfill the Law in the sense that a prophecy or promise is fulfilled—by bringing it to completion (see Rom 15:19; Matt 1:22; John 13:18)? Does loving others exhaustively complete the Law, thereby bringing the necessity of Law to an end? If so, Paul's claim here is comparable to 1 Tim 1:9 "that law is made not for the righteous but for lawbreakers." Loving others (as opposed to doing something else) fulfills the Law in the sense of perfecting it, compensating for its deficiencies, making it all God intended it to be and accomplish (see John 15:11; Phil 2:2). But "it would be premature to claim that love 'replaces' the law for the Christian, as if the only commandment both to chastise and to guide us" (Moo 1996, 815).

> What the Judaism of Paul's time sought was the keeping or performing of the law (including the provision of atonement), not some ideal of sinless perfection. . . . The dispute between Paul and his fellow Pharisees therefore was about what fulfillment = performance of the law really involves. (Dunn 2002b, 38B:777)

Paul insists that loving others fulfills the Law.

As over against the views of Jewish Christians in his audience, who had been taught to see in the Torah the sole and indispensable guide to righteousness, Paul offers love as a sufficient and more fundamental basis. Thus, he clarifies the point he made so emphatically in Rom 2:13: "It is not those who hear the law who are righteous in God's sight, but it is those who obey [*hoi poiētai*] the law who will be declared righteous." Loving others is essentially what obedience demands.

In 13:9 Paul lists four representative commandments from the Decalogue relating to conduct toward neighbors—prohibitions against adultery, murder, stealing, and coveting. These commands selected from the second table of the Decalogue (Exod 20:14, 13, 15, 17; Deut 5:18, 17, 19, 21; see Rom 2:21-22) specifically concern duties toward others. The ordering of these commandments, which does not follow either the MT or LXX, is the same as that in Luke 18:20 and Jas 2:11. Paul mentions none of the commands of the first table concern obligations toward God (including the controversial Sabbath command; see Rom 14:5-6).

Following Jesus (Matt 5:32; 19:8; Mark 10:11-12), and unlike most of his Jewish and Greco-Roman contemporaries, Paul understood the command, **"Do not commit adultery,"** to protect "the sexual rights of both men and women." It strictly forbade "sexual relations for both males and females outside of covenantal boundaries" (Jewett 2007, 810). The command, **"Do not murder,"** was stressed because of "the high incidence of crime and vigilantism in the slums of Rome" (Jewett 2007, 811). Similarly, **"Do not steal"** was relevant under such conditions, since "widespread poverty made theft appealing as well as damaging" (Jewett 2007, 812). Paul's abbreviated version of the command, **"Do not covet"** (see Exod 20:17; Deut 5:21) reflects its adaptation to an urban, egalitarian setting.

Paul insists that all the commands of the second table—**whatever other commandment there may be**—are summed up in one command, not from the Ten Commandments, but from Lev 19:18*b:* **"Love your neighbor as yourself."** Paul does not mean that all commandments are reduced to love but that love expressed in this way constitutes the essence of the matter. The person who truly loves in this way will be found to have fulfilled all the commandments of the Law bearing on duties to neighbor.

Paul and Jesus before him stand within a long Jewish tradition in summarizing the entire Law in a single fundamental principle. The Christian principle is different. "Explicit references to Lev 19:18 are lacking in Jewish tradition prior to Paul, and the allusions to it show that it was given no particular prominence." But it is "the passage in all the Pentateuch most frequently cited by NT writers" (Matt 5:43; 19:19; Mark 12:31, 33; Gal 5:14; Jas 2:8; see Dunn 2002b, 38B:778-79).

Paul, following Jesus, does not limit the application of the command to **"Love your neighbor as yourself"** to fellow Israelites, as did most Jewish interpreters before him. Nor does he make self-love the basis of neighbor-love. Despite the claims of some popular contemporary preachers, high self-esteem is not the foundational truth of the Christian gospel. The gospel calls for honest self-examination (Rom 12:3; Gal 6:3-4; Phil 2:3), not self-exaltation. But Paul would not consider self-love a mark of human sinfulness (against Cranfield 1979, 2:677).

■ **10** The following statement—**Love does no harm** [*kakon, **evil;*** see Rom 2:9-10] **to its neighbor** (v 10)—seems negative and inadequate at first glance (see Tob 4:15). Surely love demands more than not harming another person. But the negative is precisely the point. The illustrative commandments cited are prohibitions; they all proscribe things that would harm the neighbor. Together they proscribe what would restrain harmful actions (see Rom 7:7).

Love, as a positive prescription, includes and goes beyond what the Law prohibits (see 1 Cor 13:4-7). It invites us to place ourselves precisely in the position of our neighbors and allow our actions to flow from the question, "What would I desire in this situation?" rather than "What ought I to do, or to refrain from doing, with reference to this person?" Love fulfills the Law because those who love do nothing the Law forbids, and more than the Law requires (Gal 5:23*b;* see Matt 5:43-48). Paul's concern is not "a sentimental but unrealistic idealism" (Dunn 2002b, 38B:783), nor the proper observance of *agapē* meals (Jewett 2007, 813-15), but concrete expressions of self-giving love like that modeled by Christ (see Rom 15:1-3).

FROM THE TEXT

In view of the central thesis of Romans that believers are essentially freed from the Law (3:21—4:25; 7:1—8:4), readers might puzzle over Paul's insistence that the Law is something to be "fulfilled." Paul clearly expected Christians to obey God. Did he believe that the central ethical values of the Law—as distinct from the ritual prescriptions regarding circumcision, dietary rules, and calendar regulations—remained in force for believers? He nowhere makes explicit such a distinction within the Law. In fact, nowhere does such a distinction between the moral and ceremonial law appear to have been made in Judaism as a whole.

Rather than distinguishing "within" the content of the Law, Paul appears to affirm in the present passage that there is a distinction between what the Law prescribes as law and the values it enshrines as the ethical requirements of the Law. The moral law is not something imposed upon believers from without. Rather, it is "accomplished" within believers through the gift of the indwelling Spirit (8:4, 9-11), who realizes the promises for the eschatological age found in passages such as Jer 31:33 and Ezek 36:24-27.

Despite John Wesley's emphasis on "Christian perfection" and the optimism of grace that promised the experience of "perfect love" in this life, he was equally adamant that he did not mean by this "sinless perfection." The grammar of Rom 3:23 must be taken seriously: all—presumably, including believers, even entirely sanctified ones—continually fall short of the glory of God.

Perhaps 13:8-10 calls for an extension of what Wesley called "the repentance of believers." The call to love others as we love ourselves must be the constant aspiration of the truly sanctified. But when does this aspiration become perfect achievement?

In Wesley's sermon "The Scripture Way of Salvation" (1979, 6:43-54), he treats the self-knowledge and repentance that should occur when the Spirit reveals remaining sin in the hearts of believers and enables them to turn completely to Christ to be thoroughly sanctified.

Wesley believed that the sanctified enjoy and express "pure love to God and man" (1979, 11:397, in *A Plain Account of Christian Perfection*). In "The Scripture Way of Salvation," he defines "perfect love" as "love excluding sin, love filling the heart, taking up the whole capacity of the soul" (1979, 6:46).

Wesley carefully qualifies his teaching on Christian perfection throughout his sermons and letters. He cautions those who profess "pure love to God and man":

> Remember, on the other hand that you have this treasure in an earthen vessel. . . . Hence all your thoughts, words, and actions are so imperfect, so far as coming up to the standard . . . that you may say till you go up to Him you love,
>
> Every moment, Lord, I need
> The merit of thy Death. (1931, 4:208)

13:8-10 Elsewhere Wesley acknowledges, "A perfection such as enables a person to fulfill the whole law, and so needs not the merits of Christ—I acknowledge no such perfection; I do now and always protest against it" (1979, 12:257). In *A Plain Account of Christian Perfection* he further qualifies his distinguishing doctrine:

> The best of men still need Christ in his priestly office, to atone for their omissions, their short-comings, (as some not improperly speak,) their mistakes in judgment and practice, and their defects of various kinds. For these are all deviations from the perfect law, and consequently need an atonement. Yet that they are not properly sins, we apprehend may appear from the words of St. Paul, "He that loveth, hath fulfilled the law; for love is the fulfilling of the law." (Rom. xiii. 10.) Now, mistakes, and whatever infirmities necessarily flow from the corruptible state of the body, are noway contrary to love; nor therefore, in the Scripture sense, sin.
>
> To explain myself a little farther on this head: (1.) Not only sin, properly so called, (that is, a voluntary transgression of a known law,) but sin, improperly so called, (that is, an involuntary transgression of a divine law, known or unknown,) needs the atoning blood. (2.) I be-

lieve there is no such perfection in this life as excludes these involuntary transgressions which I apprehend to be naturally consequent on the ignorance and mistakes inseparable from mortality. (3.) Therefore sinless perfection is a phrase I never use, lest I should seem to contradict myself. (4.) I believe, a person filled with the love of God is still liable to these involuntary transgressions. (5.) Such transgressions you may call sins, if you please: I do not, for the reasons abovementioned. (1979, 11:396)

For too long, Wesleyans have quibbled among themselves and with believers from other Christian traditions over whether a particular failure of love is to be labeled a sin or only a mistake. This misses Wesley's central point: We all continually need the atoning merit of Christ's death. A more contemporary ethical doctrine of "the repentance of believers" will take into account the crying needs of today's world for justice and compassion.

We need not debate whether we bear individual guilt for (say) the bloated-bellied children whose images on the evening news briefly grab our attention until forgetfulness sets in again. Do we imagine that entire sanctification means that there is nothing more God longs to do within our communities of faith to conform us to the likeness of Christ?

The tension in Christian perfection is that between the "already" and the "not yet" of Rom 8:18-27. In this "time between the times," the "glory" of the divine image lost in the fall is being progressively restored in those who walk in loving obedience until they are finally and perfectly "conformed to the likeness of his Son" (v 29).

In light of the scriptural paradox—perfect and not yet perfect (Phil 3:7-16)—we must locate our profession of holiness on this side of the polarity of "this present age" and "the age to come." Awareness that we have not yet reached the goal should keep us "straining toward what is ahead, . . . the goal to win the prize for which God has called [us] heavenward in Christ Jesus" (vv 13-14). "For in this hope we were saved" (Rom 8:24).

The paradox of perfection found in the NT should urge contemporary Wesleyans to seek Wesley's balance between insisting upon the possibilities of grace and acknowledging the tragic realities of modern life, lest we fall into the trap of perfectionism. We cannot lightly dismiss the overwhelming demands of loving our six and one-half billion neighbors in a global village in which two-thirds lack the basic necessities of life. Can we conform to the conspicuous consumption of our culture? Can we claim to have fulfilled the law of love by merely treating well those we know personally?

Modern Western employment patterns have fundamentally replaced the patronage system. Vestiges of it linger on in, for example, the implicit expectations of equitably reciprocated wedding and Christmas gifts. But do we know the joy of spontaneous, unselfconscious, love-motivated generosity that gives so that the left hand does not know what the right hand is doing and expects nothing in return (see Matt 5:43-48; 6:2-4)?

We can only guess what Paul (or Wesley) might say to modern Western believers (including Wesleyans), entangled by the enslaving chains of consumerism and acquisitiveness. Have love of money, self-absorption, and conspicuous consumption replaced other-love as the motivating principles of our families and churches?

How many believers do you know who find themselves so strapped with debt they are obliged to work long hours just to make ends meet? who are committed to lengthy commutes so they can afford "the right house"? who are drowning in a sea of expensive "toys" and perpetual noise? who have no time for the all-consuming kind other-love Paul commends here? Are you one of them?

Do we even know our neighbors, much less love them? The temptations of easy credit are no less dangerous than those of the patronage system within which Paul advised, "Owe nothing to anyone except to love one another" (Rom 13:8 NASB).

3. An Ethic of the Dawn (13:11-14)

BEHIND THE TEXT

These verses bring to a conclusion what Paul began in 12:1-2. He opens this exhortation to practical Christian living on an eschatological note. This is reminiscent of his appeal for his audience not to be conformed "any longer to the pattern of this world" but to "be transformed by the renewing of [their] mind[s]" (12:1-2). Here, he concludes his general parenesis on the same eschatological note. Appeal to eschatological accountability as the basis for exhortation is comparatively widespread throughout the NT (see Matt 24:37—25:46; Mark 13:33-37; Eph 5:16; Phil 4:4-7; Col 4:5; 1 Thess 5:1-11; Heb 10:26; Jas 5:7-11; 1 Pet 4:7).

Brendan Byrne characterizes the exhortation as a swift flow of associated metaphors, all proceeding from the basic image of people awakening from sleep at dawn. The text appears to be a baptismal hymn, which Paul elaborated to serve his immediate purposes. Byrne reconstructs the original from Rom 13:11-12:

It is already the hour for you to wake from sleep;

The night is far spent, the day is at hand.
Let us then cast off the works of darkness
And put on the armor of light. (Byrne 1996, 398; compare Jewett 2007, 817-18; see Eph 5:14)

Paul's elaborations on the hymn would consist of the introductory Rom 13:11*a* and the explanatory v 11*c*, then the more specific exposition of "the works of darkness" in v 13 and the exposition of "the armor of light" in terms of "clothing yourselves with the Lord Jesus Christ" (Byrne 1996, 398).

The entire paragraph has a hortatory tone, although the first imperative verbs (in the second person plural—"you") do not appear until v 14—**clothe yourselves** and ***do not make.*** In v 11, the command to **do this** actually translates an adverbial participle, the imperative force of which depends entirely on its context. In vv 12 and 13, Paul's first person plural hortatory subjunctive verbs—**let us put aside** and **let us behave**—modestly include himself with his audience in the exhortation to appropriate behavior.

IN THE TEXT

■ **11 And do this, understanding the present time** (v 11). Paul reinforces the appeal by calling attention to the particularly significant **present time** 13:11
(*kairon;* see 3:26; 5:6; 8:18; 9:9; 11:5; 1 Cor 7:29)—the now (*nyn;* see Rom 3:21; 5:9) in which believers stand—the "overlap of the ages." Outwardly the old age still lingers—suffering and death persist, and the "flesh" continues to allure (13:14*b;* see 8:5-8). Inwardly, however, believers already discern in the resurrection of Jesus and the gift of the Spirit the dawning of a new age, ushering in a total transformation of relationships—with God and one another.

Paul takes for granted that his audience shares this **understanding** [*eidotes,* ***knowing***] of generally accepted Jewish-Christian apocalyptic convictions (e.g., 5:3; 6:9; 1 Cor 15:58). Those who glimpse **the present age** through the thin outer shell of the old age that is passing (see 7:31*b*) discern the dawning but not-yet here new reality (see Rom 8:22). As a result, this new reality, which will soon outwardly and finally prevail (see 1 Cor 15:24-28), already begins to reshape their lives.

Paul develops the call to such discernment of **the present time** by introducing the imagery that controls the entire paragraph—a person awaking from sleep at dawn. The clinical intensification comes from the sense that the decisive, divinely appointed final **hour has come** (see Dan 8:17,

19; 11:35, 40; John 4:23; 5:25; 1 John 2:18; Rev 3:3, 10; Dunn 2002b, 38B:785). It is time **to wake up** [*egerthēnai, **to be raised***] **from *our* slumber, because our salvation is nearer** [*engyteron*] **now than when we first believed** [*episteusamen, **we exercised faith***]. Paul returns to the theme of the letter announced in Rom 1:16, reminding his audience that "the salvation of everyone who believes" has a point of beginning (see 10:9, 14, 16; 1 Cor 3:5; 15:2; Gal 2:16). This probably explains the aorist tense.

The imagery of **slumber** (*hypnos*) under a variety of terms is common among NT authors (Matt 24:43; 25:5; Mark 13:35-36; Luke 12:37; John 11:11-15; 1 Cor 15:6, 18, 20, 34, 51; Eph 5:14; 6:18; Rev 3:2-3; 16:15). Paul is capable of using it in multiple senses, even within the same passage. For example, in 1 Thess 4 and 5, "those who fall asleep [*tōn koimōmenōn*]" refer to "the dead in Christ" (4:13, 16; see also vv 14, 15), in contrast to the living, who are "awake" (5:10). Those "who are asleep [*katheudōmen*]" (v 6) are morally insensitive and undisciplined unbelievers, who are "drunk" (v 7). Believers, who are alert and sober, "belong to the day" (v 8).

Perhaps Paul's eschatological expectations of the future resurrection of believers closely associated the physically and morally dead. The Greek infinitive translated **to wake up** elsewhere in the NT refers only to the resurrection of Christ (see, e.g., Matt 16:21). Paul's appeal should not be taken to suggest that he considered the Roman Christians morally lax or
13:11 lethargic and in need of revitalization. By alluding to a familiar hymn, he merely reminded them of what they already knew. Reminded of their past baptism, the present privilege of participating in the love feast, they are to celebrate the critical hour in which they live, anticipating the Parousia and messianic banquet yet to come (Jewett 2007, 820).

As elsewhere in Paul, **salvation** refers, negatively, to the final rescue of believers from God's wrath at the time of the Judgment (Rom 2:5, 8, 9; 5:9; see Gal 1:4; 1 Thess 1:10; 5:8-9). Positively, it means full entrance into all the blessings in store for the eschatological people of God—"the glory that will be revealed in us" (Rom 8:18), "the redemption of our bodies" (v 23), "glory, honor and immortality . . . eternal life" (2:7). Paul personalizes this as **our salvation**—the rescue and redemption we hope for (see 8:24-25; 2 Cor 1:6; Phil 1:28; 2:12).

There is a sense in which the old age has already ended and the new begun (2 Cor 5:17), or at least nearly so (1 Cor 7:31). On the other hand, the two ages seem paradoxically to coincide and collide (vv 29-31; 2 Cor 6:8-10). Here Paul suggests that presently, believers live between "justification" (in which their relationship with God has been established by faith) and salvation in the full future sense. Thus, the appropriateness of the imagery of awakening at dawn: The evidence that the night is over is palpable on the eastern horizon. But the darkness lingers.

The "gap" between initial justification and final salvation has, for believers from Paul's day to the present, stretched wider than he apparently envisioned. But this does not undercut his essential argument, which is anchored in the hope created by the resurrection, not upon a particular calculation of time (Rom 13:11). In the Christ event, God apocalyptically invaded the old age to bring into being the community of the new age.

This eschatological conviction is the underlying assumption of all early Christian ethics. In the Spirit, Christians have already experienced "the powers of the coming age" (Heb 6:5). Ethical exhortation does not fall upon the deaf ears of helpless slaves to Sin. The indwelling Spirit makes genuine obedience possible. Convinced of this, contemporary believers may still share Paul's conviction that the new age is dawning, transforming those who see in Christ the decisive turning of the ages. The passing of nearly two millennia since Paul wrote these words should not dull the sense of ethical and missional urgency for believers today. Should it not motivate us all the more? We still have time—unexpected time—for progress in Christlikeness.

■ **12** The "hymn" resumes with the announcement, **The night is nearly over; the day** [*hēmera*] **is almost here** (v 12*a*). **The night** refers to the old age; **the day,** to the new (see John 9:4; 11:10; 1 Thess 5:2-8; Rev 21:25; 22:5). The verb *proekopsen,* **is nearly over,** refers to time that has ***advanced*** to the point of being ***far gone*** (Bauer 1979, 707). It is now later than it has ever been! The bright light of the resurrection of Christ and the gift of the Spirit were evidence enough that morning was coming. Even in the deep darkness of **the present time** Paul's hope was buoyed by the conviction that it was always darkest before dawn (Stählin 1968, 6:716).

Paul's point was neither to curse the darkness, nor to predict its immediate end. It was, instead, to identify the lingering **present,** dark as it was, as an opportune, blessed, fortuitous, favorable time for making progress (see Stählin 1968). Unexpectedly, although the end has drawn near, we still have time to act in the present. The perfect tense verb *ēngiken* (**is almost here;** see *engyteron,* **nearer,** in Rom 13:11; Phil 4:5*b*) has the same impression it has in Jesus' announcement of the imminent coming of the kingdom of God (Matt 4:17; Mark 1:15; see Rom 14:17). The new age has drawn near, but it is not yet here. The eschatological conviction of the paradoxical dawning and delay of the new age serves as the basis for Paul's ethical summons that follows.

Given the simultaneous proximity and postponing of the eschaton,

Paul exhorts: **So let us put aside the deeds of darkness and put on the armor of light** (v 12*b*). In the ancient world (and still in societies where electricity is unavailable) the prudent rose at dawn in order to take full advantage of the light of the day. "Early morning, before the heat of day, was and is a period of great activity in the east" (Dunn 2002b, 38B:787). The imagery of awaking from sleep may continue with a call to put aside the bedcovers and prepare for the day's activity. But if the baptismal imagery used elsewhere (Eph 4:22, 25; Col 3:8) is present here, the image shifts to that of changing clothes, putting off nightwear and putting on work clothes, more specifically arming oneself for battle.

At the same time, the imagery of night and day has subtly shifted to **darkness** and **light**. In the phrase **the deeds** [*ta erga*, ***the works***] **of darkness,** those who have followed the argument of the entire letter to this point may hear faint echoes of Paul's earlier warnings against reliance on ***works of law*** (see Rom 2:15; 3:20, 28). These works similarly represent adherence to the doomed structures of the old, passing age.

But ***works of darkness*** refer not to counterproductive human efforts at self-salvation, but, as 13:13 will make clear, to the evil deeds of godless humanity (see chs 1—3; esp. 2:9). "More than in our own times it was believed among the Romans that during the night everything was permitted" (M. J. Lagrange cited in Dunn 2002b, 38B:789). Darkness was thought to
13:12 cloak "activities understood to be shameful or unlawful" (Jewett 2007, 822). But Paul calls upon Christians to live their lives as if in the open light of God's coming day (see 1 John 1:5-10).

Believers must shed entirely all such garments of their old lives as slaves to Sin. "The imagery of putting off/putting on was common in earliest Christian parenesis . . . perhaps reflecting a widespread pattern of exhorting new converts and baptisands" (Dunn 2002b, 38B:784). Such imagery strongly hints at the original baptismal context for this "hymn," which serves to remind believers to live out the implications of their conversion and baptism (see Matt 4:16; John 3:19; Acts 26:18; 2 Cor 4:6; 6:14; Eph 4:22, 25; 5:8-14; 6:11, 14; Col 1:12-13; 3:8, 12; 1 Thess 5:4-9; Jas 1:21; 1 Pet 2:1, 9-10).

On the positive side, Paul does not invite his audience to don "works of light." Instead, he urges them figuratively to **put on** [*endysōmetha*] **the armor** [*hopla*] **of light** (see Job 29:14; Ps 132:9; Wis 5:18; 2 Cor 5:3; 6:7; Eph 6:11; Col 3:12; 1 Thess 5:8). Of course, baptized Christians are to avoid evil and do good (Rom 2:7; 6:1-4; 13:3). They are to be "blameless and pure, children of God without fault in a crooked and depraved generation, in which [they] shine like stars in the universe" (Phil 2:15).

Although they "were once darkness" (Eph 5:8), believers are now to have "nothing to do with the fruitless deeds of darkness, but rather expose [*elenchete*] them"—i.e., to bring them into the light (v 11). The new clothing Paul invited Christians to put on was not to be a disguise. It was to reveal their true identity in Christ as the transformed people of God (Jewett 2007, 832).

Furthermore, believers have a crucial mission to accomplish in the unexpected time granted by the overlap of the ages. They are to take God's side in the final apocalyptic struggle against the rebellious forces that resist his right to rule (see 1 Cor 15:20-28). They are not merely to be spectators in the struggle between the forces of light and darkness. They have been enlisted as soldiers. They are to equip themselves to do battle with the demonic forces ruling the "present evil age" (Gal 1:4; see Eph 6:10-17; 1 Thess 5:5-8). Elsewhere in Romans, *hopla* appears only in 6:13. There Paul exhorts believers:

> Do not offer the parts of your body to sin, as instruments [*hopla*] of wickedness, but rather offer yourselves to God, as those who have been brought from death to life; and offer the parts of your body to him as instruments [*hopla*] of righteousness.

This is one of the images Paul exploits to characterize the life of sanctification in ch 6. Holy living entails more than separation from evil. As people wholly possessed by God, Paul invites believers to enlist in God's struggle to bring all of rebellious creation into subjection to Christ (see 1 Cor 15:20-28, 57-58; 2 Cor 6:7; 10:4). The ongoing process begins, of course, with their offering to God the part of the world they are (see Rom 12:1-2).

By submitting to their rightful Lord, they become his ***weapons*** in final eschatological battle. Only those thus "armed" to face the lingering darkness will be able to survive and overcome in the present time (Rom 13:12-13). In light of vv 1-7, the battle in which believers are engaged is not to be conceived in terms of literal warfare. They are not invited to take up the same weapons used by Rome, but instead the metaphorical **armor** that consists of **light** (see 2 Cor 10:3-5; Eph 6:10-18).

■ **13** Paul explains what it means to **put on the armor of light** (Rom 13:12) in more prosaic terms in v 13*a:* **Let us behave decently, as in the daytime** [*hēmera, **day***]. Paul expects all believers to conduct themselves in an ethically appropriate manner. The verb he characteristically uses to describe this literally refers to walking (*peripatēsōmen:* ***Let us walk;*** see 6:4; 8:4; 14:15), following standard LXX practice (see Seesemann 1964).

The adverb **decently** translates *euschēmonōs* (see 1 Thess 4:12), which is derived from the same Greek root translated "conform"—*syschēmatizō*—in Rom 12:2. Conformity involves character formed by reference to (*syn-*, ***together with***) ***the pattern of this age.*** Respectable behavior (Mark 15:43; 1 Cor 14:40), however, calls for character formed by reference to the good (*eu-*).

Paul does not hesitate to call his audience "to observe the conventional respectability of his day; he does not press for a Christian ethic distinctive in every element" (see Rom 12:17; 13:3; Dunn 2002b, 38B:789). Christian morality is not necessarily always countercultural; but it is always appropriate to God's new age that is dawning.

In v 13*b* Paul illustrates the nature of indecent, improper behavior—**the deeds of darkness.** He mentions three pairs of forbidden vices: **not in orgies and drunkenness, not in sexual immorality and debauchery, not in dissension and jealousy.** The first four terms are all in the plural. *Kōmoi*, festal banquets honoring Dionysus, the Greek god of wine, associated, as they always were, with **drunkenness** (*methais; **drunkennesses***), caused Jews and Christians to characterize all such uninhibited "wild parties" (NCV) and "revelry" (NKJV) negatively as **orgies** and "carousing" (NASB; see Wis 14:23; 2 Macc 6:4; Luke 21:34; Gal 5:21; 1 Pet 4:3). Perhaps the two words should "be translated as a hendiadys—'drunken revelry'" (Dunn 2002b, 38B:789).

The term *koitē* is used in the NT in an entirely neutral sense referring to a bed (Luke 11:7) or by metonymy to marital intercourse (as in the English "coitus"; see Rom 9:10; Heb 13:4; see 1 Cor 7:2-5). But in the present context, its plural form must refer to *"sexual excesses"* (Bauer 1979, 440), "sexual promiscuity" (Rom 13:13 NASB), or **sexual immorality,** as in the contemporary euphemism "sleeping around" (TM). Its twin sexual vice, *aselgeia,* refers to **debauchery,** promiscuous, violent, and licentious indulgence in sensuality (see 2 Cor 12:21 and Gal 5:19, linked with *akatharsia, **impurity,*** and *porneia, **fornication***). "Perhaps again translation as a hendiadys is appropriate, 'debauched sexual excess'" (Dunn 2002b, 38B:789).

The third set of twin terms (see 1 Cor 3:3; 2 Cor 12:20; Gal 5:20; Jas 3:14, 16) are social vices. The Greek term *eris,* translated **dissension** here, may also be rendered "strife" (Rom 1:29), "quarrels" (1 Cor 1:11; see 3:3), "discord" (Gal 5:20), "rivalry" (Phil 1:15), or "arguments" (Titus 3:9). Like several other terms in the list, *zēlos* may be used in a favorable sense (religious zeal or fervor in John 2:17; Rom 10:2; 2 Cor 9:2; Phil 3:6). But here it has the negative sense of **jealousy** or "envy" (NKJV)—competition run amuck. As a hendiadys, the pair might be translated "jealous infighting."

■ **14** Abandoning the filthy "wardrobe" of their old, pre-Christian lives, Paul urges his hearers: **Rather, clothe yourselves with** [*endysasthe,* "put on"

NASB] **the Lord Jesus Christ, and do not think about how to gratify the desires of the *Flesh*** (v 14). To "put on" Christ is to be transformed by the renewed humanity of the new age, modeled and facilitated by "the last Adam," the risen Lord (Rom 5:12-21; 8:29-30; 12:1-2; 1 Cor 15:45-49, 53-54; 2 Cor 3:18; Gal 3:27; Phil 3:21). As in Col 3:9-12 and Eph 4:24, the "indicative" associated with conversion and baptism appears here as an "imperative"—"put on." As in ch 6, Paul's Roman audience is urged not to seek rebaptism but to take seriously all their baptism symbolized.

The conformity to the risen Lord is radically established in conversion. Baptism marks the beginning of a lifelong task of allowing that conformity to find expression in a Spirit-transformed pattern of life (see Rom 6:3-5; 12:1). In fact, Paul refers to the entire Christian life from justification to glorification, the process of sanctification, as progressive conformity to the image of Christ (8:29; see 2 Cor 3:18). Paul's invitation to the pursuit of Christlikeness is not contingent on the correctness of his imminent expectation of the end in Rom 13:11.

Clothing oneself with the Lord Jesus Christ requires taking a firm stance against ***the Flesh*** (*sarx;* see Gal 5:16, 24; Eph 2:3; 2 Pet 2:10, 18; 1 John 2:16; and the sidebar following the commentary on Rom 7). The list describing behaviors typically associated with the night closely resembles "the works of the flesh" (NRSV) in Gal 5:19-21. They are all manifestations of the Flesh, i.e., humanity left to its own devices, weak, vulnerable to Sin, hostile to God, and oriented toward Death (Rom 8:5-8).

There is a fundamental difference between life dominated by the Spirit (7:6; 8:1-13) and life dominated by Sin (7:5-8, 14-25). Formerly, believers lived in the Flesh, for selfish ends, as helpless slaves to Sin. Paul insists that believers have been freed from Sin to live a new kind of life in Christ (ch 6). It is actually possible for believers to heed the imperative: **do not think about how to gratify the desires** [*eis epithymias;* see 6:12] ***of the Flesh.*** But how?

The expression translated **do not think about** in Greek, *pronoian mē poieisthe,* is literally ***do not make plans.*** The English verb **think** translates a Greek compound, consisting of the prepositional prefix *pro-* and the noun *voia,* literally "forethought" (see the verb *pronoeō* on 12:17). Paul continues to describe the transforming work of God in the lives of believers in terms of renewed minds (*noos* in 12:2; see the words associated with thinking in 12:3 and 16 in the commentary).

Empowered by the Spirit (ch 8), the renewed minds (*vous*) of believers are being progressively transformed (see 12:1-2) so that they may actually and already live as citizens of the new age (see 6:4-7). Scriptural holiness involves the actualization of the confession of **the Lord Jesus Christ** (see 1:7). Where the Lord-designate of the new age (see 1 Cor 15:20-28) actually rules, the eschatological community already exists as the holy people of God.

Thus, it is not surprising that Paul turns next, in Rom 14:1—15:13, to practical guidance for life within the new community. There, it will become clear that to be clothed **with the Lord Jesus Christ** and to refuse **to gratify** self-centered individual interests of ***the Flesh*** demands that everyone within the community "accept one another . . . just as Christ accepted" them (15:7).

FROM THE TEXT

One summer day in the year A.D. 386 the brilliant but licentious Augustine of Hippo in North Africa, professor of rhetoric at Milan, sat weeping in the garden of his friend Alypius. Having fled the prayers of his godly mother, Monica, he had, in answer to those prayers, come under the influence of Bishop Ambrose's preaching in Milan.

As he sat that day in the garden, almost persuaded to break with his
old life of sin, he heard the voice of a child chanting in an adjoining gar-
13:11-14 den. He thought he caught the Latin words, *Tolle lege*! *Tolle lege*!—"Pick it
up, read it; pick it up, read it." Receiving this as a voice from God, he took
up a Bible, and his eyes first lit on the words of Rom 13:13-14: ". . . not in
orgies and drunkenness, not in sexual immorality and debauchery, not in
dissension and jealousy. Rather, clothe yourselves with the Lord Jesus
Christ, and do not think about how to gratify the desires of" the flesh.

"I wanted to read no further, nor did I need to. For instantly, as the sentence ended, there was infused in my heart something like the light of full certainty and all the gloom of doubt vanished away" (1955, 8:13). Who can estimate the far-reaching effects upon the church and the world of this illumination of Augustine's heart and mind?

Believers are persuaded that the power of Christ's gospel is undiminished since Augustine was converted more than 1,600 years ago by Paul's call to awaken to the dawning of God's new eschatological day. In view of the unexpectedly extended time "gap" between the apostle's time and ours, however, it is imperative that we read this passage with the reminder of 2 Peter in mind: "With the Lord a day is like a thousand years, and a thousand years are like a day" (3:8).

Has the lingering darkness of the old age and the delayed appearance of the full light of the new day Paul believed he saw dawning two millennia ago diminished the truth of his more fundamental insight? Has the visibly imperceptible apocalyptic invasion of God into the present age in Christ changed nothing or changed everything? (see Polkinghorne and Welker 2000, and Hill 2003).

4. Love Expresses the Acceptance of Christ in Community Life (14:1—15:13)

Paul concludes the body of his letter and his closing "exhortations with a lengthy plea for mutual acceptance" (Moo 1996, 826). Paul seems to be sufficiently informed about the situation in Rome to be aware of divisions, falling largely along ethnic lines. "The division between the 'strong' and the 'weak' is a practical example of the problem of the relationship between Jew and Gentile, law and gospel, OT and NT, that is basic to Romans" (Moo 1996, 832).

Questions with which Paul has been obliged to deal since the opening of Romans—the place of the Law in the faith and practice of the community—appear in new form in 14:1—15:13. One question is, What role, if any, does the Torah's ceremonial law play in the NT ethic? Another is, What is the proper relationship between Jews and Gentiles within the Christian community? Paul addresses these and other common problems faced by communities that take seriously an understanding of God's will for themselves and the fellowship of faith.

From Paul's perspective, the final answer to all these questions and problems is the application of the law of love: "Welcome one another, therefore, just as Christ has welcomed you" (15:7 NRSV). The noun **Lord** (*kyrios*), which appears nine times in this passage, is a reminder that everyone must answer to Christ.

Although lengthy and complex, this passage may be treated as a unit. This unit consists of three major subsections: (a) The Strong and the Weak (14:1-12), (b) Walking in Love Despite Community Differences (14:13-23), and (c) Accepting One Another as Christ Accepted Us (15:1-13).

BEHIND THE TEXT

Although its origins are shrouded in mystery and anonymity, it appears that Christianity was first introduced to Rome in the Jewish synagogues of the Imperial City. These synagogues almost certainly had among their numbers Gentile proselytes and the more casual adherents called

"God-fearers" (see Acts 2:10-11). It was most often Israel's monotheistic faith and moral code, particularly the Decalogue, that attracted Gentile converts. In these synagogues they found the call to a way of life in sharp contrast to the polytheism and moral laxity of Rome. Gentiles were drawn to Judaism as a moral oasis in a spiritual desert. Jewish synagogues throughout the empire served as the bridge over which Christianity passed into the Roman world.

There is evidence suggesting that the introduction of Christianity into the synagogue of Rome was socially disruptive. As elsewhere, the claim that Jesus was the Christ created violent reaction in the synagogues (e.g., Acts 17:1-8). In Rome, riots in A.D. 49 instigated by disagreements over *Chrestus* (probably a misspelling of *Christus* based on the common slave-name prompted Claudius's edict to evict all Jews from Rome (see Acts 18:2). In the years following 49, the Gentile minority grew. After Claudius's assassination (by his wife, Agrippina, and her son Nero) in 54, the edict was treated as a dead letter.

By the time Jews began to drift back into the city and the synagogues, Gentiles constituted a majority in the Christian community (see Rom 1:5-6 and Watson 1991, 213). Back in Rome, these Jews were probably dislocated from the ethnically defined ghettos where they had earlier lived. This and the realities of urban life, perhaps, forced some to buy meat in pagan markets or to avoid meat altogether. This created a situation not unlike that Paul addressed in 1 Cor 8:4—11:1.

Although other plausible theories exist, a majority of interpreters believe that Rom 14:1—15:13 supports the thesis that questions Paul addresses here arose from Jewish congregations disturbed by the Gentile disregard of Jewish kosher regulations and the observance of the Sabbath and other sacred days of their calendar (14:5-6; for Jewish scruples against wine-drinking see Dan 1:8-17). Specific support of such a Jewish-Gentile mix in the Christian congregations of Rome may be found in 15:1-13. In ch 16, where Paul addresses house churches of both varieties, the above contention seems to be adequately supported.

The issues Paul uses to illustrate the divisive and futile debates about opinions he urges the Romans to avoid in 14:1-12 are apparently Jewish in origin. For Diaspora Jews "the boundaries which marked them off in their distinctiveness as the elect people of the one God were most emphatically and visibly drawn in the daily lifestyle expressed in diet and festivals" (Dunn 2002b, 38B:797). It would be overly simplistic to assume that the boundaries separating "weak" and "strong" in the Roman house and tenement churches fell neatly along ethnic lines. Those Gentiles who had converted to

Judaism before becoming Christians may have been as rigid and inflexible on issues preserving their newly acquired Jewish identity as ethnic Jews, perhaps more so. Lest we forget, Paul, who clearly numbers himself among the "strong" (15:1), was of Jewish descent. Socioeconomic factors almost certainly were part of church dynamics.

Just as Paul insists that the ethnic distinction between Jews and Gentiles is not decisive for salvation in chs 1—11, he refuses here to allow inconsequential cultural and religious distinctions to divide the church. He seems willing to allow Jews to maintain their unique identity, while refusing to allow their Jewishness to become a basis for false notions of ethnic separation or superiority (see 2:28-29; 4:1; 9:3). In 13:13 Paul insists that immoral eating and drinking practices are strictly off limits for all believers. But in ch 14 he is equally insistent that other such practices are totally amoral and must not be elevated to a level of importance that would allow them to become divisive.

Addressing these ethical issues as he does, Paul writes as a self-conscious Christian *theologian*, not as an ethicist. Not many years earlier, Paul had written that "in Christ Jesus . . . there is neither Jew nor Greek" (Gal 3:26, 28). "We were all baptized by one Spirit into one body—whether Jews or Greeks, slave or free—and we were all given the one Spirit to drink" (1 Cor 12:13). Paul was convinced that faith in Christ removes the barriers based on human differences and expresses itself in indiscriminate love for all (Gal 5:6). Their shared faith immersed believers into the mutual love of Christ's body. Love is the basis for the Christian theological ethic (esp. Rom 14:15) as he has already insisted repeatedly in the general parenetic section of the letter (12:1—13:14).

IN THE TEXT

a. The Strong and the Weak (14:1-12)

Up to this point, except for his instruction concerning civil authorities (13:1-7), Paul's exhortations have been general. Now he addresses his readers specifically concerning eating and drinking and reckoning of certain days as holy as they affect intercommunity relations. Although the opening exhortation of the chapter addresses the majority, who are *not* ***weak in faith,*** about their responsibilities to the minority who are, most of what Paul writes here (except 14:3*a*, 10*b*) challenges the judgmental tendencies of the ***weak in faith.***

■ **1** Paul begins abruptly: **Accept him whose faith is weak** (v 1*a*). Paul's description of some believers in his audience as ***weak in faith*** was not intended as a compliment. It seems unlikely that this was how they perceived or designated themselves. Clearly, there is something defective and deficient in their faith. But what? From 4:19 we would conclude that those who are weak in faith "fail to trust God completely and without qualification. . . . In this case the weakness is trust in God plus dietary and festival laws" (see 1 Cor 8:7-10; 9:22; Dunn 2002b, 38B:798).

Those who are ***weak in faith*** apparently do not understand that salvation is by faith from first to last—that saving faith is not secured by superior human understanding or by the intensity with which one's convictions are held, or by scrupulosity of conscience. Far from enjoying peace and reconciliation that comes with trusting God (5:1-11), the ***weak in faith*** are fearful. Just the same, such persons are to be accepted as full members of the community of faith.

Paul uses the verb *proslambanesthe* (**Accept;** "Welcome" NRSV) elsewhere to refer to God's gracious welcome of all who come to him in faith. If God welcomes the wavering person, so must we (see 15:7; see Phlm 17). Jewett considers the command to ***welcome*** the weak to urge the various house and tenement churches to open the table at their common meals for other believers—"to treat them as brothers and sisters in Christ, as equal beneficiaries of God's grace" (2007, 835-36). In the letter's original setting Paul called for the Gentile-Christian majority in Rome to extend full social standing (see Bauer 1979, 717 s.v. *proslambanō* 2.b) within their communities, to incorporate into their fellowships the Jewish Christians who were trickling back into the city following the death of Claudius.

Acceptance of believers with different opinions and practices is not an endorsement of relativity; Paul does not consider every opinion equally true and valid. He regards the opinions of "the weak" as immature and in need of change. But the issue is not who is right; it is: How are Christians to deal with the inevitable differences among them? Godet notes that Paul uses the substantive adjectival participle *ton asthenounta,* ***the one who is weak,*** rather than the substantive adjective *ton asthenēn*, "the weak one." The present tense of the verbal form implies that weak believers are only temporarily weak; they may become strong (1883, 454). The verb *a-sthenoō* literally means "un-strengthened." With education and edification provided by the welcoming community of faith (1:12; 14:14, 20; 15:14), these weak persons may come to a more adequate understanding of the gospel and thus to the "full assurance of faith" (see Heb 10:19-23). But argument will not effect the needed maturity.

Weak brothers and sisters must be welcomed, but **without passing judgment on disputable matters** (Rom 14:1*b*), or more accurately, ***but not for the purpose of quarrels*** [*diakriseis;* see 1 Cor 12:10] ***about opinions*** [*dialogismōn;* see Phil 2:14; 1 Tim 2:8]. "The opinions/reasoning (*dialogismoi*) of the 'weak' . . . are under scrutiny by the dominant group" (Jewett 2007, 836).

Paul insists that the church is not to become a debating society with winners and losers. The weak and strong are not competitors, but colleagues within a unified community. Neither side was to imagine that they could simply argue the others out of their views. In fact, arguments would only confirm the weak in their opinions. The weak must be allowed to *outgrow* their limited ideas. But even before they do, they should not be criticized or censured, but loved (see 1 Thess 5:14). And even if they never change, they are to be loved (Rom 14:15).

Although Paul uses the singular throughout, he describes two classes of believers, the "strong" and the "weak" respectively (although he does not explicitly use the term "strong" until 15:1). The weak might consider themselves the "cautious" in contrast to the "unconventional." We should recall that the "freedom fighters" and "martyrs" of one group are the despised "terrorists" of the other. Paul's language clearly indicates which side he is on.

■ **2** It is not at all uncommon in Greek to use an articular singular noun (*ton asthenounta,* ***the weak one***) to indicate a collective, generic, or gnomic usage, whereas English customarily uses anarthrous plural nouns (***weak ones***) for the same purpose (BDF 1961, 77). Although Paul contrasts just two individuals—**One man's faith allows him to eat everything, but another man, whose faith is weak, eats only vegetables** (v 2), he actually has in mind two groups. For rhetorical purposes, Paul has created "an exaggerated and somewhat ludicrous paraphrase" of the opposing positions (Jewett 2007, 837).

One group has ***faith to eat all things*** (*pistuei phagein panta*). ***But*** another group, ***the weak,*** merely ***eat only salad greens*** (*ho de asthenōn lachana esthiei*). The change in Paul's Greek construction does not explicitly credit ***the weak*** with acting on the basis of trust in God at all, not even deficient faith. The "strong" grasp the implications of the Christian faith; the weak do not. Without reference to faith, ***the weak eat only salad greens.*** Paul caricaturizes both **the weak**—as hyper-scrupulous vegetarians—and the strong as eating anything and everything. This is lampoon: It is doubtful that any group in Rome took their opinions to such laughable extremes.

Vegetarianism

"The practice of vegetarianism for religious or philosophic reasons was quite well known in the ancient world" (Dunn 2002b, 38B:799). It was not specifically or primarily Jewish. Neo-Pythagoreans, ascetic gnostics, and various Hellenistic mystery religions were more likely to ***eat only lettuce*** than were Jews.

Nonetheless, concerns about kosher—"clean" (*kathara,* v 20) vs. "unclean" (*koinon,* three times in v 14)—foods were distinctively Jewish (see Lev 11:1-23; Deut 13:3-21) and considered particularly crucial for preserving Jewish identity in the Diaspora (see 1 Macc 1:62-63; 2 Macc 5:27; Tob 1:10-12; Jdt 12:2, 19; Acts 10:13-16; 11:3; Gal 2:11-14). The scrupulously Jewish diets of Daniel and his three exiled friends consisted of vegetables and water only (Dan 1:3-16), and specifically involved the refusal of wine (see Rom 14:21). Eusebius reports that James, the brother of Jesus and leader of Jewish Christianity, was a vegetarian (*Church History* 2.23.5).

Distinctive dietary regulations and Sabbath observance were among the most widely recognized boundary markers separating Jews from Gentiles in antiquity. Perhaps Paul selected vegetarianism, the most cautious approach to Jewish kosher laws, as representative of them all (see 14:21). Jewish dietary regulations concerned not only what Jews ate but also with whom and where (see Acts 10), how food was prepared (see Acts 15:20, 29), its source (see 1 Cor 8—10), etc. That most contemporary Christians consider such regulations irrational and trivial is testimony to how far removed we are from the religious context of earliest Christianity.

Paul gives suitable advice to both classes of believers. But this is more than prudential counsel; his Greek verbs are in the imperative mood. These are matching commands. All English imperatives are implicit second person commands—"Do not look down on such a person" is clearly an order directed toward "you." English has no exact equivalent to third person singular imperative commands. "He not look down on such a person!" would strike us as merely an odd statement. Every attempt to translate such constructions (as in vv 3 and 5; see 3:4; 6:12; 11:9, 10; 13:1; 14:16; 15:2, 11) must inevitably resort to paraphrase.

■ **3 The man who eats everything must not look down on him who does not, and the man who does not eat everything must not condemn the man who does, for God has accepted him** (14:3). Persons "in the know" find it easy to **look down on** [*exoutheneitō, **make nothing of, dismiss, despise,*** or

reject with utter contempt; see v 10; 1 Cor 6:4; 2 Cor 10:10; Gal 4:14; 1 Thess 5:20) their overly scrupulous brothers or sisters. The "strong" must accept and refuse to disdain the "weak."

Paul challenges the hyper-conscientious to resist the temptation to **condemn** (*krinōn, **judge/criticize as unacceptable to God;*** see Rom 2:1, 3; 14:4, 10, 13, 22; Matt 7:1; Luke 6:37; 1 Cor 4:5; Col 2:16; Jas 4:11, 12) those who do not accept their rigorous scruples. Christians must not de-Christianize other believers who fail to observe their customs. "The frown of the legalist is just as inappropriate for the realm of Christ as the disdainful smile of the liberated" (Jewett 2007, 840). Anyone **God has accepted** (*proselabeto;* see Ps 27:10)—i.e., given equal status, we, too, must likewise ***welcome*** (Rom 14:1; 15:7).

■ **4** The sharpness of Paul's rebuke in v 4 shows that, despite all his love and consideration for the weak, the apostle was alert to the ever-present tendency of the hyper-conscientious to lapse from scrupulosity about their own conduct into loveless criticism of others: **Who are you to judge someone else's servant** [*oiketnēn, **household slave***]? (v 4*a*). His diatribe-like rebuke, framed as a rhetorical question, has the force of accusing the weak of playing God, much as he implicitly challenged the Jewish judge in 2:1-11 of self-idolatry. Noting that the verb **judge** appears twice as often in Rom 2 and 14 as in any other chapter in the NT, Dunn (2002b, 38B:803) considers the echo deliberate.

Finally, Christians do not answer to one another, but to God (see 1 Cor 4:3-5): **To his own master** [*kyriōi, **lord***] **he stands or falls** [*piptei;* Rom 11:11, 22]. **And he will stand, for the Lord is able to make him stand** (Rom 14:4*bc;* see 1 Cor 10:22). "Who are you to set yourself up as your fellow Christians' judge or master?" Paul insists that the criticized fellow believers remain in the Lord's good graces. His point is not that Christ excuses the immoral behavior of believers; he does not. And it is not that he is unable to restore those who fall into sin; he can. His point is that what the "weak" consider a fall from grace actually is not. If the Lord is satisfied with his slave's behavior, the opinions of others are inconsequential.

Paul trusts the Lord's power to enable his people actually to do his will (see Rom 12:2). Here, the verb *histēmi,* **stand,** has the metaphorical force of being made steadfast and firmly established (Bauer 1979, 382 s.v.; see 3:31; 10:3; 1 Cor 10:12; 15:1; 2 Cor 1:24; 13:1; Gal 5:1; Phil 1:27; 4:1; 1 Thess 3:8). "Do not take too gloomy a view of your fellow Christians' chances of salvation. The grace of God is sufficient to uphold them." The apostle is aware of the dangers of imagined spiritual sophistication (see 1 Cor 8:1-3; 10:12)—yet he is confident that authentic Christian liberty, through the grace and power of Christ, is sufficient to sustain the "strong" in faith for the Day of Judgment.

■ **5** In v 5 Paul turns from food laws to another question of much the same nature—the religious observance of days. On this subject, as well, he identifies two contrasting groups of Christians: **One man considers one day more sacred than another.** Paul considered the preference of one day above others a characteristic of the "weak." He apparently refers to those who insist on observing the Jewish Sabbath and feast days.

In Galatians Paul expressed concern for his converts' calendar concerns: "You are observing special days and months and seasons and years! I fear for you, that somehow I have wasted my efforts on you" (Gal 4:10-11). Their observances undermined Christian freedom (1:6; 3:1-3; 5:1, 13), making them slaves to the calendar (4:8-11); and, as such, these amounted to a fall from grace (5:4). Paul seems to be genuinely nonchalant about both the rigid and relaxed positions on the calendar.

Another man considers every day alike. This does not mean that "strong" Christians treat every day as secular. The strong regard *every day* as sacred, dedicated to the service of God. In light of the appeal that opens the parenetic section of the letter (Rom 12:1-2), Paul almost certainly thought of "strong" Christians as offering themselves as living sacrifices in true worship on a daily basis.

14:4-6 What solution does Paul propose to this potentially divisive issue? The English translation of his answer: **Each one should be fully convinced** [*plērophoreisthō;* see 4:21; 14:22-23) **in his own mind** (v 5*c*), is another attempt to communicate the force of the third person singular imperative. Paul orders his readers to decide for themselves such debatable issues as food and festival regulations on the basis of their personal relationship with the Lord.

■ **6 He who regards** [*phronein, **thinks of;*** see 12:3, 16] **one day as special, does so to the Lord** (v 6*a*). The scrupulous observe the Jewish Sabbath or the emerging Christian practice of Sunday worship (and any other festival day in the calendar) because they think that is what **the Lord** requires of them. The same is true of those who think that the resurrection changed everything, sacralizing every day. On all such matters of scruples about private opinion believers must decide for themselves. But they do so under the lordship of Christ, not with licentious autonomy.

Paul continues v 6 by returning to the potentially divisive issue of food laws, insisting that matters of personal opinion need not be resolved in favor of one side or the other. **He who eats meat, eats to the Lord, for he gives thanks to God; and he who abstains, does so to the Lord and**

gives thanks to God (v 6*b*). Both what we do and don't do in the realm of private ethical behavior may be done as **to the Lord.** Paul legitimates the thinking of both sides as responsibly Christian.

■ **7** From the context it is evident that Paul does not mean **none of us lives to himself** (v 7) in the popular sense that our actions inevitably affect our fellow humans to a greater or lesser extent. In Greek usage, "to live 'for oneself' is to live selfishly" (Dunn 2002b, 38B:807). Christians, as followers of Christ, cannot live selfishly, but in the interests of the community (2 Cor 5:15).

■ **8-9 For this very reason** [*eis touto hina*], **Christ died and returned to life** [Rom 14:9; see 5:10; 8:34; 1 Cor 15:3-4; 2 Cor 4:10; 5:15; Gal 1:4; 1 Thess 4:14]: because of human selfishness. The purpose (*hina,* **so that**) of his death and resurrection was so that he might begin to reign as **Lord of both the dead and the living.** Both his life and death modeled genuine love: life lived sacrificially for God and others. Paul's point is that we all live out of our shared communion with Christ, whether or not we recognize it. Both our lives and our deaths belong **to the Lord** (Rom 14:8). We are his property and must live consistent with this reality. Nothing in life or death exists apart from our answerability to him, nor can anything separate us from him (see 8:35-39). No one and nothing is excluded from his right to reign. Paul does not answer our curious questions about the place or the state of **the dead.**

ROMANS

14:6-10

So long as we are alive, Christ's exemplary life and death call for imitation (15:7-9; 1 Cor 11:1; 2 Cor 5:14-15; Gal 2:19; Phil 2:5-11; 1 Thess 1:6; 5:10). But Paul's concern is less Christ's model than his lordship.

> If Christ rules over everything from life to death, he certainly is the final arbiter in matters of calendar and diet. This eliminates the final shred of credibility on the part of either the weak or the powerful in their attempts to lord it over each other. (Jewett 2007, 849)

The crucified and risen Lord alone has the right to determine what obedience demands of each of his subjects. Christian liberty of conscience—the right to decide for oneself on matters of private opinion (Rom 14:6)—must not be confused with autonomy. The obedience we owe the Lord takes precedence over any differences we may have with fellow believers. And this alone is a matter of life-and-death importance. Disagreements over diet and days pale by comparison (Dunn 2002b, 38B:807).

■ **10** In v 10 Paul applies the argument pointedly to the questions under discussion. In v 4 his accusing question challenged the right of scrupulous believers to sit in judgment on their more "liberal-minded" brothers and sisters. In v 10 he again confronts "conservative" believers who challenge the Christian standing of the "strong." But he also takes on the "liberals" who despise the "weak" and simply dismiss their views as inconsequential. **You** [*Sy*], **then, why do you judge** [*krineis*] **your brother? Or why do you** [*sy*] **look down on** [*exoutheneis*] **your brother *and sister?* For we will all stand before God's judgment seat** (v 10; see v 3, where the same verbs appear in reverse order; see 2:5-16).

We are **all** responsible to Christ: **we will** appear **before** him to be judged by him (see 2 Cor 5:10). There is, therefore, no place for uncharitable judgments or self-righteous exclusiveness among Christians. We are to judge things (Rom 14:5), but leave the judgment of people—our ***Christian brothers and sisters*** and even ourselves (vv 3, 4, 10, 13, 22; 1 Cor 2:15; 4:3-5; Jas 4:12)—to God.

■ **11** Paul solemnly warns of the universal scope of God's judgment by echoing Isa 45:23: **It is written: "'As I live,' says the Lord, 'every knee will bow before me; every tongue will confess to God'"** (v 11). Paul did not understand Isaiah to suggest that everyone will finally worship God and consequently be saved, as some have misunderstood the echo of Isa 45:23 in Phil 2:9-11. On the contrary, his point is that *everyone* will answer to God/Christ as their rightful Judge.

Paul introduces his quotation with an allusion to a formula that appears frequently in the prophets (see Isa 49:18; Jer 22:24; etc.), but not in Isa 45:23—"**'As I live,' says the Lord.**" Not only those who refuse to acknowledge the lordship of Christ (Phil 2:9-11), but also those who usurp the authority of the living God and install themselves as judges of their fellow believers can expect to pay the penalty exacted of other idolaters (Rom 1:21-25; 14:6).

■ **12 So then** [*ara*], **each of us will give account of himself to God** (v 12). Paul easily passes from **Lord** to **God.** The Father and the Son were so united in Paul's mind that they are often interchanged. "God, or Christ, or God through Christ, will judge the world. Our life is in God, or in Christ, or with Christ in God. The union of man with God depends upon the intimate union of the Father and the Son" (Sanday and Headlam 1929, 389). But Paul's essential point here is not christological. It is to emphasize that **each of us**—"weak" and "strong"—without exception, finally answers to God, not to one another.

FROM THE TEXT

Paul's advice for his first readers provides a model that may still be appropriated, as Dunn observes:

> What comes to expression . . . is a keen pastoral concern: that newcomers should not be subjected to demanding discussion about their common faith and its outworking. . . . The liberty of the Christian assembly should be able to embrace divergent views and practices without a feeling that they must be resolved or that a common mind must be achieved on every point of disagreement. (2002b, 38B:798)

Paul acknowledges that differences of opinion exist within the church. But he calls for settled personal convictions, not the imposition of debatable private opinions on others. He apparently actually believes that human minds transformed and renewed by the Holy Spirit (8:5-6; 12:2) can reliably guide Christian decision-making in disputed matters. "Paul does not expect differences of opinion within the Christian congregations to result in these differences being held less firmly or with less assurance" (Dunn 2002b, 38B:806). He is untroubled by the fact that members making up the body of Christ are many and have gifts that differ in proportion to their faith (12:5-6). Just so, Paul presumes that, even in a community committed to genuine love (12:9), differing convictions on nonessentials will arise from the relative strength or weakness of one's faith.

Such differences need not prevent the church from together giving **thanks to God** (v 6). God can give us such "a spirit of unity" as we follow Christ "that with one heart and mouth [we] may glorify the God and Father of our Lord Jesus Christ" (15:5-6). It is by honoring God as God, giving him thanks (1:21), worshipping him, and serving him alone (1:25), that we fulfill our calling as creatures to live in right relationship with our Creator. Thus, we must resist the temptation to idolize human opinions and ideologies, which are as unworthy of worship as any of the creatures venerated by fallen humanity (1:18-30).

Although circumcision and kosher laws have their place in the OT, they clearly assumed an importance within the Judaism of Paul's day, which far exceeds that assigned them in the OT. Outsiders to Judaism saw these regulations as decisive boundary markers distinguishing Jews from non-Jews. By placing inordinate importance on such externally visible ritual concerns, Jesus claimed that some of his Jewish contemporaries missed the more important issues of the heart (see Mark 7).

But the OT repeatedly and forcefully commands Sabbath observance (Gen 2:2-3; Exod 20:8-11; 31:16-17; Deut 5:15; Neh 9:13-14; Isa 56:6; Ezek 20:16). Given Paul's obvious respect for the authority of the Scriptures, it seems remarkable that he was able so easily to treat its observance as optional. He makes no appeal to Jesus' challenge in word and deed to the Jewish observance of Sabbath as contrary to God's intentions for it (see, e.g., Matt 12:1-12; Mark 2:23—3:4; Luke 6:6-9; 13:10-16; 14:1-6; John 5:1-18; 7:22-23; 9:1-16).

His reference to the authority of **the Lord** (in Rom 14:4, 6, 7, and 8) on the subject, however, clearly appeals to Jesus, rather than to God as the basis for his tolerant stance. Perhaps Paul's stance is based solely on his refusal to allow Jewish identity markers—whether food laws or festival customs, even the venerable observance of the Sabbath—to become divisive within the body of Christ comprised of both Jews and Gentiles. He reached such confidence based on an even more basic conviction: "We have the mind [*noun*] of Christ" (1 Cor 2:16; see Phil 2:5).

b. Walking in Love Despite Community Differences (14:13-23)

BEHIND THE TEXT

In contrast to 14:1-12, directed primarily to the "weak," 14:13-23 is addressed primarily to the "strong." Paul endorses the position of the "strong" (15:1) that Jewish food laws do not apply to Christians (14:14, 20*b*). But he especially emphasizes the responsibility of the "strong" to put the need of the "weak" for loving consideration ahead of being right. Romans 13:1-12 and 13-23 are linked by the use of the verb *krinō* in vv 10 and 13 and 22-23—genuine love requires the exercise of good "judgment."

Romans 14:13-23 may be divided into four parts. Each of the first three begins with the inferential particle *oyn*, "therefore." Paul repeats his main points several times, reinforcing the special responsibilities of the "strong":

- Do not cause the "weak" to stumble (vv 13-15).
- The kingdom of God is not about eating and drinking (vv 16-18).
- Do not destroy the church (vv 19-21).
- Be true to your faith (vv 22-23).

Paul's focus with the passage shifts back and forth between the community as a whole—or to the "strong" or "weak" parts of it—and the individuals within it, whether offender or offended. The first person plural, "let us," in v 13*a* gives way in 13*b* to the second person plural: "[You all] make up your mind." This is replaced by the second person singular in v 15 only to return to the second person plural in v 16. The generic ***siblings*** (*tōi adelphōi* in v 13 becomes **anyone** (*ti*) and ***that one*** (*ekeiniōi)* in v 14 and ***your brother or sister*** (*ho adelphos sou*) in v 15. In v 16 the third person singular imperative addresses a plural audience (*hymōn*, ***your*** [plural]). The first person plural reappears in v 19 only to be replaced by the second person singular in vv 20 and 21. This issue is not just about others; it concerns us all. How will we relate to our fellow believers?

IN THE TEXT

■ **13** With the opening exhortation—**Therefore, let us stop passing judgment on one another** (v 13*a*)—the thought of the previous paragraph (vv 1-12) is assumed and summarized. Since God alone is qualified to judge, neither the "strong" nor the "weak" are in a position to judge the other group. Although in 14:3*b*-4 and 10*a*, only the "weak" are accused of presuming they are fit judges of the behavior of others, Paul uses the first person plural ("we") hortatory subjunctive, including himself and others among the "strong" in his polite command. All critical and censorious feelings and actions—including judgmental attitudes and words—toward others must cease.

Paul uses the word "judge" in a play on words, clear in Greek but obscured by the NIV translation. ***Therefore, let us no longer judge*** [*krinōmen;* see vv 3, 4, 5, 10, 22] ***one another. But judge*** [*krinate*] ***this instead: Do not put anything that causes fellow-believers to stumble*** [*proskomma;* see v 20] ***or puts an occasion to fall*** [*skandalon;* see 9:32-33; 11:9; 16:17; Matt 18:6-7; 1 Cor 8:9-13; 10:32; 2 Cor 6:3] ***in their way.*** Instead of being critical of one another, we are to critique our own behavior to be sure we do not cause another believer to do wrong and experience a spiritual downfall (see Gal 6:1-5).

■ **14** In Rom 14:14 Paul addresses the "strong" as one of them (see 15:1): ***I know and am persuaded in the Lord Jesus*** [*oida kai pepeismai en kyriō Iēsou*], **that no food** [*ouden,* ***nothing***] **is unclean in itself. But if anyone regards** [*logizomenōi,* ***reckons, considers;*** see 3:28; 4:3, 4, 5, 6, 9, 11, 22; 8:18] **something as unclean** [*koinon,* ***common***]**, then for him it is unclean** [*koinon*].

Paul seems to know Jesus' teaching on this subject in Mark 7:14-23. Thus, the phrase **in the Lord Jesus** might mean ***by means of the Lord Jesus;*** i.e., that traditions originating with the earthly Jesus were the source of this insight. But **in the Lord Jesus** may mean only "as a Christian" (Rom 14:14 NEB) or "in virtue of the authority of the Lord Jesus" (Dunn 2002b, 38B:818, citing Käsemann 1980). In a letter addressed to both "weak" and "strong," Paul's emphatic certainty (see 8:38) about the total irrelevance of Jewish kosher regulations for Christians makes transparently clear the view he wants his readers to adopt as their own.

Paul's "liberal" stance, asserting that ***nothing* is unclean** [*koinon*] **in itself** (see Mark 7:15), must not be wrested from its context. Paul is speaking of food (*brōma*, vv 15 and 20; see Acts 10:13-15; 11:2-3) here. He does not endorse an "anything goes" policy on morality in general. The word *koinos* in ordinary Greek means simply "common" or "shared." Only in the context of Jewish food regulations does it have the force of "profane" or ritually "unclean," as here. Paul is not concerned about food sanitation or nutrition. The issue is Jewish kosher laws that identify certain kinds of food (preparation methods, combinations of food, etc.) as unfit for human consumption for religious reasons (see Rom 14:2, 5; see Lev 11:4-8; Deut 14:7-10; Ezek 22:26; 44:23).

The open stance Paul takes toward kosher regulations is not simply a rejection of the continuing relevance of the so-called ritual law for Christians. "At stake was the whole Jewish conception of holiness" (Dunn 2002b, 38B:819). Paul refused to define "holiness" in negative terms as merely a separation of the holy community from those outside.

Paul's goal was not to deny the sacredness of certain food or days so that everything was rendered secular. It was to insist that all of life might potentially enter the realm of the holy, be sanctified, and thereby come under the rule of the Holy One. Paul does not call for an end to the distinction between clean and unclean, between the holy and the profane. His goal is to abolish the artificial boundaries dividing groups on the basis of superficial differences.

Genuine love should enable believers, despite their diverse viewpoints on such matters, to embrace one another within one community. Liberty of conscience and sensitivity to others are not incompatible (Dunn 2002b, 38B:820).

So far as Paul is concerned, the decisive issue is not food itself but how one "thinks" about it. Those who regard a food as ritually **unclean** become defiled by eating it, not because the food itself is morally contaminated but because they are convinced that eating it is an act of disobedience to God. By doing what they were persuaded is wrong, their eating offends their "conscience" (see Rom 14:23). To them, **it is unclean;** for those who are doubtful cannot give God thanks (v 6).

■ **15** Verse 15 begins with an explanatory *gar* ("For" NASB), clarifying the implications of causing Christian friends to stumble (v 13). **If your brother *or sister* is distressed** [*lypeitai*, ***grieved, hurt, made sad***] **because of what you eat, you are no longer acting** [*peripateis*, ***are . . . walking***] **in love** [*agapēn*] (v 15*a*). Paul's concern is not with kosher laws but with the demands of **love,** which continues to serve as the touchstone of Christian virtue (see the commentary on 12:9-21 and 13:8-10). How may the eating of "unclean" food by a "strong" believer cause a "weak" one to be deeply **distressed?**

First, it may pain their sensitive consciences to see a fellow believer eat at a communal meal what they (however wrongly) regard as sinful. If "love does no harm to its neighbor" (13:10), causing Christian friends to suffer grief cannot be lightly dismissed as inconsequential—"That's just their problem." Paul's language does *not* picture the pain inflicted as merely a matter of momentary irritation, annoyance, or shock. This is no superficial flesh wound, but a deeply inflicted mortal injury (see Matt 18:31; Käsemann 1980, 376).

Second, witnessing the "strong" eating unclean food may embolden the "weak" by this example to do what they believe God forbids *them* to do. Those who eat with a bad conscience are self-condemned by their wavering doubts (Rom 14:23). The "strong" can do less than their consciences will allow; the "weak" cannot do more. It must be acknowledged that, unlike the parallel in 1 Cor 8 (vv 7, 10, and 12) and 10 (vv 25, 27, 28, and 29), Paul does not here mention the "conscience" (*syneidēsis;* but see Rom 2:15; 9:1; 13:5). Are we simply to equate the ***weak in faith*** (14:1, 2) with those in 1 Corinthians he calls weak fellow Christians (1 Cor 8:11; 9:22) or weak in conscience (1 Cor 8:10, 12)?

Paul warns the "strong": **Do not by your eating** [*tōi brōmati sou,* ***by*** 14:15-16
your food] **destroy** [*apollye*] **your brother** [*ekeinon,* ***that one***] **for whom Christ died** (v 15*b;* see 5:6, 8). "So this weak brother, for whom Christ died, is destroyed by your knowledge. When you sin against your brothers in this way and wound their weak conscience, you sin against Christ" (1 Cor 8:11-12).

When we fail in our daily conduct (***walking;*** see Rom 6:4; 8:4) to do what **love** demands, we have not chosen to be neutral; we are actively seeking to bring down those Christ died to raise up, to lose those he died to save. Such indifference about our personal influence not only injures fellow believers but also offends Christ and puts us in rebellion against his purposes for humanity. If God's love led Christ to give himself up to death for the "weak" (5:8), surely the "strong" can give up some of their freedom in the interests of saving the "weak."

■ **16** In v 16 Paul recognized that this issue was not merely a matter of cordial vs. contentious internal relations within the Christian house churches in Rome. A divided community would not commend itself well to outsiders. This is his concern in v 16: **Do not allow what you consider good** [*to agathon,* see 2:10; 7:13, 18; 12:2; 13:3, 4; 14:16; 15:2; 16:19] **to**

be spoken of as evil [*blasphēmeisthō*]. The already difficult third person imperative is made even more difficult to translate in English by its passive voice. A more literal translation would be, ***Therefore, your good must not be allowed to be blasphemed!***

Good in this context surely means primarily "your Christian freedom." The freedom of conscience that has been won by Christ will inevitably get a bad name, if it is exercised in an inconsiderate, loveless manner. But **good** may refer more broadly to all that God has done in the life of the community (see 8:28). The "weak" may be entirely wrong in their opinions. But the "strong" are entirely wrong when they disregard their primary responsibility to love the "weak." And the "weak" are entirely wrong when they insist that what they consider right for them must be the criterion of judgment for all. Regardless of who is right or wrong, when the church fails to be the loving community it was called to be, no wonder it is discredited by unbelievers. The "strong" and the "weak" must defer to one another not only for their own **good** but also in the interests of the community's reputation in the eyes of the world (see 2:23-24).

■ **17** To insist on one's freedom without regard to the conscientious scruples of others is not only to fail God but also to misunderstand the nature of Christian experience. **For** [*gar*] **the kingdom** [*basileia*] **of God is not a matter of eating and drinking, but of righteousness, peace and joy in the Holy Spirit** (v 17). Since Paul does not define what he means by **the kingdom of God,** we can only assume that he takes for granted that his original audience understands what he means.

Paul seldom uses *basileia* in his letters (see Donfried 1987, 175-90). When he does, **the kingdom of God** usually refers to the *future* inheritance of God's people (see 1 Cor 6:9-10; 15:50; Gal 5:21; Eph 5:5; Col 4:11; 1 Thess 2:12; 2 Thess 1:5; 2 Tim 4:1, 18). But in 1 Cor 4:20; 15:24; and Col 1:13 it refers to *present* realities. Many average Bible readers mistakenly equate "the kingdom" with popular notions of "heaven," conceived as an ethereal place of eternal bliss reserved for the righteous dead somewhere out there. Unfortunately, most popular notions about the afterlife have little biblical basis and even less for equating it with **the kingdom of God** (see Russell 1998; Wright 2003; and McGrath 2003).

Jesus and Paul agree that **the kingdom of God** is not about a place but about God's eschatological rule. Both emphasize its future coming. Thus, e.g., Jesus urged his disciples to pray for God's kingdom to come (Matt 6:10; Luke 11:2; see 1 Cor 6:9-11). But both also recognize that with the coming of Jesus, the kingdom has already entered the present (e.g., Matt 12:28; Luke 14:12-24). "For both Jesus and Paul the Spirit is the presence of the kingdom, still future in its complete fulfillment" (Rom 8:17, 23; see Gal 4:6-7; Eph 1:13-14; Dunn 2002b, 38B:822).

Since the phrase **a matter of** has no basis in the Greek text, Paul seems to offer a definition of **the kingdom of God** both negatively and positively:

The kingdom of God
is not ***food*** [*brōsis*] ***and drink*** [*posis*]
but ***righteousness and peace and joy***
in the Holy Spirit.

This is no mere equation allowing us simply to substitute the three terms —**righteousness, peace, joy**—for the expression **kingdom of God.**

Is Paul denying an understanding of the **kingdom** actually held by some Christians or Jews in Rome or elsewhere? Did some take the expectation of the **kingdom** as a messianic banquet with such wooden literalism as to elevate **eating and drinking** in anticipation of its full coming to issues of central ethical importance? Or, was Paul's denial rhetorically conditioned by the preceding discussion of the issue of diet dividing "weak" and "strong" believers? If so, his point is that ***food and drink*** do not ultimately matter to God. Thus, he claims, in effect: "This is not what Christianity is all about!"

If **righteousness, peace,** and **joy** are what truly matters when and where God rules, what does Paul mean by these terms? And what is the effect on these terms of the added phrase **in the Holy Spirit**? These abstract qualities characterize the Spirit-filled life as Paul describes it elsewhere (see Rom 5:1-5; 8:4, 6, 10, 30, 33; 15:13, 32; see Gal 5:22; 1 Thess 1:6). He identifies the **Holy Spirit** as the divine source of these realities in human experience. Thus, these qualities are already potentially operative in the lives of wholly committed believers in this present age. But Paul's eschatology is not so fully realized as to reserve nothing for the age to come (see the commentary on Rom 8:18-25 and 13:11-14).

Despite Paul's theologically significant terminology, his essential point is completely practical and relevant to the potentially divisive issue of diet in the Roman house and tenement churches. "Faith is not 'faith to eat all things' (v. 2); Christian privilege is not the privilege to eat and drink what one likes" (Barrett 1957, 264). Rather, faith is that relation to God that produces "the fruit of the Spirit" (see Gal 5:22-23).

Generally, in Paul's letters **righteousness** and **peace** describe an objective relation to God; but **joy** is certainly something subjective and probably determines the sense of the other two words. **Righteousness** involves doing what God considers right; and **peace** with God inevitably brings a state of mind arising from the awareness of reconciliation with God (Rom 5:1-11).

But both **righteousness** and **peace** have profound implications for human relationships as well. Righteousness seeks justice; and peace, reconciliation with other humans. Both dimensions are essential to the life of holiness (see 14:19; Heb 12:10-14). **In the Holy Spirit** believers anticipate the blessings of the coming **kingdom of God** (see Rom 8:11, 23). But **in the Holy Spirit** its future blessings can be known here and now (Bruce 1963, 252). It is this **joy in the Holy Spirit** that we should seek, rather than the temporary pleasures of eating and drinking.

■ **18** Paul presumes that knowing the true character of the **kingdom** will not merely inform but also motivate Christians to appropriate action—**because** [*gar*] **anyone who serves** [*douleuōn*] **Christ in this way is pleasing** [*euarestos;* see 12:1] **to God and approved** [*dokimos*] **by men** (14:18; see 12:17; 13:3, 13). That is, to do in the power of the Holy Spirit what is required to live in a right relationship with God and at peace with God and one another is finally what serving Christ involves (see 1:1; 7:6; 12:11; 14:19; 16:18; 1 Cor 7:22; Gal 1:10; Eph 6:6; Col 3:24).

Those who serve Christ in this way please God by being just, conciliatory, and charitable toward others, not by selfishly insisting on their rights to Christian liberty (see 1 Cor 9:1-23). Humans, believers and unbelievers alike, validate and approve the genuineness of the faith of those who live in this way. Paul picks up this theme again in Rom 16:17-18, contrasting "those who cause divisions and put obstacles" in others' way by "serving . . . their own appetites" with those who genuinely serve "our Lord Christ."

■ **19** In v 19 Paul applies his brief parenthetical theological exposition (in the indicative mood) in vv 17-18 by means of resumed ethical exhortation. As in v 13, he employs the first person plural hortatory subjunctive, including himself among those called to action. **Let us therefore** [*ara oun*] **make every effort to do** [*diōkōmen*] **what leads to peace** [*eirēnēs*] **and to mutual** [*tēs eis allēlous*] **edification** [*tēs oikodomēs*] (v 19).

The Greek verb *diōkō* describes the vigorous pursuit of someone or something. When this has destructive intent, it refers to persecution (see, e.g., 12:14). Here, however, it clearly refers to a constructive pursuit, the striving for or aspiring to achieve some worthy goal (see, e.g., righteousness in 9:30-31; hospitality in 12:13; love in 1 Cor 14:1; the heavenly prize in Phil 3:14; good in 1 Thess 5:15; faith [etc.] in 2 Tim 2:22; peace and holiness in Heb 12:14). Paul recommends that we aspire for **peace** in our relationships with one another. The reciprocal pronoun *allēlōn* emphasizes that this pursuit must be **mutual;** all of us are to seek this in all of our relationships ***with one another.***

For the first time in Romans (but not the last; see 15:2, 20), Paul introduces the concept of **mutual edification** (see 1 Cor 3:9-10; 14:3, 5, 12, 26; 2 Cor 10:8; 12:19; 13:10; Eph 4:11-12, 16, 29). The imagery echoes the metaphor of God's constructive work in behalf of his people frequently used in Jeremiah (12:16; 31:4, 28; 33:7; 42:10; 45:4). Paul describes his ministry in terms of ***building up*** his churches (Rom 15:20; 1 Cor 3:9-10; 2 Cor 10:8; 13:10). But **mutual edification** must be on the agenda of every believer. In 1 Corinthians Paul especially emphasizes the goal of ***building up one another*** as the most crucial expression of love within the Christian community (1 Cor 8:1; 10:23; 14:3, 4, 5, 12, 17, 26). **Edification** is not about making others feel good about themselves. It is actually benefiting the harmony and spiritual health and contributing to the numerical growth of the community (Acts 9:31; 20:32).

■ **20** In Rom 14:20, neglecting the call to build up one another is to mean achieving its opposite—tearing down (see Mark 13:2; 14:58; 15:29; Gal 2:18). To open the door to conceit and self-centeredness destroys community; particularly victimizing the most vulnerable. This explains Paul's second person singular (you) imperative in Rom 14:20*a,* once again addressing primarily the "strong."

Do not destroy [*katalue;* see v 15] **the work of God for the sake of food.** The **work of God** describes what God has done in Christ to redeem individual Christians (as in v 15), but more importantly the Christian community, the church as the earthly dwelling place of God (see 1 Cor 3:9-17; 9:1; Eph 2:10-21; 1 Pet 2:4-5). Before we act independently on our own personal convictions, we must ask how such actions will affect the peace of the church and the Christian growth of others and of the church as a whole.

As a "strong" believer (Rom 15:1), Paul insists that **All food is clean** [*kathara*] (14:20*b;* see Mark 7:19; Luke 11:41; Titus 1:15). This repeats the point he had made negatively in Rom 14:14*a:* **No food is unclean in itself.** In v 14*b* he adds that this strong conviction does not change the way other people may think about a certain food; it is unclean for those who consider it so.

In v 20, having insisted that **All food is clean,** Paul concludes, **but it is wrong** [*kakon, **evil, wicked***] **for a *person* to eat anything that causes someone to stumble** (v 20*c*). This paraphrasing translation essentially repeats the point Paul had made in vv 13 and 15. But what he writes in Greek may make again the point of v 14*b:* ***All food is clean, but it is evil for***

those people who eat it and stumble. Both interpretations are plausible. It is wrong for the "strong" to cause the "weak" to stumble. But it is also wrong for the "weak" to stumble by violating their conscience.

■ **21** If the first interpretation of v 20*c* is correct, Paul basically repeats himself again in v 21: **It is better** [*kalon, **good;*** see 12:17; 1 Cor 7:1] **not to eat** [*phagein*] **meat** [*krea, **meats;*** 1 Cor 8:13] **or drink** [*piein, **to drink***] **wine or to do anything that will cause your** [*sou,* singular] **brother to fall** [*proskoptei, **causes to stumble***] (see 1 Cor 8:11-13). Paul expands the application of the ethical principle outlined in Rom 14:20*c* to include in v 21 his first specific reference to particular kinds of food—**meat** and **wine.**

Jewish practice did not prohibit the moderate consumption of wine, except to Nazirites (Num 6:4; Judg 13:4; Amos 2:12), Rechabites (Jer 35:6-7) and priests serving at the temple (Lev 10:9-10; Ezek 44:21-23). But under extraordinary circumstances, some expressions of Jewish scrupulosity demanded abstinence (Dan 1:3-16; 10:3). This does not seem to have been a matter of concern to avoid the "intoxicating or enslaving potential of alcohol, but because they were afraid that the wine had been contaminated by association with pagan religious practices" (Moo 1996, 856).

"Jews would sometimes abstain from wine out of concern that it had been tainted by the pagan practice of offering the wine as a libation to the gods" (Moo 1996, 831). If some of the "weak" avoided all **meat** (see Rom 14:2, 21) to assure they ate nothing that had been associated with pagan sacrifices, they may well have avoided **wine** for the same reason.

There is no basis in Greek for adding the infinitive **to do** in v 21; and the infinitives ***to eat*** and ***to drink*** are in the timeless aorist tense. These facts suggest that Paul's point may have been that you should never eat or drink **anything** that might offend the "weak." You should prefer death by starvation or thirst to causing another Christian to sin. Paul calls for the serious self-discipline of Christian love. But if abstinence out of deference for the "weak" is perpetual, Christian liberty seems to have vanished entirely. Only the "weak" will survive. But Paul has not finished.

■ **22** With v 22*a* Paul emphatically reinforces his exhortation in 14:1 not to quarrel about opinions on nonessential but potentially divisive matters. But he expands his point as well. He seems to advise the "strong": You, "strong" believers, keep your private opinions to yourself! Practice your freedom privately, out of the view of the "weak"! Church gatherings are not the place for parading your differences. But remember, God knows what you do in private.

What Paul says might be misunderstood: **So whatever you** [*sy* (an emphatic pronoun in the singular)] **believe about these things keep between yourself and God.** His point can hardly have been to keep their faith in Christ quiet. Nor does he seem to require them never to mention their views. His concern is that they do what they must to avoid controversy that would scandalize the "weak."

In v 22*b* Paul pronounces a blessing (see 4:7-8) on those who do not ***judge*** (*krinōn*) themselves by what they approve. Paul gives no license for the "strong" to sin in private. "The happiness of 'the strong' need not be disturbed if the weak condemns him, only if he were to condemn himself" (Dunn 2002b, 38B:828).

True faith is a matter between God and yourself, a confidence so complete that to have it is to be so secure in your relation to God that no scrupulosity can add to it. But the moment such faith begins to parade itself as a selfish demonstration of freedom it ceases to be faith. Paul clearly writes from the perspective of the "strong" in faith, as he has tacitly done throughout the chapter. Those who are sure of their freedom in Christ, however, make no offensive display of their freedom.

■ **23** In v 23 Paul cautions those who imagine themselves to be "strong" yet really are not. **But the man who has doubts** [*ho . . . dikrinomenos,* ***the one who wavers;*** see 4:20] **is condemned** [*katakekritai*] **if he eats, because his eating is not from faith; and everything that does not come from faith is sin.** The condemnation that "weak" Christians incur by acting against their conscience is not only subjective—a matter of so-called false guilt. But those who cannot act out of firm conviction that they are acting in full obedience to and trust in God (see v 5*c*) in matters of debated morality should avoid such questionable behaviors. Even if one's conscience/faith is not adequately informed, it is always right to follow one's conscience/faith.

Paul's claim that **everything that does not come from faith is sin** was not to make every deed of unbelievers "sinful by definition" as later church fathers were to claim (e.g., Augustine). It was to insist again, as he does in 1:19-32, that the human failure to live in total dependence on God is what it means to be a sinner. The church is not defined by the narrow-minded uniformity expected by the "weak," nor by the generous views of the "strong." As the body of Christ, we must depend exclusively on Christ and obey him, if we are to avoid sin.

All sin is a violation of the law of love and disrupts our relationships with one another as members of Christ's body. Thus, to sin willfully against God is to sin against those to whom we belong. Something precious dies in our relationship, not only with God, but also with others, when our relationship with Christ is corrupted by sin. As members of the body of Christ, "each member belongs to all the others" (12:5).

Romans' so-called wandering doxology—traditionally found in 16:25-27—appears instead following 14:23 in some late manuscripts. In still others it appears both at this point and after 16:23.

FROM THE TEXT

Paul clearly identifies himself with the "strong" in faith (see 15:1). He does not expect mature Christians to live forever in bondage to the excessive scrupulosity of the immature. As the "weak" are edified, their faith will grow. Until it does, the "strong" may continue to practice their faith privately before God, avoiding unnecessary offense of the "weak."

The Christian conscience must be "trued" by the mind of Christ. To study the Gospels is to be struck by the fact that, for Jesus, the great issues of faith and life are at the opposite pole from such matters as dietary taboos (Mark 7:18-23) and the punctilious observance of the Sabbath (Matt 12:1-13). For our Lord "the weightier matters of the law" (NRSV) have to do with God's requirement for "justice, mercy and faithfulness" (Matt 23:23).

14:13-23 Believers who are "weak in faith" must come to understand that salvation is wholly by grace though faith. It is, therefore, not dependent on a scrupulous keeping of every jot and tittle of the Law. "The just requirement of the law" is the obligation to express in all relationships the spirit of Christian love (see Rom 13:8-11). "Weak" Christians must hear the prophetic call: "He has showed you, O man, what is good. And what does the LORD require of you? To act justly and to love mercy and to walk humbly with your God" (Mic 6:8).

Life within the kind of community Paul calls for on the terms outlined in Rom 14 would be incredibly demanding of the "strong." I say "would be" because such Christian communities are rare indeed, if they actually exist. Has the church failed to hear and heed Paul's unbending call for the strong to bear the burden of the weak as demanded by genuine love? Or does the biblical canon as a whole allow for less rigorous expectations? Paul is certainly much more accommodating to narrow-minded conservatives here in Romans than in Galatians. Still, after maligning them as "weak," we can only wonder whether they appreciated how much he required the "strong" to compromise in the interests of keeping them happily within the same community.

c. *Accepting One Another as Christ Accepted Us (15:1-13)*

BEHIND THE TEXT

Paul refuses to allow Christian unity to be confused with lowest-common-denominator agreement. The "weak" and "strong" may exist together within the same community, provided that Christ is the author of the Trinitarian doxology they sing together in perfect harmony. Remarkably, Paul does not insist on either comprehensive creedal or ethical uniformity. He is enough of a realist to reckon with the possibility that the presence of "weak" and "strong" in faith may not be a passing stage within the church. But he is insistent that Christ's model must set the agenda for the unity of the community.

Jewett notes that this section of the letter

> resonates with the "ethic of reciprocity" that was considered binding in the Roman world. . . . Having received the supreme gift of salvation, granted freely to the undeserving, each recipient has the reciprocal obligation of gratitude to the divine Giver and of passing on the gift with similar generosity to others who are equally undeserving. (2007, 875-76)

In vv 1-6, Paul continues to address the "strong," reminding them of their responsibilities to the "weak." He describes pleasing others rather than oneself (v 2) and glorifying God the Father in word and deed (v 6) as hallmarks of the church that is both diverse and of the same mind (v 5). As the christologically centered Scriptures are given their rightfully instructive place within the community, endurance, and encouragement sustain the church's hope (vv 3-4).

In vv 7-13, Paul continues to emphasize the glory of God (vv 7, 9, and 11) and the exemplary model of Christ (v 8). He reiterates in v 7 the call to mutual acceptance with which he began his appeal in 14:1. For the first time, he makes explicit that the motivation of 14:1—15:13, as of the entire letter, is the unity specifically of Jews (15:8) and Gentiles (vv 9-12) within the one people of God. Here, Paul identifies the Holy Spirit as the author of the joy and peace that unifies the believing church in its sure hope (v 13).

(1) Unity in Accordance with Christ (15:1-6)

IN THE TEXT

■ **1** Paul for the first time specifically identifies himself with the "strong":

We [*hēmēis*] **who are strong ought to bear with the failings of the weak, and not to please ourselves** (v 1). Even without the personal pronoun We in Greek, the English translation would be unchanged. Its presence in Greek is noteworthy, however, because it emphatically stresses Paul's sympathies with the **strong** (*hoi dynatoi, **the powerful, those who are able***). "The language of weak and strong appears to have been adapted from Roman congregational usage, reflecting the socioeconomic, political, and probably numerical predominance of the Gentile Christians" (Jewett 2007, 876; see Dunn 2002b, 38B:837).

The language of "weak" and "strong" conveys a patronizing air of arrogance and presumption. Perhaps, Paul accommodates himself to such labels in the interests of reconciling the divided factions. He certainly does not refer to the "right" and the "wrong." And his advice to the "strong" is to follow Christ's model of apparent weakness in the interests of the "weak" (see 1 Cor 1:18-25). Dunn suggests, "Paul here is simply working out the implications of the whole Christian understanding of 'strength.'"

> Strength is illusory if it means claiming independence of God; only in the weakness of confessed dependence on God is there real strength. And strength as a believer is equally illusory if it means claiming independence of other believers; only in the weakness of mutual interdependence as members of one body in Christ is there the full strength of grace. The message then could be as much for the weak, or more precisely for anyone who thinks he is strong and able to discount or disregard others. (Dunn 2002b, 38B:843)

Paul's implicit command in Rom 15:1 is not in the imperative mood but in the language of socioeconomic obligation. The verb **ought** (*opheilomen*) is from the cognate family translated "debtor" (*opheiletēs*) in 1:14 (KJV)—Paul was "obligated" to preach the gospel to all (see 4:4; 8:12; 13:7; 15:27). Our "continuing debt [*opheilete*] to love one another" (13:8) accounts for his insistence that the "strong" [*hoi dynatoi, **the powerful, those who are able***] owe it to the "weak" (*tōn adynatōn*, the ***powerless***) to **bear with** (*bastazein;* see Gal 5:10; 6:2, 5, 17) their ***weaknesses.*** Paul does not expect the "strong" "to adopt the scruples of the 'weak.'" Bearing their weaknesses means entering sympathetically into their attitudes, refusing to despise them, and doing what love requires to strengthen them (Moo 1996, 866).

If we have correctly identified the "strong" and the "weak" as the Gentile-Christian majority and the Jewish-Christian minority respectively, there may be an additional explanation for Paul's socioeconomic language. In his image of the olive tree in 11:18, the only other instance of the verb *bastazō* in Romans, he reminds Gentile Christians of their indebtedness to Israel: "You do not support [*bastazeis*] the root, but the root supports you." He will make a similar point later in ch 15. Noting the generous "contribution" (*koinōnian*) of his Gentile churches "for the poor [*ptōchous*] among the saints in Jerusalem" (15:26), he adds: "They . . . owe [*opheiletai*] it to them. For if the Gentiles have shared [*ekoinōnēsan*] in the Jews' spiritual blessings [*pneumatikois*], they owe it to [*opheilousin*] the Jews to share with them their material blessings [*sarkikois*]" (15:27). Beyond the continuing debt of love, Paul considered the debt of the "strong" Gentile Christians to the "weak" Jewish Christians as a matter of simple reciprocity. By bearing with **the failings of the weak,** the "strong" repay a spiritual debt for the privilege of becoming a part of God's people. (See the commentary on 13:8.)

The Greek term translated **failings** (*asthenēmata*, ***weaknesses***) here is from the same cognate family as "weak" in Rom 14 (*asthenounta* in v 1; *asthenōn* in v 2; see the commentary). Perhaps there also is a faint echo of Isa 53:4 and 11 (read christologically as in Matt 8:17), so that just as Christ bore "our infirmities" (*odynatai* LXX), we ***ought to bear the weaknesses of the weak*** (see Gal 6:2). But Paul uses a different Greek term to designate the "weak" here—*tōn adynatōn*, ***the unstrong/powerless.*** This suggests that it is an ad hoc creation rather than an existing label. For Jewish-Christians in Jerusalem, at least, "the poor" (Rom 15:26) was their preferred self-designation.

The unthinkable alternative to putting up with the weaknesses of **the weak** would be for ***the strong*** **to please** (*areskein*) themselves. In v 3 Paul will appeal to the teaching (see Mark 8:34-36; 10:42-45) and example of Jesus (see 1 Cor 10:24; 10:33—11:1; 13:5; Phil 2:4-10; Dunn 2002b, 38B:837). Here his admonition overturns the cultural assumptions that only the strong can please themselves and that "slaves and members of the urban underclass could only hope to please their masters. . . . In Christ it is the powerful who are obliged to serve the powerless" (Jewett 2007, 877).

Paul implies that the scrupulosity, poverty, and lack of social status of the weak are burdens to be borne by the **strong.** If the **weak** need to be reminded of their deficiency in faith, the **strong** in faith need to be reminded that an excess of faith will never compensate for a deficiency in love. Paul warned the knowledgeable of Corinth, "Knowledge puffs us, but love builds up [*oikodomei*]" (1 Cor 8:1). What Paul expects as an appropriate expression of love is apparently "mutual assistance between house and tenement churches, involving material as well as theological and spiritual resources" (Jewett 2007, 877).

Paul pleads for love that edifies (see Gal 6:2). **Not to please ourselves** (Rom 14:1) means to refuse to insist on our rights and privileges (see 1 Cor 9—11 and Phil 2). Self-serving and self-pleasing not only lead to sin (Rom 7:7) but also destroy the potential for healthy relationships with God and others.

■ **2** In v 2 Paul employs the third person singular imperative, commanding every individual in the Roman house churches: **Each of us should please** (*aresketō*) **his neighbor for his good** [see 2:10; 9:11; 12:9, 21; 13:3, 4; 14:16; 16:19], **to build him up** (15:2; see 1 Thess 5:11). "Paul does not expect the strong to please the weak in an undiscriminating way" (Dunn 2002b, 38B:842). His concern is self-denial in the interests of achieving what is in the best interests of the "weak" and for the benefit of the community as a whole.

Mutual acceptance (14:1; 15:7) is the least that might be expected of those who have been accepted by God (14:3). By pleasing others rather than ourselves within such a community, we serve Christ and are well-pleasing (*euarestos*) to God (14:18; see 8:8). To please only oneself is "the inversion of human existence and evasion of God" (Otto Michel cited in Bietenhard 1976, 354 n. 4). "Pleasing God is incompatible with ignoring one's neighbor." And yet, "God's good pleasure" must not be "lost for the sake of human sympathy" by "mere conformism or accommodation. . . . Renewed reason has to find out whom to please and in what way" (Käsemann 1980, 381).

Eating and drinking as we see fit may please our palates, but as Christians we must seek first to **please** our **neighbor.** Whatever else the all-encompassing commandment to love our neighbors (Lev 19:18, cited in Rom 13:9-10; see Gal 5:14; Eph 4:25) may demand, it must include pleasing them. Here Paul echoes the teaching of Jesus (see Rom 13:9).

Of course, pleasing God must take precedence over pleasing people (see 8:8; Gal 1:10; Eph 6:6; Col 3:22; 1 Thess 2:4), although it may be possible to do both (Rom 14:18; 1 Cor 10:33). Aware that we may please our **neighbor** to his or her hurt, Paul cautions us to **please** them in pursuit of worthy goals: ***for*** [*eis*] ***their good*** and ***in order to*** [*pros*] ***build them up*** [*oikodomēn;* see Rom 14:19; 1 Cor 12:7, 25].

> The phrase does not have the individual as such in view ("for his edification") but, as the metaphor implies, the growth to maturity of the whole congregation *pros oikodomēn*—1 Cor 14:12, 26; Eph 4:29; *eis oikodomēn*—2 Cor 10:8; 13:10; Eph 4:12, 16); or more precisely, the growth to maturity of the weaker brother *as part of* the body of Christ (see 1 Cor 14:4). (Dunn 2002b, 38B:838)

To **please** one's **neighbor** does not mean a facile attempt to make the neighbor happy at all costs. It means to put ourselves at the task of "the common good" (*eis to agathon*) in a way that makes for mutual upbuilding. If each house and tenement church "seeks constructively to encourage the development of integrity and maturity in other groups, rather than trying to force them to conform to a single viewpoint, the ethnic and theological diversity in Rome would no longer be divisive and destructive" (Jewett 2007, 879).

■ **3** As a rationale for self-denial, Paul appeals to the countercultural example of Jesus (Mark 10:42-45 [in contrast to typical Gentile ways]; John 13:1-15; 2 Cor 8:9; Phil 2:5-10; 1 Thess 1:6; 2:14; 1 Pet 2:21). **For even Christ did not please** [*ēresen*] **himself** [see Rom 15:1]. The aorist tense of the verb may imply that Paul thought primarily of the suffering and death of the Messiah (Jewett 2007, 879).

Paul finds OT precedent for the crucifixion in Ps 69:9, **as it is written** [see the scripture quotation formula in Rom 1:17]: **"The insults of those who insult you have fallen on me"** (15:3, citing Ps 69:9). This psalm is echoed throughout the NT with reference to Jesus (see, e.g., Matt 27:34; John 2:14-17; 15:25; Acts 1:20; 2 Cor 5:21; 1 Pet 2:22, 24; 3:18). Despite a lack of Jewish precedent for understanding it messianically (Dunn 2002b, 38B:838), because of Jesus' experience and his resurrection from the dead, Christians read the psalm as messianic.

Read in this light, the psalm describes Christ as so identified with the cause of God that he endures in his own person the assaults of the enemies of God. **Insults** were Christ's lot because he **did not please himself** but lived to please the Father in the work of redemption. If self-pleasing had been the guide to his life, he would have escaped the shame and reproach that was heaped upon him. But living as he did to please God, to serve his will for our salvation, these **insults** came; and, thus, they were *God's* (Isa 53:4-5).

But Christ's refusal to **please himself** is not about just one isolated act. The pattern he followed throughout his "career" on our behalf only culminated in his death on the cross. The other-pleasing Christ did not cling selfishly to the "likeness to God," which was his "by nature"—but "emptied himself" and took on "the very nature of a slave," even to the point of dying the most shameful of deaths on the cross (Phil 2:6-8; see Gal 2:20). Thus, believers are not simply to *imitate* Christ. We must allow his self-emptying "mind-set" to transform us from within so that our very *existence* is "in Christ" (Phil 2:5; Rom 6:10-11) and cruciform (1 Cor 2:1-5; 2 Cor 4:7-12; Gal 2:20; 6:14, 17; Phil 3:17-21).

■ **4** Paul justifies (*gar,* **For**) his use of Scripture on the principle: **For everything** [*hosa,* ***whatever***] **that was written in the past was written to teach us, so that** [*hina*] **through** [*dia*] **endurance and *through*** [*dia*] **the encouragement of the Scriptures we might have hope** (Rom 15:4). Paul's call for us to emulate the model and "mind-set" of Christ (see Phil 2:5-10) is a hermeneutical principle. All Scripture is to be read in the light of Christ (see Rom 4:23-24). And all Scripture is intended to transform those who hear it (see 1 Cor 9:10; 10:11). Hence everything written **in the past** (see Rom 1:2; 3:21) was written ***for the purpose of instructing us*** (*eis tēn hēmeteran didaskalian;* see 12:7; 1 Tim 4:13, 16; 2 Tim 3:10, 16; Titus 2:7), more specifically, ***in order that we*** **might have hope** (echoing 1 Macc 12:9).

Paul's Interpretation of Scripture

Paul, as a first-century Hellenized Jew, often interprets Scripture in ways that defy modern Western expectations. But his approach is not arbitrary, frivolous, or self-serving. Richard B. Hays identifies three criteria consistently applied in the apostle's appropriation of Scripture. (1) "No reading of Scripture can be legitimate if it denies the faithfulness of Israel's God to his covenant promises." There are not two gods. The new thing God is up to is the fulfillment of the old, not a replacement of it.

(2) "Scripture must be read as a witness to the gospel of Jesus Christ. No reading of Scripture can be legitimate if it fails to acknowledge the death and resurrection of Jesus as the climactic manifestation of God's righteousness." These principles are faithfully adopted by early church fathers in their biblical hermeneutics (see O'Keefe and Reno 2005).

(3) "True interpretation of Scripture leads us into unqualified giving of our lives in service within the community whose vocation is to reenact the obedience of the Son of God who loved us and gave himself for us." Scripture may not be read legitimately for information alone; its object is transformation (all of the quotations are from Hays 1993, 191).

The purpose (*hina*) of scriptural instruction is **so that . . . we might have hope** (see Rom 5:2-4; 8:24). Paul's mention of **hope** presupposes an allusion in the psalm he quotes to the **endurance** of Christ as a righteous sufferer in God's cause. It throws light also on the sufferings believers endure in union with Christ (see 8:17; Phil 3:10). In this context the psalm is calling on the **strong** to take the attitude pioneered by Christ, suffering for the **weak** (Rom 15:1; see 5:6). It thus partakes of the **hope** accompanying all suffering for Christ (see 8:18). What Paul says about **hope** elsewhere suggests that its specific content is eschatological. Thus, we need not decide whether he has in mind "eternal salvation" (Meyer 1889, 334), "the fulfillment of Israel's eschatological hope" (Dunn 2002b, 38B:840), or "the conversion of the nations" (Jewett 2007, 883).

The two distinct (note the repeated prepositions) *means* **through** which **the Scriptures** mediate **hope** are **endurance** and **encouragement.** In 5:3-4 Paul claimed that "suffering produces perseverance" (*hypomonēn, **endurance***) and ultimately "hope." Paul similarly associated **endurance** and Christian **hope** in 8:24-25. The only other instance of the noun **encouragement** (*paraklēsis*) in Romans outside the present context is in 12:8, which identifies **encouragement** as among God's gifts to the church, perhaps actualized through scriptural preaching (see 1 Cor 14:13; 1 Thess 2:3; 1 Tim 4:13). Outside Romans, Paul associates **encouragement** and **hope** in 2 Cor 1:7 and 2 Thess 2:16.

> Both moral qualities that Paul derives from Scripture are highly relevant for the congregational situation: divinely granted steadfastness in bearing one another's burdens while living in the midst of reproaches; godly encouragement to seek responsible forms of upbuilding through pleasing others. (Jewett 2007, 882)

■ **5** After the digression of the previous verse, Paul returns to his subject and summarizes his plea for the unity of the Roman community: **May the God who gives endurance** [*tēs hypomonēs*, lit. ***of patience/endurance***] **and encouragement** [*tēs paraklēseōs*, lit. ***of encouragement***] **give you a spirit of unity among yourselves as you follow Christ Jesus** (Rom 15:5). Paul does not conceive of the Scriptures as a magical book that independently of God acts upon its readers or hearers. The Scriptures are not the source of **endurance** and **encouragement,** but God's means of making these qualities available (v 4) to those who find the personal divine reality behind the ink and paper.

That Paul addresses the Romans (*hymin,* **you** [plural]), not God, requires that his words here are not a prayer (note the rare optative mood) as such, but an intercessory prayer report (see Wiles 1974). Leaving aside his description of God for the moment, Paul's wish in behalf of the Roman Christians is simply: ***May God give you the same mind*** [*to auto phronein;* lit. ***to think the same thing;*** see 12:16] ***among one another*** [*en allēlois*] ***consistent with Christ Jesus*** [*kata Christon Iēsoun*]. (See the sidebar "Prepositions" with the commentary on Rom 8:4.)

God is the source of the **endurance and encouragement** mediated through the Scriptures (15:4) and fellow believers (see 1:12; 12:1-8). God comes alongside us and gives us the strength we need to persevere to eternal life (see 2:7), final salvation (see 8:24-25). Paul's letters are obviously not a modern systematic theology. Nonetheless, his descriptions of God reveal some of his basic theological convictions. God is the one "who justifies the wicked" (4:5), "who gives life to the dead and calls things that are not as though they were" (4:17), ***who gives hope*** (15:13), ***who gives peace*** (15:33; 16:20; Phil 4:9; 1 Thess 5:23; 2 Thess 3:16; see Heb 13:20), who is the source "of compassion and . . . of all comfort" (2 Cor 1:3) and "of love and peace" (2 Cor 13:11), "who reconciled us to himself through Christ" (2 Cor 5:18; see 1 Pet 5:10), "who . . . blessed us . . . in Christ" (Eph 1:3), who faithfully "calls" us to holiness, and who "will do it" (1 Thess 5:23-24).

The paraphrase, **May . . . God . . . give you a spirit of unity,** obscures Paul's appeal to the language of the renewed mind initiated in 12:2. More literally, Paul prays that God may give them ***the same mind/to think the same thing*** [*to auto phronein*]. In 12:16 this idiom (*to auto . . . phronountes*) is translated **Live in harmony.** Paul assumes that the renewed Christian mind should express itself in tangible cooperation among the various churches in Rome.

Paul does *not* expect "ideological conformity" (Jewett 2007, 884). Romans 14 presumes that different opinions on vegetarianism, Sabbath keeping, etc., will persist. He prays not for cultural uniformity but for unity ***consistent with Christ.*** Such harmony should reflect the model of Christ, who endured insults for others rather than pleasing himself (v 3). To ***think the same thing*** would mean unity appropriate to their place within the new humanity Christ created (see 5:12-21; 13:14; 2 Cor 3:18; 4:4, 6; Eph 4:24), confirming their status as obedient subjects of the risen Lord (see Rom 6:17; 14:4-8; 2 Cor 11:17).

Paul is not at all uncomfortable with differences within the Christian community (see 12:3-7). But he is insistent that such differences must not be allowed to become an occasion for unhealthy and counterproductive disputes on nonessentials (see the commentary on ch 14). The unanimity he expects is not uniformity. Consensus is not the same as conformity. To most ears, the harmony of symphony is preferable to both cacophony and the monotony of unison. **Christ Jesus** alone, not the "strong" or the "weak," sets the terms of Christian unity. Christ's call of Paul to be a Jewish apostle to the Gentiles (see 15:16) taught him that true strength meant accepting those who were unlike him and to defend their right to be different from him.

■ **6** According to v 6, the goal (*hina,* **so that**) of Christian unity is not the submerging of substantial differences beneath a veneer of civility. Mere tolerance of diversity is not a worthy goal. What Paul expected was authentic communal worship (see 12:2). His prayer is that ***with one mind*** [*homothymadon,* ***same emotion***] ***and one mouth*** [*en heni stomata;* see 10:8-10] the diverse members of the Roman churches **may glorify the God and Father of our Lord Jesus Christ** (v 6; see, e.g., 2 Cor 1:3; 11:31). Based on its use in Acts, *homothymadon* "appears to be a 'technical term' for prayerful unity in the early church." Similarly, *en heni stomata* uses the language of harmonious choral singing (Jewett 2007, 884, 885).

Although it is not Paul's primary agenda, his subtle identification of Jesus with God and his equally clear distinction of Jesus from God placed creedal precision on the church's agenda for centuries to come. Disputes over the fine points of Christology and Trinity have undoubtedly been as divisive in Christian history as those over food and festivals Paul addresses in Rom 14 and 15. We can only wonder how Paul might have responded to the well-intentioned efforts of "orthodox" believers after him to identify and silence the dissenting "heretics." Surely, such matters are not nonessential! But we must not miss Paul's point in Rom 15:6: Agreement on worship alone, not opinion (see 14:1-6), is essential to Christian unity.

Paul diagnoses the root problem of fallen humanity as its ungrateful failure to glorify God (1:18-25). Perhaps, he assumes that agreement on the primacy of the glory of God will enable the "weak in faith," like Abraham, to grow strong in faith (see 4:20). True Christian unity is "the unity of the Spirit through the bond of peace" (Eph 4:3; see John 17:21-23, 26). Paul does not authorize the "strong" to suppress or deny the differences that exist among Christians. Unity is not a human achievement, accomplished in the power of the Flesh. It is the work of God in Christ "by the power of the Holy Spirit" (Rom 15:13).

(2) Unity in the Power of the Spirit (15:7-13)

BEHIND THE TEXT

In 15:7 Paul repeats the appeal with which he began this subsection of the letter in 14:1. But there is reason to believe that 15:7-13 concludes not only the parenesis of the letter (12:1—15:13) but also the body of the letter as a whole. Paul's appeal in 15:8 to **God's truth** echoes 1:18, 25; 2:8; and 3:7. The **promises made to the patriarchs** in v 8 refer back to 4:9-22 and 9:4, 8-9. God's **mercy** to the Gentiles reiterates the emphasis of 9:15-18, 23, and 11:30-32. **Trust** (*pisteuein,* **to have faith in/believe**) in 15:13 harks back not only to 14:1, 2, 22, and 23, but to the theme of the letter announced in 1:16-17 (Jewett 2007, 887).

IN THE TEXT

■ **7** In 15:7 Paul broadens his plea sounded first in 14:1. Here he urges not only the "strong" but also the entire community: **Accept** [*proslambanesthe,* see 14:1] **one another** [*allēlous*]. In 14:3, Paul refers to God's prior acceptance of the strong as the rationale for their full acceptance of the weak. Here, the precedent is Christ. To practice mutual acceptance is to be Christlike: **just as** [*kathōs*] **Christ accepted** [*proselambeto*] **you** [*hymas* (plural)]. The first word in the Greek sentence, *Dio,* **then,** suggests that 15:7-13 concludes and summarizes 14:1—15:13.

Because the verb *proslambanō* connotes welcoming others to share a meal, one specific expression of the mutual (note the reciprocal pronoun *allēlous,* **one another**) acceptance Paul expected was that both groups would participate together in the agape meal/love feast—the more extensive common meal we now call Communion, Eucharist, or the Lord's Supper. The example of Christ (see 15:3), who invites all to his table, continues to provide the model for both "weak" and "strong." **Accept one another . . . as Christ accepted you.**

The previous paragraph concluded with a call for "unity" (v 5) "so that . . . you may glorify [*doxazēte*] . . . God" (v 6). In v 7 Paul makes essentially the same point: Unity expresses itself as mutual acceptance for one *purpose:* ***to the glory*** [*eis doxan*] ***of God*** (v 7*b;* see 3:7, 23; 4:20; 11:36; 15:6, 9; 1 Cor 10:31; 2 Cor 4:15; Phil 1:11; 2:11). As a verbal noun, ***glory*** presumes the human activity of praising (see the sidebar "Glory" with 8:18)—***you glorify God.***

For weak and strong Christians to accept one another would answer Paul's prayer-wish reported in v 6—**that with one heart and mouth you may glorify the God and Father of our Lord Jesus Christ.** A familiar biblical pattern of motivation is found here: what one has received from God, one is bound to extend to others: **Accept one another, then, just as Christ accepted you, in order to bring praise to God** (see 14:3; Deut 24:17-22; Matt 18:32-33).

■ **8** Up to this point, Paul has not explicitly identified the two groups—the "strong" and the "weak"—within the community. In Rom 15:8-9, however, it becomes quite clear that his focus all along has been on **God's** action in **Christ** with respect to **Jews** (*peritomēs,* ***the circumcision;*** see 3:30; 4:12) and **Gentiles** [*ta . . . ethnē;* the first appearance of the term since 11:25]. The equations in these verses challenge Nanos's claim that "the weak" in chs 14 and 15 refer to non-Christian Jews (1996, 143).

Paul's words, ***For I say,*** "introduce a solemn doctrinal declaration" (Cranfield 2004, 2:740): **Christ has become** [*gegenēsthai*—perfect tense, emphasizing a present state based on a past event] **a servant** [*diakonon, **minister;*** see Mark 10:45] **of the Jews on behalf of God's truth** (v 8*a*). Jesus' humble service (Mark 10:43-45) so transformed Jewish messianic expectations that Paul elsewhere (besides Gal 2:17) refers to it in terms of slavery (*doulou* in Phil 2:7).

Paul's allusion to Christ's ministry to "the circumcision" is more than a foil for what he is about to say concerning the Gentiles. Paul sets the two "economies of salvation" side-by-side to showcase God's faithfulness to both—"first for the Jew, then for the Gentile" (1:16). As 1:16-17 introduces the body of the letter, 15:7-13 concludes it (Dunn 2002b, 38B:847). Because justification depends first and foremost on the faithfulness of Christ, he confirms that God's promises to all Abraham's descendants can be trusted (see 4:16; see 2 Cor 1).

The perfect tense of the verb **has become** suggests that **Christ**'s service to the Jews is not limited to his earthly ministry (see Gal 4:4). His ongoing ministry to the Jews **on behalf of God's truth** [*hyper alētheias Theou*] is an expression of the faithfulness of God: God is "true" (*alēthēs*) to himself and his covenant promises, despite human unfaithfulness—by both Jews and Gentiles (Rom 3:4; see 1:18, 25; 2:8; 3:7). The risen Christ did not shed his humanity or cease to be a Jew (1:3).

Christ's "service" on God's behalf to **the Jews** demonstrates the reliability of God's **promises made** [*bebaiōsai, **established, made firm, proved reliable, fulfilled;*** Bauer 1979, 138] **to the patriarchs** of Israel (4:9-22; 9:4, 8-9; 2 Cor 1:18-21). God's promises to the patriarchs were fulfilled in the sending of his Son and his Spirit (Gal 3:14, 22), so that Abraham's seed could bless "all peoples on earth" (Gen 12:3; see Rom 4:18).

■ **9** In 15:9, Paul spells out the gracious result (**so that**) of God's demonstrated faithfulness to Israel. Through Christ's atoning sacrifice (3:9, 20, 23) and free offer of salvation (see esp. 3:21, 25-26), he opened a door of **mercy** to the **Gentiles** (see 11:30-32). For the **Gentiles** (v 9*a*) a different "economy" was operative. They had not directly received God's **promises,** as Israel had (see 3:2; 9:4), although his promise to Abraham did concern them (see 4:16-17; Gal 3:8, 14, 15-22, 29). "Paul's whole point is that Christ became servant of the circumcised *not* with a view to their salvation alone, but to confirm *both* phases of God's saving purpose: to Jew first but also to Gentile" (Dunn 2002b, 38B:848). **Jews** should praise God for his faithfulness to his covenant **promises.**

But the salvation of the **Gentiles** came as an act of **mercy** (*hyper* *eleous;* see Rom 11:30-32). This was grace, pure and simple, to those who were by definition "Gentile sinners" (see Gal 2:15), outside the covenant. The goal of Christ's "service" on their behalf is that *they,* too, **may glorify** [*doxasai*] **God,** but in recognition of his **mercy** (Rom 15:9*a;* see 9:15-23; 11:30-32).

Dunn sees in these verses Paul weaving together the major strands of his theological argument emphasized earlier in Romans. Thus, he recapitulates the central themes of his letter as he brings it to a conclusion.

> The truth of God as creator, as one with God's covenant faithfulness to Israel; no dichotomy between creation and salvation. Jesus still a Jew and servant of circumcision, even though now exalted, last Adam and Lord of all; the tension between Jewish priority and universal fulfillment maintained within Christ himself. And not least the unified concept of God's truth-and-mercy expressing that unity in the combination of his faithfulness to circumcised and mercy to Gentile. (Dunn 2002b, 38B:852)

In vv 9*b*-13 Paul closes the body of the letter with a list of scriptural quotations (see 3:10; 11:8) demonstrating that "the acceptance of the Gentiles [is] an eschatological miracle" (Käsemann 1980, 386). The inclusion of all nations within the people of God, like the resurrection of the dead, was a prophetic **hope** expected only in the last age. Thus, it is not surprising that the word **hope** appears three times in vv 12-13.

As it is written, *kathōs gegraptai* (v 9*b*), repeats the quotation formula appearing first in 1:17 (see 2:24; 3:4, 10; 4:17; 8:36; 9:13; 10:15; 11:8, 26; 15:3, 21), emphasizing Christ's role in behalf of the Gentiles. As in 3:10 and 11:8, it introduces a catena of OT citations.

In rabbinic style, Paul selects texts from each of the three main canonical divisions of Israel's Scriptures: the Law (LXX Deut 32:43 in Rom 15:10), the Prophets (LXX Isa 11:10 in Rom 15:12), and the Writings (LXX Ps 18:49 [= 2 Sam 22:50] in Rom 15:9*b* and Ps 117:1 in Rom 15:11). Such representative quotations of Scripture allow him to assert the unanimous biblical witness to God's intent, through the ministry of the Messiah—**the Root of Jesse**—to extend his **rule** to include ***the Gentiles*** (v 12).

The apostle to the Gentiles understands the words of Ps 18:49 as a prophecy of his mission (Käsemann 1980, 387). **I will praise** [*exomologēsomai*] **you** in v 9 translates the same verb rendered he **will confess** [*exomologēsetai*] in 14:11. Thus, the **I** in 15:8-9 refers to Paul. His mission is to confess Christ **among the Gentiles,** to ***sing praise*** [*psalō*] **to** his **name.** "Paul places himself in the role of the eschatological agent whose task is to initiate the crescendo of praise that will sweep over the Gentile world, responding to the conversion and pacification of the world evoked by the gospel" (Jewett 2007, 894).

■ **10** Verse 10 selectively quotes Deut 32:43 as evidence for the expectation that Jews and Gentiles will rejoice together. Paul reverses the OT eschatological hope that Israel would conquer the Gentiles, hoping instead for their conversion (see Scobie 2003, 509-40).

■ **11** In Rom 15:11, Paul quotes Ps 117:1, urging Gentiles and Jews to **sing praises** to the Lord together. "This scriptural warrant reinforces the emphasis of the preceding citation concerning ethnic groups rejoicing *with* each other rather than at each other's expense" (Jewett 2007, 895).

As a result of God's faithfulness and mercy, Israel's Messiah has become the object of **hope** for ***all the people*** of the world. "The final events are being fulfilled in the conversion of the Gentiles" (Dunn 2002b, 38B:849). As his rule progressively destroys the enslaving forces of Sin and Death, Christ prepares the way for the final victory of God's kingdom (see 1 Cor 15:24-28; Phil 2:9-11).

In recognition of his victory already in progress, believing **Gentiles** are called upon to **glorify God for his mercy** (Rom 15:9*a*). This is the goal of Christ's "acceptance" of them, ***to the glory of God*** (v 7*b;* see 1:21). In 15:9-11, Paul employs five different verbs describing the activity of giving glory to God—*exomologēsomai* (***confess,*** v 9*b;* see 14:11) and *psalō* (***sing praise*** in 15:9*c*), *euphranthēte* (**Rejoice, *be glad*** in v 10; see Gal 4:27), *aineite* (***praise***), and *epainesatōsan* (***praise*** in 15:11).

ROMANS

15:9-13

■ **12** Isaiah 11:10, which Paul quotes in Rom 15:12, was widely understood as a messianic prophecy (Isa 11:1-5; Jer 23:5; 33:15; Rev 5:5; 22:16). **The Root of Jesse,** referring to the great descendant of David (see Rom 1:3), Jesse's son, **will spring up** (*anistamenos, **arising again;*** see Acts 17:3; Eph 5:14; 1 Thess 4:14). As a result of his rising again, **Gentiles will hope in him.** In contrast to the MT, the LXX translation allows Paul to associate the resurrection of Christ and the conversion of the Gentiles. The extension of Christ's **rule** to include the **Gentiles** is the basis for their **hope in him.**

Contrary to the eschatological hope of many Jews, Christ came to save Gentiles, not to destroy them (see Pss 2:8-9; 72:8-9; 110:1). Such **mercy** should cause Gentiles to **glorify God** (Rom 15:9), to celebrate their **hope.** Paul's reading of the Scriptures has demonstrated to his satisfaction that God "promised [the gospel] beforehand through his prophets in the Holy Scriptures" (1:2; see Hays 1993, 71).

■ **13** In 15:13 a second prayer-wish report (see v 5) forms an appropriate conclusion to Paul's lengthy appeal, extending from 14:1 through 15:13: **May the God of hope** [*Ho . . . theos tēs elpidos;* see 15:4; 4:18; 5:4] **fill you**

with all joy and peace as you trust in him, so that you may overflow with hope. Once again, the rare optative mood expresses the sentiment of Paul's intercessory prayer—***May God fill you with every kind of joy and peace*** (see 14:17; 5:1-5; see the sidebar "Peace" with 5:1).

Paul prays that ***as*** Jews and Gentiles ***believe*** (*en tō pisteuein*) together, despite all their differences, they may nonetheless **overflow** [*perisseuein;* see 3:7; 5:15; Phil 1:9-11] **with hope** [*en tēi elpidi*] **by the power of the Holy Spirit** [see 1:4, 16; 5:5; 14:17; 15:16, 19]. God's divine resources are more than adequate to move the church composed of Jews and Gentiles forward "into the new world of hope" (Dunn 2002b, 38B:851, citing H. W. Schmidt).

FROM THE TEXT

From its earliest times, as Rom 14:1—15:13 reveals, Christians have differed in conscientious scruples. In nonessentials such as those over which the Christian communities in Rome were struggling, "others may, I cannot" is a valid motto. The church should have by this time, however, outgrown such contentions. As it has matured it has generally moved beyond most of such disputes—although orthodox Seventh-Day Adventists still insist that Constantine changed the church's "Sabbath" from Saturday to Sunday and continue to observe some OT dietary rules. For most denominations, however, these issues are gospel "nonessentials" that call for the loving "welcoming" urged by Paul in 15:1-7. Such ceremonial issues, however, do not rend Christ's one body.

Paul's insistence that Christ has abolished the Law is the *theological* basis for the Christian ethic. What the Law cannot do *Christ* has done, once and for all (8:1-4). This basic truth must not be forgotten when discussing matters of *ceremonial* law (see, for example, Matt 12:1-7).

In giving the Decalogue centrality in the Christian ethic (Rom 8:12-13; 13:8-10), Paul puts all ethical matters in proper perspective. Compared to *that,* the contentious issues of chs 14—15 are minuscule. Being Christian is not a matter of observing or not observing ceremonial regulations. The ethical issues of true moment are those Jesus addressed in the Sermon on the Mount—the "more important matters of the law" (Matt 23:23). The Great Commandment calls us to love God with all our heart and soul and mind and our neighbor as ourselves. "All the Law and the Prophets hang on these two commandments" (Matt 22:40; see vv 37-40). For Paul, as for virtually all Christian ethicists since, the love command is what really matters. For John Wesley, it is the substance of "Christian perfection."

Romans 14:1—15:13 concludes Paul's development of the parenetic appeal initiated in 12:1-2. Mutual relationships within Christian communities are crucial tests of the working out of renewed minds, practical expressions of worship in everyday life, and proofs of genuine love at work (12:9). Such holiness is, or should be, a distinguishing mark of the church. Practical soteriology inevitably has ecclesial implications. Wesley believed "welcoming one another as Christ has welcomed you" to be a crucial demonstration of the "catholic spirit," which should prevail in the body of Christ. Of course, Wesley referred not to the presence of the Holy Spirit within the Roman Catholic Church but to an attitude that took seriously the potentially universal inclusiveness of the church of Christ. In his sermon on 2 Kgs 10:15, Wesley found this ecumenical principle:

> Although a difference of opinions on modes of worship may prevent an entire external union, yet need it prevent a union of affection? Though we cannot think alike, may we not love alike? May we not be of one heart, though we are not of one opinion? (1979, 5:493; sermon on "Catholic Spirit")

Wesley recognized that as long as there were diverse opinions, there would be various ways of worshipping God, since a variety of opinions necessarily imply a variety of practices. Thus, he asked of those who would enter into community together only this: Is your heart right with God? Do you believe in the Lord Jesus Christ? Do you love God with all your heart, mind, soul, and strength? Is your heart right toward your neighbor? These questions alone truly matter (1979, 5:495-98; sermon on "Catholic Spirit").

Although Wesley believed the Episcopal form of government to be "scriptural and apostolical," he allowed Presbyterians and Independents their right to differ. He even received as fellow Christians those who differed with his conviction that he "ought to eat bread and drink wine, as a memorial to [his] dying Master," allowing others who differed the ecclesiastical right to "act according to the light" they had received (1979, 5:499; sermon on "Catholic Spirit"). All he asked of others was a "heart enlarged" to include all humanity. "Catholic love is catholic spirit," he concluded (1979, 5:503).

Wesley denied that his willingness to extend the label "Christian" to those who were very different from him was *"speculative"* or "any kind of *practical* latitudinarianism" (1979, 5:502). Perhaps we may speak of Wesley's view as *evangelical* latitudinarianism, which confesses with John Oxenham:

> In Christ there is no East or West,
> In Him no South or North;

But one great fellowship of love
Throughout the whole wide earth.
Join hands then, brothers of the faith,
Whate'er your race may be;
Who serves my Father as a son
Is surely kin to me.

Wesley as Catholic Theologian

> Wesley developed and changed, not only before his conversion, but also long after. So, if you see him in his maturity, say from the mid-1740s and even more from the 1760s onward, what you see is not the dogmatic high churchman of his early years or the dogmatic "evangelical" at the time of his conversion, but rather what I would call a "both-and" rather than an "either-or" theologian. This runs through his theology and practice. Thus, justification *and* sanctification; formal *and* informal worship; individual *and* collective piety; spiritual *and* social salvation. Even more challenging is his claim that church order must be subordinated to the demands of evangelism and pastoral care. (Rack 2006, 186)

Christian unity is founded on the theological understanding that through faith in Jesus Christ we become members-in-common of the one body of Christ. Christian unity is not an option; it is a gift to be received and expressed. Christian unity does not require institutional consolidation. In the midst of denominational diversity, the Holy Spirit is at work making trans-denominational Christian unity visible. In the power of the Spirit, Christians, liberal and conservative alike, may refuse to allow the comparatively petty things that divide them to divert them from the one thing that finally matters—the glory of God (Rom 15:6).

III. CONCLUSION (15:14—16:27)

Romans 15:14-22 picks up where 1:1-15 left off. Paul recapitulates his reasons for writing the letter (15:14-16) and briefly explains the missionary strategy that had made it impossible for him to visit Rome earlier (15:17-22). In 15:23-33 he announces his travel plans and requests the prayers of his Roman audience in his behalf. Final greetings to acquaintances in the several house and tenement churches of Rome fill 16:1-16. Following a warning against false teachers in 16:17-20, he sends greetings from his companions in 16:21-24, before formally closing the letter with a doxological benediction in 16:25-27.

Romans 15:14—16:27 includes all of the typical closing features of a Pauline letter, although in a far more expansive form than usual. Numerous textual variations complicate this closing section. The lengthy, wandering benediction of 16:25-27 presents particular challenges. Nonetheless, Harry Gamble's thorough investigation of the textual history of Romans offers persuasive evidence in favor of the literary integrity of the letter even in this most textually disturbed section (1979).

A. Paul's Travel Plans (15:14-33)

In 15:14-33 Paul restates and expands upon the announcement of his plans to visit Rome provocatively introduced in 1:8-15 (compare 1:8 and 15:14; 1:10 and 15:30-32; 1:11-12 and 15:23-24, 28-29; 1:13-14 and 15:15-22; 1:14 and 15:25-27). Dunn goes so far as to identify 1:16—15:13 as an extremely "long parenthesis" (2002b, 38B:866). In 1:16—15:13 Paul outlined the "theological scope" of his apostolic mission; in 15:14-33, its "geographical scope" (Dunn 2002b, 38B:867).

1. To Rome and to Spain (15:14-22)

BEHIND THE TEXT

Paul has completed his lengthy celebration of the gospel (see 1:16), which occupies the body of the letter (1:16—15:13). He has communicated to his largely Gentile audience in Rome a sense of the significance and hope of their inclusion in the eschatological people of God (see 1:16—8:39). At the same time he has made clear that the God who acted in their behalf has not excluded his ancient people Israel (see 9:1—11:36). He has invited the various churches of Rome to allow their communal life to be shaped by this vision of the gospel (see 12:1—15:13).

Presenting his gospel as a celebration of God's grace and faithfulness, Paul has, in effect, "preached the gospel" to the Romans in an anticipatory way (see 1:15). The time has now come to present *himself* more directly to them, not simply as a minister of the gospel to the Gentiles (see 1:1-5, 8-15) but now as one en route to visit them. By announcing his travel plans, sending greetings to various members of their mutual community, and offering prayers for their well-being, Paul simply follows the pattern of ancient letter writing. But this announcement is more than a conventional necessity. In fact, the central treatise of the letter (1:16—15:13) "was intended in part at least to forward and facilitate these plans" (Dunn 2002b, 38B:856).

The diplomatic way in which Paul introduces his plans in 15:14 goes well beyond conventional rhetoric (plerophoric; see 4:21; 8:38-39; 14:5; Col 2:2; 1 Thess 1:5; Heb 6:11; 10:22; 11:1). His communication with Rome at this point reaches its most delicate moment. He wants to announce his visit without alienating the community or putting them on the defensive. Paul's visit there was, after all, to be a violation of his own principle of not interfering in the affairs of churches he had not founded (15:20). At the same time, Paul needed to preserve the sense of himself as apostle to the Gentiles, looking for a future base for his missionary aspirations in the West in which the Roman community might play a crucial role.

Paul goes about this task according to acceptable rhetorical practice. He diplomatically acknowledges that he has admonished them as "competent to instruct one another" (15:14). If he has written "quite boldly" to them, it has been simply to "remind" them of the gospel they already know (v 15). At this time he gives a much fuller account of the grace given to him and its purpose, as he sees it: "to be a minister of Christ Jesus to the Gentiles with the priestly duty of proclaiming the gospel of God, so that the Gentiles might become an offering acceptable to God, sanctified by the Holy Spirit" (v 16). The cultic language of offering and sacrifice here is his first attribution in this letter of Christian believers' *sanctification* by the Holy Spirit (Acts 15:9; 1 Cor 3:16; 6:19; see Rom 12:1-2).

This cultic use of *hagiazō* is part of the way Paul conceives of the unity of the Gentiles with Israel. With similar language about Israel in 11:16, he argued, "If the root is holy, so are the branches." Gentiles who have been grafted into Israel partake of the "nourishing sap" of Israel's holiness (11:18). This cultic language also connects "the apostle to the Gentiles" and his "offering," which is the Gentiles. Elsewhere Paul refers to himself as "a drink offering on the sacrifice and service coming from your faith" (Phil 2:17).

After writing theologically of his apostolic role, Paul states what he has practically accomplished in this role. Or, more accurately, he describes "what Christ [had] accomplished" (Rom 15:18) through him by the "signs and miracles" (v 19) performed in the power of the Spirit. His ministry had been part of the mighty arc of evangelization taking in the entire eastern Mediterranean world. He had been only an agent of the gospel, impelled by the Spirit to press ever outward to regions where Christ "was not known" (v 20), laying a foundation for the future expansion of the gospel. This pressing task had "often . . . hindered" (v 21) him from coming to Rome.

IN THE TEXT

■ **14 I myself am convinced, my brothers *and sisters,* that you yourselves are full of goodness, complete in knowledge and competent** [*dynamenoi,* ***able/empowered***] **to instruct one another** (v 14). The striking contrast with the description of sinful humanity in 1:29 demonstrates how completely the gospel changes lives. By addressing his Roman audience as friends (**brothers**), Paul not only prepared them to expect a new turn in his correspondence (see 1:13; 7:1, 4; 8:12; 9:3; 10:1; 11:25; 12:1; 16:17), he assured them that he fully respected their Christian standing.

Such ingratiating expressions of confidence (*captatio benevolentiae*) were typical rhetorical devices in situations such as Paul's. To assure that his message was received favorably, he courteously flattered his audience with typical Eastern hyperbole. Sincere, albeit extravagant, praise would dispose them to receive him and his message sympathetically.

Assuming that the Roman churches were as anxious to see him as he was to see them, he hoped to overcome any distance that may have arisen from his failure to visit Rome earlier. He took seriously his own advice: "Let us therefore make every effort to do what leads to peace and to mutual edification" (14:19) and "Each of us should please his neighbor for his good, to build him up" (15:2).

To this end Paul expressed the conviction that the Roman Christians were **full** [*mestoi*] **of goodness** (v 14; see Gal 5:22; Eph 5:9; 2 Thess 1:11). Although the abstract noun **goodness** (*agathōsynēs)* appears only here in Romans, Paul has used the adjective "good" (*agathos*) throughout the letter to describe the positive behavior God approves (see 2:7, 10; 3:8; 7:18, 19; 9:11; 12:2, 9, 21; 13:3-4; 14:16; 15:2; 16:19). This description of his audience stands in striking contrast with the apostle's characterization of fallen humanity in 1:29 as "full [*mestous*] of envy, murder, strife, deceit and malice."
15:14 The Roman Christians were living proof of the saving power of the gospel.

They were **full of goodness** precisely because they were ***filled*** [*peplērōmenoi*] ***with all*** [*pasēs*] **knowledge** [*gnōseōs*] (contrast 1:29—"filled [*peplērōmenous*] *with* every kind of [*pasēi*] wickedness, evil, greed and depravity.") This knowledge had made them fully **competent to instruct** [*nouthetein*] **one another.** The Greek term for instruction refers to ethical advice and warning (see 1 Cor 4:14; 10:11; Col 1:28; 3:16; 1 Thess 5:12, 14; 2 Thess 3:15; Titus 1:11; 3:10). It is a compound verb from the same cognate family as the noun *nous,* "mind."

The renewed minds of fully committed Christians are capable of giving and receiving moral guidance (see Rom 12:2; 1:28; 7:23, 25; 14:5), a point Paul made throughout the preceding parenetic section of the letter (12:1—15:13). All rhetoric and hyperbole aside, the more restrained point of Paul's flattery was that he considered the Romans mature—well-behaved and well-informed—believers. He took seriously the presence of the Spirit among them, confirming that his letter taught them nothing they could not have known on their own. The reciprocal pronoun (*allēlous,* **one another**) presumes that every member of the congregation is capable of admonishing others and equally willing to receive admonition.

■ **15** This acknowledgment raises the need to explain why (*dia,* **because**), if his praise is sincere, Paul has written them so **boldly on some points** (v 15). This reference to frank speech may point to his urgent plea for mutual tolerance in the preceding section. But he may have had in mind those parts of the letter audaciously written in authoritative tones to a community he had neither founded nor previously visited. He politely apologizes for his forwardness, assuring them that he wrote only **to remind** them of what they already knew—i.e., with the epideictic rhetorical object of deepening their existing commitment to mutually shared convictions.

Could Paul have sincerely meant that the body of his letter to the Romans was merely a "reminder" of a universally shared Christian faith? Was it not his innovative and idiosyncratic articulation of the gospel (see 2:16, "my gospel")? The prepositional phrase *apo merous* (**on some points**) might imply that Paul acknowledges being offensively bold "in parts of the letter." But it could also imply that the letter was only "partly" a reminder. He wrote some things on the assumption that they did not already know them well enough or take them seriously enough.

Paul had taken the liberty of rehearsing the familiar and introducing new insights into and important implications of the gospel. He did this **because of** (*dia*) the **grace** bestowed on him as apostle to the Gentiles. As in 1:5 and 12:3, he does not conceive of this **grace** as distinct from his apostolic calling and authority. Apostleship is the gracious gift and sacred responsibility **God gave** (*dotheisan*—aorist passive) him when he was converted/called to be an apostle (see 1 Cor 3:10; Gal 2:9). Grace is never given merely to be possessed but to be extended to others (Dunn 2002b, 38B:867). In Rom 1:5 Paul describes his grace-empowered mission as "to call people from among all the Gentiles to the obedience that comes from faith."

■ **16** The description of his apostolic mission that follows in v 16 is the most solemn in all the Pauline correspondence. It amounts to the apostle's claim to a unique status in the Christian movement. The cultic language he employs to describe himself is an application of terminology and imagery taken from Israel's worship: **a minister** [*leitourgos;* see 13:6; 15:27; Heb 8:2] . . . **with the priestly duty of proclaiming the gospel of God** [*hieourgounta to euanggelion tou theou;* lit. ***sacrificing the gospel of God;*** see 1:1], **so that the Gentiles might become an offering acceptable to God.**

The Greek word *leitourgos,* **minister,** is the source of the English cognate "liturgy." The term is derived from two words referring to "people-work." As a minister, Paul serves the people of God, performing a **priestly** function. The compound verb *hierourgeō* means "priest-work," specifically offering sacrifices (in Philo and Josephus; Bauer 1979, 373). Paul does not portray himself as a "priest" in the sense the transliterated Greek term *presbyteros,* "elder," acquired in later church usage. Rather, he characterizes himself in terms of the original imagery of a sacrificial priest making **an offering** [*prosphora;* see Heb 10:5, 10, 14, 18] **acceptable to God** [*euprosdektos;* lit. ***well-pleasing;*** see Rom 15:31; 2 Cor 6:2; 8:12; 1 Pet 2:5].

Although the terminology varies, this is similar to the service that is the reasonable worship expected of all believers in Rom 12:1, who offer (*parastēsai*) themselves as "living sacrifices . . . pleasing to God" (*thysian zōsan . . . euareston tōi theōi*). With the dawning of the new age, "the division between cultic and secular (together with that between sacred and profane, clean and unclean—14:14, 20) has been . . . abolished" (Dunn 2002b, 38B:859).

Paul is a "priest" of the *gospel,* with divine authority to make an **offering** that consists of previously "unclean" Gentiles (echoing Isa 66:20; see Acts 21:28), **acceptable to** God (*euprosdektos;* see Rom 1:24, 26-27, 28-31; 15:31; 2 Cor 6:2; 8:12; Gal 2:15; 1 Pet 2:5). "The 'offering' is used here in a way that both fulfills and reverses Isaiah" (Jewett 2007, 907).

The priestly imagery refers not to the role Paul typically depicts himself fulfilling—as a preacher of the gospel concerned with *converting* unbelievers. His role here concerns the subsequent *sanctification* of those previously unclean Gentiles (see 1 Cor 3:16). This *first* occurrence of the verb *hagiazō* in Romans, certainly, has cultic significance, but it also has deep spiritual and ethical implications (see 1 Cor 6:9-20, esp. v 11; and the comments on Rom 12:1-2). What he says about being sanctified here must also be read in light of his use of the noun *hagiasmos,* holiness/sanctification, in 6:19 and 22.

Significantly, the perfect tense of the verb *hēgiasmenē* (**sanctified**) refers to the state resulting from a past event. The passive voice makes it clear that neither Paul nor any Gentile he serves is the agent of this sanctification. They are **sanctified** specifically **by** [*en,* ***in/with***] **the Holy Spirit** (15:16; see 1 Cor 6:11; 2 Thess 2:13; 1 Pet 1:2). God had fulfilled and transformed the Jewish hope of Ezek 36:22-28 (see Rom 2:24). Acts 26:16-18 reports Paul's sense of calling as he recounted his conversion to King Agrippa in the words of the risen Christ:

> "I have appeared to you and appointed you as a servant . . . I will rescue you from your own people and from the Gentiles. I am sending you to them to open their eyes and turn them from darkness to light [see Isa 49:6], and from the power of Satan to God, so that they may

receive forgiveness of sins and a place among those who are sanctified [*hēgiasmenois*—also a perfect passive] by faith in me."

In some NT passages (e.g., 1 Cor 1:2; Heb 2:11) "to be sanctified" has only the cultic sense of being set apart as God's people, i.e., "to become Christians." This does not seem to be the case here, however, as Rom 15:16 and the parallel with Acts 26:18 demonstrate. But, Jewett correctly insists that ethical sanctification should not be confused with individualistic notions of sanctification as merely a private "striving toward high ethical ideals" (2007, 907). Paul's concern is with the holiness of the Gentile churches as communities, with the transformation of their social life that comes from the empowering and hallowing presence of the Holy Spirit among them (as Rom 12:1—15:13 shows).

■ **17** Paul took appropriate pride in his God-given assignment. **Therefore** [*oun;* ***consequently, for this reason***] **I glory in Christ Jesus in my service to God** (v 17). Literally, Paul writes, ***Therefore, I boast*** [*kauchēsin;* see 3:27; 5:11; contrast 4:2] ***in Christ Jesus about the things that concern God*** [see Heb 5:1]. The flow of Paul's argument is best served if his "boasting" is seen as preparing the way for the account of his ministry that is to follow in Rom 15:18-19. **In Christ Jesus** is a familiar phrase indicating that Paul's "boast" is entirely founded upon and controlled by his existence, as a Christian, within the sphere of Christ as risen Lord. His boast is not of *his* success, but of Christ's. And it is all about what God has accomplished, not about Paul as his competitor.

Paul walks a diplomatic tightrope in these verses. He is merely a *representative* of Christ. But he is a representative of *Christ;* his is no small or inconsequential assignment. And he is a representative of Christ *to Gentiles,* whose favor he seeks to win for the cause of God. But his assignment is finally not about his priestly function or about the offering—the Gentiles or their sanctification; it is about *the glory of God* (see 15:6).

■ **18-19*a*** Thus he writes in vv 18-19*a:* **I will not venture** [*tolmēsō;* ***dare/presume;*** 2 Cor 10:2, 12; 11:21] **to speak of anything except what Christ has accomplished** [*kateirgasato*] **through me in leading the Gentiles to obey God** [*eis hypokoēn ethnōn*] **by what I have said and done—by the power of signs and miracles, through the power of the Spirit.**

Paul claimed that Christ worked **through the power of the Spirit** (see 15:13; 1 Cor 2:4) in his preaching and ministry—***in word and deed*** (see Luke 24:19; Acts 7:22; 2 Cor 10:11; Col 3:17; 2 Thess 2:17). The Spirit validated Paul's apostolic credentials **by the power of signs and miracles** (see Rom 1:16; 2 Cor 12:12; Gal 3:1-5; 1 Thess 1:5; 2:13: Heb 2:4).

Paul nowhere explicitly identifies the wonders that confirmed to his churches that his message was actually the word of God. The OT (e.g., Exod 7:3; 8:19; Deut 13:1-2) and the Acts of the Apostles (see 2:19, 22, 43; 4:30; 5:12; 6:8; 7:36; 14:3; 15:12) might lead us to think of miraculous healings and awe-inspiring charismatic gifts. Although Paul credited the Spirit with powerful manifestations (1 Cor 12:10, 28-29), this was not his typical emphasis.

Paul found wonder in the unexpected juxtaposition of human weakness and divine power. To the Corinthians he was willing to cite a failed prayer for healing as evidence of God's power at work in his life (2 Cor 12:1-10) and to boast of his weaknesses as the occasion of Christ's power residing in him (2 Cor 11:30; 12:9). To the Thessalonians he identified the power of the Holy Spirit in his experience of joy in spite of severe persecution (1 Thess 1:6) and in his courage to preach in spite of great opposition (1 Thess 2:1-2). He reminded the Galatians that despite the illness that brought him to them, they received him as an angel of God, as Christ himself (Gal 4:12-14). Paradoxically, their response of faith to his vivid portrayal of Christ crucified had resulted not only in their receiving the Spirit but in the Spirit's working miracles among them (Gal 3:1-5).

Paul's concern here is not to prove his apostolic claim to the Romans. It is to admit that *everything* of which he could boast was *solely* the achievement of Christ through him, through the Spirit's empowerment (= by "the grace of God" in 1 Cor 15:9-10). Perhaps, the paradoxical wonder
15:18-19a here may be that unclean Gentiles have been cleansed by the sanctifying presence of the Spirit of God in their midst.

The proximity of Paul's definition of his role in facilitating the sanctification of the Gentiles in Rom 15:16 and the definition of his mission as **leading the Gentiles to obey God** in v 18 makes it abundantly clear that he does not think of them as **sanctified** in a merely cultic, positional sense. The Spirit had effected a moral transformation (see 12:1-2) in the lives of these former pagans. In both 15:16 and 18, of course, Paul acknowledges that he serves merely as God's messenger; it was **the Holy Spirit** who **sanctified** and led **Gentiles to obey God.** Jewett helpfully observes:

> This use of the term "obedience," which was so characteristically related to biblical religion, entails the claim that "in Christ" all converted Gentiles "could now enter into covenant relation with the God of Israel and be accounted faithful by him apart from the necessity of first becoming and then remaining Jewish" [quoting Garlington 1990, 255]. Being granted righteousness through faith, thus being made holy through the power of the Spirit, these Gentile communities have been brought to a new form of obedience through Paul's gospel. (2007, 909-10)

■ **19*b*** Paul's effective evangelism throughout his eastern Mediterranean mission field was the result [*hōste* = ***so that***] of what God had done through him. **So** [*hōste*] **from Jerusalem all the way around** [*kyklōi, **in a circle***] ***to*** [*mechri*] **Illyricum, I have fully proclaimed the gospel of Christ** (v 19*b*). Acts mentions nothing of Paul's ministry in **Illyricum;** and this brief note is all we know about it from Paul.

The Roman province of Illyria was to the northeast of Italy, across the Adriatic Sea, in the Latin-speaking region where the modern Baltic nations north of Greece (including all or parts of Albania, Bosnia and Herzegovina, Croatia, Kosovo, Macedonia, Serbia and Montenegro, and Slovenia) are located. Paul's ministry in Jerusalem and Judea was quite limited, based on his own testimony (Gal 1:15-24). (See Jewett 2007, 911-12, for a discussion of Paul's description and ancient maps.)

Paul's two geographical references may simply indicate the outer limits *within* which his ministry took place. The preposition *mechri* may indicate that he ventured ***up to*** but not "into" Illyricum. But we cannot be certain (see 2 Tim 4:10, which reports Titus' mission to Dalmatia, a part of Illyricum; Jewett 2007, 913). Paul's imprecise and broadly representative terms probably refer to his extensive ministry throughout the entire eastern Mediterranean region. Within these boundaries, Jerusalem would represent a starting point, not because Paul preached to Gentiles there, but in accordance with the early Christian view of the gospel as emanating outward from Jerusalem "to the ends of the earth" (Acts 1:8).

It is difficult to assess precisely what Paul meant by his claim to have **fully proclaimed** [*peplēōkenai*] **the gospel of Christ** throughout the eastern Mediterranean. Bauer interprets *peplēōkenai* to mean that Paul brought the preaching of "*the gospel to completion* by proclaiming it in the most remote areas" (see Col 1:25; Bauer 1979, 671 s.v. *plēroō)*. The evidence of the full extent of Paul's preaching preserved in his letters and in Acts is hardly exhaustive. That he mentions apparently lost letters in his preserved letters (see 1 Cor 5:9; 2 Cor 2:3-4; 7:8, 12; Col 4:16) suggests that he may have written still others for which no trace lingers. We know, for example, from Gal 1:16-17 that Paul spent some time preaching in Arabia. But this is nowhere mentioned in Acts; and no letters to churches there survive, if he wrote any. We can only guess where else Paul traveled and preached.

In Rom 15:23, Paul will insist: **now . . . there is no more place for me to work in these regions.** This would be no more or less hyperbolic than his claim in 1:8 that the faith of the Roman church was known everywhere in the world (see 1 Cor 1:2; 1 Thess 1:8). But in Rom 15:19 his explicit claim is not that he had preached **the gospel of Christ** (see 1:1) in every Roman province between Judea and Italy, in every major city in the area, nor in "the most remote areas," much less to every Gentile in the eastern Mediterranean (see 11:25). It is instead that he ***filled full*** **the gospel of Christ** there. Since the good news *about* Christ is not an empty container, the precise meaning of his extravagant metaphorical language remains unclear.

Perhaps Paul meant no more than that he had completed his God-assigned mission in the east (Jewett 2007, 914) and was now ready to move on to Rome and the as-yet-unevangelized Latin-speaking far western extremes of the empire—Spain (15:24, 28) in particular. Now that there were thriving Christian communities throughout the Greek-speaking east, he could entrust the evangelization of the remaining unbelievers there to these congregations (see, e.g., 1 Thess 1:6-10). Before he could undertake his ambitious new venture in the west, he had urgent business to attend to in Jerusalem (15:25-32).

■ **20** The force of the first word of v 20 (omitted in the NIV translation), *houtōs*—***thus***—is difficult to determine. **It has always been my ambition** [see 2 Cor 5:9; 1 Thess 4:11] **to preach the gospel** [see 1:15] **where Christ was not known** [see Eph 1:21; 2 Tim 2:19], **so that** [*hina*] **I would not be building on someone else's foundation** (v 20; see 1 Cor 3:10-12). Paul had aspired to follow the principle of always seeking fresh pastures. His *purpose* [*hina* = **so that**] for doing so was that he might cover as much unreached territory as possible in his missionary work, not merely to avoid personal conflicts and competition with other missionaries (see 2 Cor 10:13-16; 11:1-6, 12-15; 12:11-13).

The goal of Paul's adherence to his nonintervention rule was not to secure his own comfort or his reputation as a successful evangelist. It was to bring the name of Christ to places where it had previously been unknown (*ouch . . . ōnomasthē*, **was not known,** means literally ***not named***).

■ **21 Rather** than preaching where others had already planted churches, Paul made it his mission to follow the dictum of Isa 52:15: **as it is written** [see 1:17 for this quotation formula]: **"Those who were not told about him will see, and those who have not heard will understand"** (v 21). Paul understood the word **those** to refer to the Gentiles and **him** to Christ.

Paul accounted for the vast sweep of his activity by pointing to the policy that had guided his distinctive apostolic mission. His task was to be a pathfinder, a pioneer of the Christian mission of his day. He chose to go where Christ **was not known,** that is, where other missionaries had not gone. Paul was essentially a foundation-layer (see 1 Cor 3:10). He spoke of his career in terms of a text that originally referred to Isaiah's "Servant" (echoing Isa 52:15; see Acts 26:18). Without referring to himself as *the* Servant of the Lord, the apostle represented his own career as the fulfillment of the prophecy inherent in this text, a career proclaiming the good news of the Servant's saving mission for all humankind.

■ **22** Paul understood his calling to be that of a pioneer missionary and church planter. In this way he communicated to the Roman communities his distinctive role within salvation history and how he assessed his progress in fulfilling that role. It also explained his long-delayed visit to Rome (see 1:11-15). **This is why I have often been hindered from coming to you** (15:22)—I have merely been doing what God called me to do.

Verse 22 serves a transitional function, concluding this section discussing Paul's past pursuits while simultaneously introducing his future plans. The inferential conjunction *Dio* (***Therefore;*** see 4:22) prepares for his explanation that the committed pursuit of his God-given mission (15:19), not negligence or unwillingness to minister within a community founded by another (vv 20-21), was the reason why he had not favored Rome with a visit earlier: **This is why I have often been hindered from coming to you.** It was not for lack of interest or effort.

The comparatively rare imperfect tense of the verb *enkoptō* (**have . . . been hindered;** ***kept being cut off;*** see Gal 5:7; 1 Thess 2:18; 1 Pet 3:7) with the accusative adjective *polla* (**often,** ***many times***), used adverbially, coheres with Paul's claim in Rom 1:10, 13 that his plans had been regularly or repeatedly (*pollakis*) frustrated. He does not indicate who or what was responsible for complicating his plans (in 1 Thess 2:16—Jewish opposition—and 1 Thess 2:18—Satan; in Acts 16:6—the Holy Spirit; see 2 Cor 11:24-29). Perhaps the delay had been due to repeated crises in Corinth (compare 2 Corinthians), now behind him (see Rom 15:26; 16:1). Acts 21—28 indicates that even these plans to visit Rome had to be delayed for several years as a result of Paul's arrest in Jerusalem and his extended imprisonment in Caesarea, both occasioned by Jewish opponents.

FROM THE TEXT

"In the priestly service of the gospel of God" (NRSV), Paul had offered the Gentiles as a sacrifice "acceptable to God, *sanctified* by the Holy Spirit" (15:16, emphasis added). This first occurrence of the verb *hagiazō* ("I sanctify") in Romans merits special attention. Does this text have anything in common with passages in Acts emphasizing the work of the Spirit, as understood within the American Holiness Movement?

Acts reports that the risen Jesus promised his apostles, "In a few days you will be baptized with the Holy Spirit" (Acts 1:5). This was fulfilled in Jerusalem within the experience of Jewish believers at the first Pentecost after the crucifixion and resurrection (Acts 2:1-21). Luke reports Peter's understanding of the subsequent baptism with the Holy Spirit of Gentiles at Samaria (Acts 11:15-17): "God, who knows the heart, showed that he accepted them by giving the Holy Spirit to them, just as he did to us. He made no distinction between us and them, for he purified their hearts by faith" (15:8-9).

Both Acts and Romans suggest that the Spirit's work within the lives of believers has cultic and moral consequences. When, in response to hearing the gospel, sinners are enabled to trust Christ for their salvation, God baptizes them with the Holy Spirit. That is, he immerses them into Christ's body, the church, where the Spirit dwells. Christian theologians of every tradition agree that this begins within their hearts the divine work of inward sanctification (see 1 Cor 12:13).

Wesleyans distinctively insist that as the grand work of sanctification proceeds within believers, they come to a second "instant." This logically subsequent movement of divine grace within the lives of fully consecrated believers Wesley sometimes called *entire* sanctification (in the language of 1 Thess 5:23). We have attempted to demonstrate the plausibility of the Wesleyan understanding in our commentary on Rom 6:13-22 and 12:1-2.

Paul's appeal for believers to offer themselves unreservedly to God in these passages has both cultic and ethical implications. What will we do with this call to full consecration, this final showdown between *Self* and *God*? Will we be a part of God's solution or a part of his problem? Will we respond obediently to Paul's call to make the members of our bodies "instruments of righteousness" for the advancement of the gospel? Will we "offer them in slavery to righteousness leading to holiness" (6:19)? Will we go on muddling along as half-Christians? Or, will we reap the benefit that "leads to holiness, and the result . . . eternal life" (6:22)? Wesleyans believe that every serious Christian eventually faces this issue, regardless of how he or she may label it.

Paul invites believers to allow God to transform cultic sanctification into ethical reality. This deeper work of sanctification, like justification, is entirely God's doing. But neither movement of God's sanctifying grace is initiated apart from human cooperation. The logical necessity of both cultic and ethical sanctification is compelling; but the consequence is not inevitable. Paul urges: Just as believers once presented their body parts as slaves to impurity and to greater and greater iniquity, so they should now also present their body parts "as slaves to righteousness for sanctification [*hagiasmon*]" (6:19 NRSV). Believers should allow the grand work of inward sanctification the Spirit *initiates* at justification to be *perfected* in the "through and through" sanctification he promises in 1 Thess 5:23-24. Wesley came to understand this reading of the biblical evidence to be substantiated in broad Christian experience, by longstanding Christian tradition, and appeal to reason.

A Wesleyan Understanding of Sanctification by the Holy Spirit

Wesley came to understand scriptural holiness to be "perfect love." This was the result of years of Bible reading and preaching, enlightened by the works of the early Eastern fathers, the musings of saints and mystics, the insights of certain Christian teachers, and the critical NT studies of Lutheran scholar Johannes Bengel (1687-1752) (see 1979, 5:2-4; "The Life of the Rev. John Wesley" by Thomas Jackson). This he took to be what was demanded by carefully following the classic Christian hermeneutic known as the "analogy of faith" (1950, 569-70; see the commentary on Rom 12:6).

Wesley defended his doctrine often, by reminding his hearers that it was but the substance of the familiar Anglican Collect in the service of Holy Communion (quoted in From the Text on 12:9-16). Wesley found a witness to his doctrine of Christian perfection—*in experience*—through personal examination of hundreds who professed to have received "perfect love." Answering critics who claimed "all this salvation is given at once," he testified: "But we do not know a single instance, in any place, of a person's receiving, in one and the same instant, remission of sins, the abiding witness of the Spirit, and a new, a clean heart" (1979, 11:380). In his *Plain Account of Christian Perfection,* Wesley insisted that if he were convinced no one in Britain had experienced love made perfect, "after what had been so clearly and strongly preached for so long a time," he "would preach it no more" (1979, 11:405). But he *was* convinced of the truth of his doctrine and continued to preach it to his death.

In this light, what does "sanctified by the Holy Spirit" in Rom 15:16 mean within the broader context of biblical and Wesleyan theology?

First, this sanctification is *ethical.* The proximity of Rom 15:16 and 18 make sanctification "by the Spirit" and obedience to God "through the power of the Spirit" mutually interpretive. Sanctification must entail more than the cultic dimension of being set apart as people who belong to God. The obvious parallels between Rom 1:5; 15:18; and 16:26 suggest that the ethic of obedience to God is the ongoing evidence of Christian faith, which expresses itself through love (Gal 5:6).

Central to Paul's understanding of obedience to God is the fulfillment of the Law in the power of the Spirit (see Rom 8:1-11). Thus, he insists, "Love does no harm to its neighbor. Therefore love is the fulfillment of the law" (Rom 13:10; see Gal 5:14). "Love excluding sin; love filling the heart, taking up the whole capacity of the soul" Wesley prefers to call Christian perfection. Wesley exults, "How clearly does this express the being perfected in love! How strongly imply the being saved from all sin! For as long as love takes up the whole heart, what room is there for sin therein?" (1979, 6:46, 52; sermon "The Scripture Way of Salvation").

Second, this sanctification is *social.* Loving God with "all your heart and with all your soul and with all your mind," *and* loving "your neighbor as yourself" (Matt 22:37-39) requires a community. But "Christian perfection" requires the holy community to extend its mutual love beyond itself. Sanctification is incomplete unless it also includes loving enemies, as God does (Matt 5:43-48). Wesley insisted that we may be perfect Christians "in kind, though not in degree, 'even as [our] Father which is in heaven is perfect'" (1979, 5:293; sermon "Upon Our Lord's Sermon on the Mount. Discourse III" on Matt 5:8-12). In Wesley's view, "Christianity is essentially a social religion; therefore to turn it into a solitary one is to destroy it" (1979, 5:296; sermon "Upon Our Lord's Sermon on the Mount. Discourse IV" on Matt 5:13-16).

Third, this sanctification is *personal.* Methodist missionary statesman E. Stanley Jones expressed this truth unforgettably: "Christianity that does not begin with the individual does not begin; Christianity that ends with the individual ends." Thus, holiness, while it is always social, is also intimately personal. "It is a personal relationship with God, which involves a change (gradual or sudden) from the kingdom of self to the Kingdom of God through the grace and power of Christ" (Jones 1942, 325). "It is a harrowing journey, a death to self—the false self—and no one wants to die. But it is the only path to life, to freedom, to peace, to true love" (Benson and Benson 1989, 73). To insist that this sanctification is *personal* must not be mistaken to undermine its essentially corporate or social character.

Fourth, this sanctification is *corporate* and *comprehensive,* embracing the totality of the Spirit's work in the regeneration, sanctification, and glorification of the entire church (Rom 8:1-30). It is symbolized by water baptism (Eph 4:4-6) and accomplished by Spirit baptism. "For we were all baptized by one Spirit into one body—whether Jews or Greeks, slave or free—and we were all given the one Spirit to drink" (1 Cor 12:13). All justified believers "drink" of the Spirit when by faith they are baptized into Christ's body, receiving the Spirit. When they go on to "thirst" for the *fullness* of the Spirit, and "drink" to satisfaction (John 7:37-39), their hearts are completely "purified . . . by faith" (Acts 15:8-9) and perfected in love (Acts 2:4, 14-18, 42-47). The river of the Spirit flows through them to water other parched and thirsty souls (see Acts 2:32-39).

In sum, *ethical* sanctification is what Wesleyans mean when they refer to *entire* sanctification. As Christian perfection, it "is nothing higher and nothing lower than this—the pure love of God and man. . . . It is love governing the heart and life, running through all our tempers, words, and actions" (Wesley 1979, 11:397).

Charles Wesley expresses every serious Christian's cry for this purity and perfection—to be "sanctified by the Holy Spirit"—in these plaintive words. We might improve upon them theologically by replacing his words "me" and "my" with "us" and "our."

Jesus, Thine all-victorious love,
Shed in my heart abroad;
Then shall my feet no longer rove,
Rooted and fixed in God.
O that in me the sacred fire
Might now begin to glow,
Burn up the dross of base desire,
And make the mountains flow!
Refining Fire, go thro' my heart;
Illuminate my soul.
Scatter Thy life thro' ev'ry part,
And sanctify the whole.
My steadfast soul, from falling free,
Shall then no longer move,
When Christ is all the world to me,
And all my heart is love.

Like the term *sanctification* in Paul's letters, the expression *baptism with the Holy Spirit* is a *holistic* and *corporate* concept in the book of Acts, which has parallels in Paul's letters. It encompasses *all* the Spirit accomplishes in the lives of believing communities. This corporate concept allows Wesley to embrace Fletcher's more flexible use of the phrase—of both the new birth and entire sanctification—*so long as the latter remains within NT categories.*

Although Wesley had chosen Fletcher as his "designated successor," he nevertheless cautioned him against preaching the baptism with the Spirit as "receiving the Holy Ghost." In a letter to Fletcher's associate Joseph Benson, dated December 28, 1770, Wesley cautioned against "some persons at Trevecca," who, following Fletcher, "were speaking frequently of the baptism with the Holy Spirit." "If they like to call this 'receiving the Holy Ghost,' they may; only the phrase in that sense is not scriptural and not quite proper; for they all 'received the Holy Ghost' when they were justified" (Wesley 1931, 5:215; see 1950, 393 on Acts 1:5).

Wesley believed adherence to NT language relative to the Spirit's *inclusive* work is important for teaching and preaching "full salvation" (including emphasis upon entire sanctification). But he also believed in adhering to the *specific* language of Scripture concerning the Spirit's work in Christians' lives when preaching and enforcing the gospel (see 1 Cor 2:12-13). Wesley maintained this faithfulness to NT language in his maturity, when he strongly emphasized the message of full salvation, while still adhering to the categories that had defined his doctrine from the early days of his evangelical ministry.

2. But First to Jerusalem (15:23-33)

BEHIND THE TEXT

Paul's successful completion of his eastern ministry sufficiently accounts for his next statement. His efforts in the regions surrounding the Mediterranean Sea had so occupied his time and energy that he had been unable to visit the Christian churches in Rome. "But now that there is no more place for me to work in these regions, and since I have been longing many years to see you, I plan to do so when I go to Spain" (15:23-24*a*). Paul has a sense of closure on the past and is turning his attention to the future.

As in the typical conclusion (peroration) of an ancient speech or letters, Paul brings Romans to a climax "by inciting the audience to action," but "gently and indirectly," as is appropriate to a demonstrative letter (Jewett 2007, 919). Paul's future plans to evangelize Spain will require participation from the Romans. He hopes they will **assist** him on his **journey there**, **after** he has **enjoyed** their **company for a while** (15:24*b*) and been "refreshed" by them.

Paul's euphemistic diplomatic language politely requests them to supply staff, provisions, and monetary support for his journey. Paul alerts them that he intends to ask for their financial backing for his proposed evangelistic mission to Spain. In the opening of the letter Paul's reference to reaping "a harvest" among them (1:13) may have subtly hinted at this desire. Since it was apparently impossible for the Roman house churches to participate in the Jerusalem-collection project, Paul offers them an alternative opportunity. He implicitly asks them to become the base of his missionary operations for the West. This may explain Paul's concern for the unity of the Roman Christians (15:6); a divided community would be less equipped to fund his vision for a Spanish mission.

Before Paul can turn his attention to these long-range plans, however, he needs to complete the project that has preoccupied him during much of the previous ministry: "Now, however, I am on my way to Jerusalem in the service of the saints there" (15:25). Paul intends to deliver to the church in Jerusalem the funds he had been collecting for many years to fulfill his pledge to the "pillars" at Jerusalem "to remember the poor, the very thing I was eager to do" (Gal 2:10). The Jerusalem Christians were notoriously poor and in need of financial support (Acts 11:27-30).

Paul certainly envisioned the offering as a sacramental gift from the law-free Gentile churches to the Torah-observant Jewish Christian community in Jerusalem with whom they were, nevertheless, one in Christ. Paul had invested himself in the effort for years. He must have been anticipating the relief of bringing the long-standing project to a conclusion. As he writes, Paul is able to report that his fund-raising efforts with his churches (see 2 Cor 8—9) was so far successful (Rom 15:26-27)—signed, sealed, and ready to be delivered. Only the uncertain outcome of its reception in Jerusalem remained to be seen (vv 30-32).

IN THE TEXT

■ **23** Paul stands at the threshold of a new stage of his apostolic career. He has completed his pioneering evangelism, founding self-sustaining churches in the eastern Mediterranean region, which have contributed in solidarity toward his collection for poor Christians in Jerusalem. **But now there is no place for me to work in these regions, and since I have been longing for many years to see you, I plan to do so when I go to Spain** (vv 23-24*a*). See the comments on Paul's claim that there remained **no place for** [him] **to work** in the East in connection with 15:19 above.

Paul cannot possibly have meant that there was nothing left to be done in the East, that the entire population had come to faith, or that there was no room for improvement in the existing churches. All he claims is the conviction that *his* work there is done. He does not indicate that the Spirit (see Acts 13:1-4; 16:6) or a vision (see Acts 16:9-10) impelled him elsewhere. He mentions only his longstanding personal desires (*epipothian . . . echōn: **having a desire;*** see Rom 1:11; 2 Cor 7:7, 11) and hopes (*elpizō:* **I hope,** in Rom 15:24*b*). But he certainly expected Christ to bless his plans (see the comments below on v 29).

■ **24** This radical redirection of Paul's ministry affords him the opportunity to fulfill his long-cherished desire to visit Rome (1:10, 13) en route to **Spain** (15:24, 28). The mention of **Spain** as his ultimate destination is almost incidental. Does he assume that his Roman correspondents already know of his plans and understand the urgency of evangelizing the West? He never says why his heart was so set on reaching Spain. We cannot be sure whether Paul was ever able to do so. The claim that he did in *1 Clem.* 5:7 may be merely wishful thinking, based only on Paul's plans announced here.

Why Spain?

Jewett proposes three plausible reasons why Paul chose Spain as the next stage in his mission. First, "Spain was both Gentile and barbarian, par excellence. It lacked any Jewish population and remained stubbornly resistant to Greco-Roman culture." It would allow Paul to fulfill his debt to "barbarians" (1:15). Second, Spain completes the missionary circle Paul mentions in 15:19, as ancient maps of the Mediterranean indicate. Third, Paul may have interpreted Isa 66:19 as identifying Tarshish with Spain and "the ends of the earth" (Pss 71:8, 10; 72:8). Thus, successful evangelism there would complete the offering of the Gentiles (see Rom 15:16) and prepare the way for the Parousia (2007, 924).

Paul's more pressing and immediate need is to explain the objective
of his planned intermediate visit to Rome, now that news of it has been finally broached. Clearly, he had no intention of violating his longstanding
pioneer-missionary principle (see 15:20). Rome was not to be his final destination but only an intermediate stop on his journey. In mid-sentence
Paul breaks off what he is saying to explain precisely what he has in mind:
I hope to see you on my way and to be helped by you on my journey
there [*propemphthēnai ekei*] (v 24*b*). The sentence remains grammatically
15:24 incomplete, although Paul's meaning is clear enough from v 28 and 1:11-
15. His broken construction

> acknowledges the uncertainty of future plans and diplomatically leaves the door open for the Roman congregations to decide whether to receive Paul or not. . . . Paul's choice of terms opens the possibility of polite acquaintance and consultation with the Roman churches within the restricted scope of a short visit. (Jewett 2007, 925)

The Greek technical term *propempō* (***helped on my journey***) was used to refer to personnel, provisions, etc., necessary for a journey (see 1 Macc 12:4; 1 Esd 4:47; Acts 15:3; 20:38; 21:5; 1 Cor 16:6, 11; 2 Cor 1:16; Titus 3:13; 3 John 6). In Rom 15:32 Paul will express his hope to be **refreshed** (*synanapausōmai*) by them, using another word with monetary implications. He not too subtly but politely and diplomatically requests financial assistance from the community to fund his prospective venture. Since Greek was not used in Spain, Paul may also have hoped that some Latin-speaking Romans would accompany him to serve as translators. **After I have enjoyed** [*emplēsthō*] **your company for a while** also suggests that he has more than rest and relaxation in mind. The verb *empimplēmi* literally means to be filled to satisfaction. Paul trusts the Romans' hospitality to provide all he needs to make his mission to Spain possible, while politely asking for nothing specific.

■ **25** In vv 25-27 the apostle transitions sharply to another matter weighing heavily on his mind. **Now, however** [*nyni de;* see v 23; 3:21, 26; 5:9], **I am on my way to Jerusalem in the service of** [*diakonōn,* ***to serve;*** see 12:7; 15:31; 2 Cor 8:4, 19-20; 9:1, 12-13] **the saints** [*tois hagiois,* ***the holy ones = Christians;*** see Rom 1:7] **there.** Between him and Rome—and ultimately Spain—he is faced with an intermediate task—a journey to **Jerusalem** with relief for **the saints** there. The uncertainty of the subjunctive mood of the verb *poreuomai* in v 24 ("whenever I go to Spain" NASB) is replaced with the indicative mood of fact in v 25 ("I am going to Jerusalem" NASB). Paul is about to leave for Jerusalem, but a lot of contingencies remain to be resolved before he goes to Spain (see Jewett 2007, 926).

References in other letters (1 Cor 16:1-3; 2 Cor 8—9) attest to the high premium Paul placed on collecting and delivering to the Jerusalem church the monetary contribution from his Gentile churches. This was no mere relief measure to a community in particular need; it was the fulfillment of a commitment Paul had made to the "pillars" of the Jerusalem church when they recognized the apostle's unique ministry to the Gentiles (Gal 2:8-10).

But the collection may well have represented an even more momentous undertaking in Paul's mind. Did Paul see the delivery of the collection as at least a partial fulfillment of prophetic expectations that in the eschaton the wealth of the Gentiles would flow into Jerusalem (see Rom 9:26; Isa 45:14; 60:5-17; 61:6; Mic 4:13; Tob 13:11)? It was obviously important for Paul that the Roman community sense the symbolic significance of this offering. Therefore, he enlisted their prayers and moral support for the enterprise in Rom 15:30-31. It is unclear whether the Jerusalem church saw the collection as Paul did.

■ **26** In vv 26-27 Paul explains the nature of the collection. It was something the churches of **Macedonia and Achaia** had contributed as a gesture of solidarity—solidarity (*koinōnan,* ***a sharing,*** **a contribution;** v 26) with one another and with the recipient community—for the relief of **the poor among the saints** [*tous ptōchous tōn hagiōn*] **in Jerusalem.** By referring to the collection as *koinōnia,* he emphasized that this was not an act of charity but an expression of the commonality of the churches involved—both those giving and receiving aid. The donor communities must have included Paul's churches in Philippi, Thessalonica, Corinth, and Cenchrea. But his churches in Galatia (see 1 Cor 16:1; Gal 2:10) and Asia (see Acts 20:4-5; 24:17) seem also to have been involved. Jewett speculates that Paul may not have mentioned them because they had not yet arrived in Corinth when he dispatched his letter to Rome (2007, 928-29).

Paul identifies the intended recipients using a Greek phrase, which might be translated ***the poor, that is, the saints.*** **The poor** may have been a self-designation of the entire Jewish-Christian community in Jerusalem (see Pss 69:32; 72:2, 4), rather than an economically distressed group within it. It seems obvious that the antecedent of the third person plural pronouns ("they" in English) in Rom 15:27 and 28—**them** (*autōn*—twice) in v 27 (translated **the Jews'** by the NIV in its second appearance) and **with them** in v 27 and **they** in v 28 (*autois* in both instances in Greek) and 28—refers to all the members of the Jerusalem church. In v 31 he refers to the beneficiaries of his service as merely in behalf of **the saints** who are **in Jerusalem.**

Paul makes a special point of emphasizing that the contribution from **Macedonia and Achaia** had been voluntarily (*eudokēsan,* **were pleased** in vv 26 and 27) given. This was not a tax, implying that the Gentiles were second-class Christians. On the contrary, Paul's frequent designation of the collection using the Greek term *koinōnia* (**contribution** in v 26; see the verb *ekoinōnēsan*—**have shared** in v 27; see 2 Cor 8:4, 23; 9:13) identifies it as an expression of community solidarity, involving mutuality and equality, not subservience. It is a freely given **service** (*diakonia* or *diakonos; see* Rom
15:26-27 15:25 and 31; 2 Cor 8:4, 19, 20; 9:1, 12, 13)—a ministry, not a mandate.

■ **27** But on another level, Paul concedes that the Gentiles (*to ethnē*) were somehow "indebted" (*opheiletai . . . opheilousin,* **they owe;** v 27; see 1:14; 4:4; 8:12; 13:7-8; 15:1) to the Jerusalem church in this matter. The cultural assumptions of the patronage society that dominated Mediterranean life, particularly reciprocity among friends, were universally taken for granted, even by Christians (see 1 Cor 9:11; Gal 6:6; Phil 4:15; Phlm 19). "To the ancient mind there was no necessary contradiction between goodwill and obligation." Paul and his Gentile churches would have thought of the collection as "an uncoerced decision that derives from grateful hearts, transformed by divine righteousness, rather than from any form of social or political pressure" (Jewett 2007, 930). Ingratitude in response to a debt of grace is disgraceful. Through God's great mercy (see Rom 11:16-18, 30-31; 15:8-9) the Gentiles had **shared** (*ekoinōnēsan;* see 12:13) **in the Jews' spiritual** [*pneumatikois;* see 1:11] **blessings.** Their gift, as generous as it had been, was merely **material** [*sarkinois,* **fleshly**).

Gentiles are and will always remain the "wild olive branch" that has been grafted into and continues to draw its life from the original "root" (the patriarchs of Israel; see 11:16-18). The privilege of having shared in these "superior" spiritual blessings—the blessings of salvation—creates for them an "obligation" to ensure that a similar kind of sharing takes place on the "fleshly" level. The Gentile churches had freely recognized—undoubtedly by much urging from Paul (see 2 Cor 8:9; 9:6-10)—their obligation **to share with** (*leitourgēsai*, ***to minister to;*** compare the noun from this cognate family in Rom 13:6, describing public servants, and in 15:16, describing Paul's priestly apostolic ministry) the Jerusalem community in this material way.

Solidarity of Jews and Gentiles in the People of God

> What Paul subtly communicates here to the Roman community is a sense that the collection symbolizes recognition on the part of the Gentile communities of the "priority" of the Jewish-Christian Jerusalem church as regards the history of salvation (cf. 1:16: "the Jew first, but also the Greek"). The Gentile communities may be more prosperous in numerical and material terms than the mother church is. But they cannot supplant its role as the first hearer and proclaimer of the worldwide gospel. At the same time, the acceptance of the collection on the part of the Jerusalem community will represent *its* recognition of the full citizenship of the Gentile communities in the eschatological people of God. (Byrne 1996, 442)

■ **28** Paul stressed the importance of his mission to Jerusalem in hopes that the Romans would share the urgency he sensed of conveying the collection and indulge this further postponement of his projected visit to Rome. But he assured them (too optimistically, as it turned out): **So after I have completed this task . . . I will go to Spain and visit you on the way** (v 28). A more literal translation of the Greek sentence reveals a noteworthy omission in the NIV: ***When I have fully perfected*** [*epitelesas;* see 2 Cor 7:1; 8:6, 11; Gal 3:3; Phil 1:6] ***this and have sealed*** [*sphragisamenos;* see John 6:27; 1 Cor 9:2; 2 Cor 1:22; Eph 1:13; 4:30; 2 Tim 2:19] ***to them this fruit*** [*karpon;* see Rom 1:13], ***I will go through you to Spain.*** (See Acts 21—28, which explains why Paul's visit to Rome was delayed longer than he could have expected when he wrote Romans.)

By referring to the collection metaphorically as ***this fruit,*** Paul suggests that it represents a token of how richly the "spiritual seed" of the gospel, originating in Israel, had produced successful results among the Gentiles. ***This fruit*** had to be totally ***completed*** and ***certified as genuine*** (on this meaning of ***sealed,*** see 1 Cor 16:3) before he could feel released to undertake new work in the West. Paul also was aware of the more mundane responsibility of assuring that all the money collected for Jerusalem would be delivered to its intended recipients as promised (see 2 Cor 8:20-23).

■ **29** Once the collection was delivered, Paul was confident that he would **come** to Rome **in the full measure of the blessing of Christ** [*en plērōmati eulogias Christou;* see Rom 11:12, 25; 2 Cor 9:5-8]. This phrase in Rom 15:29 is ambiguous—perhaps intentionally. Did he mean only that the collection's delivery would cause Christ to look favorably on his future plans? Did he expect that Christ's gracious blessings received in fulfilling his obligations in Jerusalem would especially equip him to impart grace to the Romans (see 1:11)? Did he expect that success in Jerusalem could lead to the conversion of the whole world and usher in the Parousia of Christ (Jewett 2007, 933)?

Paul's confidence—modest or grandiose—arises from God's mandate to reap "fruit" among the Gentiles (1:13), something the collection fully attests. Paul, apostle to the Gentiles, is confident that the benefits mentioned early in this letter (1:11-13) will come with him when he finally arrives in Rome. Some ancient manuscripts insert "of the gospel" in 15:29, before "of Christ." Did Paul think of the "sealing" of the unified church comprised of Gentiles and Jews, accomplished in the favorable reception of the Gentiles' collection in Jerusalem, as a *sacramental* "fullness of the blessing *of the gospel* of Christ"?

■ **30** Paul's desperate plea for the Romans to intercede in prayer for the success of his mission to Jerusalem in vv 30-32 indicates both its importance to him and his realization that success was far from certain. **I urge** [*Parakalō;* see 12:1] **you, brothers, by our Lord Jesus Christ and by the love of the Spirit, to join me in my struggle by praying to God for me. Pray that I may be rescued from the unbelievers in Judea and that my service in Jerusalem may be acceptable to the saints there, so that by God's will I may come to you with joy and together with you be refreshed** (vv 30-32). Essential as it was to his mission in the East (and perhaps even to God's plans for the end times), Paul had some foreboding of the precarious nature of his collection-visit to Jerusalem. The solemn character of his request for intercessory prayer may be indicated in part by its (probably unconscious) Trinitarian formulation, referring to the **Lord Jesus Christ,** the **Spirit,** and **God** together in v 30 (as in vv 15-16).

In v 30, on the basis of the bond they share in their common **Lord Jesus Christ** (see 5:1) and the mutuality of **the love *the Spirit inspires among them,*** Paul entreats the Romans to **join** him in his **struggle** [*synagōnisasthai moi, **to strive with me***—the compound with the prepositional prefix *syn-* appears only here in biblical Greek, but see the cognates in 1 Cor 9:25; Phil 1:30; Col 1:29; 4:12; 1 Thess 2:2; 1 Tim 4:10; 6:12; 2 Tim 4:7] **by praying to God *in my behalf,*** for a twofold purpose (employing a single *hina*, ***in order that,*** suggesting their close relationship; see Dunn 2002b, 38B:879). The imagery of athletic and military contests emphasizes the need for disciplined, strenuous, and unceasing prayer to meet this challenge of apocalyptic proportions.

■ **31** *First,* in v 31 Paul begs the Romans to join with him ***in intercessory prayer*** (*en tais proseuchais;* see 1:10; 8:15-16, 26-27; 12:12) that he may be **rescued—*spared destruction*** [*hina rhysthō;* see Matt 6:13; Luke 11:4; 2 Cor 1:10; 2 Thess 3:2; 2 Tim 3:11; 4:17-18] at the hands of **unbelievers** [*tōn apeithountōn, **the disobedient, the unpersuaded;*** see Rom 2:8; 10:21; 11:30-31]—non-Christian Jews **in Judea** (15:31; see 1 Thess 2:14). "Paul fears for his life" (Dunn 2002b, 38B:878)—as we see from Acts, with good reason. Paul expected opposition **in Judea.** But

> he did not anticipate the assassination plot en route to Judea (Acts 20:2) that later caused him to change travel plans. As in 1 Thess 2:14, he anticipates the possibility of anti-Christian persecution . . . , in this instance probably motivated by hostility against his missionizing and particularly against his goal of unifying the Gentile and Jewish branches of the church, which in the eyes of zealous revolutionaries would further pollute Israel. Such hostility could only be increased by Paul's missionary rationale expressed in 11:11-24, converting Gentiles in order to provoke Jews to zeal. (Jewett 2007, 936)

Second, and more poignantly, he urges them to pray that the collection **may be acceptable** [*euprosdektos;* see 15:16 and the commentary there] **to the saints** in Jerusalem. He fears that the Jews and the Jewish-Christian community there may spurn either the collection (*hē diakonia mou: **my ministry;*** see the comments on vv 26-27 and 11:13; 12:7) or what its acceptance would symbolize—the acknowledgment of Law-free Gentile-Christians as full citizens in the eschatological people of God.

Acts 21:20-21 indicates that Paul's fears were not unfounded. Jewett speculates:

> When one examines the "remarkable silence" of Acts about the delivering of the offering and the strange story about Paul paying for a Nazarite vow (Acts 21:23-24), it appears that a kind of religious money-laundering scheme was in fact adopted that sanctified the Jerusalem offering by assimilating it into legalistic devotion. It is very likely that Paul's fears about the acceptability of the offering to the

> Jerusalem church, under extreme pressure from nationalistic zealots, were fully justified. (Jewett 2007, 937)

The Jewish nationalism that would result in revolution in A.D. 67 was already on the rise in Israel a decade earlier when Paul wrote Romans. Josephus claims that "the action which made the first Jewish revolt inevitable was the decision that the Temple should accept no further gift or sacrifice from a foreigner [*J.W.* 2.409-10])." This "provides the most coherent context and explanation for Paul's fears that his gentile gift (v 27) would be refused" (Dunn 2002b, 38B:880).

Failure in Jerusalem "would clearly jeopardize any prospect of overcoming the ethnic tensions between the house and tenement churches in Rome, . . . which the . . . cross-cultural mission to Spain requires" (Jewett 2007, 933). Such high stakes called for serious intercession. Paul considers his private prayers alone insufficient to the seriousness of his need. He coveted the communal prayers of his as-yet-mostly-unknown Roman Christian friends. But he also recognizes that a favorable answer to their combined prayers involves contingencies beyond their control.

■ **32** Paul knew that success depended supremely on **God's will** (Rom 15:32; see 1:10). And he reckoned with the reality that his mission would have to **be acceptable to** (15:31) the Jewish-Christian community in Jerusalem for their prayers to be answered. The *purpose* or *expected result* (*hina:* **so that**) of their answered prayers—his rescue from unbelievers and the success of his mission—will mean that he will be able to **come to** them **with joy** (see 14:17; 15:13; Isa 55:12). This will assure that both he and they **together** ***may be mutually*** **refreshed** (*synanapausōmai,* ***rest together*** —only here and Isa 11:6 in the Bible) by their time together. Paul eagerly looks forward to relaxation in Rome after the tensions involved with completing the collection and before the new demands of his mission to the far West.

■ **33** The benediction in Rom 15:33 is missing in some ancient manuscripts of Romans. Whether or not it is original here, its sentiment, May the **peace** [see 1:7; 5:1] of **God be with you all,** is a characteristic Pauline prayer-wish (see 15:5-6, 13; 16:20, 24; 2 Cor 13:11, 13; Phil 4:9; 1 Thess 5:23; 2 Thess 3:16, 18; Heb 13:20), fittingly concluding this final section of the letter. The final **Amen** invites the Romans to respond with vocal agreement to Paul's request, ***May it be so!*** Only ***God's peace*** could reconcile the divided factions in Rome and Jerusalem and create a unified church comprised of Jews and Gentiles.

FROM THE TEXT

What we know of the outcome of Paul's ambitious plans sadly illustrate the truth of Robert Burns' line from "To a Mouse": "The best laid schemes o' mice an' men / Gang aft a-gley" (The best-laid plans of mice and men often go awry)! Paul's was certainly a "Purpose-Driven Life" (Rick Warren). But what he hoped and prayed and planned for did not come to pass as he envisioned.

Who does not regret the ethnic and religious divide that continues to separate believers in the God of Abraham? The parting of the ways that led Judaism and Christianity to emerge as competitors during the late first and early second century was certainly not Paul's dream. The divisions among seventh-century Christians that contributed to the emergence of Islam, the separation of the Orthodox and Roman Catholic churches during the eleventh century, and the disarray of the Catholic church that prompted the Protestant Reformation of the sixteenth century are only a few of the tragic chapters in a story that bears witness against Paul's grand vision of a united people of God. But perhaps we would not be here today if it had.

Paul's unshaken confidence in the imminence of the Parousia stands in stark contrast to increasing eschatological skepticism among affluent Western believers today. If Paul's eschatological optimism was mistaken, was his sense of the urgency of mission to those who have not yet heard the good news also flawed? Why did Paul's purposes for Jerusalem, Rome, and Spain fall apart? Was Paul not only overly optimistic but misguided in other respects as well? Did the Romans fail to unite in the kind of intercessory prayer the occasion demanded? Did God have other plans? Did even the purposes of God go awry? Did deep-seated ethnic resentments frustrate God's plans? Did political realities compromise gospel imperatives?

Romans does not answer these questions. But we must take them seriously. Paul knew full well that human plans could be hindered (Rom 15:22). Repeated experiences with frustrated plans did not cause him to abandon his faith; instead, they motivated him to make alternative plans. He was not forgetful of what God had already done through him to accomplish his purposes for human salvation.

We might learn from Paul to strategize and scheme to put the implications of the gospel into practice, making plans that cannot be achieved apart from divine intervention. Of course, Paul feared failure, but he was willing to risk it. Thus, he bears witness to the truth of the truism, "Nothing ventured, nothing gained." He did not make the mistake of too many well-intentioned contemporary Christians, flippantly claiming God as the source of all his pious purposes. He was willing to admit that he sometimes pursued only his own thoughtful plans, motivated by God-inspired desires and hopes, but fully aware of the myth of certainty.

We might also learn from Paul to seek the "cooperation" of others in the pursuit of grand missionary ventures. And we should not hesitate to ask for financial and other substantial forms of assistance with the same diplomacy he practiced. Paul refused to be a beggar or to use guilt to manipulate generosity. His fund-raising approach seems to have been designed to leave his readers the freedom to decide whether and how to participate in his missionary vision.

Although Paul did not achieve all he envisioned, the relief for the poor saints in Jerusalem did meet urgent needs there. Thus, his mission was not a total failure. What loss did the churches of Macedonia and Achaia experience as a result of their failed gesture of solidarity toward unknown Jewish believers in Jerusalem? Is it not still "more blessed to give than to receive" (Acts 20:35) even when the recipients are not appropriately grateful?

Even if Paul never succeeded in evangelizing Spain himself, later Christian missionaries inspired by his zeal for evangelism did. And a similar passion for mission continues to inspire comfortable believers to give
16:1-2 themselves and their resources in behalf of the gospel to unknown people in parts of the world Paul could not have imagined existed. Perhaps Paul succeeded after all.

B. Paul's Recommendation of Phoebe (16:1-2)

IN THE TEXT

■ **1** Before Paul begins his farewell greetings to his Roman acquaintances, he first writes a brief epistolary recommendation (compare 1 Cor 16:15-18; 2 Cor 3:1-3) in behalf of a woman named Phoebe, a church leader in the nearby city of **Cenchrea,** the Aegean (eastern) port serving Corinth, from where he writes (Rom 16:1). Paul's opening words, *synistēmi de hymin,* **I commend to you,** was a technical epistolary expression used to introduce a friend to other acquaintances. The particle *de* (***and/but***) implies that ch 16 was not an independent composition (contrary to earlier text-critical contentions).

The designation **our sister** (*adelphē hymōn;* see 1 Cor 7:15; 9:5; Phlm 2) probably identifies the bearer of the letter as a fellow Christian. Paul's recommendation assures the Romans that Phoebe is authorized to speak in his behalf. Her name *Phoibē* [***shining, beaming,*** or ***bright***] suggests that her background was pagan (in Greek mythology, Phoebe was the Titan grandmother of Apollo, often called Phoebus because of his identification with the sun; Fitzmyer 1993, 729). The description of her as **a servant** (*diakonon,* ***deacon/minister***) may designate her generically as a member of a special leadership group within the church. We cannot be certain that the term refers to the diaconal "order" that emerged later in the apostolic church (see Phil 1:1; 1 Tim 3:8, 12; Titus 1:7).

In 1 Tim 3:11 *gynaikes,* "women," are mentioned in the instructions given *diakonoi,* but it is unclear whether they are themselves *diakonoi* or the "wives" of deacons. That the generic masculine gender of the noun *diakonos* is applied to Phoebe gives evidence against its traditional translation as "deaconess" (Rom 16:1 RSV, NJB), a subordinate ministry open to women. Significantly, Paul uses the same noun to refer to his own office/ministry role in Rom 15:8 (see 11:13; 12:7; 13:4; 15:25, 31; 1 Cor 3:5; 2 Cor 6:4; 11:15, 23). Thus, she may well have been "the leader of the congregation" in Cenchrea (Jewett 2007, 944).

Remarkably, the word *ekklēsia* (**church**) appears for the first time in Rom 16:1. It designates a local, organized Christian community, probably one that gathered in Phoebe's private house **in Cenchrea.** The word in 16:4, 5, 16, and 23 refers to local congregations. There is no reference in Romans to the universal church, which some interpreters find in Ephesians and Colossians (and 1 Corinthians). Paul never refers to "the church in Rome" (contrast 1 Cor 1:2; 2 Cor 1:1; 1 Thess 1:1; see Gal 1:2).

■ **2** Paul has two purposes (*hina,* ***in order that***) he hopes to achieve from his recommendation of Phoebe in Rom 16:2. First, he expects the Romans to **receive** [*prosdexēsthe;* see Phil 2:29 and *proslambanesthe,* **Accept/*Welcome*** in Rom 14:1 and 15:7] **her in the Lord** [see 16:8, 11, 12, 13, and 22] **in a way worthy** [*axiōn,* ***honor consistent with;*** see Eph 4:1; Phil 1:27; Col 1:10; 1 Thess 2:12; 2 Thess 1:11] **of the saints** (Rom 16:2*a;* on **saints,** see 1:7). They should give Phoebe a reception **worthy** of Christians, not because she deserves it, but because it is only appropriate that **the Lord**'s people should receive fellow believers as graciously as **the Lord** received them. The hospitality Paul expects for Phoebe would include lodging and other help (Käsemann 1980, 411).

Phoebe is to be warmly and respectfully welcomed into the Roman Christian community as one of its members. The manner of the reception as **in the Lord** (again in vv 8, 11, 12, 13, and 22; see 6:23 and 8:39: "in Jesus Christ our Lord") connotes a mode of Christian hospitality ***consistent with*** the close relationship believers share because of their common Lord.

Second, Paul expects the Romans **to give her *whatever practical*** [*pragmati, **matter***] **help** [*parastēte;* translated "offer" in 6:13, 16, 19; and 12:1] **she may need** (v 2*b*). Jewett suggests that the unspecified help Paul has in mind is "integral to the purpose of the letter" she is delivering in his behalf and not related to her business dealings in Rome (2007, 946).

The apostle explains why (*gar,* **for**) he hopes both purposes will be accomplished: **for she has been a great help** [*prostatis, **protectress/patroness***] **to many people, including me** (v 2*c*). The Romans are to offer Phoebe the reciprocity expected of clients, as if they had personally benefited from her patronage of Paul (see Jewett's survey of the evidence for upper-class benefactors in early Christian communities; 2007, 946-47).

As a patroness, Phoebe was almost certainly a person of social prominence within the churches of Achaia—a financial supporter of the Christian community in Cenchrea or a leader there. She probably owned her home and was wealthy and influential. Her travel to Rome suggests that she was involved in commerce. Thus, she was in a position to assist missionaries and other Christians who traveled to and from Corinth (see Lydia's role in Acts 16:11-15; and also Acts 17:12).

Paul's indebtedness to Phoebe may indicate she had served as a hostess to him when he visited Cenchrea during his eighteen-month stay in Corinth (see Acts 18:1-18). Perhaps she "had agreed to underwrite a project of vital significance to Paul"—even "the Spanish mission" (Jewett 2007, 947).

Perhaps her service consisted in delivering his letter to Rome. Rome had no postal service for ordinary citizens. Letter writers depended on the willingness of people with the means to travel to deliver their mail. Otherwise, they hired private couriers or assigned the responsibility to trusted slaves.

FROM THE TEXT

Women like Phoebe and Lydia played prominent roles in the life of the early church and in Roman society. Christian women emerged as vocal opponents of the widespread practice of infanticide and abortion in the empire. Growing evidence suggests that women made up the majority of most early Christian congregations. This underscores the significance of

Christian women's influence in the Roman world. In this light, it seems strange that some contemporary Christians have launched virulent attacks against the reemergence of women as church leaders in recent decades as an unfortunate accommodation to modern culture. Nothing could be farther from the truth.

C. Paul's Greetings to Acquaintances (16:3-16)

BEHIND THE TEXT

In antiquity private individuals typically placed greetings at the end of their personal letters. Jewett identifies three types: (1) a first person (I) greeting from author to recipient; (2) a second person (you) greeting, asking the recipient to greet another; and (3) a third person (he/she) greeting from another to the recipient (2007, 949). The greetings here are of the second type. They are uncharacteristically in the plural, urging the community as a whole to greet the named individuals: (***You all***) ***greet*** . . . ! (*aspasasthe* in vv 3, 5, 6, 7, 8, 9, 10 [two times], 11 [two times], 12 [two times], 13, 14, 15, and 16). "In this context, to greet is to honor and welcome one another, probably with the hug, kiss, handshaking, or bowing that gave expression to greeting in the ancient world" (Jewett 2007, 952).

Paul's randomly arranged greetings to various persons in the Roman churches name 24 individuals. These commendations of his Roman contacts indirectly prepare the way for his own coming visit. Some he greets as close personal friends, acquaintances, and longtime coworkers: Priscilla, Aquila, Epenetus, Mary, Andronicus, Junia, Ampliatus, Urbanus, Stachys, and Apelles. Paul probably met them all in the East after their eviction from Rome with the Edict of Claudius in A.D. 49.

Other names apparently belong to previously unknown Roman church leaders, familiar to Paul by reputation only: Herodion, Asyncritus, Phlegon, Hermes, Patrobas, Hermas, Philologus, and Julia. Of those singled out as active in the service of the gospel, eight are women: Priscilla, Junia, Tryphena, Tryphosa, Persis, the mother of Rufus, Julia, and the sister of Nereus. Jewett (2007, 953) identifies five house or tenement church groupings: those meeting with Priscilla and Aquila (v 5), slaves of Aristobulus (v 10), slaves of Narcissus (v 11), brothers with Asyncritus (v 14), and the saints with Philologus (v 15).

Among those named, some have Greek names, some have Latin

names. Scholars dispute which are which, since all are in their Greek forms. Even known Jews in the list, like Paul, have Greek or Latin names. Some names denote prominent persons; others are otherwise unknown. Many are common slave names or names common among freedmen, craftsmen, and simple folk of the lower middle class. The persons greeted in the letter furnish Phoebe with a list of persons from whom she could expect to receive hospitality and assistance in Rome. But few seem to have been people of affluence or influence beyond the Christian community.

In letters Paul wrote to churches he had himself founded he rarely greets individuals as he does here. This fact strengthens the argument that this letter is being sent to Rome, to a congregation he did not found personally but in which he knows that a number of friends now reside.

IN THE TEXT

■ **3** **Greet Priscilla and Aquila** (v 3; see 1 Cor 16:19; Acts 18:1-3). In Acts 18 Aquila is identified as a Jew (although Paul fails to mention this; contrast Rom 16:7) originally from Pontus in Asia Minor. Priscilla, who is not identified as a Jew in Acts, may have been a freeborn woman of noble Roman descent, which may explain why her name is mentioned first (see Acts 18:18, 26; 2 Tim 4:19; see Jewett 2007, 955, for the evidence).

When Paul met this husband and wife team, they had recently come to Corinth after being banished from Rome by Claudius's decree. They were already Christians when Paul met them. Like Paul, the couple engaged in tentmaking for a livelihood. They moved from Corinth to Ephesus and served the church there, instructing others, including Apollos, an Alexandrian orator who had become a Christian convert (Acts 18:26). When Paul wrote 1 Corinthians, he sent greetings to the Corinthian church from the house church of Priscilla and Aquila in Ephesus (1 Cor 16:19).

The greeting in Romans indicates that Priscilla and Aquila had returned to Rome. As **fellow workers in Christ Jesus,** they shared Paul's mission of evangelism as colleagues, not assistants. It is "likely that they shared a theological and congregational orientation compatible with that of the apostle" (Jewett 2007, 957). They were law-free Paulinists who had probably informed Paul about the contemporary situation in the Roman community.

■ **4** We cannot know how or under what circumstance Priscilla and Aquila **risked their lives** to save Paul's (lit. ***they risked their neck for my soul;*** v 4). Perhaps they stuck out their necks (risked beheading, the quick means of execution that was the privilege of Roman citizens) by using their wealth and high social status to intervene with the authorities in Paul's behalf (Jewett 2007, 957). Paul expresses his gratitude for some unspecified, selfless intervention. Did this occur sometime during Paul's eighteen-month ministry in Corinth about which Acts 18:1-18 offers few details? Or did the incident occur at Ephesus—perhaps in the riot of the silversmiths reported in Acts 9:23 or during another Ephesian imprisonment (see 1 Cor 15:32; 2 Cor 1:8-9; Acts 19:23-31)?

All the apostle adds is this: **Not only I but all the churches of the Gentiles are grateful to them.** Paul effusively praises Priscilla and Aquila as exemplary leaders and generous patrons of the Gentile Christian communities in Rome, Corinth, Ephesus, and elsewhere. Paul hints that the rest of the Roman church would do well to imitate their example.

■ **5 Greet also the church that meets at their house** (v 5*a*). Over time Christians increasingly found themselves unwelcome in Jewish synagogues. Centuries passed before buildings were constructed specifically for church gatherings. Thus, early Christians often gathered in house churches made available by wealthy patrons such as Priscilla and Aquila. There they met for prayer, preaching, and observance of the Lord's Supper (see Acts 2:43-47; 20:7-12).

Although the argument from silence is a particularly weak one, Jewett notes that "the congregation led by Prisca and Aquila is the only one known to Paul that is called a 'church' and meets in the private home of patrons" (Jewett 2007, 959). Paul implies that other such gatherings met in family-like settings in tenement apartment buildings: those of the household of Aristobulus (16:10) and of Narcissus (v 11); those associated with Asyncritus (v 14) and Philologus (v 15). But Paul does not identify these as churches (see 1 Cor 16:19; Phlm 2; Col 4:15) nor mention their patron-leaders.

All of the references to **the church** or **churches** in Rom 16 are to local communities of Christians who met together in individual houses or tenements (vv 1, 4, 5, 16, 23). The reality of space limitations and the restraints of walking distances meant that in larger cities more than one such meeting place was necessary to accommodate growing numbers of believers. Of course, social and ethnic differences then (as now) also accounted for the necessity of multiple meeting places.

In v 5*b* Paul greets an otherwise unknown male Gentile believer, identified as his **dear friend** [*ton agapēton mou;* see vv 8, 9, and 12] **Epenetus** ("praiseworthy"—a slave name). He is distinguished as **the first convert to Christ in the province of Asia** (*aparchē tēs Asias eis Christon, **the firstfruits of Asia for Christ;*** see 1 Cor 16:15). Perhaps he is mentioned in proximity to Priscilla and Aquila because he became a believer under their influence in Ephesus before Paul arrived (see Acts 18:19-21, 24-26; 19:1-7). **Asia** was located in the far west of today's Turkey.

■ **6** Paul begins Rom 16:6 with a call to **Greet Mary,** an otherwise unknown Christian woman, probably of Jewish background. The name "Mary" is probably from "Miriam," the sister of Moses (Exod 15:20). "Since the Jewish community in Rome began primarily with 'the enslaved prisoners of war' brought by Pompey in 62 B.C.E., Miriam probably derived from a family of slave background" (Jewett 2007, 960). But the Latin name, Maria, is found in Roman records associated with slaves of the Marius family. So she may have been a Gentile of pagan background. Paul commends her as one **who worked very hard** [*ekopiasen*] **for you,** apparently as a missionary church leader (see Jewett 2007, 961).

■ **7 Greet Andronicus and Junias, my relatives who have been in prison with me. They are outstanding among the apostles, and they were in Christ before me** (v 7). Despite the familiar transliteration, the second name is clearly feminine, ***Junia.*** Early commentators (e.g., Chrysostom) believed she was the wife of Andronicus and that both were prominent apostles.

Paul's reference to the two as **my relatives** [*tous syngeneis mou;* see vv 11 and 21; 9:3], who **were in Christ before I was** implies that they were Jews who became Christians before Paul did ("prior to 34 C.E."—Jewett 2007, 964). They may have been among the "visitors from Rome" in Jerusalem (Acts 2:10) who returned after Pentecost to found the church there. Could ***Junia*** be the Latinized form of the Jewish name Joanna, one of the female witnesses of the risen Christ (Luke 24:10)? (see Witherington 2004, 389, following Richard Bauckham).

By referring to Andronicus and Junia as ***my fellow prisoners*** (*synaichmalōtous mou*) Paul implies that they had **been in prison with** him. Where was this imprisonment—in Ephesus (1 Cor 15:32), or Philippi (Acts 16:23), or elsewhere (2 Cor 11:23)? Clement of Rome speaks of seven imprisonments of Paul but never says where (*1 Clem.* 5:6).

Paul's use of the term "fellow prisoner" of Epaphras in Phlm 23 and of Aristarchus in Col 4:10 suggests that he was imprisoned at the same time and place with them, not merely that they, too (at some time and place), had been imprisoned for the faith. Jewett (2007, 962) suggests that Paul's twofold solidarity with the couple may have been intended to counter the prejudicial treatment of the Jewish Christian minority by the Gentile Christian majority within the Roman Christian community.

That Andronicus and Junia were **outstanding among** [*en:* in, with, by—see the sidebar "Prepositions" with the commentary on Rom 8:4] **the**

apostles probably meant that people considered them **outstanding . . . apostles** (see 3 Macc 6:1). But it might mean that **the apostles** considered them an **outstanding** couple but not apostles. The author of Acts restricted the application of the title "apostle" to the Twelve. But Paul and most early Christians used the term more generously to include other itinerant evangelists, who were eyewitnesses of the risen Christ. Thus Paul may well have considered Andronicus and Junia male and female apostles (Fitzmyer 1993, 737-39).

Francis Watson speculates that Andronicus and Junia were probably "the founders of the Roman congregation" and "the most important and influential members of the Jewish Christian congregation" in Rome. He also implausibly conjectures that they evangelized only Jews (see Gal 2:7-9) and "shared the Jerusalem church's deep suspicion of Pauline 'freedom from the law'" (Watson 1991, 210). This ignores Paul's emphasis on his solidarity with the couple.

■ **8-9 Greet Ampliatus** ["ample"], **whom I love** [*ton agapēton mou;* see vv 5*b*, 9, and 12] **in the Lord** (v 8). Beyond the fact that the name was frequently used for slaves or freedmen, nothing is known of Paul's friend **Ampliatus.** Paul next urges the Roman church to greet **Urbanus** ("cultured," v 9), whose name was also common among Roman slaves. Paul's identification of him as his **fellow worker** [*synergon*] **in Christ** is the same he applies to Priscilla and Aquila (v 3), Apollos (1 Cor 3:5-9), Titus (2 Cor 8:23), Epaphroditus (Phil 2:25), Clement (Phil 4:3), Jesus-Justus (Col 4:11), Timothy (1 Thess 3:2), and Philemon (Phlm 1), Mark, Aristarchus, Demas, and Luke (Phlm 24).

The name of Paul's **dear friend** [*ton agapēton mou;* see vv 5*b*, 8, and 12] **Stachys** ["ear" of corn] was used in Latin for a slave in the imperial household at Rome (see Phil 4:22).

■ **10** In Rom 16:10*a* Paul greets **Apelles,** whom he characterizes as **tested and approved** (*ton dokimon;* see 12:2; 14:18; 1 Cor 11:19; 2 Cor 10:18; 13:5-7; 2 Tim 2:15) **in Christ.** His name was common in Greek, but he is otherwise unknown. Paul was probably "personally acquainted with Apelles, because it would not have been rhetorically convincing to recommend someone as genuine whom one had never met" (Jewett 2007, 966).

Greet those who belong to the household of Aristobulus [*tous ek tōn Aristoboulou,* lit. ***those from among Aristobulus;*** Rom 16:10*b*]. "Paul does not greet Aristobulus, but only the Christian part of his household. He may have been a pagan, otherwise unknown" (Fitzmyer 1993, 740). Byrne notes that "a prominent member of the Herodian dynasty, [named] Aristobulus, [was a] grandson of Herod the Great, brother of Agrippa I." A friend of

Emperor Claudius, this Aristobulus had died a decade earlier. But, "it is possible that his household lingered on. Paul would then be greeting Christian members of his household" (Byrne 1996, 454). Since Paul fails to mention any of the believers in this household by name or to say anything about them, it may be that he knows them by reputation only.

■ **11** In v 11*a* Paul calls for greetings to be given a ***fellow-Jew*** (*ton syngenē mou*, **my relative;** see vv 7 and 21) named **Herodion.** This name naturally suggests some connection with the Herod family. Perhaps Herodion was one of the slaves or freedmen of the household of Aristobulus (Jewett 2007, 966).

In v 11*b* Paul greets members **of the household of Narcissus who are in the Lord.** As with Aristobulus (v 10*b*), it is not Narcissus himself, but the Christian members of his extended family, including its slaves, that Paul greets. Perhaps this Narcissus was the notorious freedman of the Emperor Claudius, whose wealth was proverbial and whose influence with Claudius had been practically unlimited. He had been forced to commit suicide by Agrippina shortly before Paul wrote his letter to the Romans. As a result his household probably passed into the possession of Emperor Nero (see Jewett 2007, 967).

■ **12** In v 12 Paul greets three women: **Tryphena, Tryphosa,** and **Persis.** He commends them all for their labors (using the verb *kopiaō*) **in the Lord,** apparently referring to some kind of Christian ministry (see v 6, referring to **Mary**). The first two names occur in Latin inscriptions and papyri. Paul may be attempting a wordplay on their names, both connected with Greek words connoting the soft-life of leisure, in contrast to their strenuous labors. The two may well have been twin sisters (Käsemann 1980, 395).

Paul identifies **Persis** (a typical female Greek slave name) as a **friend** (*tēn agapētēn;* see vv 5*b*, 8, and 9). The three women may have been freewomen from enslaved Jewish families, whose non-Jewish names were given by their owners. This would explain how Paul knew them well enough to commend them, thanks to their exile from Rome between A.D. 49 and 54 because of the Edict of Claudius (Jewett 2007, 968).

■ **13** In v 13 the apostle greets a son and his mother—**Rufus** ["redhead" in Latin], **chosen** [*eklekton;* see 1:6-7; 8:33; 9:24] **in the Lord, and his mother, who has been a mother to me, too.** This unique reference to an individual, rather than a community, as **chosen** suggests he was "a Gentile believer of considerable means and reputation"; a believer "who had a direct link with the historical Jesus" (Jewett 2007, 969). Mark alone, writing to Christians in Rome, describes Simon of Cyrene as "the father of Alexander and Rufus" (Mark 15:21). Paul acknowledges with gratitude that Rufus's mother had befriended Paul in a motherly way—with hospitality, etc.

■ **14** In Rom 16:14 Paul greets five men—**Asyncritus** ["incomparable"], **Phlegon** [a dog's name], **Hermes** [named after the Greek god], **Patrobas, Hermas—and** an unspecified number of anonymous **brothers with them,** all apparently members of the same communal gathering. The five leaders, judging by their names, must have been Gentile slaves or freedmen. The absence of any commendation suggests that Paul does not know them personally. That no patron is named suggests this was "a 'tenement church,' meeting somewhere in one of the multistoried dwellings where slaves and lower-class handworkers and laborers lived in rented spaces in the upper floors" (Jewett 2007, 971).

■ **15** In v 15 Paul apparently greets a family-based community—**Philologus, Julia, Nereus and his sister, and Olympas and all the saints with them. Philologus** was a common slave name. **Julia,** probably his wife (or sister), was a common Latin name, especially among slaves of the imperial (Julian) household. **Nereus and his sister** are possibly their children. **Olympas** also appears to be a male slave name. **The saints with them** would have been other members of their lower-status "tenement church" under a five-member leadership-team (Jewett 2007, 972).

■ **16** Having completed his greetings to particular individuals and the groups associated with them, Paul makes a general request to the Christians in Rome: **Greet one another with a holy kiss** (v 16*a;* see 1 Cor 16:20; 2 Cor 13:12; 1 Thess 5:26; and 1 Pet 5:14).

The earliest reference to the holy kiss as a regular part of the church's worship—between the intercessory prayer and the offertory—is found in Justin's *Apology* 65. Tertullian refers to it as "the kiss of peace." Paul requests this expression of mutual (**one another**) acceptance, customarily reserved for family members, to be extended to everyone in the Christian community, despite their disparity. Kissing non-family members welcomed them into the extended family (see Luke 7:45; Acts 20:37-38).

The adjective **holy** was probably necessary to remind all involved that this greeting was not a license for sexual promiscuity (Jewett 2007, 973). It is likely that Paul intended the letter to be read publicly when the community was assembled together for worship. Thus, his command could be immediately observed.

All the churches of Christ send greetings (v 16*b*). He feels authorized to speak for the churches for which he was responsible, that is, the Gentile communities of Galatia, Asia, Macedonia, and Achaia (see Rom 15:19*b*). Greetings in this third person form are resumed in 16:21-23.

FROM THE TEXT

Paul's greetings provide an illuminating glimpse into the demographics of the Roman Christian community and its collection of house churches. In some respects it may also offer a representative cross-section of the composition of earliest Christianity. Paul refers to a heterogeneous collection of Jews and Gentiles, men and women, slaves and free, patrons and clients, rich and poor.

What Paul says about these individuals and groupings suggests that their common life in the Lord Jesus Christ was what constituted them as a community. Paul urges the entire Roman Christian community to recognize and honor these leaders equally, despite their different social status and economic standing. And he urges all of them, leaders and ordinary church members alike, to give visible expression to their familial unity by means of the "holy kiss."

The house and tenement churches seem to be modeled after the extended family of the first-century Mediterranean world. At the center of several of these house churches are married couples: Priscilla and Aquila, Andronicus and Junia, and Philologus and Julia. But siblings, parents and children, and slaves belonging to the same household groupings are also
16:3-16 mentioned.

Paul singles out several of those he names as friends, relatives, fellow workers, and fellow sufferers. He mentions more women than men who are distinguished for their hard work in various church ministries. In this respect, not much has changed in most churches in two millennia.

It is noteworthy how Paul captures the essence of those he names in a brief descriptive phrase. Given all he might have said, what he says and what he leaves unsaid is telling. Although Acts 18 makes it clear that Aquila was a Diaspora Jew like Paul, he does not mention the fact in Rom 16. Why then does he mention his shared Jewish kinship with others—Andronicus and Junia and Herodion? Why does he not explicitly mention his special friendship with Priscilla and Aquila but make of point of identifying others as dear friends—Epenetus, Ampliatus, Stachys? What he mentions of Priscilla and Aquila is their shared labors and his gratitude for their selfless risking of their lives to save his. Most of what Paul seems to know about Roman Christianity he seems to have learned from the Jewish exiles from Rome during the period of A.D. 49-54, following the Edict of Claudius.

Someday, after we are dead and gone, those who survive us will sum up our lives in a succinct line or two: "You remember Bill Greathouse, who . . ." How will they fill in the ellipsis? How would we like them to remember us? Do we have any influence on what others will say and leave unsaid about us?

As we reflect with gratitude on those fellow believers who have significantly impacted our lives, we may do well to consider how we would describe them. And perhaps, like Paul, we would do well to commend them while they are still alive, before we eulogize them at their funerals.

Honor and mutual acceptance are comparatively inexpensive gifts. Why are we not unstinting in our sharing of these priceless expressions of community solidarity? Isn't there someone who might be encouraged by some honest words of affirmation, maybe even today?

How do we give visible expression to our acceptance of others who are part of the church but not like us? Romans 16:3-16 offers a fertile field for pastoral reflection and implicit guidance for pastoral care and congregational life, even if this part of Romans is an unlikely choice as a text for a sermon.

D. Paul's Warnings About False Teachers (16:17-20)

BEHIND THE TEXT

The admonitions contained in these verses abruptly break into the series of greetings. In 16:16*b* the focus shifts from naming individuals to be greeted in Rome in 16:3-16*a*, to naming those who send greetings from Paul's associates in Corinth to the Romans, a focus that continues in 16:21-23. The warnings in this passage inexplicably interrupt this second series of greetings.

The passage includes a significant number of Pauline *hapax legomena*—unique terms not found elsewhere in Paul's letters. More striking still is the change of tone. The Roman community is "urged" and warned to "watch out" for troublemakers, whose behavior and influence are described in dark tones.

It is by no means unusual to find such severe warnings in the apostle's letters (see 1 Cor 16:22; Gal 6:11-15; Phil 3:2-21). But the admonitions of Rom 16:17-20 remain abrupt. It is not easy to suggest a context, either in Rome or in the situation Paul faces as he writes from Corinth that would account for such a warning. In spite of the verbal affinity in content and warning of Phil 3:17-19, the language is more typical of the Pastoral Letters (1 and 2 Timothy and Titus) and the General Epistles (esp. 2 Peter and Jude).

Thus, it is not surprising that recent commentators have identified these verses as a later non-Pauline interpolation (e.g., Byrne 1996, 446, 455-56; Jewett 2007, 985-96). Even those who accept it as original acknowledge its peculiarities and inexplicable placement within the letter (Fitzmyer 1993, 745; Moo 1996, 929; Dunn 2002b, 38B:901). Despite the many textual uncertainties of chs 15 and 16, there is no surviving manuscript evidence supporting the interpolation hypothesis as applied to 16:17-20.

The first half of the passage (vv 17-18) consists of the warning and characterization of the troublemakers in negative terms. Then in vv 19-20*a*, in a positive vein, the focus turns to the recipients and the certain hope of victory that may be entertained on the basis of God's action and grace.

IN THE TEXT

■ **17 I urge** [*parakalō;* see 12:1; 15:30] **you, brothers *and sisters***
[*adelphoi, **friends;*** see 1:13], **to watch out for those who cause divisions**
16:17 [*dichostasias, **dissensions;*** see 1 Cor 3:3; Gal 5:20] **and put obstacles**
[*skandala;* see Rom 9:33; 11:9; 14:13] **in your way that are contrary to the**
teaching you have learned (16:17). It is not immediately clear whether the warning concerns invaders, who threaten the peace and faith of the community from the outside, or insiders, who cause dissensions and influence others to sin from within the community (but see v 18).

The assault of the troublemakers undermines the basic kerygmatic and catechetical **teaching** (*didachē*) in which the community has been instructed (see 6:17; 1 Cor 15:1-3; see Gal 5:20; 2 Thess 2:14-15), although no further word is said about the precise nature of the threat. Paul's advice to the Roman community is not only **to watch out for** [*skopein;* see Phil 3:17] them, but also: **Keep away from them** (*ekklinete ap' autōn, **turn away from them;*** see 1 Pet 3:11; *ekklinō* appears only here in Paul's letters). Despite Paul's call for mutual acceptance of other Christians in Rom 14:1; 15:7; and 16:16*a*, here he urges his audience to avoid all false teachers (as in 2 Tim 3:5 and Titus 3:10-11).

As frequently in the later books of the NT, the threat from false teachers is less in the erroneous theological content of their message than in their perverse ethical character (see, e.g., Phil 3:17-19; Col 2:1-23; 2 Pet

2:1-22; Jude). Such people are not truly Christians, whatever profession they may make for themselves. Paul does not specifically explain here in what their immorality consists.

■ **18** Paul instructs the Romans to shun troublemakers for this reason (*gar, **For***): **such people** [*hoi toioutoi;* see 2 Thess 3:12; Titus 3:11] **are not serving** [see 12:11; 14:18] **our Lord Christ, but their own appetites** [*koiliai, **belly;*** v 18; see Phil 3:19; 2 Tim 3:2-5]. This is the only instance in the NT of the expression **our Lord Christ** [but see Col 3:24). Paul's emphasis upon the different lord these false teachers serve identifies them as definitely *not* Christians. Thus, this threat comes from outside the Roman churches (see 2 Cor 11:13; Phil 3:18-19).

By **not serving** the risen **Lord,** the opponents fail to lead a life that is faithful to the gospel and the Christian ethic in an everyday setting (see Col 3:24; Eph 6:7; Titus 3:10-11; 2 Tim 3:5). By instead **serving . . . their own appetites,** they make themselves "slaves of their own belly." Their influence is not merely a matter of a bad example. **By smooth talk** [*chrēstologias, **sweet-talk;*** only here in the NT] **and flattery** [*eulogias, **eulogy, praise;*** only here in the NT in the negative sense of ***false eloquence;*** contrast Rom 15:29], Paul continues, **they deceive** [*exapatōsin;* see 7:11; 1 Cor 3:18; 2 Cor 11:3; 2 Thess 2:3; Eph 5:6; 1 Tim 2:14] **the minds** [*kardias, **heart***] **of naive people** [*tōn akakōn, **the non-evil, innocent;*** only here in Paul's letters; see Heb 7:26]. This patronizing characterization of the Roman believers seems particularly unexpected in light of Rom 15:14.

■ **19** Following a remark that might be taken as demeaning of his audience, in v 19 Paul resorts to hyperbolic praise, comparable to that found in 1:8. **Everyone has heard about** [*aphiketo;* only here in the NT] **your obedience** [*hypakoē*] is literally, ***For your obedience has reached to all people*** (v 19). For Paul, what matters above all, proving the validity of sincere faith, is **obedience,** a continuing adherence to the gospel (see 1:5, 8; 5:16; 6:16; 8:4; 15:18; 16:26).

Because (*oyn,* **so, *therefore***) the Romans obey God, Paul explains, **I am full of joy** [*chairō;* see 12:12] **over you** (lit. ***Therefore, I rejoice over you***). Their obedience would make them **wise about what is good, and innocent** [*akeraious, **unmixed;*** see Matt 10:16; Phil 2:15] **about what is evil.** The contrast between **good** and **evil**—*agathos* [or *kalos*] and *kakos* [or *ponēros*]—appears frequently in Romans (2:7-9; 3:8; 7:19, 21; 12:9, 17, 21; 13:3; 14:16, 20) but seldom elsewhere in Paul's letters.

■ **20** In v 20 Paul predicts: **The God of peace** [see 15:33; Phil 4:9; 1 Thess 5:23] **will soon** [*en tachei, **speedily;*** elsewhere in Paul only in 1 Tim 3:14; but see Rom 13:11-12; Luke 18:8; Rev 1:1; 22:6-7] **crush** [*syntrip-*

sei—only here in Paul's letters] **Satan under your feet** (v 20*a*). The phrase gives expression to the gospel message that the suppression of God's great adversary Satan is the prelude to the final, cosmic victory of God (see Luke 10:18-19; Rev 20:10).

Normally, we would expect Paul to express this as a prayer wish (in the optative mood) rather than in the future indicative. And we would expect Satan to be defeated under the feet of Christ, rather than of the Roman believers (see 1 Cor 15:23-26; 2 Thess 2:8). Paul only infrequently refers to the activity of Satan, usually in the context of explaining some hindrance or temporary setback (2 Cor 2:11; 12:7; 1 Thess 2:18; see 2 Cor 4:4; Eph 6:10-17). The implication here is that the false teachers, under the influence of Satan (as in 2 Cor 11:14-15), currently thwarting the progress of the Christian community in Rome, will soon be defeated.

The parenthesis closes in Rom 16:20*b* with yet another benediction (see 15:13, 33; 16:24): **The grace** [*charis;* see 1:5] **of our Lord Jesus be with you,** the usual Pauline final greeting (1 Cor 16:23; 1 Thess 5:28; 2 Thess 3:18; see 2 Cor 13:33; Col 4:18). There is no explicit verb in this sentence. In view of the future indicative in the first half of the verse, rather than an implicit optative prayer wish, the sentence might be translated: **The grace of our Lord Jesus *is* with you.**

FROM THE TEXT

Regardless of the conclusion we reach on Rom 16:17-20—Was it an original part of Paul's letter to the Romans or a later interpolation?—these verses are an indisputable part of the canonical form of the letter. Within this larger scriptural context, the warning sounded in this paragraph sets limits on the all-inclusive Christian welcome Paul recommends in 14:1—15:13. There are important restrictions on the "catholic spirit" (see From the Text on 14:7-13). Although there is room for intercultural and other nonessential differences within the Christian church, there is no room for immorality.

In chs 14—15 Paul definitely sides with the strong (liberal) branch of the church rather than the weak (conservative). But he does not de-Christianize the weak. Here, he (or a later editor) emphasizes that there must be limits to Christian liberalism. Tolerance of diversity within the church should not be unprincipled. Non-Christian ideals and immorality are not acceptable alternatives within the church.

Insisting upon such limits is not a "fundamental distortion" of the message of Romans or of "Paul's vision of the impartial righteousness of

God" (despite the claims of Jewett 2007, 996). It is a necessary reminder that God's righteousness expresses itself as wrath "against all the godlessness and wickedness" of people "who suppress the truth by their wickedness" (1:18). Divine impartiality (2:11) means that God rewards the good and punishes the evil, regardless of who they may be—Jew or Gentile, Christian or non-Christian.

E. Greetings from Paul's Companions (16:21-24)

BEHIND THE TEXT

Paul brings his letter to the Christians of Rome toward a conclusion with greetings from eight Christians with him as he writes from Corinth. Such greetings were typical features of Paul's letters (see 1 Cor 16:15-20; Phil 4:21-22; Col 4:10-17; Phlm 23-24). The letter and these greetings were no doubt formulated by Paul. But his scribe, Tertius, the amanuensis who wrote the entire letter at Paul's dictation, is given the freedom to craft his own greeting.

These individual third person greetings from the apostle's associates, which include both Jews and Gentiles, continue the collective community greeting in Rom 16:16*b*. All of these greetings are sent to all of the believers of Rome (*hymas,* **you** [plural]; vv 16*b,* 21, 22, 23 [two times]). Paul's mention of these associates suggests that they are already known to the Romans.

Paul implied in 15:26 that he was writing from "Macedonia and Achaia," a detail that fits well with Acts 20:1-5, as he prepared to leave for Jerusalem to deliver the collection. Here in Rom 16:21-23, still in Corinth (in Achaia), he mentions Timothy, Sosipater, and Gaius among his associates, all names mentioned in Acts 20:4 (although the Gaiuses in the two passages are probably not to be identified) as well-known representatives from his Gentile churches who were to accompany him to Jerusalem to deliver the collection to the poor saints there. "Their greeting lends weight to Paul's venture," suggesting "the official backing of all the churches in Achaia, Macedonia, Asia, Galatia, Syria and elsewhere" (Jewett 2007, 977).

IN THE TEXT

■ **21 Timothy, my fellow worker, sends his greetings to you** (v 21). This coworker from Lystra joined Paul on his second missionary journey. He was the son of a Jewish-Christian woman named Eunice and a Gentile father (Acts 16:1-3; 2 Tim 1:5). Timothy is listed as the co-sender of six of Paul's letters (1 Thess 1:1; 2 Thess 1:1; 2 Cor 1:1; Phil 1:1; Phlm 1; Col 1:1). He accompanied the apostle on a number of his missionary journeys. But he also served as Paul's emissary on missions to Thessalonica (1 Thess 3:1, 6), Corinth (2 Cor 1:1, 19), and Philippi (Phil 2:19-24). Thus, he was well-known among Paul's churches in Asia (Troas and Ephesus—1 Cor 4:17; 16:10; 1 Tim 1:2), Macedonia (Thessalonica and Philippi), and Achaia (Corinth). Hebrews 13:23 implies that his name was also familiar outside the Pauline circle. Now, as Paul writes from Corinth, he adds greetings from Timothy to the Christians in Rome.

Paul next mentions three others, whom he identifies only as **my relatives**—apparently fellow Jews (see Rom 9:3; 16:7, 11), who also send greetings. Jewett proposes that Paul makes a point of mentioning these Jewish Christians as a way of honoring them before the Gentile majority in the Roman church on behalf of the Jewish minority (2007, 978).

The first of Paul's fellow Jewish associates, **Lucius,** has been conjecturally identified with Lucius of Cyrene, mentioned in Acts 13:1, and with Paul's friend Luke the physician (Col 4:14; 2 Tim 4:11; Phlm 24), the presumed Third Evangelist and author of Acts (Dunn 2002b, 38B:909; Cranfield 1979, 2:805). The latter seems particularly unlikely, since this traveling companion was apparently a Gentile.

Jason, mentioned next, was possibly Jason of Thessalonica, Paul's host there according to Acts 17:5-9. **Sosipater** is in all likelihood "Sopater" of Berea, who was to accompany Paul to Jerusalem according to Acts 20:4. Lucius, Jason, and Sosipater, now resident in Corinth, are apparently delegates from Achaia and Macedonia (see 2 Cor 8:1), who are to accompany Paul to Jerusalem on his collection mission.

■ **22 I, Tertius, who wrote down this letter, greet you in the Lord** (Rom 16:22). Paul's secretary, **Tertius,** had transcribed the entire letter at Paul's dictation, which may have occupied several weeks or even months. Now Tertius adds this greeting in his own name. The Greek word order of this sentence, which begins with ***I greet you*** and concludes with **in the Lord,** suggests that Tertius identifies himself as a Christian amanuensis; it is not his greeting as a Christian.

Jewett speculates that Tertius was a slave of Phoebe (16:1-2), currently on loan to Paul for the purposes of assisting him in writing the letter as a service to the Lord. He sends greetings because he was already known to the Roman recipients of the letter through his business travels with Phoebe between Corinth and Rome (Jewett 2007, 979).

■ **23 Gaius, whose hospitality I and the whole church here enjoy, sends you his greetings** (v 23). The **I** here is presumably once again Paul (see the first person singular—**my**—referring to Paul in v 21) and no longer Tertius (the **I** in v 22). Gaius might be Gaius Titius Justus, whom Paul baptized in Corinth (Acts 18:7; 1 Cor 1:14). It is less likely that he is the Gaius of Macedonia, who was among Paul's traveling companions in Ephesus (Acts 19:29) or the Gaius of Derbe who was to accompany Paul on his collection trip to Jerusalem (Acts 20:4).

Paul identifies this Gaius as his Corinthian host, and perhaps the patron whose house was the venue of some **church** gatherings in Corinth. In this case *ekklēsia* is used in the local sense to refer to a house church (see 16:1, 5). But if the Corinthian church was composed of multiple house churches (Jewett [2007, 980] argues for six to ten such churches), it is unlikely that **the whole church** (*holēs tēs ēkklēsias*) met in the house of Gaius. Typical attriums of the houses of the wealthy could accommodate meetings of no more than 30 to 50 (Dunn 2002b, 38B:910).

As *ho xenos,* ***the one who extends hospitality to strangers,*** perhaps Gaius is hosting all the delegates from Paul's eastern churches gathered in Corinth preparing to accompany him to Jerusalem. If so, we have in **the whole church** an early use of *ekklēsia* referring to a more universal community than a local gathering.

Paul next sends greetings in behalf of **Erastus, who is the city's director of public works.** This **Erastus** may be the same person mentioned in Acts 19:22 and 2 Tim 4:20. Paul perhaps names him here because of his political prominence in the Corinthian community. This high-ranking Roman official is probably the same Erastus who paved a square in first-century Roman Corinth, according to the Latin inscription still partly visible among Corinth's archaeological ruins. Jewett suggests that Paul's mention of the greeting from this Roman official is an implicit endorsement of his proposed mission to Spain (2007, 982).

Paul's final greeting comes from an otherwise unknown person named **Quartus.** The Greek *ho adelphos,* ***the*** **brother,** might mean **our brother,** Paul's Christian friend and associate. Or it might mean ***his,*** i.e., Erastus's biological **brother.**

■ **24 May the grace of our Lord Jesus Christ be with all of you. Amen** (Rom 16:24*b* margin). Within the troubled textual tradition surrounding the termination of Romans, this benedictory prayer wish is found sometimes in 16:20*b*, sometimes here, and sometimes in both places. See the comments on 16:20*b*.

F. Doxology (16:25-27)

BEHIND THE TEXT

The authenticity of these verses has been seriously challenged by modern scholars. Some interpreters claim that the doxology was added, in its present or a briefer version, to the form of the letter shortened by Marcion, which ended with 14:23. Thus, it was added to provide a liturgically appropriate ending to round off this mutilated version of the letter.

Jewett offers a speculative reconstruction of the redactional process that led to the creation of the doxology by a later editor. He interprets the doxology as consistently undermining the essential message of Romans (2007, 1003-4). Dunn, however, argues that the doxology is "a pastiche culled from the letter itself but going a little beyond it."

> Even if the idiom is not quite Paul's . . . , the doxology succeeds quite well in summing up the central themes of the letter—God's power (1:16), Paul's gospel (2:16), the message of Christ (see 1:9), the mystery revealed (11:25), the "now" revelation (3:21), the prophetic scriptures (1:2; 3:21), and not least "the obedience of faith" "to all the nations" (1:5). (Dunn 2002b, 38B:913)

16:25-27 The textual problems associated with this doxology are complex. One group of manuscripts lacks 16:25-27 entirely. Others place it at the close of ch 14; others after ch 15; others include it at the end of both chs 14 and 16. Many critics agree that the wandering doxology, because of its intrinsic merit, was added either to a form of the letter ending at 14:23 or to a fuller form ending with 15:33.

The alleged overloading of the ideas in these verses is probably not in itself a sufficient basis for arguing that editorial expansion has taken place. Still, none of Paul's other letters conclude with a doxology. Furthermore, a significant number of Pauline or NT *hapax legomena* (unique terms) appear here. Even if the doxology did not originate with Paul, there is no good reason to deny that its origin was orthodox. It would be rash to assert unequivocally that Paul could, or could *not,* have written it. While the doxology may not be Paul's work in its present form, it certainly preserves the substance of apostolic proclamation.

Whatever its impact on its original audience, the rhetorical force of the closing greetings in 16:21-23 certainly seems a weak way to end a powerful letter to later readers. Whether this wandering doxology is a piece of liturgy that was adapted for use here or a fresh composition for the purpose of rounding out the letter, it forms a worthy appendix to Paul's most weighty Epistle.

IN THE TEXT

■ **25** The liturgically formulated doxology begins in v 25. It is, of course, directed toward God, but God is not explicitly named until vv 26 and 27. It begins by referring to God indirectly with a substantive adjectival participle—**to him who is able** (see Eph 3:20-21; Jude 24-25) **to establish** (*stērixai;* see Rom 1:11; 1 Thess 3:2, 13; 2 Thess 2:17; 3:3) believers. God can accomplish his work of confirming and strengthening us in our belief in and obedience to the gospel.

Because salvation is conditional at every stage, we *may* fall into apostasy (Heb 6:3-6); but God "is able to keep [us] from falling" (Jude 24). God *can* so **establish** us in faith and love that we may "in all . . . things [be] more than conquerors through him who loved us" (Rom 8:37). Therefore, we can proclaim with all confidence that nothing can "separate us from the love of God that is in Christ Jesus our Lord" (8:39). It is indeed a truth that calls forth doxology! ROMANS

Paul speaks of this truth as the message announced in what he calls **my gospel** (see 2:16; 2 Cor 4:3; 1 Thess 1:5; 2 Thess 2:14; 2 Tim 2:8). The 16:25
good news he preaches has become his own. It is not that Paul has a gospel different from what others preach (1 Cor 15:11). He takes for granted that the gospel of which he speaks is the same gospel the Roman believers received when they became Christians. He links his **gospel** with **the proclamation of Jesus Christ** [*to kērygma Iēsou Christou*].

Although this expression—**my gospel and the proclamation of Jesus Christ**—appears nowhere else in Paul's letters, numerous parallel expressions (see Rom 10:8, 14, 15; 1 Cor 1:21, 23; 2:4; 15:11, 12, 14; 2 Cor 1:19; 4:5; 11:4; Gal 2:2; Phil 1:15; Col 1:23; 1 Thess 2:9; 1 Tim 3:16; 2 Tim 4:2, 17; Titus 1:3) suggest that he would not object to the formulation.

The *kērygma* here could refer to the message Jesus preached during his earthly ministry or to the message about Christ all Christian preachers share. Jewett claims that this composite formulation "commences a long tradition of interpreting Romans as a doctrinal treatise, summing up the gist of orthodox theology" (2007, 1006).

We should probably take **according to the revelation** [*apokalyspin*] as modifying **the proclamation** about Christ. The **gospel** is revealed truth, not human wisdom (see 1 Cor 2:12-13). The Christian **proclamation** consists in **the mystery** [*mysteriou*] **hidden for long ages past** (see Rom 1:25; 1 Cor 2:8-10; Eph 3:3-9; Col 1:26-27). The truth is that God's Son came from heaven to live, die, and rise for us so that we might enter into salvation by faith in him alone. This is not obvious; it can only be known by us when and as God reveals it (see Gal 4:4-6).

When God is silent, he is **hidden** [*sesigēmenou, **kept silent***—a perfect passive participle]. The truth about his innermost being is not open to the scrutiny of mortals. He may choose to make himself known, but that does not mean that everything about him has been revealed. Even his supreme self-revelation in Christ is at the same time a hiding. Consider the paradox of God revealed in human flesh! There remains much about God that is beyond human perception and understanding.

Morris understands the silence endured **for long ages past** as a reference to God's eternity rather than to the time between creation and the present (1988, 546). Jewett takes it to refer to the time between creation and the coming of Christ (2007, 1007).

■ **26** In contrast to the **long** silence of the **past** stands the apocalyptic invasion of God in the present. The **mystery hidden** in the **past** has given way to the age of revelation, in which God has spoken definitively in Christ. **Now** [*nyn;* see Rom 3:21; 5:9, 11; 8:1) Christ has been **revealed and made known** (*phanerōthentos,* "has been manifested"; v 26). The aorist tense of the verb points to a completed past event, the coming of "Christ." The revealed gospel, anticipated **through the prophetic writings** [*graphōn prophētikōn;* only here in the NT; but see 1:2; 3:31], has been **made known.**

The true meaning of the OT has become apparent only through the coming of Christ (see Luke 24:25-27, 32, 45-47), who is the constant theme of the NT. Both the revelation and Paul's preaching of it took place **by the command** [*epitagēn*—in this sense only in 1 Tim 1:1; Titus 1:3] **of the eternal God.** The doxology does not suggest that humans may earn salvation by obeying the commands of God (contrary to Jewett 2007, 1001) nor that Gentile Christianity somehow replaces Israel in supersessionist fashion (contrary to Jewett 2007, 1008). On the contrary, the message of salvation by faith is proclaimed **so that all nations might believe and obey** Christ.

The once-**hidden**-but-now-revealed **mystery** of salvation for all through Christ was not contrary to God's eternal purposes. Nor is it the result of a fickle, recently conceived change of mind on the part of **the eternal God** [*tou aiōniou theou*—only here in the NT]. God has made his purposes historically known in the recent past—**so that all nations might believe and obey him** (see 1:5).

Jewett (2007, 999) claims that the application of the word **mystery** to God's eternal purpose (to include Gentiles within his saving purposes) runs counter to the association of "mystery" with the conversion of Israel in 11:25 and the crucial emphasis throughout the letter on the priority of the Jews. But this claim depends on unjustified either-or assumptions. In some instances in the LXX (e.g., Gen 17:5; 22:18; 26:4; Isa 42:5) the expression **all nations** includes both Israel and the Gentiles, as Jewett admits it does in Rom 1:5 (see 4:9-18; Gal 3:8). Furthermore, even Rom 9—11 emphasizes the special role the inclusion of the Gentiles plays within God's saving purposes for Israel. The doxology nowhere counters the emphasis elsewhere in Romans that salvation is through faith in Christ. The doxology does not suggest that salvation is by faith "in the mystery of salvation for the Gentiles."

■ **27** Only with v 27 does the doxology become explicit in a monotheistic confession: **To the only wise God** [*monōi sophōi theōi*—only here in the NT; but see 3:28-31; 11:33; 1 Tim 1:17; 6:15-16] **be glory** [*doxa;* see the sidebar "Glory" with the commentary on Rom 8:18-27] **forever** [*eis tous aiōnas;* see 11:36; Gal 1:5] **through Jesus Christ** [see Rom 1:8]! Christians incessantly praise God because of what he in his unique wisdom chose to do to make possible universal salvation through what Christ has done!

Within the worship setting in which the letter was first read, the final **Amen** was intended to invite all those gathered for its reading to give verbal affirmation: ***May it be so!***